DATE DUE

JE 1 0'00			
AG 4'00			

DEMCO 38-296

DATE DUE

Cooperative Learning

Spencer Kagan, Ph.D.

Resources for Teachers, Inc.

Cooperative Learning

Spencer Kagan, Ph.D.

© 1992

Resources for Teachers, Inc.
27128 Paseo Espada, Suite 622
San Juan Capistrano, CA 92675
1(800) Wee Co-op • (714) 248-7757

ISBN: 1-879097-10-9

Illustrated by
Celso Rodriguez (Art)
Miguel Kagan (Diagrams)

Formatted by
Ben Taylor
Miguel Kagan

BOOKS PUBLISHED:

January 1985:	1000
January 1987:	5000
June 1988:	12,000
February 1989:	20,000
July 1989:	30,000
June 1990:	45,000
November 1991:	75,000

Cooperative Learning

Spencer Kagan

Table of Contents

Part I. Cooperative Learning Theory

Chapter 1: **Ten Frequent Questions**
Chapter 2: **The Need for Cooperative Learning**
Chapter 3: **Positive Outcomes**
Chapter 4: **Six Key Concepts**
Chapter 5: **Three Schools of Cooperative Learning**

Part II. Cooperative Learning Methods

Chapter 6: **Teams**
Chapter 7: **Management**
Chapter 8: **Teambuilding**
Chapter 9: **Classbuilding**
Chapter 10: **Mastery Structures**
Chapter 11: **Thinking Skills Structures**
Chapter 12: **Information Sharing Structures**
Chapter 13: **Communication Skills Structures**
Chapter 14: **Social Skills Development**
Chapter 15: **Cooperative Projects**
Chapter 16: **Scoring and Recognition**

Part III. Cooperative Learning Lesson Designs

Chapter 17: **Mastery Designs**
Chapter 18: **Task Specialization Designs**
Chapter 19: **Project Designs**
Chapter 20: **Co-op Lesson Planning**

Part IV. Cooperative Learning Beyond the Classroom

Chapter 21: **Teachers Supporting Teachers**
Chapter 22: **Schoolwide Cooperation -- and Beyond**
Chapter 23: **Co-op Play**
Chapter 24: **Cooperative Learning Resources**

Note on Numbering

This book uses a chapter based numbering system. For example, Chapter 10 begins on page 10:1, and the fifth page of Chapter 10, is numbered 10:5.

The advantage of this system is that once you know that the Mastery Structures, for example, are all found in Chapter 10, you can turn right to those structures without looking up a page number in the Table of Contents.

Spencer Kagan: *Cooperative Learning*©
Publisher: Resources for Teachers , Inc. • 1(800) Wee Co-op

CHART OF STRUCTURES

Chapter 13: Communication Skills

Chapter 12: Information Sharing

CHART OF LESSON DESIGNS

Chapter 17: Mastery Designs

Color-Coded Co-op Cards 17:1

1. Pre-Test
2. Create Cards
3. Flashcard Game
4. Practice Test
5. Count Improvement Points
6. Flashcard Game
7. Final Test
8. Final Improvement Scoring
9. Individual, Team & Class Recognition
10. Reflection

STAD 17:6

1. Direct Instruction
2. Group Work for Practice
3. Individual Quiz
4. Improvement Scoring
5. Team Recognition

TGT 17:10

(Same as STAD except Tournament replaces Quiz, and points are based on out scoring others.)

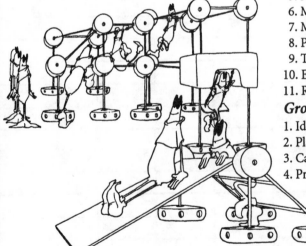

Chapter 18: Division of Labor Designs

Telephone 18:1

1. A Student Exits Room
2. Remaining Students Instructed
3. Student Returns
4. Returnee Instructed by Teammates
5. Returnee Tested

Jigsaw II 18:15

1. Direct Instruction
2. Expert Topics Assigned
3. Expert Group Work
4. Experts Teach Teammates
5. Individual Quiz
6. Improvement Scoring
7. Team Recognition

Partners 18:1

1. Form Partners Within Teams
2. Class Division
3. Materials Distributed
4. Partners Work
5. Partners Consult
6. Partners Prepare to Present
7. Teams Reunite
8. Partners Present & Tutor
9. Reflection
10. Individual Assessment

Chapter 19: Project Designs

Co-op Co-op 19:1

1. Class Discussion
2. Team Selection
3. Teambuilding/Social Skill
4. Team Topic Selection
5. Mini-Topic Selection
6. Mini-Topic Preparation
7. Mini-Topic Presentation
8. Prepare Team Presentation
9. Team Presentations
10. Evaluation
11. Reflection

Group Investigation 19:10

1. Identify Topic; Team Selection
2. Plan the Learning Task
3. Carry Out Investigation
4. Prepare Final Report

Co-op Jigsaw........ 19:10

1. Expert Topics Assigned
2. Expert Group Work
3. Experts Return, Share, Tutor
4. Prepare Team Presentation
5. Team Presentations
6. Check for Connections
7. Evaluation
8. Reflection

Rotation Learning Centers 19:16

1. Monday: Input
2. Tuesday: 1st Learning Center
3. Wednesday: 2nd Learning Center
4. Thursday: 3rd Learning Center
5. Friday: Integration & Assessment

Chapter 20: Multi-Functional Frameworks

Effective Instruction 20:3

1. Anticipatory Set
2. Instructional Input
3. Check Understanding
4. Guided Practice
5. Closure
6. Independent Practice

Johnson & Johnson 5:9

1. Direct Instruction of Content
2. Teach Social Skills
3. Students Work in Groups
4. Teacher Observes for Social Skills & Content
5. Process Social Skills & Content

Big Four.... 20:18

1. Class Building
2. Teambuilding
3. Mastery
4. Thinking Skills

Index of Structures

	Teambuilding	Classbuilding	Mastery	Thinking Skills	Information Sharing	Communication Skills	See Also
4S Brainstorming	8:10			11: 5			20: 9, 14, 16, 21: 2
Affirmation Chips						13: 2	14:13, 27, 20: 9
Blackboard Share					12: 5		20: 9, 15, 16
Blooming Worksheets				11:18			
Broken Squares						13:19	14:25
Build-What-I-Write				11: 7			
Carbon Sharing					12: 5		
Carousel					12: 6		
Choral Response			10:16				20: 9, 16, 17
Class Notebook					12: 5		
Class Projects		9: 7					
Colored Chips						13: 1	
Consensus Seeking						13: 5	
Corners		9: 8					20: 9, 17, 21: 2
Draw-What-I-Say						13: 9	
Fact Bingo		9: 7					
Fact-or-Fiction	8: 4	9: 7	10:14				
Find-Someone-Who...		9: 4	10:14				
Flashcard Game	8: 3		10: 9				14:13, 24, 25, 17:2, 20: 9, 15, 16
Formations	8: 4	9:11		11: 7			20: 9
Four-Step Interview					12: 4		
Freebies						13: 2	
Gallery Tour					12: 5		
Gambit Chips						13: 2	20: 9
Guess-the-Fib	8: 4	9: 7	10:14				
Inside-Outside Circle		9: 6	10:11		12: 7		6:10, 14:13, 20: 9, 14, 15, 16
Line-Ups		9: 6					6: 9, 20: 9
Linkages		9: 6					
Maps and Chains				11:15			
Match Mind				11:11		13:16	
Match Mine						13:16	20: 9
Mix-Freeze-Pair		9: 7					

Spencer Kagan: *Cooperative Learning*©
Publisher: Resources for Teachers, Inc. • 1(800) Wee Co-op

Index of Structures

	Teambuilding	Classbuilding	Mastery	Thinking Skills	Information Sharing	Communication Skills	See Also
Mix-Freeze-Group		9:10	10:14				20: 9, 20:17
Numbered Heads Together			10: 2				5:2, 14:13, 20:9,15,16
On-the-Line				11:10			
One & All				11:15			
One Stray, Three Stay					12: 6		
Pairs		9:10					14:26
Pairs Check			10: 5				14:13, 24, 25, 20:9, 15
Pair Discussion				11: 2			
Paraphrase Passport						13: 2	14:13, 26, 15: 2, 20: 9, 15, 17, 21: 2
People Sorts				11:14			
Pin-A-Place						13: 9	
Proactive Prioritizing						13: 6	
Q-Review			10:15				
Q-Trix				11:17			
Rallyrobin					12: 1		
Rallytable			10:13				
Rotating Review			10:15		12: 6		
Response Mode Chips						13: 2	14:26
Roam the Room					12: 5		20: 9
Roundrobin	8: 3	9: 6			12: 1		14:13, 24, 25, 26, 15:15, 20: 9, 14
Roundtable	8: 9		10:12				14:13, 24, 25, 26, 15:15, 17, 20: 9, 14
Roving Reporters					12: 6		
Same-Different						13:10	20: 9, 20:15
Send-A-Problem	8:10		10:11				20: 9, 20:15, 16
Sequencing				11: 6			
Share & Compare					12: 5		20: 9
Similarity Groups		9: 4					21: 2
Simultaneous Sharing					12: 5		
Six-Step Interview					12: 4		
Spend-A-Buck						13: 5	21: 2
Split Value Lines						13: 8	
Stand & Share					12: 5		20: 9, 15, 16

Index of Structures

	Teambuilding	Classbuilding	Mastery	Thinking Skills	Information Sharing	Communication Skills	See Also
Structured Sorts	8: 4			11:14			
Talking Chips						13: 1	14:13, 24, 25, 26, 20: 9, 17
Team Discussion				11: 2			5: 3, 15:10, 20: 9, 14, 16
Team Inside-Outside Circle					12: 6		
Team Interview	8: 2				12: 2		14:13, 15:10, 20: 9, 14
Team Notebook					12: 5		
Team Projects	8:3,5,8,11,13						
Team Statements				11: 5			
Team Test Taking			10:12				20: 9, 20:15
Team Word-Webbing				11:15			
Teammates Consult				11: 4			
Think-Pair-Share				11: 2			15:10, 20: 9
Think-Pair-Square				11: 3			20: 4
Three-Step Interview					12: 2		5: 3, 14:13, 24, 25, 15: 2, 20: 9, 14, 21: 2
Three Stray, One Stay					12: 6		
Timed Turns						13: 2	
Toss-A-Question			10:13				
Trade-A-Problem			10:12				
Turn Toss	8: 2						14:13, 14:25
Turn-4-Review			10:16				14:13, 20: 9, 20:15
Turn-4-Thought				11:23			14:13
Two-Box Induction				11: 9			
Value Lines	8:11	9: 9				13: 6	
Who-Am-I?		9:10					20: 9, 20:17
Unstructured Sorts				11:14			
Yarn Yarn						13: 2	
Venn Diagrams				11:10			
Voting						13: 5	

Spencer Kagan: *Cooperative Learning*©
Publisher: Resources for Teachers, Inc. • 1(800) Wee Co-op

Index of Lesson Designs

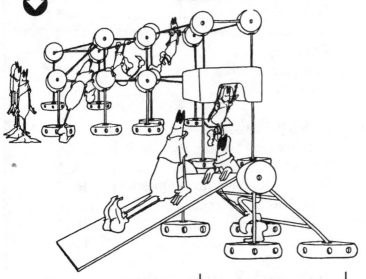

Spencer Kagan: *Cooperative Learning*©

Publisher: Resources for Teachers, Inc. • 1(800) Wee Co-op

TEACHER TOOLS

STUDENT HANDOUTS

Spencer Kagan: *Cooperative Learning*©
Publisher: Resources for Teachers, Inc. • 1(800) Wee Co-op

Preface

Back in 1980, I was begging schools to give me permission to conduct an experiment, to allow students to work together. Some were gracious enough to say yes. But they were cautious: "Try it in spelling." They knew I couldn't mess up their spelling curriculum too much.

Now it is over ten years later. Many districts are completing multi-year cooperative learning implementation plans, providing every teacher in the district competency in a variety of cooperative learning structures. Back in 1980, when I first wrote this appreciation, I expressed thanks to one principal, Roger Skinner, who opened his school to me. As I write now, I wish to express thanks to a host of individuals across the United States and Canada who have opened up whole districts to my structural approach to cooperative learning.

By 1985 my concept of a cooperative learning lesson had transformed: I moved from seeing a cooperative learning lesson as one which implemented a fully orchestrated set of learning experiences toward teacher determined learning objectives. Structures became the building blocks of a lesson.

My demonstration lessons in cooperative learning changed radically. Prior to 1985, I would demonstrate Jigsaw, or the Color-Coded Co-op Cards, or Co-op Co-op. After 1985, a typical demonstration lesson might include a half dozen structures such as Inside/Outside Circle, Three-Step Interview, and Pairs Check. The reason: I became convinced that only by multi-structural lessons can all goals be realized most efficiently.

Structures moved to the heart of my approach. Repeatedly, I found that if I gave teachers cooperative learning activities during initial training, they reported back excitedly: the activities produced enthusiastic, intense involvement and learning among their students. The teachers were hungry for more activities; they had "used up" the initial activities. In contrast, when I switched to providing teachers structures during initial training, the response was different: there was the same intense involvement and learning among students, but were the teachers not waiting for me to provide more activities. They saw numerous ways to use the structures in each of their curriculum areas all year. *Structures, unlike activities, don't get used up.*

The structures provided yet other advantages. Teachers had difficulty translating abstract concepts like positive interdependence and individual accountability into lesson plans, but they easily adopted structures like "Numbered Heads Together" and "Pairs Check." And the structures had built-in positive interdependence and individual accountability. Teachers were free to teach rather than worry about implementing abstract concepts. Training of teachers by other teachers also was facilitated: It is hard to train "cooperative learning," but easy to train one structure. Thus, schools began developing their year-long training plans, forming their Structure-a-Month Clubs.

This book is dedicated to the teachers of the future -- to those about to enter teacher training. May those kindergarten students of today experience throughout their schooling such a broad range of structures and activities that when they begin to prepare their first lesson, they would no more dream of trying to teach primarily through Teacher Talk than they would dream of going back to the 20th century.

structure; I began seeing the lesson as *composed of* structures.

We had discovered the power of multi-structural lessons, in which each structure built on the effects of the previous structures, moving students through a care-

Spencer Kagan: *Cooperative Learning*©
Publisher: Resources for Teachers , Inc. • 1(800) Wee Co-op

Cooperative learning was being learned in bite size pieces -- a structure at a time.

In this book, the structures are grouped by function; the chapters contain structures with common objectives. In ordering structures within chapters, when other considerations have not prevailed, I have begun with the simplest structures. A teacher might well start with the relatively easy four-step Numbered Heads structure for content mastery, before moving to the nine-step Color-Coded Co-op Cards. Similarly, among the thinking structures, Team Discussion is presented before Team Word-Webbing.

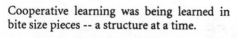

A Structure is Content Free

WHAT'S NEW?

Those of you familiar with previous editions of this book will find numerous changes. This edition is based on a more differentiated concept of the structural approach which distinguishes Co-op Activities, Co-op Structures, and Co-op Lesson Designs.

Structures, Content, and Activities. At any one time, there is always some structure being used in a classroom, whether it is Teacher Talk, Numbered Heads Together, or Silent Reading. *A structure itself is content-free.* For example, the Teacher Talk may be about the Civil War, the moral of a story, or the Pythagoras Theorem. *Any one structure can be used to deliver an infinite range of content.*

Structures hold content. *We place content into a structure to create a learning activity.* By changing either the structure or the content, we create a different activity, and a different kind of learning results. For example, a Roundrobin of favorite foods produces different learning than a Roundrobin of foods from the meat group. Similarly, holding the content constant, changing the structure changes the activity, and the resultant learning. To Roundrobin foods from the meat group produces different learning than to use Roundtable writing of the same foods. A great deal of the art of good teaching is the ability to choose the best structure/content combination to reach a given learning objective. An activity is a structure/content combination.

Lesson Designs and Lesson Plans. We have all known for some time that STAD and Co-op Co-op are different animals than structures like Roundtable and Think-Pair-Share. To call them structures is to lose sight of a fundamental distinction. Roundtable and Think-Pair-Share are Co-op Structures; STAD and Co-op Co-op are Co-op Lesson Designs. The distinction between structures and lesson designs is as important as the distinction between activities and structures.

Lesson designs are activity-free. They are frameworks, setting the goals of a lesson. A Lesson Design provides a sequenced set of sub-objectives. To reach each sub-objectives, you use an activity (a structure plus content) Lesson designs hold activities (structure/content combos).. *We place activities into a lesson design to create a lesson.* One form of Co-op Lesson planning is to find the best structure/content combination to reach each sub-objective dictated by a given Co-op lesson design.

Any one lesson design can be used to deliver an infinite number of lessons. When you are in the second step of the STAD lesson design, for example, it is time for teamwork for practice. At that point, you might use Worksheet Practice, Send-A-Problem, Turn-4-Review, The Flashcard Game, or any other of the mastery structures to have students practice in teams the content you want them to master.

Structure + Content = Activity

Spencer Kagan: *Cooperative Learning*©
Publisher: Resources for Teachers , Inc. • 1(800) Wee Co-op

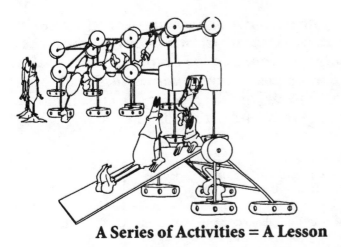

A Series of Activities = A Lesson

Following this model, in this book structures are presented before lesson designs. For example, mastery structures such as Numbered Heads Together and Pairs Check are presented together in a chapter on mastery structures (Chapter 10), whereas mastery lesson designs such as STAD and Color-Coded Co-op Cards are presented together in a chapter on mastery lesson designs (Chapter 17). In this edition of the book, you will find four chapters on structures, (one of which is entirely new), three new chapters on lesson designs, and one new chapter on Co-op Lesson Planning. Communication skills structures have been distinguished from Social Skills Development methods; and Information Sharing structures have been distinguished from Thinking Skills Structures. Other additions include new chapters on co-op projects, co-op management and cooperation beyond the classroom.

This edition of the book also introduces a new framework for categorizing thinking skills structures, and a new way to categorize cooperative sports. You will find many new structures, methods, and activities, as well as improved and broadened presentations of old structures and activities. For example, in the classbuilding chapter, you will find class meetings and class goals as well as many new classbuilding structures and activities.

Some old sections which had been dropped in recent editions have been revived because of reports from teachers regarding their successes. So, for example, Rotation Learning Centers is reintroduced in an improved version.

ACKNOWLEDGEMENTS

I am most grateful to my good friend **Celso Rodriguez,** who did the delightful drawings. In a few lines Celso expresses more than I can with many. Each time I give Celso a concept to illustrate, I look forward to seeing what that cheerful character, Professor Jelly Bean, will do next. **Miguel Kagan** helped create the conceptual framework which led to this new version of the book. He also did graphics, a major part of the formatting, a bit of writing, created the student-directed multi-structural lesson, Surface Tension, and encouraged and supported me to make the book as good as I could. Without Miguel's dedication and hard work, this radically improved edition would not have been possible. **Laurie Robertson** kept an eye on getting this abstract ex-professor to write for teachers - she got me to focus more on teachers' needs, and provided suggestions, resources and encouragement. If this version is more understandable and friendly than previous editions, it has a lot to do with her input and her insistence that I not rush to press. Laurie got me to read and edit most of what I have written - and although it has been an embarrassing experience, the book is much improved for the effort. **Jeanne Stone** did a major job in proofreading. If there are errors still in the book, it is because we added them after she got done. **Ben Taylor,** with his positive spirits and a fresh approach, turned my scribbling into formatted words, and added graphic elements and fresh layout ideas. **Catherine Gardner** joined Resources in time to do final formatting.

My thanks go to so many people who have given me ideas, support, and help. Numerous teachers have contributed ideas and are mentioned in the text. **Ted and Nan Graves** gave me Simultaneous Roundtable, Team Word-Webbing, several teambuilding activities, and contributed to the resources section. **Robert Slavin** provided the material for STAD and Jigsaw II. **David and Roger Johnson** provided the material for Learning Together. Over the years I have come to have a deeper and fuller appreciation of their

Preface

work as I have seen the power of social roles and reflection time within teams and within classrooms. **Liz Cohen** wrote the section on Finding Out. **Noreen Webb** provided the helping role play lesson as well as some helping processing forms based on her excellent work demonstrating the importance of teaching students how to help. **Dee Dishon and Pat Wilson O'Leary** provided forms from their excellent book, *A Guidebook for Cooperative Learning: A Technique for Creating More Effective Schools.* **Chris Harrison** created and allowed me to share Co-op Jigsaw I; **Dolores Sasway** contributed Workstation Jigsaw; **Doug Wilkinson** designed Leapfrog Jigsaw and suggested Team Worksheets. **Gayle Hughes** provided cooperative skill development materials and permission to reproduce materials from *Working together, Learning together! The Cooperatively Structured Classroom.* **Shlomo Sharan,** inspired me with his vision of cooperative learning which includes a concern for the total education of the student. Although my Co-op Co-op and his version of Group Investigation were developed independently, they share a similar philosophy and structure.

I owe a great debt to **Irving Balow** (Dean, School of Education, UC Riverside), who first gave me encouragement to try large scale training of student teachers and supervisors. **Sylvia Andreatta** and **James Reardon,** (Supervisors of teacher training, UCR School of Education) were inspirational. James Reardon supplied his versions of Survival in the Desert and Lost on the Moon, which are the grandparents of the versions presented in this edition..

Roger Skinner is the principal who first opened to me his school (Chaparral Middle School, Diamond Bar, California) providing me a wonderful place to experiment and learn. Chaparral has received many honors and has become a model school, leading the middle school movement. The staff continues its strong commitment to cooperative learning, serving as a visitation site for hundreds of teachers and administrators each year, and putting on trainings for neighboring middle schools.

Above all, I am deeply appreciative of the many teachers, theorists, trainers, administrators, student teacher supervisors, student teachers, and students who have had the courage to turn students around. What a daring idea: Have students face each other, rather than each other's backs. In the process of this revolution, we are all students, learning from and with each other.

Those who have allowed me to work with them on their district-wide cooperative learning implementation plans include: **Helen Fried** (ABC School District), **Frank Encinias** (Coachella Valley Unified School District), **Yolanda Gutierrez Miller** (Pajaro School District), **Dolores Sasway** (Vista Unified School District), **Bill Manahan** (Saddleback Unified School District), **Henrietta Sakamaki** (Franklin-McKinley School District), **Lu Hishman** (Los Angeles Unified School District) **John Pennoyer** (Lyons County Township) and **Diane Wallace** (Culver City Unified School District).

I have learned greatly participating in the multi-district training programs designed by **Shelly Coleman** (Los Angeles County Office of Education), **Rocio Moss** (San Diego Multifunctional Resources Center), **Tina Marinez** (Riverside County Office of Education) **Dien To** (Santa Clara County Office of Education), **Jeannie James, David Delgado, and Naeda Robinson** (Monterey County Office of Education), and **Catherine Jones** (Sonoma County Office of Education).

Individuals who contributed to previous editions of the book and whose work in some form is still included in the present edition include **Pat Lederer, Pam Betz, Chuck Wiederhold, Keith Bimson, Ann McCrocklin, Susan Paul, Amalya Nattiv, Ethel Barkelew, Simon Kagan, Monica Kagan,** and **Carlos Kagan.**

Spencer Kagan
November, 1991

Spencer Kagan: *Cooperative Learning*©
Publisher: Resources for Teachers , Inc. • 1(800) Wee Co-op

When giving initial workshops and talks on cooperative learning, following my presentation, frequently I hear questions or objections. When this happens, I wish I had answered the questions first, for I suspect that the questioner has listened to the whole presentation through the filter of their objections.

In an attempt to clear the air and hopefully allow a more open evaluation of what is contained in this book, I will begin by listing the most frequently asked questions and objections regarding cooperative learning, together with my responses.

with the interpersonal skills they will need for positive participation in economic life. That is not happening. When I used to ask my undergraduate students each quarter, how many of them had ever worked together with other students on a learning team or on part of a learning project, approximately 85% indicated they had never been part of a learning team in the classroom. Clearly the social structure of schools is out of step with the reality of the workplace. And without change, the schools will be further and further out of step because our economy is shifting toward high-technology and information-related jobs in which cooperative interpersonal skills increasingly are at a premium.

1. Isn't it wrong to teach using cooperative learning methods when we must prepare students for a competitive world?

There are two important points to be made: (1) The world is not just competitive and in some important respects is becoming less so; (2) I do not advocate exclusive use of cooperative learning methods, but rather a healthy balance of cooperative, competitive, and individualistic classroom structures to prepare students for the full range of social situations.

With regard to the first point, it is hard to imagine a job today which does not involve some cooperative interaction with others. The most frequent reason for individuals to be fired from their first job is not lack of job related skills, but rather lack of interpersonal skills. Given the reality of the job-world, it is incumbent on schools to provide cooperative, interdependent experiences in order to provide students

With regard to the first point, it is hard to imagine a job today which does not involve some cooperative interaction with others. The most frequent reason individuals are fired from a job is not lack of job related skills, but rather lack of interpersonal skills.

With regard to the second point, it would be just as unhealthy for schools to teach exclusively with cooperative methods as with competitive individualistic methods. In 1968 I began a research program examining how children in different cultures behaved in situations in which they could cooperate or compete. The experimental situations usually involved a game board on which children played for rewards. One striking result of that research program was the consistent finding that by the second grade children in urban settings persist in competition even when that strategy is not adaptive for obtaining desired rewards. This non-adaptive competition appears strongly after a few years of conventional, competitively structured schooling. Many of the competitive children are blind to the cooperative solution. They say things like "This game is too hard," or "No one can get any toys." Meanwhile their younger brothers and sisters find the game very simple and obtain almost all of the available rewards. (Kagan and Madsen, 1971)

Chapter 1. Ten Frequent Questions

Competitive cultural values and school practices do not prepare students to see and select an adaptive cooperative strategy. We found that students who experienced cooperative classroom structures (even for limited times in one subject area) more often choose adaptive cooperative strategies. (Kagan and Associates, 1985)

If our future generations are to behave rationally across the full range of social situations, our classrooms must include cooperative, interdependent learning situations along with competitive and individualistic learning situations. Because we face an increasingly complex, changing, and unpredictable future social and economic world, we must prepare our students to be flexible so they can recognize and adapt to cooperative, competitive, and individualistic social interaction situations. It would be as foolish to prepare individuals to be only cooperative as it would be to prepare them to be only competitive. We need flexible and rational individuals, who have experienced the full range of social situations and who are prepared to work and interact productively in them all.

The research on this point is clear. Studies of cross-age peer tutoring reveals tutors make substantial academic gains -- they learn almost as much as their tutees. There is no evidence that time spent tutoring others is a detriment to learning. The opposite is true.

Unfortunately, we have come to believe that learning is best promoted by being taught. In fact, learning is best promoted by being motivated to learn and being in a situation which allows learning to occur. It turns out that tutoring is such a situation, providing both the motivation and opportunity to learn.

The high achievers profit in cooperative learning in other ways. Leadership skills, self-esteem gains, conflict resolution skills, and role-taking abilities are part of the "new curriculum" inherent in cooperative learning. Ask the parents of the high achiever, "What do you most want your child to do when he/she leaves school?" They will respond by naming a position which involves leadership. Then ask, "If your student doesn't have the opportunity to work with others, where will he or she obtain the necessary leadership skills?"

As we tutor, even simple questions from the tutee make us look at our subject matter freshly. As we try to determine the easiest way to convey understanding or overcome a learning block, we ourselves gain a deeper understanding of our topic. But then, somehow, we deny that deeper understanding to our students: We do not let them teach.

2. Isn't the accelerated achievement of low-achieving students in cooperative learning bought at the expense of high-achieving students? Couldn't the high achievers learn more if they were not stuck tutoring?

This question surprises me coming from teachers. As teachers, we know that in the process of teaching others we continually learn more about the topics we teach. As we tutor, even simple questions from the tutee make us look at our subject matter freshly. As we try to determine the easiest way to convey understanding or overcome a learning block, we ourselves gain a deeper understanding of our topic. But then, somehow, we deny that deeper understanding to our students. We do not let them teach. When we look at our students, we forget our own experience which shows us how much teaching is itself a great teacher.

3. If I allow students to discuss and argue among themselves, won't I be faced with difficult classroom management problems?

If the institution of cooperative learning is not accompanied with an effective classroom management system, serious problems are likely to occur. One of the most important, but most neglected, topics in cooperative learning is classroom management. Teachers have lost control of their classrooms because they could not manage the energy which is released by teaming students and allowing them to interact.

It has become second nature to most teachers to exert energy keeping students quiet with their attention only on the teacher or text. Teachers forget that they are demanding that students not do what they most want to do -- interact with their peers. It is no wonder that teachers in a traditional classroom end up so exhausted. They are bucking the basic nature of the student. Students want to question, discuss, argue, and share. The great strength of cooperative learning is that it channels this natural intelligence toward positive academic and social outcomes. In the process, however, great energy is released among students and the effective cooperative learning teacher must know how to channel that energy in positive directions -- know how to manage a classroom of teams. One of the most important contributions of this book is the section on classroom management.

accountable for their learning or product. This means less direct instruction and a new role for the teacher as a consultant to groups. If a teacher attempts direct instruction while groups are in operation, it can interfere with students talking, working together, and learning. Depending on the cooperative learning method, however, the teacher's role can be quite different. Some methods include direct instruction, systematic observation and feedback of group process, careful assignment of students to teams, social skill instruction and creative lesson design. Some approaches demand that the teacher master a number of structures and skills, and become creative within a variety of lesson designs; other approaches rely on one method only, and the teacher has little input into the content or structure of the learning experience.

4. Isn't cooperative learning in conflict with back-to-basics and direct instruction?

No. There is a confusion in the minds of some educators. Somehow, for them cooperative learning is associated with soft, undisciplined, humanistic approaches to the classroom. In fact, the cooperative learning methods encompass the entire range of classroom objectives. Some of the methods are tightly structured and have clearly defined learning objectives which are assessed frequently by individual quizzes and exams. Direct instruction often is an important component of a cooperative learning lesson. Research reveals that students spend more time on academic tasks in cooperative classrooms than they do in traditional classrooms. When students know that their performance depends on their teammates, they make sure their teammates stay on task.

In general, during cooperative learning, the teacher delegates authority to groups while holding them

It is no wonder that teachers in a traditional classroom end up so exhausted. They are bucking the basic nature of the student. Students want to question, discuss, argue, and share. The great strength of cooperative learning is that it channels this natural intelligence toward positive academic and social outcomes.

5. Doesn't cooperative learning mean forcing some students to work with others they don't like?

No. In fact, if teachers try to make students work together, the students probably won't. In a well-managed cooperative classroom, there is never a power play. Teachers assign students to teams and provide team recognition for desired academic and social behaviors. The power of teambuilding, classbuilding, and positive group dynamics draws initially hostile and reluctant students into full participation.

6. I was involved once in a group project. The group decided on a topic and I had to go along, although I did not agree. Doesn't cooperative learning mean giving up individuality?

No. The behavioral engineering in formal cooperative learning methods is based on a respect for individual differences in abilities and values. For example, in Jigsaw each student has a unique contribution to the group; in Co-op Co-op each student has a minitopic for which he/she alone is responsible. Many cooperative learning techniques are structured so that the contributions from each member must be respected or the group cannot reach its objectives.

7. I was in a group once also. In my group a few members did all the work. Doesn't cooperative learning mean a free ride for some and extra work for others?

No. Again, the design of formal cooperative learning methods ensures that each student must contribute if the group is to reach its goal. In this way, the formal cooperative learning methods differ from informal, collaborative groups which often do not ensure that the contribution of each member is necessary for success. Cooperative learning methods are structured so that no individual can coast on the efforts of his/her teammates. Learning is individually assessed and students are individually accountable for their own learning gains.

8. If I use cooperative learning can I still "get through" the curriculum? Doesn't it focus on process at the expense of content?

Some cooperative learning methods are oriented toward mastery of basic skills and information; others are oriented toward completion of complex group projects, often with an emphasis on higher level thinking skills. Depending on the values and objectives of the teacher, cooperative learning is used in very different ways.

Even the same methods can be used with very different objectives. For example, because of the division of labor in the design, Jigsaw can be used as a very efficient way of covering a great deal of content in a short period of time. On the other hand, Jigsaw can be used within a process approach in which the goal is to promote higher level thought, without concern that a fixed amount of content be covered. In that case, each student may be assigned a point of view and discussion and thought are the outcomes.

Some educators abhor memorization and practice, but find value in the interactive aspects of cooperative learning; others find in cooperative learning efficient practice methods to ensure memory of basic facts, and skills. Cooperative learning offers methods to reach the whole range of educational objectives more efficiently than traditional methods.

Cooperative learning will take a different form in each classroom, depending on the values and beliefs of each teacher. This book is designed to provide resources from which teachers can draw. Like an artist, the good teacher draws from the available resources and creates his or her own unique masterpiece.

9. How much class time should be devoted to cooperative learning?

This question will be answered in practice very differently by each teacher. Some experienced teachers use cooperative groups most of the time and others use them one day a week in one subject only. In general, teachers training with me end up using cooperative learning more than any other approach, but this usually comes about gradually. My own research showed that very impressive academic and social gains can be obtained if cooperative learning is used only briefly. One recommendation I do make: Try cooperative learning in a very limited way at first. After you have mastered the art of managing a classroom of teams and feel competent in one structure, you may well begin to include other techniques -- eventually finding the amount and style of grouping which best fits your own style. I recommend you ease into cooperative learning; the excitement, involvement, and gains of your students will lead you to try more.

10. Should we use rewards -- tokens, points, and certificates?

Some argue that points, tokens, certificates, and even praise are reward systems which foster extrinsic motivation and erode intrinsic motivation. Others feel they are useful methods of recognizing desired behavior and communicating in a clear way a teacher's appreciation of certain behaviors and the extent to which students are making progress toward their goals.

As teachers become more versed in a range of cooperative learning structures, they come to trust the rewards intrinsic in cooperative learning. Over time, they find themselves using fewer and fewer extrinsic rewards. Whenever possible I like to design the learning task so that it is intrinsically rewarding. On the other hand, when using practice structures, such as with Pairs Check and the Flashcard Game, I emphasize liberal use of peer praise. In observing thousands of students using these methods, I know inclusion of peer praise makes learning fun and game-like. If these methods eroded intrinsic motivation, why is it that students now request Pairs Check, and ask to take their Color-Coded-Co-op Cards out to recess, to continue playing?

Tokens, special recognition systems, and structured peer praise do not necessarily weaken intrinsic motivation. Extrinsic motivators can increase motivation.. As teachers, we should design learning tasks which are as intrinsically interesting. But adding points, praisers, and games is not the problem. The problem occurs where we try to motivate students through points and praise without focusing on creating the most meaningful learning experience.

The personal values and beliefs of each teacher, the nature of the task, and the needs of the students will dictate the extent to which some form of extrinsic motivators are included.

Improvement scoring is giving students points based on how much they improve, not just based on how well they do compared to a standard or compared to each other. Although it is not a defining characteristic of cooperative learning, it is a method of scoring very compatible with cooperative learning, which can tremendously facilitate learning. If I assign one high, two middle, and one low achieving student to each team and use traditional scoring methods, the students will soon learn that no matter how hard they work with the low achiever he or she always brings in the low score. Soon students ask for a new teammate! Traditional scoring is a disaster for the self-esteem of the low-achieving student. If however, improvement scoring is used so that students bring points back to the team based on how much they have improved over their usual level of performance, then each student has the potential of bringing maximum points to the team. When improvement scoring is used teammates are pleased to work with those who need help the most.

A Bit of Philosophy

The type and amount of cooperative learning a teacher adopts is, in part, a function of what he or she sees as the goal of teaching. Some teachers have as a goal making students cooperative. Others want to make students more competitive. Personally, I do not identify with either goal. I would like students to become flexible, so they cooperate, compete, or go it on their own depending on the situation. I would be pleased if we provided for our students as wide a range of learning experiences as possible, so that they are better prepared to adapt to and modify their social and physical environment.

Thus, it would be as bad to provide only cooperative learning experiences as it would be to provide only competitive or individualistic learning experiences. Ideally, as teachers we would provide as broad a range of learning experiences to our students as possible, including a variety of structured and unstructured cooperative learning experiences, as well as a balance of cooperative, competitive, and individualistic learning experiences. Our students would be then prepared to function well across the whole range of life's settings. Following that model, ideally, during the time allotted to cooperative learning, there would also be a range of learning experiences, encompassing both the structural and process approaches, cooperative and

Spencer Kagan: *Cooperative Learning*©
Publisher: Resources for Teachers , Inc. • 1(800) Wee Co-op

collaborative models, mastery, as well as thinking skill and concept development.

One of the highest goals of education is to provide students with experiences which will allow them to structure their own future social and physical environments in positive ways, including their own continuing education. I have no problem with the occasional use of highly structured learning experiences, including point systems, tokens, and "drill and practice" methods, but I would have a problem if these methods became the only type of learning experience for our students. If teachers structured things so that there always was an extrinsic reward for learning, they would rob students of experiences in settings in which students' interests and needs provide the sole basis of learning. Similarly, if as teachers, we provide only situations in which it is adaptive to cooperate, we rob students of important learning experiences. Ultimately, students need to learn how to structure and restructure their own social environment and learning experiences. That kind of learning occurs as a function of experiencing a very wide range of classroom learning structures.

As educators, we presently face a task very different from that of previous generations of educators. We must prepare our students for a world we can only dimly imagine. The world is changing so fast that half of the students who enter school this year will have their first job in a job category not yet created. They will have many types of employment over their lifetime. We no longer have the luxury of preparing students with a set body of information which they will apply for a lifetime. The information base is changing so fast that many of the facts, and even conceptual systems, we now teach will be outdated before students graduate, and certainly over the years of their employment. Given this situation, we need to emphasize thinking skills as well as content, and we must prepare our students to act adaptively in a very broad range of social situations. ∽

References:

Kagan, S. & Madsen, M. C. Cooperation and competition of Mexican, Mexican-American, and Anglo-American children of two ages under four instructional sets. *Developmental Psychology*, 1971, *5, 32-39.*

Kagan, S., Zahn, G. L., Widaman, K., Schwarzwald, J., & Tyrrell, G. Classroom Structural Bias: Impact of Cooperative and Competitive Classroom Structures on Cooperative and Competitive Individuals and Groups. In R. Slavin, S. Sharan, S. Kagan, R. Hertz-Lazarowitz, C. Webb & R. Schmuck (Eds.) *Learning to Cooperate, Cooperating to Learn.* New York: Plenum, 1985

A Team
*Four individuals,
Giving and taking.
By interacting,
Four becomes more.*

Chapter 2

The Need for Cooperative Learning

As we approach the twenty-first century, radical shifts in our economy and demographics necessitate a reexamination of our educational system. The role our schools must play in preparing all students for full participation in the economy and society of the twenty-first century is fundamentally different than the traditional role of schools. At an accelerating rate, we move into a rapidly changing, information-based, high-technology, and interdependent economy. Along with the traditional role of providing students with basic skills and information, increasingly schools must produce students capable of higher-level thinking skills, communication skills, and social skills.

Our economy is transforming: The largest and fastest growing segment of the economy is the information segment -- generating, analyzing, and communicating information. In a high-technology economy, the norm in the workplace is interaction. Increasingly, the workplace consists of interdependent teams working on complex problems which no individual alone can solve. Thus, our schools must set as highest priority the teaching of thinking skills, communication skills, and social skills necessary for participation in our increasingly complex, interdependent society and workplace.

At an accelerating rate we move into a rapidly changing information-based, high-technology, and interdependent economy. Along with the traditional role of providing students with basic skills and information, increasingly schools must produce students capable of higher-level thinking skills, communication skills, and social skills.

As educators our primary function is to provide our students with the skills they will need for a productive and happy life. Thus we must look carefully at the forces that are shaping our economic and social world, to discern the kinds of skills our students will need and those which they are lacking, based on our present socialization and educational practices. A critical question, then, is, "What kind of an economic and social world will our students face?" As educators we must examine closely the social, economic and demographic trends, to assess whether we are providing our students with the full range of skills they will need for their future maximum development.

The change rate provides a press for change in our schools. Half the kindergarten students of today will have their first job in a job category which does not yet exist. Because technology produces ever higher-level technological advances, which in turn will transform even more radically the jobs and lives of students, the schools must provide for their students a broader base of experiences, skills, and information. Because cooperative teamwork, interaction, and communication will characterize the workplace of the future, it is

We as educators today have the unprecedented job of preparing pupils to participate in a world we can only dimly imagine.

Spencer Kagan: *Cooperative Learning*©
Publisher: Resources for Teachers , Inc. • 1(800) Wee Co-op

imperative that our classrooms include not only individualistic and competitive interaction, but also cooperative interaction. How else will our students learn the skills necessary for participation in the new economy?

Schools across the nation are dealing also with population shifts: racial, linguistic, economic, and social diversity are increasing dramatically. In California, as we enter the twenty-first century, Hispanic students will become the largest ethnic group in our public schools.

Thus, a variety of reasons compel us to consider cooperative learning as an important response to the transformations in our society. It broadens students' range of experience, including interactive learning opportunities representative of the workplace of the future. It provides a variety of ways to foster communication skills, higher-level thinking skills, and social skills -- skills increasingly in demand. The heterogeneous team in the classroom becomes a positive model of how society can cope with the demographic and economic shifts.

Transformed Socialization Practices

THE SOCIALIZATION VOID

Students today generally do not come to school with the same prosocial values once common; they are not as respectful, caring, helpful, or cooperative as they were twenty years ago. The loss of prosocial values and behaviors among students is a result of a number of converging economic and social factors.

Family Structure

Families today are mobile, separating children from the stabilizing influences of enduring neighborhood and community support systems. The two-income family is increasingly an economic necessity. Mothers have left home to enter the job-world, children spend less time in the company of the person most concerned about their posi-

tive development. The two-parent family can no longer be assumed; one quarter of American families have only one parent living at home, and it is estimated that by year 2000 the percentage of one- parent families will grow to between one-third and one-half of all families in the United States. The number of "latch key kids" is on the rise. Because families are small and not extended, children grow up having less contact with older siblings and grandparents -- older, caring others who once had a positive impact on social development.

Television

If children are less often under the guidance of adults and older siblings, where are they? What has filled the socialization void? Answer: If a student makes it to graduation from high school she/he has completed approximately 15,000 hours of classroom experience; by then she/he has completed about

If we count summer viewing hours, children now spend more time viewing television than they do in school or any other single daily activity.

18,000 hours of TV viewing. There are three problems with television as a substitute socializer.

1. Antisocial Content. It is hard to flip the channels of television without finding someone killing or at least hurting someone. The content of television programs often provides a very poor model for social development. More violent acts per minute are portrayed on children's TV programs than at any other time. Violence on prime time television has increased radically in the past decade, and it is greater during children's' viewing hours than at any other time.

2. Advertising. A tremendous fortune goes into television advertising, all designed to communicate a fundamental message: if you are unhappy, if you want to feel more potent, powerful, or successful, an easy solution awaits -- buy something. If you want to feel better about yourself, purchase a product.

Through television our youth are taught that the way to be more attractive is to buy a better deodorant; I have yet to see an advertisement for increasing one's communication or conflict resolution skills.

3. Erosion of Family Communication. When the television is on, the probability is decreased that family members will interact in ways likely to increase positive social development. Television viewing is very individualistic. As family members orient toward the television rather than each other, opportunities are lost for children to learn valuable social interaction and communication skills. Elementary school children now watch television about fifteen times as many hours as talking with their father. Television is a very poor substitute for caring family interaction.

Consequences of the Socialization Void

These changing family structures and socialization practices have resulted in students who lack social skills and attachments. The students of today do not know how to get along well with each other, care for each other, or care for themselves.

Dozens of studies have demonstrated that our students do not recognize the cooperative solution to problems. When students

"Among the personal skills that students should develop are sensitivity to the needs, problems, and aspirations of others... an understanding of people as individuals rather than as stereotypical members of a particular group; and the ability to adjust one's behavior to work effectively with others." (History-Social Science Framework, California State Board of Education, 1987, p. 24).

are placed in situations in which they can maximize their own gains only by working together, they tend to adopt a competitive strategy which produces fewer positive outcomes for both themselves and their peers. The nonadaptive competitiveness of our students has been documented through almost the whole range of development. It begins a few years after students enter school and continues throughout college years. After only a few years of traditional, competitive schooling, 7-9 year old students repeatedly fail to employ the adaptive cooperative strategies which 4-5 year old children (who have not yet been subject to years of competitive classroom structures) easily adopt (Kagan & Madsen, 1971; Kagan, 1977).

The need for a positive socialization program in schools is indicated also by a variety of statistics. Among an average group of 640 high school students this year, one will commit suicide; ten will make a serious attempt to do so; and 100 will contemplate doing so. Suicide rates among our nation's youth have climbed drastically in the last twenty years. Crimes against persons and property in school are at an unprecedented rate. Schools must devote substantial resources to repair vandalism; some have been forced to hire security forces. Many students leave today's schools without the social skills necessary to hold a job. Numerous studies examining the reasons for job loss among first-time employees reveal that the most common cause of losing a job -- far more common than lack of job-related skills -- is lack of social skills. Today, students finish their education unprepared for the social demands of our modern economy.

Schools must Fill the Socialization Void

Forces have combined to thrust on the schools -- like it or not -- the job of socializing our nation's youth. Schools must pick up the job of socializing students in the values of caring, sharing, and helping. Schools cannot stay out of the arena of moral and social development. The evidence on this point is extremely clear. If exclusively traditional classroom structures are used, children become more competitive; if cooperative classroom structures are used, children become more cooperative. And we must choose some type of classroom structure! The only real question is not if, but how, we are going to impact on the social development of our students.

Cooperative learning groups involve more facilitative and encouraging interaction among students than do competitive or individualistic learning situations. Dozens of studies have demonstrated that when students are allowed to work together they experience an increase in a variety of social skills; they become more able to solve problems which demand cooperation for solution, better able to take the role of the other, and are generally more cooperative on a variety of measures, such as willingness to help and reward others.

It is hard to imagine how students can obtain skills like "adjusting one's behavior to work effectively with others" if they are not allowed to work together. Unfortunately, at present, most schools still rely almost exclusively on competitive and individualistic classroom structures. The ethnographic research reveals that teachers do about 80% of the talking in most classrooms. Students are expected to passively orient to the teacher -- they literally have little or no say regarding what and how to study. It is remarkable that a nation which prides itself on democracy has settled on an educational system which effectively socializes its youth to be passive participants in an autocracy.

During the seventeen years I was a professor at the University of California, I used cooperative learning in my classes. When I asked students how many had ever worked with other students on a cooperative learning project, never more than 15% of the students raised their hands. The implications are staggering: most students manage to go through the whole educational system without ever working with anyone else! There is a large void in our socialization practices. Nowhere are students learning how to work effectively with others. It is no wonder employers find a lack of social skills among employees the number one problem. The need for social skills in the economy and society of the future will be even greater.

Transformed Economy
TOWARD A PEOPLE-ORIENTED ECONOMY

It turns out that the world of the near future, the world in which our present students will work and interact, will be radically different from that of our grandparents, parents, and even ourselves. Many of the ways in which our world is transforming have been detailed by John Naisbitt in *Megatrends*. The first, and perhaps most important, of these megatrends is the transformation from an industrial to an information-based economy.

From Agriculture to Industry

At the turn of the century more than one-third of the total labor force in this country was engaged in farming. Now less than 3 percent of the work force are farmers, and over 10% of them are at or near insolvency. The number of persons engaged in agricultural occupations in the future will be even lower than at present. The shift from an agricultural to an industrial society was very fast in historical terms -- taking less than 100 years. In the last 30 years another shift has taken place. We have entered, as sociologist Daniel Bell calls it, the "post-industrial age." A nation of farmers turned industrialists and laborers, has undergone, in the last thirty years, yet, another radical transformation.

If we are not a nation of farmers as we once were, and we are not a nation of manufacturers and laborers, as we most recently were, what are we?

From Industry to Information-Management

Almost without noticing, in the last thirty years Americans have again radically transformed their economic base. The manufacturing portion of the economy has shrunk radically. As of May 1983, David L. Birch of MIT reported that only 12 percent of our labor force is engaged in manufacturing.

It turns out that we are a nation of professionals. In 1956, for the first time, white-collar workers in technical, managerial and clerical positions outnumbered blue-collar workers. In 1950, only 17 percent of the nation worked in information-related jobs.

We have become a nation of secretaries, clerks, teachers, accountants, and managers. By 1970 the information-management-service sector of the economy accounted for more than half of the GNP and income earned.

And the trend is continuing. Legal services, not apparel, are now New York City's leading export. The nation's work force grew 18% in the 1970's, but the number of

Of the 20 million new jobs created in the 1970's, 5% were in manufacturing, and almost 90% were in information, knowledge, or service. Now more than two-thirds of the work force deals primarily with information and/or other people.

Spencer Kagan: *Cooperative Learning*©
Publisher: Resources for Teachers , Inc. • 1(800) Wee Co-op

administrators and managers grew about 60%. The shift in our economic base is exemplified by the percentage of growth in health administrators versus engineers: In the 1970's the number of engineers grew by almost 3 percent. In contrast, the number of health administrators grew by 118 percent. In the seven year period ending 1976, 9 million new workers were added to the work force, but the work force in the Fortune 1000 largest industrial concerns did not increase.

Interdependence in Manufacturing

Increasingly, industry is adopting a cooperative model. For example, recent versions of hand-held calculators most often consisted of electronic chips from the United States. They were assembled in Singapore, Indonesia, or Nigeria, placed in a steel housing from India, and stamped with a label, "Made in Japan," upon arrival in Yokohama.

In view of the very radical shift in the economic and social world in which our students will function, it is frightening to realize that the structure of our classrooms has not changed. We still structure our classes as if our students will work within static and individualistic economic structures.

Modern hotels in Saudi Arabia are built with room modules made in Brazil, construction labor from South Korea, and management from the United States. We are seeing the dawn of a global economy and an interdependence previously not imagined.

In the new General Motors in Fremont, California, production, product quality, worker satisfaction, and earnings are all up. What is the "New General Motors?" It is cooperation in the workplace: labor-labor and labor-management teams.

The Change Rate Accelerates

Another radical shift in our society is in the rate at which information is produced. At present, the sheer volume of scientific and technical information doubles every 5 years. And that doubling rate for new information is projected to dwindle to only two years before the end of the century.

The rate of economic change itself also has accelerated tremendously. The transformation from an agricultural to an industrially-based economy took about 100 years, but the transformation from an industrially-based to an information-service based economy took only thirty years. Thus, we can predict that our students are likely to see numerous radical changes in our economic structure -- even if we cannot predict with confidence the nature of those changes. Students entering school today will have numerous jobs over their lifetimes - many in job categories not yet created!

Schools Must Prepare for the New Economy

The radical transformation of our economic and information base, as well as the rate of change itself, has very serious implications for education. If we are to be successful educators, we must look beyond the scores on narrowly defined achievement tests. We are now called upon to prepare our students for a very different world, including different kinds of skills if they are to be successful.

Because of the very rapid change rate in our information base, much of the content we teach will be outdated by the time our students leave school. As educators, we must make a radical shift in our approach to teaching. We must balance our emphasis on content with an emphasis on process. Increasingly, we must teach our students not just what science knows, but how it knows.

The very rapid change rate in our economic base means we must prepare our students to be flexible -- to be prepared to work under a wide range of economic and social task and reward structures. They must learn not only how to be competitive, cooperative, and/or individualistic as task and reward structures demand, but also they must learn the skills associated with transforming existing task and reward structures, not just responding to predetermined structures. Increasingly, economic success -- at both the individual and company levels -- will come by transforming competitive task and reward structures into cooperative structures.

It was once true that, with a fixed set of skills and an individualistic orientation, many of yesterday's students could function very well. In an agricultural economy in which production was based on traditional skills, the more land a man cleared and worked the more he could produce.

That world is gone. Schools must now prepare students for a social and economic world which is changing so fast that it is relatively unpredictable. In the rapidly changing, high-technology, management and information oriented economy of the future, there will be a premium placed on individuals with a variety of social skills. To succeed, students of today must learn to communicate and work well with others within the full range of social situations, especially within situations involving fluid social structures, human diversity, and interdependence.

Transformed Demographics
THE NEW MAJORITY

Our population is shifting in three ways: First, an increasing percentage of students are living in urban centers. Second, racial diversity is increasing. Third, in many key cities and states, we are about to hear loud and clear from a "new majority."

Urbanization

The rate of urbanization, world-wide is increasing logarithmically. In 1800 only 2.4% of the world were living in urban centers; by 1900 the percentage was about 10%; by 1950 the figure was 25%. There has been a massive world-wide rural to urban migration because technological improvements in agriculture have left a substantial portion of the rural population at a large relative disadvantage. This urbanization of our population has serious implications for the evolution of social character and the socialization demands placed on schools.

There has been a long history of speculation regarding the effects of urbanization on social character. Since before the turn of the century sociologists began warning about the consequences of living and working in close proximity with many others with whom there is no sentimental, emotional, or economic interdependence. They spoke of urban life as fostering a spirit of competition, self-aggrandizement, and mutual exploitation. A large number of urban-rural comparisons of cooperativeness among chil-

Students in the future will more and more often need to know how to find out and how to produce knowledge. They will less often be called upon to draw from a stable storehouse of knowledge.

dren all over the world revealed that, almost without exception, children developing in an urban environment grow up valuing less the prosocial behaviors of caring, sharing, helping, and cooperating.

Putting these two pieces of information together -- (1) that we are becoming more urban and (2) that children in urban environments are less cooperative -- it is possible to predict with some confidence the direction of the evolution of social character. Unless we change our socialization practices, people in the future will be less cooperative. This evolution of social character away from prosocial values and behaviors comes at an historical moment when more cooperative values and behaviors are needed. The job of living together in a world in which economic decisions have world-wide implications will demand a new overriding consciousness of interdependence.

Racial Diversity and the "New Majority"

In the last twenty years we have seen a transformation of our basic demographics -- a transformation which in many places will make us redefine our descriptors for students. This transformation is quite profound in the southwestern states, but is being felt in other parts of the United States as well.

In describing students, as recently as 1967, we could use the terms "majority" and "minority" with no ambiguity: 75% of the students in California schools were white or "majority" students 25% were of other races,

Old teaching methods which assume a single language, and shared homogeneity of proficiencies, learning styles, and motivational systems are increasingly inadequate and inappropriate. Cooperative learning methods, which assume heterogeneity, are better designed to cope with the diversity of today's students.

Spencer Kagan: *Cooperative Learning*©
Publisher: Resources for Teachers , Inc. • 1(800) Wee Co-op

Education Completed by Ethnic Group In California

	Complete High School	Enter College	Complete College
Whites	83%	38%	23%
Blacks	72%	29%	12%
Hispanics	55%	22%	9%
Native Americans	55%	17%	6%

mentary school non-white students are about half a grade behind white students in math and a full grade behind in reading. By the end of junior high school, the gap has doubled so that white students score a full grade higher in math and two full grades higher in reading. Beyond that, it is impossible to get accurate comparison figures because there are differential drop-out rates -- non-white students begin dropping out of the educational pipeline much earlier than do white students. By age 17, three times as many Hispanic students (one in five) have dropped out of school compared to whites (one in fifteen). About half of the Hispanic students who enter high school today will drop out before graduation. The education drop-out rates are staggering, see box.

The depth of the forthcoming achievement crisis is clear. Consider two facts: (1) By the year 2000, Hispanics will comprise the largest single segment of school-aged children in the State of California; (2) Presently almost half of all Hispanic students drop out of formal education before they finish high school, and less than 10% finish college.

and were meaningfully referred to as "minority" students. Today both the California population statistics and school enrollments reflect a radically different picture: Just under 50% of the students in California public schools are Anglo, the old minority

The new majority does not come to school with the same values and background as did the old majority. They are not responding well to traditional educational structures.

has become the new majority! By year 2000 the break even point will be past: In public schools only 42.7% of the students will be Anglos. And in the State of California as a whole, over 53% of the population will be "minority;" Hispanics will be the single largest "minority" group in California. As our "minority" has become our majority we need to redefine our terms. And the New Majority is about to have a tremendous impact on public education

The Achievement Crisis

We have across the United States a "majority-minority progressive school achievement gap." Each year non-white students fall farther behind white students: While there is little or no difference in achievement scores at or near entry to school, by the end of ele-

We are moving simultaneously toward a greater need for higher education and a population in which higher education will be less common.

The reason for the poor record of schools in educating and holding nonwhite students has not been established. One plausible explanation is the structural bias hypothesis. In brief, the hypothesis states that traditional classroom structures, because they rely heavily on competitive task and reward structures, provide a bias in favor of the achievement and values of majority students who are generally more competitive in their social orientation than are minority students. This hypothesis has received some support. Minority students, especially Hispanic students, are more cooperative in their social orientation than are majority students, and cooperative students achieve better and feel better about themselves and school in less competitive classrooms. The differential effect of cooperative versus traditional class structures on achievement of minority and majority

Thus we are facing a future population far less educated than the present population. This prospect is especially frightening given the increased educational demands of our future high-technology oriented economy.

Spencer Kagan: *Cooperative Learning*©
Publisher: Resources for Teachers , Inc. • 1(800) Wee Co-op

students can be quite dramatic, as pictured in the graph.

The graph in the box represents the results of a twelve week pretest - posttest study of gains in standardized junior high school English grammar proficiency among black and white students in inner-city school classrooms. Perhaps the most important implication of the results is that the minority-majority achievement gap can be attributed to classroom structure -- not to lack of motivation or ability among minority students. Four major studies which examined the gains of minority and majority students in traditional and cooperative classrooms found similar results. In all four studies, minority students gained far more in cooperative than traditional classrooms. It is important to note that the dramatic achievement gains of non-white students in classrooms using student learning teams are not bought at the expense of white students -- the white students also gained more in the cooperative than the traditional classrooms. Although high achieving students spend considerable time in cooperative learning working with weaker students, they achieve as well or better than if they were working on their own all of the time. Apparently, as they teach they learn. Alternatively, it may be that if students find that if learning allows them to teach, if it empowers them, they may be more motivated to learn. The finding has its parallel in studies of cross-age peer tutoring: Tutors who are sent to lower grades to work with low achieving students gain as much as tutees in both academics and liking for school -- both groups show substantial gains compared to students who do not engage in the tutoring process.

Whatever the reasons, the dramatic gains of low achievement students in cooperative learning is our best hope to respond successfully to the challenge provided by the progressive school achievement gap and the achievement crisis in general.

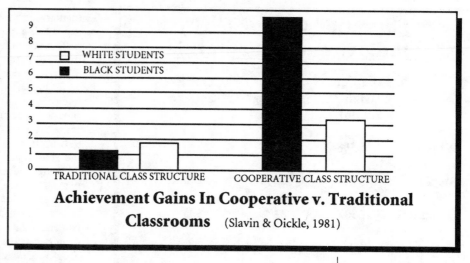

Achievement Gains In Cooperative v. Traditional Classrooms (Slavin & Oickle, 1981)

Race-Relations

Our changing demographics means increased racial diversity. Schools generally have not adopted effective practices to create positive race-relations.

As with the school achievement problem, the problem of poor race-relations among students is progressive. Each school year students choose fewer friends outside their own ethnic or cultural group. In the early years of elementary school, children play and work easily in mixed-racial groups, but by the end of elementary school they begin to segregate themselves along race lines. Racial divisions and tensions increase through middle school, culminating by high school in students isolated from those in other racial groups. Whether or not there is the appearance of racial gangs, there is racial tension. Students are not prepared by our schools to work well in a racially integrated, democratic society.

Consider two facts: (1) By the year 2000, Hispanics will comprise the largest single segment of school-aged children in the State of California; (2) Presently almost half of all Hispanic students drop out of formal education before they finish high school, and less than 10% finish college. We are moving simultaneously toward a greater need for higher education, and a population in which higher education will be less common.

The potential for a race-relations crisis is frightening. Increased racial diversity in the absence of programs which promote positive cross-race relations could be associated with race-relation problems so severe that they could threaten the fabric of our democratic society.

Numerous studies now indicate that progressive deterioration of race-relations among students is not inevitable.

Following cooperative learning, students choose more friends from other races, and interact in a more integrated pattern. Slavin (1983) examined 14 experiments involving students from grades 3 through 12. Cross-ethnic friendships increased in the cooperative learning classrooms over control classrooms. In the studies using the original Jigsaw method, only one of the five ethnic relations measures showed improvement in cooperative over the control classrooms. In the remainder of the studies, however, 63 percent of the 19 tests of ethnic relations showed better ethnic relations in cooperative than control classrooms. The remaining comparisons showed no difference. Never were ethnic relations significantly better in control classrooms.

Our courts have mandated desegregation, but they have not provided resources or training so that our schools can create integration. We have court-mandated desegregation, but within our classrooms students segregate themselves along race lines.

The improvement in ethnic relations among students in a number of the studies is quite dramatic. For example, in one study in traditional classrooms, students listed 9.8% of their friends as from a race other than their own; in contrast, students in the cooperative classroom listed 37.9%. In some studies there have been very dramatic reductions or elimination of self-segregation among students following relatively brief cooperative learning experiences (Kagan, Widaman, Schwarzwald, & Tyrrell, 1985).

In classrooms which use integrated student learning teams, positive race relations among students increases.

Increased Numbers of Limited English Proficient Students

With our changing demographics, there is an increasing number of students limited in English proficiency. Cooperative learning responds to the needs of those students as it allows improved comprehension, as well as production of language, and these outcomes both aid subject matter gains. As input is made more comprehensible, the probability of acquiring language increases, as does access to the curriculum. As language output over subject matter increases, so does the probability of obtaining and retaining new linguistic abilities as well as the new subject matter. Further, as students interact during cooperative learning, the goals of increasing comprehensibility of input and increasing the quantity and quality of language production complement each other. Through the negotiation process, the language production of one student becomes the comprehensible input for another. Thus, cooperative learning simultaneously serves to aid both understanding and practice of both language and content (Kagan, 1990).

Unless there is a change in our educational practices, increased non-white student populations and increased racial diversity will result in two crises within school: (1) a failure to hold and educate most students, and (2) increased racial tension and segregation along race lines among students. We are failing to educate our non-white students. As they become our new majority, our schools will become elitist, effective for only the white minority of our population. If we continue along our present path, we are likely to experience an achievement crisis and a race-relations crisis the likes of which we have not yet imagined.

In Conclusion

We are facing a severe crisis in education. If we do not change our educational practices, we are headed toward a break-down in race relations, both in our classrooms and in the society as a whole. If we do not change, we will face the inability to hold and educate the majority of our population to the minimum educational standards.

We are facing another critical choice-point. We can allow social character to evolve in ways discrepant with our projected needs,

Chapter 2. The Need for Cooperative Learning

or, as educators, we can have a direct positive impact, changing our schooling practices in ways which will prepare our students for the interdependent world they will face. As we have seen, the question is not whether schools will impact on social development, but what direction that impact will take. At present, schools contribute heavily toward socializing our future generation toward a less caring and more competitive social orientation. As educators we can make a different choice. We can restructure our classrooms so that students experience, for some of the time, situations in which it is adaptive to help, rather than hinder, each other.

As educators, we have not taken responsibility for the competitive socialization which we are providing for our students. Competitive classroom structures, at present, are an assumed given. But in fact, they are not a given; they are something we create each day. And as we do so, we create negative race-relations, poor achievement -- especially for non-white students, and a social character ill-equipped to meet the demands of an increasingly interdependent social and economic world.

We need to include cooperative learning experiences in our classrooms, because many traditional socialization practices are now absent, and students no longer come to school with an established caring and cooperative social orientation. Traditional, competitive classroom structures contribute to this socialization void. Thus, students are left ill-prepared for a world which increasingly demands highly developed social skills to deal with increasing economic and social interdependence.

Additionally, we need cooperative learning if we are to preserve democracy. Exclusive use of autocratic, teacher-dominated classroom structures leaves students unprepared for participation in a democratic society. Democracy is not nurtured by a system which fosters racial cleavages, educates only an elite group, models autocratic decision making, and expects passive obedience among pupils.

Cooperative, interdependent educational experiences in our classrooms are necessary if we hope to make possible the democratic ideal of informed and equal participation.

∿

References:

California State Board of Education. *History- Social Science Framework.* California State Department of Education, Sacramento, 1988

Kagan, S. & Madsen, M. C. Cooperation and competition of Mexican, Mexican-American, and Anglo-American children of two ages under four instructional sets. *Developmental Psychology,* 1971, 5, 32-39.

Kagan, Spencer. Social motives and behaviors of Mexican-American and Anglo-American children. In J. L. Martinez (Ed.), *Chicano Psychology.* New York: Academic Press, 1977.

Kagan, Spencer. Cooperative Learning for Students Limited in Language Proficiency. In M. Brubacher, R. Payne, & K. Rickett (Eds.) *Perspectives on Small Group Learning.* Oakville, Ontario, Canada: 1990.

Kagan, S., Zahn, G.L., Widaman, K.F., Schwarzwald, J. & Tyrrell, G. Classroom Structural Bias: Impact of cooperative and competitive classroom structures on cooperative and competitive individuals and groups. In R. E. Slavin, S. Sharan, S. Kagan, R. Hertz-Lazarowitz, C. Webb & R. Schmuck (Eds.) *Learning to Cooperate, Cooperating to Learn.* New York: Plenum, 1985.

Naisbitt, John. *Megatrends.* New York: New York, Warner Books, 1988.

Slavin, R.E. & Oikel 1981. Effects of cooperative learning teams on student achievement and race relations: Treatment by race interaction. *Sociology of Education,* 1981, 54, 174-180.1981.

Slavin, Robert, E. *Cooperative Learning.* New York: Longman, 1983.

Chapter 3

Positive Outcomes

Cooperative Learning is the most extensively researched educational innovation of all time. And the results are clear.

Hundreds of lab and field research studies demonstrate that cooperative learning has a number of very positive outcomes. The three most important of these are (1) academic gains, especially for minority and low achieving students; (2) improved race-relations among students in integrated classrooms; and (3) improved social and affective development among all students. There is also evidence that cooperative learning has a positive impact on classroom climate, self-esteem among students, internal focus of control, role-taking abilities, time on task, attendance, acceptance of main-streamed students, and liking for school and learning. References to reviews of the extensive research are provided. The following is a brief summary of the effects of cooperative learning and an examination of possible explanations of the many positive effects.

What Does Cooperative Learning Do and Why?

ACADEMIC ACHIEVEMENT

Cooperative learning promotes higher achievement than competitive and individualistic learning structures across all age levels, subject areas, and almost all tasks. This conclusion is based on a number of major literature reviews including those of David and Roger Johnson (1981) who conducted a meta-analysis on 122 achievement-related studies and Robert Slavin (1983b) who analyzed 46 controlled research studies which were conducted for an extended time in regular elementary and secondary school classrooms. Among the studies examined by Slavin, 63% showed superior outcomes for cooperative learning, 33% showed no differences, and only 4% showed higher achievement for the traditional comparison groups. Achievement gains were found in almost all (89%) of the studies which used group rewards for individual achievement (individual accountability). When individual accountability was absent, achievement overall was about the same as in comparison classrooms.

The lowest achieving students and minority students in general benefit most, but the benefit obtained for the lower achievers is not bought at the expense of the higher achievers; the high achieving students generally perform as well or better in cooperative classrooms than they do in traditional classrooms.

ETHNIC RELATIONS

A consistent finding in cooperative learning research has been improved ethnic relations among students. In my own research involv-

Spencer Kagan: *Cooperative Learning*©
Publisher: Resources for Teachers , Inc. • 1(800) Wee Co-op

ing about 1000 students and almost 1 million bits of data, improvements in ethnic relations were greater than any other outcome from cooperative learning (Kagan and Associates, 1985). In summarizing the literature, Robert Slavin (1983a) examined 14 experiments involving students from grades 3 through 12. Overall, cross-ethnic friendships improved in the cooperative learning classrooms over control classes. In the studies using the original Jigsaw method, only one of the five ethnic relations measures showed improvement in cooperative over the control classrooms. In the remainder of the studies, however, 63 percent of the 19 tests of ethnic relations showed better ethnic relations in cooperative than control classrooms. The remaining comparisons showed no difference. Never were ethnic relations significantly better in control classrooms.

SOCIAL AND AFFECTIVE DEVELOPMENT

Social Skills

The ability to adjust one's behavior to work effectively with others and to communicate with others can be learned only in the process of working and interacting with others. Thus, cooperative learning becomes a necessary component of curriculum reform if we are to prepare our students for a job world of the future. Johnson and Associates (1981) and Slavin (1983a) have summarized the research: Cooperative learning results in more positive social development and social relations among students at all grade levels.

Dozens of studies have demonstrated that when students are allowed to work together, they experience an increase in a variety of social skills; students become more able to solve problems which demand cooperation for a solution, better able to take the role of the other, and are generally more cooperative on a variety of measures, such as willingness to help and reward others.

Self-Esteem

Almost all studies which compare the self-esteem of students following cooperative and traditional interaction, show significant gains favoring students in cooperative classrooms; the remaining studies show no sig-

nificant differences; none of the studies had results which favored traditional structures. This outcome is probably related to improved peer relations and to improved academic achievement.

Self-Direction

Students in cooperative learning classrooms become more internal in their sense of control in contrast to students in traditional classrooms who feel more externally controlled. Students from cooperative learning classrooms also have a greater sense of intrinsic, rather than extrinsic, motivation.

Liking For Class

Liking for class and improved classroom climate was found in about half of the studies comparing cooperative and traditional classrooms. Only one study favored traditional structures; in the remaining studies there was no difference.

Role-Taking Abilities

Cooperative learning results in increased cognitive and affective role-taking abilities. Theoretically, role-taking and cooperative interaction opportunities have been related to the development of a higher level of morality. Experiences in situations in which bilateral and multilateral communication are necessary probably increases the general sense of interdependence among students which, in turn, increases their understanding of the experience of others.

The positive results are caused in so many ways cooperative learning is a teacher's dream, and a researcher's nightmare.

Why Does Cooperative Learning Work?

In all honesty, we do not know very much about why the use of small cooperative teams in the classroom produces such general and large positive academic and social gains. There has been considerable theorizing and speculation, but few definitive explanatory studies. In reviewing the literature on that topic, I am struck by the great number of plausible explanations for the observed gains. In fact, there are so many possible ways in which the cooperative techniques produce gains, that the topic is a nightmare for the serious researcher: It is probable that each technique works differently with different groups of students, and that there are many reasons for the gains observed with each technique. In this case, however, the nightmare for the researcher is a dream for the educator. There are so many positive elements in cooperative learning that adoption of cooperative classroom structures is bound to impact favorably on a number of educational outcomes. The following is a very brief outline of possible causes for observed gains in cooperative learning.

TUTORING & PRACTICE

The learning task in cooperative classrooms is different from that in traditional classrooms in a number of ways that are likely to foster academic achievement. Those ways include, as indicated, the amount of comprehensible input, complexity of input, and amount of comprehensible output. In addition the following are increased: quantity and quality of tutoring and practice, clarity of task structure, subdivision of learning unit, time-on-task, practice opportunities, and frequency and quality of rewards.

Peer Tutoring

Peer tutoring results in positive outcomes for both tutees and tutors. A meta-analysis of 65 objective studies of peer tutoring concluded that peer tutoring was effective in producing positive academic and social outcomes for both tutors and tutees. In 87 percent of the studies, students from classes that included tutoring programs outperformed students from controlled classes. The aver-

age effect size across studies was equivalent to raising the performance of students from the 50th to the 66th percentile. Importantly, in all of the eight studies that included tutee attitudes toward subject matter, student attitudes were more positive in peer tutoring classes. The effects on tutors were equally impressive. Tutors moved in achievement an equivalent of from the 50th to the 63rd percentiles and their increases in positive attitudes toward the subject matter exceeded that of the tutees.

Frequency and Type of Practice

In the well-structured mastery oriented cooperative learning methods, students spend a great deal of practice on the items they most need to learn. The students use flash cards and worksheets to master and practice skills and information, receiving repeated contact with missed items. There also is an opportunity for drill and practice also in the Jigsaw methods following the expert presentations. This structured, frequent, and often interactive practice in cooperative learning methods is probably superior for most students to group-paced work on worksheets or in workbooks. There is evidence that cooperative learning groups involve more frequent helping, tutoring, and practice than do competitive or individualistic class structures.

Time-on-Task

A consistent finding in cooperative learning research has been that students spend more time-on-task. Of ten studies examining time-on-task in cooperative and control classrooms, seven showed time-on-task is greater in cooperative classrooms. As with academic achievement, those cooperative learning methods that provided group rewards based on individual achievement most consistently related to increased time-on-task. Increased time-on-task has been associated with increased achievement across a variety of learning methods.

Increased time-on-task in the cooperative learning methods results from the game-like nature of the learning tasks, the clarity of task structures, the

The desire to express oneself to a peer, a constant problem in the traditional classroom, is channeled in the cooperative classroom toward academic achievement.

subdivision of the task into easily mastered parts, and most importantly, the interactive nature of the task. Students like to talk. The desire to express oneself to a peer, a constant problem in the traditional classroom, is channeled in the cooperative classroom toward academic achievement. So, rather than taking time away from task in the cooperative formats, peer interaction directs students toward the academic task. This is especially true because of the incentive reward structure; peers are motivated to keep their teammates on task because that behavior will result in higher rewards for their team.

MOTIVATION AND REWARDS

The reward structure in cooperative learning classrooms is radically different from that found in traditional classrooms. Rewards in cooperative learning classrooms are frequent and peer supported. In most of the methods rewards are group based. In some of the methods, the rewards are also individually-normed and equally accessible. Although in most cooperative learning methods, there are no explicit rewards for cooperative behavior (because cooperative behavior is instrumental in achieving group success), peers become supportive and rewarding of cooperativeness among their teammates; therefore, a social reward system evolves which is parallel to the academic reward system.

Pro-Academic Peer Norms and Rewards

Of eleven studies which have examined peer norms, over half showed students in cooperative learning develop significantly more positive pro-academic norms; no study revealed students in traditional classrooms to have more positive peer norms for achievement. Over a dozen studies demonstrate that cooperative learning groups involve more facilitative and encouraging interaction among students than do competitive or individualistic learning situations. This finding is particularly important as there has been a relative shift in the importance among students of peer norms as opposed to parental and teacher norms.

Frequent, Immediate Rewards

Rewards for achievement in the cooperative learning methods are more frequent and immediate than individual or competitive classes. In many of the approaches there is immediate reinforcement from peers following academic gains. In addition, there are weekly quizzes, newsletters, and/or classroom bulletin boards that give recognition to team and individual achievements. The frequency and immediacy of rewards in cooperative learning classrooms are in contrast to those received in traditional classrooms. If rewards are grades and/or written praise by the teacher following a good test performance, the rewards probably follow the learning by days. Such rewards are pitifully weak in contrast to peer praise immediately following learning successes.

Rewards for Improvement and Equal Reward Opportunity

In a number of the cooperative learning methods all students have an equal opportunity to receive rewards each week, but for different reasons. In STAD and Jigsaw II, each student's performance is compared with his or her past performance; therefore, weak and strong students have an equal chance to earn top grades. In TGT it is the bumping system that ensures that students compete against those of equal ability. In TAI, progress through the individual workbooks can occur at an equal rate for those working on beginning or advanced workbooks. Students bring their new knowledge to each workbook; therefore, difficulty remains relatively constant as students progress through the individual learning materials. With the Color-Coded Co-op Cards, students earn improvement points, as each student works on material he or she has not yet mastered. That rewards are equally accessible to all students is quite in contrast to a traditional classroom in which grading is on the curve and the basis for comparison is not individual past performance but rather the performance of other students.

Spencer Kagan: *Cooperative Learning*©
Publisher: Resources for Teachers , Inc. • 1(800) Wee Co-op

Group-Based Rewards

Some cooperative learning methods include group-based rewards. A revealing set of experiments demonstrated that group rewards have a direct effect on peer tutoring and student achievement. The experimenters manipulated which students' scores would be used to determine the group grade and also how many students in a group would receive the group grade. As more students' grades were dependent on the scores of the lowest three members in the group, peer tutoring and student achievement rose. When the group grade was contingent on the scores of the highest achievers, it was the highest achievers who learned most; when the group grade was contingent on the scores of the lowest achievers, it was the lowest achievers who learned most. The group grade motivates achievement among those students who are responsible for it. Group rewards also promote prosocial behaviors; group rewards create interdependence among students which increases cooperative behaviors.

Culturally Appropriate Rewards

Certain cultural groups place a special value on working for the group -- individuals in those groups are more motivated to work hard it if will benefit the group than if it benefits only themselves. If a culture places a strong value on cooperative work and the school chooses to use competitive and individualistic structures to the exclusion of cooperative structures, there is a mismatch between home/culture values on one side and school/classroom values on the other. The school, without intending, devalues the home culture, and undermines the identity of the pupil. The likely consequence of this mismatch is alienation of minority students. Tragically, these students may be caught be

tween the two value systems, and end up alienated to some extent from both home and school values. When there is alienation from the school value system, there is a consequent alienation from the language of the school. In the struggle to form an identity which expresses the mismatch between home and school values, some minority students may avoid acquisition of speech patterns provided by the school; part of the formation of a counter culture is the formation of speech patterns which distinguish it from the mainstream culture. If schools respect the range of home cultural values represented by students, there will be less of a need for oppositional identities.

The cooperative classroom structure is more compatible with the social values of minority and other cooperative students. Students who value helping and sharing will find achievement rewarding in a cooperative classroom, whereas they will have little motivation to achieve if achievement is associated only with gains for themselves. Considerable research demonstrates that minority students are relatively more cooperative than majority students in their social orientation. Thus the particularly strong gains of minority students in cooperative classrooms may be due to the compatibility of the classroom structure with the individual social values of minority students. The choice of exclusively competitive and individualistic classroom structures may bias academic and social outcomes against the achievement of minority students.

PEER SUPPORT; LOWERED ANXIETY

In the traditional classroom almost all content related student talk occurs in one situation: Students respond to a teacher's question, speaking with the whole class as an audience. In this situation there is usually a strong competitive element. The teacher's question has a right or wrong answer, and a wrong answer is met with the waving of hands of other students more than ready to prove their ability by correcting the mistake.

If a culture places a strong value on cooperative work and the school chooses to use competitive and individualistic structures to the exclusion of cooperative structures, there is a mismatch between home/culture values on one side and school/classroom values on the other. The school, without intending, devalues the home culture, and undermines the identity of the pupil.

Spencer Kagan: *Cooperative Learning* ©
Publisher: Resources for Teachers , Inc. • 1(800) Wee Co-op

In the cooperative classroom most content related student talk occurs either in pairs within teams, or in the small group. Team-members are supportive, hoping their team-mates will perform well. If there is correction, it is in the process of negotiation of meaning, not in the process of evaluation. In such a situation, talking is adaptive -- it leads to content and language acquisition. And to the thing which means most to most students -- peer support and recognition.

TEACHER ROLES AND BEHAVIORS

Teachers in cooperative classrooms are freed from the responsibility of always lecturing and directing. They can become consultants and gravitate to those students who can benefit most from their attention. Further, in the properly managed cooperative learning classroom teachers are freed from many of the problems of management inherent in keeping most students quiet most of the time. In cooperative classrooms students are allowed to do what they most want to do -- communicate with their peers, and teachers are not forced to fight the natural tendencies of their pupils. The teacher in the cooperative classroom is on the same side as the students, serving not to dam up their natural expressiveness, but rather to channel it in positive directions.

STUDENT ROLES AND BE-HAVIORS

Students in cooperative teams are more active, self-directing, and expressive, all of which may be associated with achievement gains. Students take direct responsibility for teaching each other and receiving help from each other. There is structural support for peer tutoring and mutual support, so peer norms for achievement emerge. Importantly, students are often given differentiated roles so that students of different ability levels have relatively equal status within their groups. ∾

References:

Johnson, D.W., Johnson, R., & Maruyama, G. Interdependence and interpersonal attraction among heterogeneous and homogeneous individuals: a theoretical formulation and a meta-analysis of the research. *Review of Educational Research*, 1983, 53, 5-54.

Johnson, D.W., Maruyama, G., Johnson, R., Nelson, D. & Skon, L. Effects of cooperative, competitive and individualistic goal structures on achievement: a meta-analysis. *Psychological Bulletin*, 1981, 89, 47-62.

Kagan, Spencer. Cooperative learning and sociocultural factors in schooling. In Bilingual Education Office, California State Department of Education: *Beyond Language: Social and Cultural Factors in Schooling Language Minority Students.* Los Angeles: Evaluation, Dissemination and Assessment Center, California State University, Los Angeles, 1986.

Kagan, S., Zahn, G.L., Widaman, K.F., Schwarzwald, J. & Tyrrell, G. Classroom Structural Bias: Impact of cooperative and competitive classroom structures on cooperative and competitive individuals and groups. In R. E. Slavin, S. Sharan, S. Kagan, R. Hertz-Lazarowitz, C. Webb & R. Schmuck (Eds.) *Learning to Cooperate, Cooperating to Learn.* New York: Plenum, 1985.

Sharan, Shlomo. Cooperative learning in small groups: recent methods and effects on achievement, attitudes, and ethnic relations. *Review of Educational Research*, 1980, 50, 241-271.

Sharan, S., Kussell, P., Hertz-Lazarowitz, R., Bejarano, Y., Raviv, S., & Sharan, Y. *Cooperative Learning in the Classroom: Research in Desegregated Schools.* New York: Erlbaum, 1984.

Slavin, Robert, E. *Cooperative Learning.* Review of Educational Research, 1980, 50, 315-342.

Slavin, Robert, E. *Cooperative Learning.* New York: Longman, 1983. (a)

Slavin, Robert, E. *When Does Cooperative Learning Increase Student Achievement?* Psychological Bulletin, 1983, 94, 429-445. (b)

R. Slavin., S. Sharan,. S. Kagan., R. Hertz-Lazarowits., N. Webb., R. Schmuck. (Eds.) *Learning to Cooperate, Cooperating to Learn.* New York: Plenum, 1985.

Traditional classroom organization is characterized by competitive or individualized social organization; collaborative group work includes students working together, but does not necessarily include the key concepts of cooperative learning.

Cooperative learning refers to a set of instructional strategies which include cooperative student-student interaction over subject matter as an integral part of the learning process. Cooperative learning practices vary greatly. Interaction over subject matter can be as simple as having students in pairs briefly discussing points of a lecture. Or the cooperative learning can be very complex, including the following: development of student teams, including a variety of complex teambuilding activities; development of a

Not all cooperative learning lessons implement all six of these key concepts, and some aspects of a cooperative learning lesson may include none. Nevertheless, competence in the following six key areas define a teacher's ability to successfully implement cooperative learning.

cooperative class atmosphere, including classbuilding activities; special training in social roles, communication skills, and group skills; assignment of specialized roles for students within teams; specialized tasks for teams; students consulting with students from other teams; complex, multi-objective lesson designs for mastery of curriculum and thinking skills; and special scoring, recognition and reward systems for individuals, teams, and classes.

Underlying the diversity which is cooperative learning are six simple concepts. Not all cooperative learning lessons implement all six of these key concepts, and some aspects of a cooperative learning lesson may include none. Nevertheless, competence in the following six key concepts defines a teacher's ability to successfully implement cooperative learning.

1. Teams

What is a Team? A group may be of any size, does not necessarily have an identity or endure over time. Cooperative learning teams in contrast, have a strong, positive team identity, ideally consist of four members, and endure over time. Teammates know and accept each other and provide mutual support. Ability to establish a variety of types of cooperative learning teams is the first key competency of a cooperative learning teacher.

The most common cooperative learning team formation method assigns students to maximize heterogeneity. The heterogeneous team is a mirror of the classroom, including, to the extent possible, high, middle, and low achievers, boys and girls, and an ethnic and linguistic diversity. Heterogeneity of achievement levels maximizes positive peer tutoring, and serves as an aid to classroom management. With a high achiever on each team, introduction and acquisition of new material becomes easier. Mixed ethnicity dramatically improves ethnic relations among students.

How are Teams Formed? There are a variety of methods of teamformation. Students can group themselves by friendships or interests, random teams may be formed by the luck of the draw, or teachers can assign students to teams. Almost all theorists prefer heterogeneous teams (mixed in ability level as well as race and sex), at least most of the time, because heterogeneous teams maximize the probability of peer tutoring and improving cross-race and cross-sex relations.

One very important exception to the general use of heterogeneous teamformation methods is use of homogeneous language teams for specific objectives.

There is some disagreement about whether to create heterogeneity by forming random teams and having students become members of many teams over time, or by carefully as-

Spencer Kagan: *Cooperative Learning*©
Publisher: Resources for Teachers , Inc. • 1(800) Wee Co-op

signing students to teams mixed in ability level as well as racial and sex composition. An argument for membership in many random teams is that students learn and transfer cooperative skills to many situations. A disadvantage of random teams is that the luck of the draw can place the four lowest achievers together on a team! Unless you have a very homogeneous class, random teams generally cannot stay together very long without substantial differences in achievement among teams.

An argument for teacher assignment is that teams can be held together for a long time and students can form a strong team identity. Teams learn to learn together.

Teachers can have the best of both worlds by having heterogeneous teams and occasional random teams. The methods and issues of teamformation are covered in Chapter 6: Teams.

How Long Should Teams Last? If random teamformation is used, teams must be changed frequently, because the luck of the draw could result in "loser teams" -- the four lowest achievers in the class could end up on the same team. If teams are carefully designed by the teacher, they can stay together for a long time and students can learn how to learn together. I suggest changing teams after five or six weeks, even if they are functioning well. It enables students to transfer their new social and academic skills to new situations.

How Big Should Teams Be? Teams of four are ideal. They allow pair work which doubles participation and open twice as many lines of communication compared to teams of three. Teams larger than four often do not lead to enough participation and they are harder to manage.

∼ See Chapter 6: Teams ∼

2. Cooperative Management

Efficient management of a classroom of teams involves quite a number of skills not necessary in the traditional classroom. The room is arranged so that each student has equal and easy access to each teammate (ideally each student on a team can easily put both hands on a common piece of paper) and all students are able to easily and comfortably orient forward toward the teacher and blackboard.

The teacher establishes a quiet signal which at any time quickly focuses all attention away from peer interaction and toward the teacher. Extensive use of teacher and student modeling is an efficient cooperative management technique, as is extensive use of structuring. Noise level is managed while teamwork is in progress. Efficient methods of distributing materials are established, and class rules or norms establish team as well as individual responsibilities.

∼ See Chapter 7: Management ∼

3. Will To Cooperate

There are three ways in which the will to cooperate is created and maintained: teambuilding, classbuilding, and use of cooperative task and reward structures including recognition systems.

Teambuilding and Classbuilding. What appears like time off task can be viewed as a very important investment in creating the

Although for many theorists teambuilding and classbuilding activities are not a defining characteristic of cooperative learning, my own experience, and that of teachers with whom I have worked, leads me to encourage teachers to use a great deal of teambuilding and classbuilding.

social context necessary for teams to maximize their potential. Again and again, I have seen greater long run efficiency, learning, and liking of class, school, and subject matter if teachers take time for teambuilding and classbuilding. When there is a positive team identity, liking, respect, and trust among teammembers and classmates, there is a context within which maximum learning can occur.

Teambuilding and classbuilding activities provide unique learning experiences not afforded by traditional exclusive emphasis on academic content. Today in the workplace, Americans are learning the value of teambuilding, as they follow the successful lead of the Japanese. When teambuilding and classbuilding are neglected, especially in classrooms in which there are preexisting tensions, teams experience serious difficulties.

〜 See Chapter 8: Teambuilding and Chapter 9: Classbuilding 〜

Task and Reward Structures. The will to cooperate is determined to a large extent also by the task and reward structures. Understanding task structures and reward structures allows a teacher to design cooperative learning activities in which there is an high motivation to cooperate among all students.

Cooperative task structures are created when no one individual can complete the learning task alone. The most common way of creating a cooperative task structure is to require a group product -- a product which no one group member can produce without the help of the others. Another way, as in Jigsaw, is to provide each student with a unique portion of the learning material and make it the job of the group to master all the material.

The reward structure describes how rewards are distributed. Rewards can be given to individuals, teams, or to the class as a whole. If a reward is given to the best individual in the class, competition will almost certainly result -- each student attempting to be better than each other. Weak students compared to strong students will fail over and over and will sooner or later "drop out" of the race. Setting students in competition is a prescription for drop out.

If rewards are based on individual improvement, an individualistic reward structure is created, and students will not necessarily feel in competition with each other, especially if it is clear that all students can improve and receive recognition. On the other hand, they will have little or no motive to cooperate.

If rewards are given based on team or class improvement or performance, then a cooperative reward structure is created and students will begin to encourage and help each other.

Group Grades. Cooperative reward structures are commonly created by making the grades of students dependent on each other. For example, you might give a group grade based on the sum of the individual achievements of the members of the group. Research reveals that cooperative reward structures are very powerful in directing the efforts of the group. For example, if the grade of the lowest achiever in a group contributes heavily to the group grade, the lowest achiever will receive a great deal of tutoring and support, and his/her achievement will improve.

Although group grades can motivate students, they create two major problems. First, if one student consistently performs poorly, resentments will build up among the other students. They will see the weaker student as preventing them from achieving a goal -- a good team score. A solution to this problem is to use improvement scoring so all students can perform well, regardless of initial ability level. The second problem with group grades occurs when group grades feed into a report card. If so, a student's report card grade can be raised or lowered by the work of another student! This is never acceptable. A solution to this second problem is to have team scores, but to use them as part of a recognition system, never as part of a report card grade.

Warning!

Group Grades

Although group grades can motivate students, they create two major problems:

Problem 1: If one student consistently performs poorly, resentments will build up among the other students. They will see the weaker student as preventing them from achieving their goal -- a good team score.

Problem 2: When group grades feed into a report card, a student's report card grade can be raised or lowered by the work of another student! This is never acceptable.

Spencer Kagan: *Cooperative Learning*©
Publisher: Resources for Teachers , Inc. • 1(800) Wee Co-op

Motivating Cooperation Among Teams. Cooperative learning methods range from fostering intense between-team competition, sometimes even including intense tournaments, to an emphasis on between-team cooperation. The amount of cooperation or competition within and between-teams is a function of the reward and task structures, as summarized in the following table. The most cooperative classroom has cooperative reward and task structures within and among teams.

Reward Structures. Relations among teams are largely a function of the between-team reward structure. If the team grades are summed and result in a class reward when the sum reaches a certain total, there is a cooperative between-team reward structure. In this case, teams will be motivated to help and encourage each other. In contrast, if only the best teams receive recognition there is negative interdependence among teams and there exists a competitive between-team

One of the easiest and most certain ways of improving class climate when using student teams is to include class goals and class rewards. If teams are always set against each other by recognizing the best teams, a "civil war of teams" results; if instead class goals are set up, a positive "our classroom" feeling emerges. Each student feels a belonging to the class, encouraging the gains of others.

reward structure. In the short run we can motivate students by setting them against each other, but in the long run that strategy is counter-productive because it necessarily produces losers, peer norms against achievement, alienation, and drop-out.

One of the easiest and most certain ways of improving class climate when using student teams is to include class goals and class rewards. If teams are always set against each other by exclusive use of competitive between-team reward structures, a "civil war of teams" results; if cooperative between-team rewards are used, a positive "our classroom"

Creating Cooperative and Competitive Relations by Task and Reward Structures

Relations	Reward Structure	Task Structure
Cooperative Within-Team	Team Score & Team Reward	Team Product; Division of Labor Among Teammates
Cooperative Among Teams	Team Scores Contribute to Class Score which Lead to Class Celebration	Each Team makes A Unique Contribution to the Class Product
Competitive Among Teams	Team Score & Reward - Best Team Wins	Identical Team Products Invite Comparisons

Note: Cooperative Relations Within-Teams can occur with either Cooperative or Competitive Relations Among Teams.

feeling emerges in which each student feels a belonging to the class, and is identified with the gains of each other student. Occasional between-team competition can be healthy if it is in the context of fun and within a larger context of a basically cooperative classroom in which all teams feel themselves to be on the same side, encouraging each other to do their best.

The reward structure is easy to manipulate. For example, it is simple for teachers to change the competitive between-team reward structure of STAD or Jigsaw II into a cooperative between-team structure. All that is necessary is to have the improvement points of each team contribute to a class score, and to provide a class reward when the class score reaches a certain level.

Task Structure. The between-team task structure also can be cooperative, competitive, or independent as well. For example, the work of each team may contribute to the goals of the other teams, or there may be competition for limited resources between teams. Division of labor among teams (unique team products which contribute to a class goal) is the easiest way to create a cooperative between-team task structure; identical team goals for each team and competition for limited resources are ways to create a competitive between-team task structure.

See Chapter 16: Scoring and Recognition

4. Skill To Cooperate

Some theorists include social skill development as a defining characteristic of cooperative learning -- others do not. There is no social skill component to the STAD and Jigsaw II structures. The need for instruction in social skills depends in part on the classroom and in part on the kind of cooperative learning which is to occur. When very highly structured methods are used such as the the mastery methods, which include drill and practice and little unstructured social interaction, little cooperative skill development is necessary. On the other hand, when students move to complex cooperative projects, they need help in learning how to

listen to each other, resolve conflicts, set and revise agendas, keep on task, and encourage each other.

There is a variety of ways of fostering the development of social skills, including modeling, defining, role-playing, observing, reinforcing, processing, and practicing specific social skills. It is also possible to structure for skill acquisition by role assignment and use of specific structures. The four most important methods are modeling and reinforcement, role assignments, structuring, and reflection.

See Chapter 14: Social Skills

5. Basic Principles

There are three basic principles fundamental to cooperative learning. These principles, Simultaneous Interaction, Positive Interdependence, and Individual Accountability are built into cooperative learning structures. If a teacher wishes to modify the structures, or create new cooperative learning projects activities, an understanding of the three basic principles is fundamental. For how to apply the principles to cooperative projects, see Chapter 15: Cooperative Projects.

1. Simultaneous Interaction

Cooperative learning involves simultaneous interaction among students. This simple fact goes a long way toward explaining the advantage of cooperative learning over traditional teaching.

In the traditional classroom, one person at a time speaks, usually the teacher, but occasionally a student, as the student is called on by the teacher. This is a sequential structure, in that each person participates in turn, one after the other in sequence.

The mathematics of sequential structures are disastrous because they leave unacceptably little time per pupil for active participation. Let's examine the mathematics of sequential structures -- it goes a long way toward explaining the failure of traditional teaching methods.

Spencer Kagan: *Cooperative Learning*©
Publisher: Resources for Teachers , Inc. • 1(800) Wee Co-op

In the largest study of schooling ever conducted, John Goodlad (1984) demonstrated that teachers on the average do almost 80% of the talking in a classroom. Because some time is taken for management, less than 20% of the time is left for student talk.

At first glance, it does not seem disastrous that out of every 50 minutes the students will be allowed 10 minutes for active participation. But because the 10 minutes are spent in a sequential structure, as one student after another is called upon, the average per pupil active participation time is 10 minutes divided by 30 or just a third of a minute per student! No wonder that the dominant emotion of many students going through traditional education is boredom. They are allowed to express themselves on the average of 20 seconds a class period and listen to others, mostly the teacher, for the remaining 49 minutes and 40 seconds!

Contrast that outcome with what happens when we reorganize the classroom using the simultaneity principle. Although in the cooperative classroom the teacher would never take 40 out of the 50 minutes for him/herself to speak, for purposes of comparison, let's take the same ten minutes of time for student talk. If we abandon the sequential organization of the classroom and adopt a simultaneous structure, say a pair discussion, then active participation is not occurring for just one student at a time. At any one time half the class is talking. Thus, during the ten minutes, the average speaking time per pupil is not just 20 seconds, but rather a full five minutes. There is 15 times as much student language production over subject matter. Further, the other five minutes is also far more active than in the traditional classroom, because students are far more involved when one is speaking directly to them than when another student somewhere in the classroom is answering a question the teacher has posed.

Thus knowledge of and ability to apply the simultaneity principle is another key to max-

Sequential v. Simultaneous Structures

Goal	Sequential Structure	Simultaneous Structure
Distribute Supplies	Teacher or student walks around and hands out materials one at a time.	Materials Monitor from each team distributes materials to teammates.
Discuss Topic	One student at a time states their viewpoint.	All students discuss views in pairs.
Form Teams	Sequential reading by the teacer of students' names and assignments.	Students simultaneously look for names placed on tables.
Share Answers	Teacher calls on one student at a time.	All students engage in Choral Response.
Receive Help	Students raise hands and wait for teacher to come over.	Students ask a teammate and receive immediate help.

imizing positive outcomes in cooperative learning. Essentially, when all else is equal, pair work is better than teamwork, team work is better that whole-class work, and smaller teams are better than larger teams.

~ See Chapter 7: Management ~

2. Positive Interdependence

A second basic principal of cooperative learning is positive interdependence. Positive interdependence occurs when gains of individuals or teams are positively correlated. If a gain for one student is associated with gains for other students, the individuals are positively interdependent. Similarly, if the gains of one team contribute to the probability that another team will be successful, then the teams are positively interdependent.

It is important to distinguish strong and weak forms of positive interdependence. If the success of every teammember depends on the success of each member (if one fails, all do), then a very strong form of positive interdependence is created and teammembers are very motivated to make sure each student does well. For example, if our team rewards depend on all of us scoring 80% or better, we will work hard to make sure everyone performs above 80%. In contrast, if the team has to average 80% to receive the reward if we have two students who usually get around 100%, we won't be too worried if some of our teammates fall below 80%. Thus, if the success of each member depends on the success of every member, strong positive interdependence is created. If, in contrast, the team can receive a reward even if one student does very poorly, then only a weak form of positive interdependence exists, and teammate encouragement and tutoring of the weakest members is less certain. Therefore, the type of positive interdependence created has a dramatic impact on the tutoring and encouragement teammates give each other. When there is strong positive interdependence, cooperation follows.

Positive interdependence can be created by the task structure (having a single team or class product, including division of labor among teams or individuals, limiting resources, or having a rule that a group cannot progress to a new learning center until all the students have completed an assignment). Positive interdependence can be created also by the reward structure (creating a team score which is an average of individual scores or the sum of how many students reached a predetermined criterion, choosing a randomly selected individual paper as the team score, selecting the lowest score on the team as the team score). Other ways of creating positive interdependence involve roles, goals, and resources. See box on next page.

If positive interdependence exists, students have the subjective experience of "being on the same side" and will behave cooperatively toward each other. If, for example, I know our team will receive a grade on our team report, I will hope my teammates do well on their portions of the report and I am likely to offer encouragement and help.

A competitive social organization of the classroom exists if students are negatively interdependent. Negative interdependence exists when the gains of one are associated with losses for another. Ways to create negative interdependence are grading on the curve, posting only a few best papers, or calling on only one student when a number of students raise their hands. In situations of

---

Types of

Positive Interdependence

Weak Forms
1. The success of each teammember is likely to contribute to success of others.
2. The success of teams is likely to be facilitated by success of individual members.

Intermediate Forms
1. The success of each teammember contributes to success of all teammates, but a teammember could succeed on own.
2. The success of a team is facilitated by the success of each member, but team could succeed without success or contribution of every member.

Strong Forms
1. The success of every teammember is not possible without success/contribution of each.
2. The success of a team is not possible without success or contribution of each member.

---

negative interdependence, as the teacher recognizes or rewards one student the probability of recognition or reward for other students is decreased and individuals feel competitive toward one another. For example, if I know only five papers will be posted, I am unlikely to hope for five other students in the classroom to do extremely well on their essay, and I am unlikely to offer them encouragement and help.

An individualistic social organization exists when there is non-interdependence. Non-interdependence occurs when there is no correlation between the outcomes of individuals. For example, if all students are working alone at their own pace in individual work books, and the grades of each student have no relation to those of the other students, there is non-interdependence among students; we may then speak of individualized instruction. It is important to note, however, that the students often feel competitive toward each other during individualized instruction because of the social comparison process. For example, it is unlikely that all students will receive top grades, and those who do not are unlikely to hope for the continued success of those who do -- by the comparison process the top students make the other students appear less successful, even if the outcomes of one student do not actually influence the outcomes of others.

Two ways to avoid a competitive social comparison process if there are individualized grades are (1) to have students taking different tests, and (2) use improvement scoring.

See Chapter 16: Scoring and Recognition

3. Individual Accountability

Including individual accountability contributes to academic gains in cooperative learning. Methods which provide a group grade or a group product without making each member accountable for his or her contribution, do not consistently produce achievement gains (Slavin, 1983).

Individual accountability can take different forms, depending on the content and cooperative learning method. One form is reward accountability. For example, if each student takes an individual test and a team grade is formed by summing or averaging the individual quiz scores of teammembers, there will be reward accountability if each student knows the contribution of his/her teammates to the team score. A second form of individual accountability is task accountability which occurs if each student is made accountable to the group for her/his portion of a project.

Students can be made individually accountable by having each student receive a grade on his or her portion of the team essay or project; by having each student responsible for a unique portion of a team learning material, presentation, or product; or by instituting the rule that the group may not go on to another learning center until everyone finishes his/her task at the present learning center. Whatever the form of individual accountability, the contribution of each individual is made known to the team.

If evaluation is not based on individual products or tests, it is possible for a freerider and/or a workhorse to develop. The freerider is an individual who will accept the team grade but who does no work. The workhorse does more than

Structuring

Positive Interdependence

1. Goals
We all have same goal: A team mural, essay, model, or report.

2. Rewards
Team recognition based on the contributions all make.

3. Task
The task is structured so we can't do it alone: We need eight hands for this job; division of labor is more efficient; we all have important mini- topics.

4. Resources
I have the scissors, you have the paper, Jim has the glue, and Mary has the marker.

5. Roles
Complementary and necessary roles: Materials Monitor, Question Commander, Coach, Encourager, Reflector, Quiet Captain, Praiser, Cheerleader, Checker, Gatekeeper, Taskmaster, Recorder .

his/her share. After all, if I am on a team which will have one grade on a group product, and there is no accountability for who does what, I will do different things depending on my achievement level. If I am a very bright student, I may decide the best way to ensure continued high marks is to do it all myself. If I am a low achieving student, I may decide the road to success is to let the bright student do what he or she does well -- in fact, do it all. To this end, I might loaf or even play dumb or helpless. If there is individual accountability, everything changes. If our grade is to be based on the individual work of each of us, then I and my teammates know that if each of us does not do our share, we will be letting down our teammates. This line of reasoning indicates that group test taking should be reserved for "Thursday practice time." The bottom line toward which the students are working must be improved individual achievement.

Individual accountability may exist not just for academic achievement. For example, if the teacher lets students know that following a discussion they will be asked to list ideas they have heard from others, then there is individual accountability for listening and the group will be less likely to have everyone talking and no one listening.

All of the formal cooperative learning structures except Team Discussion and Brainstorming have built-in individual accountability, but in different ways. For example,

the third step of Three-Step Interview makes students accountable for listening; the last step of Numbered Heads Together makes students individually accountable for academic achievement, as they must respond on their own when their number is called. Similarly, individual accountability is provided in cooperative lesson designs: by the mini-topic presentations in Co-op Co-op, the individual quizzes in STAD, and the expert presentations in Jigsaw.

6. *Structures*

As we have seen there are many cooperative learning structures, each with a different domain of usefulness. Much of this book is an introduction to structures. Because each of the structures presented performs at least one function better than any other structure, knowledge of each structure is essential if a teacher is to be as efficient as possible in reaching the range of learning objectives. ∼

∼ See:

Chapter 5: Three Schools of Cooperative Learn ing

Chapter 10: Mastery Structures

Chapter 11: Thinking Skills Structures

Chapter 12: Information Exchanges Structures

Chapter 13: Communication Building Structures ∼

Structuring
Individual Accountability
For Achievement
1. Color code individual contributions
2. Team scores based on individual scores
3. Give teams time to reflect on individual progress & role performance
4. Assign & grade Mini-Topics
5. Use structures like Numbered Heads Together

For Participation
1. Use Talking Chips
2. Have students summarize their participation
3. Have students take time to reflect on participation

For Listening
1. Use Paraphrase Passport, Three-Step Interview
2. Share ideas heard from others "I heard from..."

References:

Slavin, Robert, E. *When Does Cooperative Learning Increase Student Achievement?* Psychological Bulletin, 1983, 94, 429-445.

Goodlad, John, I. *A Place Called School.* New York: McGraw-Hill Book Company, 1984.

Six Key Concepts

1. Teams

2. Management

3. Will

4. Skill

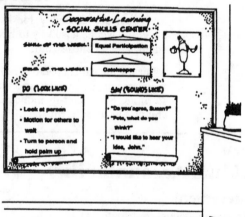

5. Principles

6. Structures

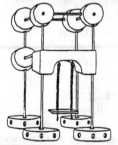

Chapter 5

Three Schools of Cooperative Learning

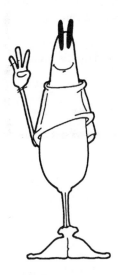

Three major schools of cooperative learning can be distinguished: The Structural Approach, Learning Together, and the Curriculum Specific Packages. To some extent, each approach complements and draws from the others. Both the Curriculum Specific Packages and the Learning Together models include structures to some extent. Whereas the Structural Approach and the Learning Together model emphasize social skills, some of the curriculum specific approaches do not. Nevertheless, there are important differences among the approaches.

Some of those who have emphasized the Curriculum Specific Packages have taken the stance that without curriculum materials especially designed for cooperative learning, quality learning is not likely. In contrast, the

The three schools of cooperative learning are sufficiently distinct that they are associated with very different approaches to teacher training, lesson planning, lesson content, and the relation of curriculum to cooperative learning.

Structural Approach and Learning Together are premised on the idea that quality cooperative learning can occur with little or no specially designed curriculum materials. The

---

Structure:

Whole-Class Question-Answer

1. The teacher asks a question.
2. Students who wish to respond raise their hands.
3. The teacher calls on one student.
4. The student attempts to state the correct answer.
5. The teacher responds to the student's attempt.

---

three approaches are sufficiently distinct that they are associated with very different approaches to teacher training, lesson planning, lesson content, and the relation of curriculum to cooperative learning.

1. The Structural Approach

The Structural Approach to cooperative learning is based on the definition and use of many distinct ways of organizing the interaction of individuals in a classroom, called structures. The definition and analysis of structures allows systematic design of cooperative learning lessons; the structures have predictable outcomes in the academic, linguistic, cognitive, and social domains. Structures are building blocks of a lesson; they are combined to form multi-structural lessons with predictable results. Quite a number of individuals have created structures; new structures continue to be developed and old structures continue to evolve.

STRUCTURES

A structure is a content-free way of organizing the interaction of individuals in a classroom. There are numerous distinct structures, such as Pairs Check, Numbered Heads Together, and Inside-Outside Circle.

Structures describe the social interaction patterns of individuals. For example, one of the most common structures teachers now use may be called Whole-Class Question-Answer. See box.

Whole-Class Question-Answer is a competitive structure because the students compete for the attention and praise of the teacher and there is negative interdependence among students -- as one student is called on, the others lose their chance to be called on. Further, a failure to give the desired response increases the chances for other students to receive attention and praise. Thus, students in this struc-

Spencer Kagan: *Cooperative Learning* ©
Publisher: Resources for Teachers , Inc. • 1(800) Wee Co-op

ture actually get excited and wave their hands with joy when they realize another student missed a question. They know that another student's failure increases their own chance for recognition. Students in this structure begin to hope for the failure of their classmates and set peer norms against achievement.

Numbered Heads Together is a simple four-step cooperative structure. Numbered Heads Together meets the criteria of being a structure because it is a content-free way of organizing the social interaction in the classroom. It can be used with almost any subject matter, at all grade levels, and at various places in a lesson. Structures are ways of organizing the classroom, not sets of curriculum materials.

Numbered Heads is a cooperative structure. It includes all the essential elements of cooperative learning: teams, a management system, motivation and ability for students to cooperate, positive interdependence, individual accountability, and simultaneous interaction. Positive interdependence is built-in. If any student knows the answer, the ability of each student is increased. Individual accountability is built into the structure also because all the helping is confined to the heads together step; students know that once a number is called, there is no more helping, each student is on his or her own. The simultaneous interaction during Numbered Heads Together is quite in contrast to the sequential interaction in Whole-Class Question-Answer, rather than one student responding, when a question is posed, all students interact.

When Numbered Heads is used, students cooperate. The high achievers share answers, because they know their number might not be called, and they want their team to do well. The lower achievers listen carefully, because they know their number might be called. Numbered Heads Together is quite in contrast to Whole-Class Question-Answer in which only the high achievers need participate; the low achievers can (and often do) tune out, leaving the student participation time more like a private conversation between the teacher and the highest achieving students.

Structure:

Numbered Heads Together

1. The teacher has students number off within groups, so that each student is a 1, 2, 3, or 4. (Colors or letters also can be used.)
2. The teacher gives a directive to the group, such as, "Make sure everyone on the team can name the capital of California?" or "Be sure each person on the team knows how to build 1/2 + 1/16 using fraction bars."
3. The teacher tells the students to put their heads together to make sure everyone on the team knows.
4. The teacher calls a number (1, 2, 3, or 4) and only the students with that number can respond.

STRUCTURES, CONTENT, AND ACTIVITIES

An important cornerstone of the Structural Approach is the distinction between structures, content, and activities. A structure is the content-free "how" of instruction. It is the social organization of the classroom, involving a series of steps or elements which define interaction patterns. A structure can be used to deliver a wide range of academic content. The content is the "what" of instruction, ranging from letter sounds to calculus. When you plug content into a structure you have an activity. Content is delivered via structures. At any moment in a classroom the activity is defined by a combination of a structure and the content:

Structure + Content = Activity

When you use Numbered Heads Together (Structure) to practice map reading (content) you have an activity. There are many excellent cooperative activities which teachers can design, such as making a team mural, paper tower, or quilt. Activities almost always have a specific objective, such as creating a tri-part team creature as a prewriting activity; having students take a "care walk" as a trust building activity; or creating a class banner in order to build a positive class identity. Activities are specific and content-bound, they cannot meaningfully be repeated many times. In contrast, structures are content-free ways of structuring group interaction; structures may be used repeatedly with a variety of curriculum materials, at various places in the lesson plan, and across a wide range of grade levels.

If a teacher new to cooperative learning learns learns five activities, he/she might well report back after a week, "Those worked well, what should I do next week." If instead the teacher learns five structures, he/she could meaningful include cooperative learning in lessons all year, to further the academic progress of students in any subject matter.

WHY SO MANY STRUCTURES?

There are dozens of structures. In this book I have categorized structures into six types, by function: Teambuilding, Classbuilding, Communication Building, Information Exchange, Mastery, and Thinking Skills. And, within these categories there are numerous structures. So, for example, a teacher wishing to have students master some content might choose among some dozen and a half structures.

Why so many? Each structure has a different impact on students. Knowing the domains of usefulness of many structures allows teachers to choose the best structure for a given outcome.

The definition and analysis of structures allows teachers to intelligently design cooperative lessons because each structure has predictable outcomes in the academic, linguistic, cognitive and social domains. There are dozens of structures and variations on structures. This variety of structures is necessary because they have different functions or domains of usefulness.

This is illustrated by contrasting two similar simple structures, Team Discussion and Three-Step Interview. See box. In Team Discussion there is no individual accountability -- in some groups some individuals may participate little or not at all. Also, there is no assurance that teammembers will listen to each other -- in some groups all individuals may be talking, while none are listening. Further, at any one moment, if one person at a time is speaking, one-fourth of the class is involved in language and idea production.

In contrast, in Three-Step Interview each person must produce and receive language; there is equal participation; there is individual accountability for listening, because in the third step each student has a time to share what he has heard; and for the first two steps, students interact in pairs, so one-half rather than one-fourth of the class is involved in language production at any one time.

Team Discussion v. Three-Step Interview

STEPS

1. Teacher asks a question. 2. Teacher tells the groups to talk it over.	1. In pairs, one student interviews another. 2. Reverse roles: interviewer becomes interviewee. 3. Roundrobin: Each student shares with the group what he/she learned in the interview.

BASIC PRINCIPLES

Individual Accountability	None	High (for listening)
Simultaneous Interaction	Medium: 1/4 Participate at a time	High: 1/2 Participate at at time
Equality of Participation	Unequal	Equal

DOMAIN OF USEFULNESS

Usefulness for:		
Reaching Consensus	High	Low
Brainstorming	High	Low
Sharing Personal Info	Medium	High
Increasing Listening Skills	Low	High

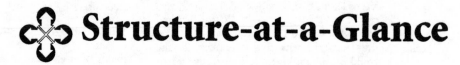 Structure-at-a-Glance

Structure: _____

Steps:	**Variations:**

Functions:

Teambuilding:

Classbuilding:

Communication:

Info Sharing:

Mastery:

Concept Development:

Where are the Principles?

Interdependence:

Accountability:

Simultaneity:

Social Skills/Roles:

Sponge Idea:

Notes:

Structure-at-a-Glance:
Content Ideas

Language Arts	**Science**

Math	**Social Studies**

Other:

Spencer Kagan: *Cooperative Learning*©
Publisher: Resources for Teachers , Inc. • 1(800) Wee Co-op

Thus structural analysis reveals profound differences between apparently similar simple cooperative structures. The Three-Step Interview structure leads to almost twice as much language production as well as more listening, when compared to Team Discussion. Team Discussion is the structure of choice for brainstorming and for reaching group consensus; Interview is far better for developing language and listening skills. When the teacher is aware of the effects of different structures, she/he can intelligently design lessons with predetermined outcomes.

DOMAIN OF USEFULNESS

Different structures are useful for different objectives. In this book most structures are categorized by their primary functions: Classbuilding, Teambuilding, Communication Building, Mastery, and Thinking. Multi-functional structures are described in more than one chapter.

The most important considerations when determining the domain of usefulness of a structure are:

1. *What kind of cognitive development does it foster?*

2. *What kind of social development does it foster?*

3. *Where in a lesson plan does it best fit?*

4. *With what kind of curriculum is it best used?*

Some structures have a very specific domain of usefulness, such as Talking Chips which serves to regulate communication within a group. In contrast, other structures, like Three-Step Interview can be used in many places in a lesson plan. Each structure has a different domain of usefulness, good for some but not all steps in a lesson plan, and for some but not all kinds of cognitive and social development. A teacher knowledgeable in a number of structures can choose the most efficient structures for a particular goal. For example for acquiring a new skill among the mastery structures Pairs Check works well, but for memorization the Flashcard Game is superior. In contrast, Numbered Heads is a far better structure than either Pairs Check or the Flashcard Game if

the goal is for the teacher to check for understanding.

Cooperative learning goes wrong most often because of a mismatch of structure, objective, skills, and/or cognitive level. Examples of these mismatches are assigning students a group project which involves conflict resolution before they have conflict resolution skills or using a mastery structure when the objective is concept development. Part of the art of structuring successful cooperative learning lessons is analyzing the objective of a lesson, and then knowing which structures to use, given the cooperative skills of the students and the cognitive and social objective of the lesson.

On the previous two pages are the Structure-at-a-Glance Forms which are used to process each structure. During training in the Structural Approach, participants receive a binder which is formatted to allow them to process many structures -- essentially they write their own book about structures. With each structure they define the essential steps or elements of the structure, variations, functions of the structure, how it operationalizes the basic principles of cooperative learning, the social skills or roles involved, and how to use it across the curriculum. Some structures, such as Inside-Outside Circle, are multi-functional. Inside-Outside Circle can be used for classbuilding, information exchange, mastery, and thinking skill development. Other structures are narrower in their domain of usefulness, such as Talking Chips, which is a good communication regulator, but serves little else.

Moving Up from Structures:
MULTI-STRUCTURAL LESSONS

A very competent cooperative learning teacher is fluent in many structures and moves into and out of them as appropriate for reaching certain learning objectives. Thus, the teacher designs multi-structural lessons. For example, a lesson might begin with some content-related classbuilding using a Line-up, followed by content-related teambuilding using Roundtable. The lesson might then move into some Direct Instruction, followed by Paired Reading for information input. To check for comprehension and emphasize key concepts, the teacher might choose Numbered Heads Together. Next might come some Team Discussion or Team Word-Webbing for concept development. No one structure is most efficient for all objectives, so the most efficient way of reaching all objectives in a lesson is a multi-structural lesson.

Excellent books of multi-structural lessons in specific content areas and grade levels are listed in the references. Forms for multi-structural Lesson Planning are provided in the chapter on lesson and planning design.

〜 See Chapter 20:
Co-op Lesson Planning 〜

Moving down from structures:
ELEMENTS

Structures can be analyzed into their components, called elements. An element consists of an action or interaction occurring within a group size. For example, the structure, Think-Pair-Share consists of three elements: Individual thinks, Pair Discusses, Individual shares. Once teachers are fluent in structures and their domain of usefulness, they begin to work at the element level, to modify and create their own structures. A Think-Pair-Share, for example, may be modified to create more individual accountability, becoming a Think-Pair-Roundrobin. It is important, though, to base work at the element level on a very thorough understanding of structures which can occur only by extensive classroom experience.

Miguel Kagan and I have developed the Element Matrix which facilitates work at the element level. An explanation of that work is beyond the scope of this book, and will be

Blank Element Matrix
Group Size

Action or Interaction	Individual	Pair	Team	Class
Creative (Low Consensus, Divergent)				
1. Brainstorm				
2. Construct				
3. Draw		■	■	■
4. Discuss	■			
5. Think		■	■	■
6. Write	Individual Writes		■	■
Mastery (High Consensus, Convergent)				
1. Check				
2. Instruct/Present	■			
3. Question (review)				
4. Solve Problem				■
Info Exchanges				
1. Interview	■			
2. Question (true)				
3. Read				
4. Share	■			
Social Exchanges				
1. Celebrate			Team Celebrates	
2. Paraphrase	■			
3. Praise				
4. Reflect/Process				
Transitions				
1. Clean				
2. Distrubute Mats	■			
3. Move				

Spencer Kagan: *Cooperative Learning* ©
Publisher: Resources for Teachers , Inc. • 1(800) Wee Co-op

Putting it all Together

In sum, in the Structural Approach there are Elements which combine to form Structures which organize the social interaction of students over subject matter. When Content is placed into a Structure, a learning Activity is created. A lesson is merely a series of Activities designed to reach teacher determined objectives. Below, the popular Elements of Effective Instruction Lesson Design is illustrated. In Chapter 20, Co-op Lesson Planning, a variety of cooperative learning lesson designs are presented. Note: Many possible structures could be used to implement most elements of a lesson design. For example, if the design element is Guided Practice, many structures can be used. Numbered Heads, Pairs-Check, Send-A-Problem, and Turn-4-Review are but a few possibilities. See Chapter 10: Mastery Structures.

Structural Approach Key Concepts

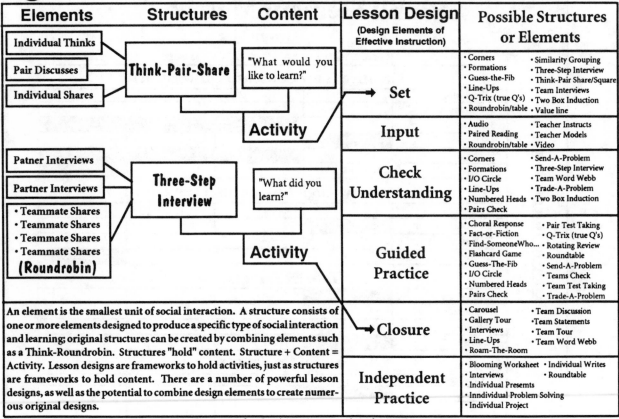

Elements	Structures	Content	Lesson Design (Design Elements of Effective Instruction)	Possible Structures or Elements
Individual Thinks / Pair Discusses / Individual Shares	Think-Pair-Share	"What would you like to learn?" → Activity	Set	• Corners • Similarity Grouping • Formations • Three-Step Interview • Guess-the-Fib • Think-Pair Share/Square • Line-Ups • Team Interviews • Q-Trix (true Q's) • Two Box Induction • Roundrobin/table • Value line
			Input	• Audio • Teacher Instructs • Paired Reading • Teacher Models • Roundrobin/table • Video
Patner Interviews / Partner Interviews / • Teammate Shares • Teammate Shares • Teammate Shares • Teammate Shares (Roundrobin)	Three-Step Interview	"What did you learn?" → Activity	Check Understanding	• Corners • Send-A-Problem • Formations • Three-Step Interview • I/O Circle • Team Word Webb • Line-Ups • Trade-A-Problem • Numbered Heads • Two Box Induction • Pairs Check
			Guided Practice	• Choral Response • Pair Test Taking • Fact-or-Fiction • Q-Trix (true Q's) • Find-SomeoneWho... • Rotating Review • Flashcard Game • Roundtable • Guess-The-Fib • Send-A-Problem • I/O Circle • Teams Check • Numbered Heads • Team Test Taking • Pairs Check • Trade-A-Problem
An element is the smallest unit of social interaction. A structure consists of one or more elements designed to produce a specific type of social interaction and learning; original structures can be created by combining elements such as a Think-Roundrobin. Structures "hold" content. Structure + Content = Activity. Lesson designs are frameworks to hold activities, just as structures are frameworks to hold content. There are a number of powerful lesson designs, as well as the potential to combine design elements to create numerous original designs.			Closure	• Carousel • Team Discussion • Gallery Tour • Team Statements • Interviews • Team Tour • Line-Ups • Team Word Webb • Roam-The-Room
			Independent Practice	• Blooming Worksheet • Individual Writes • Interviews • Roundtable • Individual Presents • Inndividual Problem Solving • Individual Project

Resources for Teachers, Inc. • 1(800) Wee Co-op

Spencer Kagan: *Cooperative Learning*©
Publisher: Resources for Teachers , Inc. • 1(800) Wee Co-op

presented in a future book: Kagan and Kagan, *The Element Matrix: Creating Cooperative Learning Structures.*

2. *Learning Together*

Learning Together is a framework for applying cooperative learning in any subject area and any grade-level. The focus is on five principles: Positive Interdependence, Face-to-Face Interaction, Individual Accountability, Interpersonal Skills, and Group Processing. Each lesson has specified academic and social skills objectives. A detailed presentation of the philosophy and techniques may be found in Johnson, Holubec & Roy (1984). The Johnsons have emphasized the following principles in establishing cooperative learning: Shared Leadership; Shared Responsibility; Direct Instruction of Task Related and Social Relationship Skills; Teacher Observation and Intervention (including structured observation and feedback on specific academic and social skills); and Group Processing. In Learning Together, teachers follow 18 steps, divided into five main types, as follows:

SPECIFYING OBJECTIVES

Specifying Academic and Collaborative Skill Objectives. Both the academic and cooperative skill objectives are specified before each lesson begins.

MAKING DECISIONS

Deciding on Group Size. Depending on the objectives and the nature of the learning task, cooperative groups range in size from two to six.

Assigning Students to Groups. Decisions are made regarding homogeneous or heterogeneous ability grouping; separating or grouping non-task-oriented and task-oriented students; allowing student input into grouping; and length of time before reassignment.

Arranging the Room. Members sit in a circle and are close enough to communicate without disrupting the other learning groups.

Planning Materials. Materials are distributed in carefully planned ways to communicate the assignment is a joint effort.

Assigning Roles. Interdependence may be arranged though the assignment of complementary and interconnecting roles to group members. For example, one student may be assigned the role of "the praiser", another "the checker."

COMMUNICATING THE TASK, GOAL STRUCTURE, AND LEARNING ACTIVITY

Explaining the Academic Task. Teachers set the task so students are clear about the assignment; explain the objectives of the lesson; relating the concepts; define relevant concepts; explain procedures, and give examples; and ask specific questions to check students' understanding of the assignment.

Structuring Positive Goal Interdependence. The group goal is emphasized, and it is made clear that students must work collaboratively to reach the group goal.

Structuring Individual Accountability. There is frequent assessment of the level of performance of each group member. Thus, students know which members need encouragement and help.

Structuring Intergroup Cooperation. Positive outcomes found within cooperative groups are extended throughout the whole class by structuring intergroup cooperation.

Explaining Criteria for Success. Teachers explain at the beginning of the lesson clear criteria by which the students' academic work will be evaluated.

Specifying Desired Behaviors. Teachers also define cooperative work by specifying the behaviors that are appropriate and desirable within the learning groups.

MONITORING AND INTERVENING

Monitoring Students' Behavior. After group work begins, teachers spend most of their time observing group members to determine what problems they are having in completing the assignment and working collaboratively.

Providing Task Assistance. Teachers clarify instructions, review procedures and strategies for completing the assignment, answer questions, and teach task skills as necessary.

Teaching Collaborative Skills. Teachers also intervene to suggest more effective procedures for working together.

Providing Closure. Teachers summarize the major points of a lesson, ask students to recall ideas, and answer final questions.

EVALUATING AND PROCESSING

Evaluating Students' Learning. Whatever the product of the lesson, it is always evaluated by a criteria-referenced system. Group members also receive feedback on how effectively they collaborated.

Assessing How Well the Group is Functioning. Even if class time is limited, some time should be spent talking about how well the groups did, which things were done well, and which could be improved.

3. Curriculum Specific Packages

Whereas structures are content free and can be used to facilitate acquisition of a large range of content, packages are content bound. Packages are one or more structures combined with curriculum materials specially designed for cooperative learning. In some cases, development of the package has involved very substantial curriculum development. Adoption involves a change, not only in the social organization of the classroom, but also in the content to be taught. The curriculum specific or package approaches represent a mixed set of task and reward structures which have evolved to meet the needs which arise in applying cooperative learning to specific content areas.

Team Accelerated Instruction (TAI)

In math it is often the case that different students need to work on quite different skills, and that students can progress at quite different rates. Team Accelerated Instruction (TAI) was designed to allow each student to progress at his or her own rate, working on the skills he or she most needs, but at the same time to have each student be part of a team, caring about and encouraging the progress of teammates.

TAI was designed to create a happy marriage between cooperative and individualized learning. Details are provided by Slavin (1985). As students progress at their own pace through carefully designed individualized learning modules they earn points for their teams. Unlike typical individualized programs, in TAI students do the routine checking and management. TAI uses heterogeneous teams and team recognition, much like in STAD.

There is some peer tutoring in TAI (team members are to turn to their teammates for help), but because the individual learning modules are designed to be self-explanatory and because teammembers are usually working at quite different levels, cooperative interaction is minimal. There are some starred learning modules which students receive as a group, but the groups are of students of similar academic ability. TAI is available for grades 2 through 8, and as remedial instruction in high school and community college..

Finding Out/ Descubrimiento

(Description provided by *Elizabeth Cohen,* Stanford University)

Finding Out/Descubrimiento (FO/D) was originally designed by *Edward DeAvila* (Linguametrics Group, Corte Madera, CA..) as an instructional approach using activities from science and math. The materials were specifically designed for developing thinking skills in Spanish/English dual language settings; all materials are in both languages. The methods of classroom management, the methods of teacher training, and a complete model of organizational support were developed by the Program for Complex Instruction at Stanford under the direction of Elizabeth G. Cohen. In its present form, there are 130 activities grouped around 17 themes or units. Each unit's activities are on a theme such as optics, electricity, or measurement. For example, in the unit of probability, students graph the height of a bouncing ball, the frequency of outcomes on a flipped coin, and the frequency of outcomes of spinning a polysided object.

Finding Out exposes the students grades 2-5 to concepts of mathematics, physics and chemistry in the context of highly demanding tasks. The curriculum materials consist of intrinsically interesting manipulatives. Activity cards contain instructions for students to engage in such activities as experimenting with electricity, and plotting coordinates. For each activity there is a worksheet which requires the child to describe what happened, to make estimates and computations, or to form inferences about why things happened the way they did.

Children are assigned to linguistically and academically heterogeneous small groups at learning centers. Each learning center has a different activity card and worksheet. Each student must complete the worksheet from each learning center. Students are trained to take responsibility for each other with each person playing a different role. Roles are rotated. At a given learning center, one teammember may be a facilitator whose job it is to see that everyone in the group gets the help that he or she needs. Other roles are Checker, Safety Officer, Clean Up Coordinator, and Reporter. The classroom management system requires a blend of individual accountability and collective responsibility.

Students are trained to use each other as resources, asking questions, explaining, offering assistance, and helping others without doing things for them. In this way, students are enabled to understand the activity cards and to gain access to the learning tasks. Because of the peer interaction, they understand the nature of tasks at their learning centers; they receive assistance in filling out their worksheets. (There are no individual grades assigned.)

Because these tasks are so varied and challenging, children who do not have basic skills find that they can make intellectual contributions while accepting help from classmates with better academic skills in reading the activity card and in writing on the worksheets. For example, children who are lacking in basic skills may make accurate estimates, keen observations, or clever predictions. Teachers are trained to incorporate status treatments which result in improved expectations for competence by such children.

As a result of engaging tasks in which the basic skills of reading, writing, and computation are integrated with higher order thinking skills, students make broad gains in achievement and in English language proficiency. Evaluation has documented the capacity of the approach to bring students up to grade level in math and science (as well as in reading) according to national norms on standardized achievement tests. Achievement results are the most impressive for grades 2-4. Implementation has been studied in great detail and teachers and supportive evaluators are trained to monitor classroom implementation with systematic observations.

Stanford University's program for Complex Instruction has developed a method of teacher training and organizational support that enables teachers to use this general approach for Finding Out or for other curricula employing multiple groups with activities requiring higher order thinking skills. These methods are currently being disseminated in collaboration with the California State University system. At the present time there are dissemination centers in operation at CSU Sacramento, Fresno, and San Diego. More are being developed at CSU San Bernardino and Long Beach. School districts in California can or will be able to receive training through the Schools of Education at each of these campuses.

At the school and district levels, this program offers a model of organization support that takes into account how schools need to alter the isolation of teachers if more sophisticated instruction is to survive over time.

Methods of collegial problem-solving and evaluation are integrated in the training. A year-long process of follow-up takes place after an initial two weeks of training. FO/D curriculum materials are now available through Santillana, a commercial publisher.

Cooperative Integrated Reading and Composition (CIRC)

CIRC was developed by *Robert Slavin* and associates at (Johns Hopkins University, Slavin, 1986). The program represents a bold attempt to apply to the principles of cooperative learning and other recent research in the areas of reading, writing, spelling, and English language mechanics. In CIRC all of these skills are integrated, in a fashion, so that instruction in each reinforces the others. The approach also incorporates training in metacognitive strategies for comprehension, retention, and thinking skills.

The class is divided into two reading levels: a "code/meaning" group which receives instruction in phonic decoding skills, vocabulary, and comprehension; and a "meaning" group which has adequate decoding skills and receives instruction on vocabulary, comprehension, and inference. Sometimes the "meaning" group is subdivided into two levels.

Students are assigned to 4-5 member teams. They are assigned in pairs to teams so that they have a partner on their reading level to work with during the reading activities. The team, thus, usually has both "code/meaning" and "meaning" ability pairs within it; the work of all members contributes to a team score and team recognition.

Students work in their teams to assess mastery of vocabulary, decoding, and content presented in each basal story. Materials are prepared to accompany specific commercial basals (At present materials are available to accompany the latest versions of Holt, Ginn, Houghton-Mifflin, and Macmillan). There are written pretests and final tests for each unit, and an oral reading list for each story.

The study of reading and writing is integrated. For example, when students are studying quotation marks, they write dialogues. A peer editing approach is used to facilitate writing for revision and evaluation of writing.

Where to Start

Each of the three approaches to implementing cooperative learning has been used widely and successfully; very experienced cooperative learning teachers draw from all three. But the question remains for a beginning teacher, "How do I start?" Is it better to receive training in one package, concentrate on one structure or complex lesson design, or is it better to learn basic principles and begin designing lessons, following the Learning Together model? My own answer to the question has been the Structural Approach. I feel strongly that teachers need to be experienced in a variety of cooperative learning structures. In this approach the best place to start, is with a simple structure like Round-table or Think-Pair-Share. With those structures, there is no need for prior work on cooperative skills, communication skills, or role assignments. Further, the very simple structures can be used with almost any curriculum content. I recommend leaving the Division of Labor and Cooperative Projects designs until the students have developed some cooperative and communicative skills -- when the groups are functioning well. As you become comfortable with one structure and have used it in a variety of ways, move to a second structure. Before long you will be doing complex multi-structural lessons, going to each structure for what it does best. See Chapter 20: Co-op lesson Planning.

If we are to provide a truly rounded education for our students, we need to move from the simple to the complex structures and to cooperative skill development. If we have only the noble, but somewhat limited goals of getting students to cooperate, improving academic achievement, and improving race relations, we can accomplish those goals with a strictly Structural Approach, and with only the simple structures. In a few hours a teacher can learn to use effectively Pairs Check or Numbered Heads Together. Those methods are relatively rigid ways of structuring the classroom so that cooperation will result, and associated with the cooperation is improved achievement, race-relations, and classroom climate. If however, we have the more noble and more difficult goals for our students of not just increasing the amount of cooperation in the classroom but rather increasing the cooperative skills in the students, then we must travel a more difficult road. If the latter, much more difficult goal is adopted, then just getting students to cooperate is not enough. The goal is to provide students with a large range of cooperative skills and practice opportunities so later they can transfer or apply those skills to many of life's situations such as in their jobs and marriages.

Almost everyone will cooperate if a situation is structured so that it is in that person's interest to cooperate. It is quite another thing to prepare our students with a variety of cooperative skills, so that if they choose to, they have the skills to transform otherwise competitive situations and work cooperatively with otherwise competitive individuals. It is a yet untested belief of a number of us working in the area of cooperative learning that the Structural Approach alone is not enough to produce in students the ability to apply the principles of cooperation to new situations -- that they also need to learn a range of cooperative skills. If we want our students to transfer cooperative skills to new situations, then we must included cooperative skills as part of the curriculum and place students in relatively unstructured situations. We must then allow reflection time so they can internalize the need for the cooperative skills. See Chapter 14: Social Skills Development.

Curriculum Specific Packages offer something neither of the other two approaches offer: Curriculum specifically designed to be implemented with cooperative learning. The idea is fundamental. No teacher has the time to do comprehensive curriculum development. And why should each teacher have to reinvent the same materials? What have we gained if we use The Structural Approach or the Learning Together model to deliver weak curriculum? There will be in the coming years more and more curriculum especially designed for cooperative learning. But, on the other side, the teacher who does not know a range of structures and the basic principles and processes emphasized in the Structural and Learning Together models, will not deliver even the best curriculum as efficiently as possible.

What then can we conclude? Each of the three approaches to cooperative learning has evolved for important reasons -- each fills important needs. ◡

References & Resources:
Structural Approach:

Resources for Teachers publishes and distributes books, videos, materials, and posters on the Structural Approach, and provides a wide range of training institutes.

For more information on the Structural Approach, or to receive information on training and new materials, contact: **Spencer Kagan**, Resources for Teachers, Inc., 27128 Paseo Espada, Suite 622, San Juan Capistrano, CA 92675. Toll Free: 1(800) Wee Co-op, or (714) 248-7757.

Books:

Andrini, Beth. *Cooperative Learning and Mathematics: A Multi-Structural Approach.* 1991

Curran, Lorna. *Cooperative Learning Lessons for Little One.* 1991

Kagan, Spencer. *Same-Different. Holidays Edition.* 1990

Kagan, S. & **Kagan, M.** *The Book of Structures. (In Preparation, expected September, 1992)*

Kagan, S. & **Kagan, M.** *The Element Matrix: Creating Cooperative Learning Structures. (In Preparation, expected September, 1992)*

Shaw, Vanston. *Communitybuilding. (In Preparation, expected January 1992)*

Stone, Jeanne M. *Cooperative Learning and Language Arts: A Multi-Structural Approach.* 1991.

Wiederhold, Chuck. *Cooperative Learning and Critical Thinking, The Question Matrix.*

Binders:

Kagan, Spencer. *Transparencies for Teachers. (Transparency Binder)* 1991.

Kagan, Spencer. *Cooperative Learning Structures. (Workshop Binder)*. 1991.

Kagan, Spencer. *Co-op Lesson Designs. (Workshop Binder)*. 1991.

Kagan, Spencer. *Co-op Facilitators' Handbook. (Workshop Binder)*. 1991.

Videos:

Co-op Co-op - Exploring the Lesson design in depth.

Fairy Tale Express - A Multi-Structural Language Arts Lesson.

Foundations of Cooperative Learning: Interview with Spencer Kagan.

Just a Sample - A Multi-Structural Math Lesson.

Numbered Heads Together - Exploring the Structure in Depth.

Pairs Check - Exploring the Structure in Depth.

We Can Talk - Cooperative Learning for LEP Classrooms.

Materials:

Base 10 Kit
Fraction Bar Kit
Match-Mind
Numbered Heads Together Spinner
Q-Materials Packet
Quality Q-Dials
Social Roles Packet
Turn-4-Learning Kit
Team Formation Wheel

Learning Together:

For more information on Learning Together contact **David and Roger Johnson,** Cooperative Learning Center, 202 Pattee Hall, 150 Pillsbury Dr. Se, Minneapolis, MN. 55455. Phone: (612) 831-7031.

Books:

Johnson, D. & Johnson, R. *Learning Together and Alone.* Edina, MN. Interaction Book Company, 1987.

Johnson, David and Roger, & Edythe Holubec. *Circles of Learning: Cooperation in the Classroom.* Edina, MN: Interaction Book Company, 1986.

Johnson, D., Johnson, R. & Holubec, E. *Advanced Cooperative Learning.* Edina, MN: Interaction Book Company, 1988.

Videos:

Circle of Learning. University of Minnesota.
Belonging. University of Minnesota.

Curriculum Specific Packages:

TAI:

For more information about TAI contact: **Barbara Bennett** (408) 270-9551 or **Marshall Leavey**, TAI Mastery Education, 2D Nobility Court, Owings Mills, Maryland 21117 (301) 363-1948.

Finding Out/Descubrimiento:

For more information about FO/D, contact either **Dr. Edward De Avila**, Linguametrics Group, PO Box 3495, San Rafael, CA 94912 (415) 459-5350 or **Dr. Elizabeth Cohen**, School of Education, Stanford University, Palo Alto, CA 94306 (415) 723-4661.

Books:

DeAvila, Edward. *Finding Out/Descubrimiento.* Compton, CA:. Santillana Publishing.

CIRC:

For further information about CIRC, contact **Dr. Robert Slavin**, Center for Research on Elementary and Middle Schools, Johns Hopkins University, Baltimore, Maryland 21218 (301) 338-8249.

Slavin, R. E. *Using Student-Team Learning.* Baltimore MA: The Johns Hopkins Team Learning Project, 1986.

Videos:

Cooperative Integrated Reading and Composition. The Johns Hopkins University: Baltimore, MA.

Team Accelerated Instruction. The Johns Hopkins University: Baltimore, MA.

Chapter 6

Teams

Heterogeneous teams maximize the potential for cross-ability tutoring, positive race relations, improved cross-sex relations, and efficient classroom management. If we always use heterogeneous teams, however, the high achievers would never interact (missing important academic stimulation) and the low achievers would never be on the same team (missing leadership opportunities). Thus, there is a need for additional teamformation methods which provide a variety of ways of producing each of the four types of teams. There are four major types of cooperative learning teams and assorted methods to produce them. The four most common cooperative arrangements are: (1) Heterogeneous

Heterogeneous teams maximize the potential for cross-ability tutoring, positive race relations, improved cross-sex relations, and student-assisted classroom management. If we always use heterogeneous teams, however, the high achievers would never interact (missing important academic stimulation) and the low achievers would never be on the same team (missing leadership opportunities).

Teams, (2) Random Groups, (3) Interest Teams, and (4) Homogeneous Language Teams. Each of these types of teams is useful for different purposes.

When first announcing team assignments, name tags placed on the team tables indicating where students are to sit, can save a lot of confusion. Rather than a sequential reading by the teacher of each student's name and team assignment, the teacher simply places a team list (usually four names) on each team table and the students simultaneously move to find where they sit. Numbered mobiles above each team table make good signs for students and for teachers.

Team reformation and parting methods also merit attention.

RATIONALE FOR HETEROGENEITY

A number of researchers and theorists have taken heterogeneity of teams as a defining characteristic of cooperative learning. Heterogeneous teams are usually formed by having a high, two middle and a low achieving student on each team, and attempting to make sure the team is composed of males and females as well as an ethnic diversity. In general, heterogeneous teams have been preferred because they (1) produce the greatest opportunities for peer tutoring and support, (2) improve cross-race and cross-sex relations and integration, and (3) make classroom management easier -- having a high achiever on each team can be like having one teacher aide for every three students. Non-heterogeneous teams can be formed in a variety of ways, including self-selection (allowing students to group themselves by friendships or interests) or random selection (students draw a number from 1 to 8 for team assignments). Self-selection runs a strong risk of promoting or reinforcing status hierarchies in the classroom ("in-" and "out-groups"); random selection runs the risk of the creation of "loser" teams (the four lowest achievers in the classroom may end up on the same team if it is left to the luck of the draw). Thus, in general, heterogeneous, teacher-formed teams have been preferred, and some theorists have referred to heterogeneity of teams as a basic principle of cooperative learning.

The teamformation methods each allow certain important benefits. Although I prefer the heterogeneous team as a mainstay, there are important benefits derived from breaking out from the heterogeneous teams to sometimes form random, interest, or homogeneous language teams.

Spencer Kagan: *Cooperative Learning* ©
Publisher: Resources for Teachers , Inc. • 1(800) Wee Co-op

RATIONALE FOR THE FOUR-MEMBER TEAM

Much of the rationale for cooperative learning is based on the benefits of active participation. In the whole-class, when a student is called on and responds, 1/30th of the class is actively participating. If we make two large groups in the class, and allow one person at a time to talk within each group, during the discussion time we double the amount of active participation --1/15th of the class is talking. As the group size is made smaller, the percentages get better. Groups of four allow 1/4 of the class to produce language at any one time -- from the perspective of participation, they are twice as good as groups of 8. Given this rationale, why not move to groups of 3 or even pairs. Why does Spencer call for groups of 4? There are three reasons.

1. Allow Pair Work. Very often I will do pair work within teams, doubling the amount of participation. With groups of three there is an odd-man-out with pair work. Pairs Check, Paired Reading and the Flashcard Game are among the structures which maximize simultaneous interaction through pair work.

2. Avoid Odd Man Out. The social psychology of a group of three is often a pair and an outsider. Two people hit it off well and talk to each other often, leaving one left out.

3. More Learning Pairs. Compared to a group of three, a group of four doubles the probability of an optimum cognitive and linguistic mismatch. Both the Piagetian moral development work and linguistic development work indicates that we learn well from someone only somewhat different from our own level of development. In a group of three there are three possible pairs; in a group of four, there are six.

WHEN THE CLASS DOESN'T DIVIDE BY FOUR

If your class does not divide evenly by four, use the following guidelines:

Teams of Four Double The Lines of Communication

Teams of 3 = 3 Pairs

Teams of 4 = 6 Pairs

With one student left over, look around and place that student where he or she would best learn or help others. With two students left over, look around and steal a student from one of the teams of four so that you have two teams of three. With three students left over, keep those three as a team.

MORE BOYS THAN GIRLS ?

If there are more boys than girls or more girls than boys, the best strategy usually is not to share the scarce resources equally, assigning one boy to each team or one girl to each team. One boy and three girls often amounts to one student receiving an inordinate amount of attention. One girl and three boys often is a team with one student being ignored by three others. Solution: Assign students to teams of two boys and two girls until you run out of boys or girls and then have the remaining teams be either all boy teams or all girl teams.

Odd-Man-In

1 left over = 1 Team of 5

2 left over = 2 Teams of 3

3 left over = 1 Team of 3

Spencer Kagan: *Cooperative Learning*©
Publisher: Resources for Teachers , Inc. • 1(800) Wee Co-op

A NOTE ON SEATING:

Some teachers report better luck if during initial team assignments they have students sit so that the high achiever is next to a middle achiever and across from a middle achiever; they place the low achiever furthest from the high achiever. Some high achievers have difficulty initially working with students far below their level.

How to Form Teams

1. Heterogeneous Teams

Heterogeneous Method 1:

TEACHER ASSIGNED TEAMS

Step 1. Rank Order Students. Produce a numbered list of students, from highest to lowest achiever. The list does not have to be perfect. To produce the list, use one of the following (in order of preference): pretest, recent past test, past grades, or best guess.

Step 2. Select First Team. Choose top, bottom, and two middle achievers. Assign them to Team 1, unless they are:

a. all of one sex;

b. all one ethnicity in a mixed ethnicity group;

c. worst enemies or best friend;

d. unfavored choices on the Sociometric Grid (if using the Sociometric Approach to be described).

To make switches, move up or down one student from the middle to readjust.

Step 3. Select Remaining Teams. To produce Team 2, repeat Step 2 with the reduced list. Then use the even more reduced list to assign students to Teams 3, 4, and so on. A worksheet for forming heterogeneous teams is provided on the following page.

Note: For ease, some teachers place the students' names on pink and blue post-it slips to easily move the names about while assigning teams. See also the Teamformation Wheel on page 6:15.

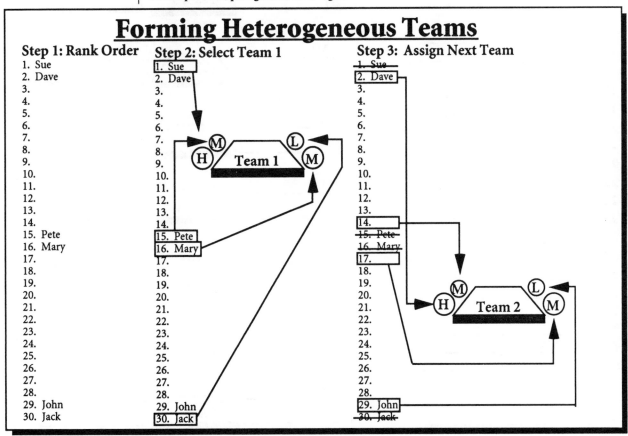

Forming Heterogeneous Teams

Step 1: Rank Order
1. Sue
2. Dave
3.
4.
5.
6.
7.
8.
9.
10.
11.
12.
13.
14.
15. Pete
16. Mary
17.
18.
19.
20.
21.
22.
23.
24.
25.
26.
27.
28.
29. John
30. Jack

Step 2: Select Team 1
1. Sue
2. Dave
3.
4.
5.
6.
7.
8.
9.
10.
11.
12.
13.
14.
15. Pete
16. Mary
17.
18.
19.
20.
21.
22.
23.
24.
25.
26.
27.
28.
29. John
30. Jack

Team 1

Step 3: Assign Next Team
1. Sue
2. Dave
3.
4.
5.
6.
7.
8.
9.
10.
11.
12.
13.
14.
15. Pete
16. Mary
17.
18.
19.
20.
21.
22.
23.
24.
25.
26.
27.
28.
29. John
30. Jack

Team 2

Forming Heterogeneous Teams

Step 1. Fill in your students' names in the class list marked 1 through 36. Attempt to rank order your students so Number 1 is the highest achiever and so on down the list. The rank order does not have to be perfect.

Step 2. Place the highest, two middle, and the lowest achievers on Team 1. Make switches among the middle achievers to avoid teams of all one sex or one race. Avoid also best friends and worst enemies.

Step 3. Cross out the names of Team 1 students from the class list. Repeat Step 2 with the reduced class list to form Team 2. Repeat for each remaining team.

Step 4. Assign left over students to teams of three or five.

Class List

1. _____
2. _____
3. _____
4. _____
5. _____
6. _____
7. _____
8. _____
9. _____
10. _____
11. _____
12. _____
13. _____
14. _____
15. _____
16. _____
17. _____
18. _____
19. _____
20. _____
21. _____
22. _____
23. _____
24. _____
25. _____
26. _____
27. _____
28. _____
29. _____
30. _____
31. _____
32. _____
33. _____
34. _____
35. _____
36. _____

H = High • M = Medium • L = Low

(M) _____   (L) _____
(H) _____ Team 1 (M) _____

(M) _____   (L) _____
(H) _____ Team 2 (M) _____

(M) _____   (L) _____
(H) _____ Team 3 (M) _____

(M) _____   (L) _____
(H) _____ Team 4 (M) _____

(M) _____   (L) _____
(H) _____ Team 5 (M) _____

(M) _____   (L) _____
(H) _____ Team 6 (M) _____

(M) _____   (L) _____
(H) _____ Team 7 (M) _____

(M) _____   (L) _____
(H) _____ Team 8 (M) _____

(M) _____   (L) _____
(H) _____ Team 9 (M) _____

Spencer Kagan: *Cooperative Learning*©
Publisher: Resources for Teachers , Inc. • 1(800) Wee Co-op

The Sociometric Approach

The Sociometric Approach is an optional adjunct when using the Ranked List Approach. This approach was developed by *Susan Masters* and *Lucile Tambara* (Maple Hill Elementary School, Diamond Bar California). It allows consideration of the relations among students.

Step 1. Students Fill in Preferences. To use the Sociometric Grid, first present students with a list of their classmates and have them place a plus by the names of the three persons they would most like on their team and a check mark by the names of the three persons they would least like to be on their team.

Student Handout:

Name:_____

Team Preference Sheet

Instructions: We will form new teams. To form the best teams possible, I would like to know your preferences. Here is a list of your classmates. Please put a plus by the names of the three classmates you would most like to have on a team for the next six weeks, and a check mark by three people you would prefer not to be on a team with this time. You may want to make new friends, so you might place a check mark by the names of old teammates and your best friends. I cannot promise you will be on a team with someone you have given a plus, or that you will not be on a team with someone you have given a check, but I will consider your preferences when I make the new team assignments.

Class List

1. _____
2. _____
3. _____
4. _____
5. _____
6. _____
7. _____
8. _____
9. _____
10. _____
11. _____
12. _____
13. _____
14. _____
15. _____
16. _____
17. _____
18. _____

19. _____
20. _____
21. _____
22. _____
23. _____
24. _____
25. _____
26. _____
27. _____
28. _____
29. _____
30. _____
31. _____
32. _____
33. _____
34. _____
35. _____
36. _____

Step 2. Teacher Records Preferences on Sociometric Grid. Record the information on a zerox copy of the Sociometric Grid on the following page.

The example sociometric grid below illustrates how the Sociometric Grid should look after recording the students preferences. The choices of each student toward each other student are indicated by a +, -, or blank. The black squares are filled in to in dicate that students cannot nominate themselves. Thus, Miguel indicated he would like to have as teammates students 2 (Pat), 5 (Carlos), and 9 (Jason), and that he would prefer not to have as teammates students 3 (Tom), 7 (Monica), and 10 (Simon). Note, the chart is filled out with the choices for only the first ten students. Jason is very popular; Monica is very unpopular; and Scott is an isolate.

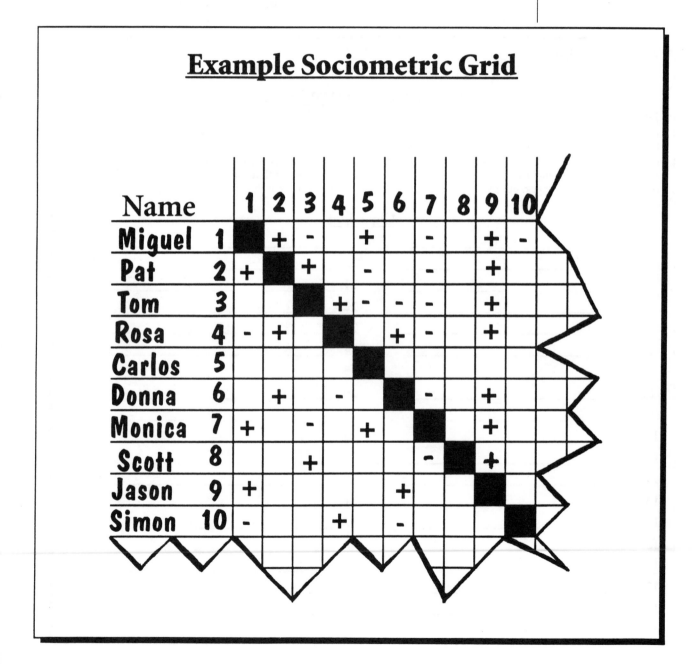

Example Sociometric Grid

Name		1	2	3	4	5	6	7	8	9	10
Miguel	1	■	+	-		+		-		+	-
Pat	2	+	■	+		-		-		+	
Tom	3			■	+	-	-	-		+	
Rosa	4	-	+		■		+	-		+	
Carlos	5					■					
Donna	6		+		-		■	-		+	
Monica	7	+		-		+		■		+	
Scott	8			+				-	■	+	
Jason	9	+					+			■	
Simon	10	-			+			-			■

The Sociometric Grid

For teacher's use. Write in the three pluses and three minuses following the name of each student, indicating that student's preferences. While assigning teams you may wish to avoid pairing students if a minus occurs. Although some students may not be a favorite of anyone, and may have quite a number of students who do not want to be on their team, it is almost always possible to find at least three others who have not indicated they would mind having the student as a teammate. You may want also to avoid certain pluses as they represent "best friends" who can pair, minimizing interaction along many lines within teams.

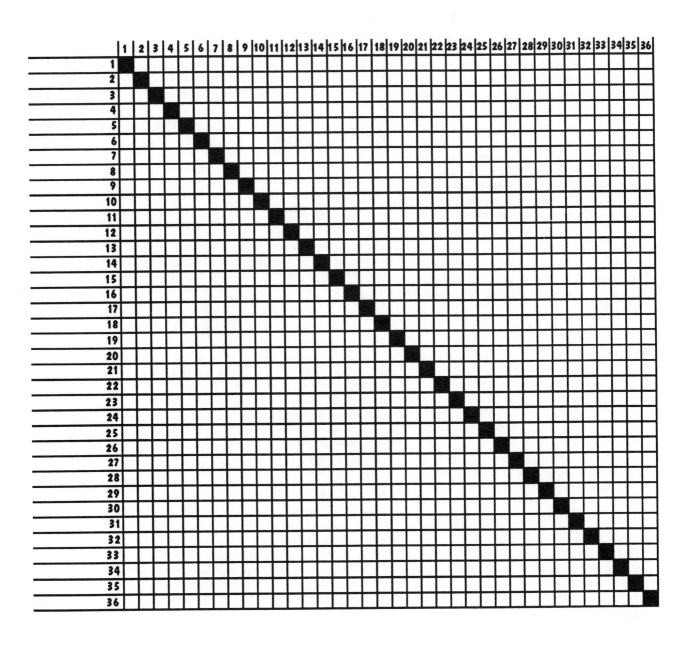

Spencer Kagan: *Cooperative Learning*©
Publisher: Resources for Teachers , Inc. • 1(800) Wee Co-op

Heterogeneous Method 2:
TEAM LEADER APPROACH
The following is a version of a method developed by *Richard Shetley* (Alta Loma Junior High School, Alta Loma, CA).

Step 1. Select Team Leaders. Select the top 7 or 8 students (highest achievers) as team leaders, one per team.

Step 2. Leadership Meeting. Meet with the leaders as a group. Explain to them that the success of the team approach depends on mixed ability-level teams. Have them decide which of the 6 or 7 lowest ability students will be on each team. Explain to them what they are to do the next day.

Step 3. Leaders Choose Teammates. The next day in class announce that there will be student teams and announce the team leaders. Ask the team leaders to choose someone to be on their team. As per agreement, the team leaders each go up to one of the low ability students and say something like, "I want you to be on my team."

Be prepared. Many of the low ability students have never been selected by their peers for anything. They are used to being the leftovers. There may be tears or at least moist eyes.

Step 4. High-Low Pair Choose Middle. The leader and his/her first selection sit down together and decide on a second choice from the pool of remaining middle ability-level students.

Step 5. High-Low-Middle Triad Choose Last Teammate. The three members choose the remaining teammate.

Students are informed that they cannot choose teams all of one sex. The teacher maintains the option to make final decisions and adjustments if necessary.

Richard Shetley has come up with an easy way to have students assign themselves to teams which not only is fair, but which for some students provides the most powerful peer inclusion experience of their life! Thanks, Richard.

Heterogeneous Method 3:
PAIRS PAIR
Julie High (Consultant, Resources for Teacher) developed Pairs Pair. Students are divided into four groups, High, High/Middle, Low/Middle, and Low. The High and Low groups meet on one side of the room and the two middle groups meet on the other. The students then form pairs (High-Low on one side of the room and High/Middle-Low/Middle on the other). Next the pairs pair. Thus the students have selected heterogeneous teams. Julie is a very experienced cooperative learning teacher and facilitator, and she reports that Pairs Pair has produced the best functioning teams in her classroom. It would seem that Pairs Pair will work well only in classrooms which are relatively homogeneous. In many classrooms it would be undesirable to have low achievers stand as a group.

Heterogeneous Method 4:
TOPIC-SPECIFIC TEAMS
One way to ensure a diversity of opinions and a provocative discussion on a topic is to form topic-specific heterogeneous teams. My favorite approach is to do a folded folded value line. See graphic on the next page.

First, have the students line up on a value line on the issue, from agree to disagree. Have them mark their position first on a piece of paper and then take their stance so they don't just go where their friends stand. Next, have them discuss with a person next to them why they took the stance they did (similar positions reinforce and support each other). Now fold the value line so that the strongest agree person is standing across from the strongest disagree person. Have students play Paraphrase Passport and or Affirmation Passport to make sure they respect and understand each others' point of view. Now comes the fun part. Fold this folded value line so that the strongly agree and strongly disagree pair walk over and stand with the two at the other end of the folded value line (these two were two who either saw two points of view or did not care strongly about the issue). These four students sit down as a team. The remaining pairs at both ends of the line in turn each join together as a group of four and sit down. You have just formed Topic-specific Heterogeneous Teams and they are ready for a lively and informative project or discussion!

2. Random Teams

Random Method 1:
SOCIAL ROLES PACKET

Use a Social Roles Packet which comes with nine sets of twelve role cards, one color-coded set per team.

Step 1. Pick Roles. Pick four important social roles, such as Gatekeeper, Quiet Captain, Recorder, and Praiser.

Step 2. Mix-Freeze-Trade. Have students walk around the room in a random order, each with a role card. Tell them to "freeze" and "trade" with the person nearest them. Do this several times.

Step 3. Pair and Interview. Students form pairs with one other student with the same color role card. For example, ask the Gatekeepers and Praisers of the same colors to form pairs while the Recorder and Quiet Captain do the same. Students interview each other on a getting acquainted topic.

Step 4. Pairs Pair. Pairs find the pair with the corresponding color. They sit down as a group and each introduce the partner they have just interviewed.

Students are now in teams of four, with their roles preassigned!

Random Method 2:
PUZZLED PEOPLE

Step 1. Tear Picture. Have students tear a picture into four parts.

Step 2. Mix and Trade. Have students mill around the room and trade pieces -- each with one other person. (They keep their hand raised until they have made a trade, so those who have not yet traded can see who to trade with.)

Step 3. Solve Puzzle. Then let students solve the puzzle by grouping with the others who hold pieces of the same picture.

The new teams are thus formed.

Alternative versions: use four sentences in a content-related statement, or four lines of a proverb or poem.

Forming Heterogeneous Teams:
Topic-Specific Teams

Step 1. Students Line Up. Students line up on a value line.

Step 2. Fold Value Line. One end walks so opposing opinions meet.

Step 3. Pair Promenades. The pair on one end of the folded value line promenade to the other end so pairs pair up.

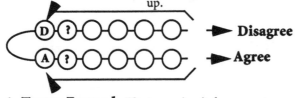

Step 4. Teams Formed. The two pairs sit down as a team of four.

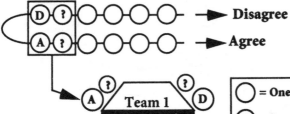

Step 5. Repeat 3 and 4. Steps 3 and 4 are repeated to form each additional team.

○ = One Student
Ⓐ = Strongly Agree
Ⓓ = Strongly Disagree
(?) = No Strong Opinion

Random Method 3:
INSIDE-OUTSIDE CIRCLE

Inside Outside Circle is a powerful mastery structure (students rotate to practice with partners) - See Chapter 10: Mastery Structures. Random teams can be formed from the circle, as follows:

Step 1. Fun Interviews. Have students rotate and interview their partner on a get-acquainted topic such as "Dream Vacation," "Favorite Food," or "Ideal Profession."

Step 2. Pairs Pair. Have one pair join another pair next to them to sit down as a team. Next, have the two pairs on either side of the pair which left the circle walk forward, meet each other and sit down. Each of the remaining pairs does the same, in turn, in promenade fashion.

Step 3. Roundrobin. When seated, students each introduce the partner they have interviewed. If there is an extra pair, have them split and have two teams of five, or borrow an extra person from one of the groups of four and have two teams of three.

Forming Random Teams:

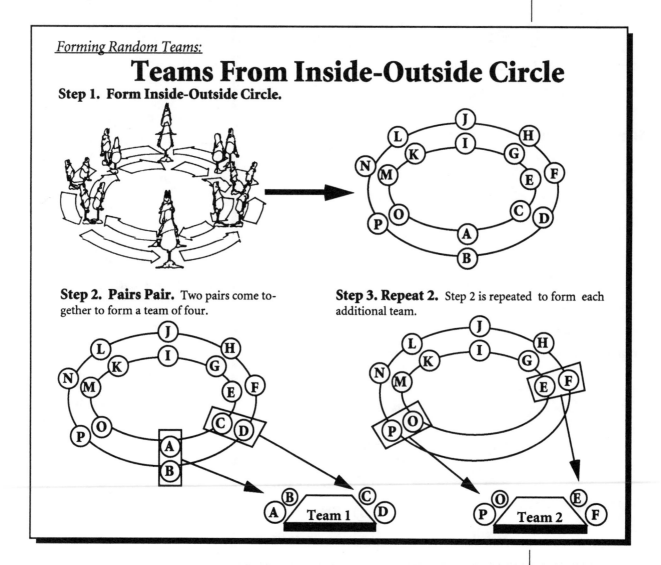

Teams From Inside-Outside Circle
Step 1. Form Inside-Outside Circle.

Step 2. Pairs Pair. Two pairs come together to form a team of four.

Step 3. Repeat 2. Step 2 is repeated to form each additional team.

Domains of Usefulness
Random vs. Heterogeneous Teams

Frequent random teamformation has much to offer including variety, perception of fairness, opportunity to transfer skills to a new group (see box below). On the other hand, random selection could lead to the four lowest achievers in the class on the same team. Thus, random teams generally cannot stay together for long periods. And the carefully designed, long-standing team has a great deal to offer, including learning to learn together, maximum tutoring, and easy management. To get the best of both worlds, use a basic long-standing heterogeneous team with an occasional random breakout team.

Teamformation Methods

	Heterogeneous	**Random**
Advantages	• Balanced • Maximum cross-race, cross-sex, & cross-ability team contact • Low achievers carefully placed to maximize tutoring • Language ability grouping • Management (student aid for each three) • High achiever for every team	• Side-steps stereotypes • Classbuilding and networking • Built-in roles & teambuilding • Quick and easy • Can form teams without knowing student status (beginning of year) • Variety, stimulation, fun • Avoid resistance; perception of fairness • Many transference opportunities • Leadership opportunities
Disadvantages	• Teacher time • Fewer transference opportunites • No high-high & low-low contact • Possible teammate overdependence • Implicit tracking • Negative stereotypes • Negative metacommunication (we can't work with everyone)	• Team where no one knows content well • Possible intense conflicts • Language incompatibilities • Teams of one sex or one race • Limited bonding opportunities; weaker team identity • Limited opportunities to learn how to learn • Imbalance: "Winner" and "Loser" teams.

Spencer Kagan: *Cooperative Learning*©
Publisher: Resources for Teachers , Inc. • 1(800) Wee Co-op

The use of Random and Heterogeneous teams is interfaced with the curricular cycle. When introducing new and demanding material, use heterogeneous teams to maximize tutoring. Later when the goal is practice and review, a random team can work fine - even the four lowest achievers in the class can function well as a team if the goal is practice.

3. Interest Teams

On an occasional basis, allowing students to form their own teams can provide learning opportunities not otherwise possible. For some projects, having students group by interests will allow students with similar interests to explore a topic in depth. Allowing best friends to work together can bring new energy to academics.

4. Language Teams

HOMOGENEOUS LANGUAGE TEAMS

A general principle of instruction, in settings in which there are Limited English Proficient students, is that students with different levels of English language proficiency need different kinds of input -- lower level students need more context and less cognitively demanding materials. Therefore, at certain points in the instructional cycle, and especially when there is a large range of language abilities and demanding content, teams homogeneous by English language ability are desirable, and the homogeneity principle should override the heterogeneity principle. Thus, a fourth and often desirable basis of teamformation exists: homogeneous grouping by language proficiency.

While homogeneous by language, an attempt is still made to make the team heterogeneous on other dimensions such as content ability, sex, and, if possible, ethnic background. Thus the team is really a homogeneous language/heterogeneous ability team.

In general, occasional or even frequent use of homogeneous grouping of students by language ability facilitates instruction in dual or multiple language classes. Whole class instruction in settings involving Limited English Proficient students often leads to teaching to one group at the expense of others; cooperative learning with exclusively heterogeneous groups may not allow language appropriate input and production; homogeneous language groups can allow students appropriate language acquisition opportunities more of the time.

The use of both heterogeneous and homogeneous teams, properly balanced, can maximize the positive academic, linguistic, and social outcomes for language minority students. In general, the use of homogeneous groups functions to provide comprehensible instruction, equal access to the curriculum for all students, early acquisition of language and content, and the context for later work in heterogeneous groups in which primarily English is used. The heterogeneous language group functions to facilitate social and racial integration, as well as opportunities for practice and application of both language and content.

With demanding or unfamiliar content, low English language abilities, and a greater range of English language proficiencies, a teacher must forego exclusive use of heterogeneous groups in favor of occasional or even frequent use of groups which are homogeneous by language proficiency. Nevertheless, even if homogeneous language groups are used, there probably should be some use of heterogeneous or random groups. Exclusive use of homogeneous grouping by language will lead to the formation of undesirable stable status hierarchies and a polarization of the class. Thus, even in classrooms in which homogeneous language groups are desirable much of the time, there is a need to avoid fixed stereotypes by use of occasional random and or heterogeneous team formation and classbuilding.

There are some interesting ways to obtain the positive outcomes associated with both homogeneous and heterogeneous teams:

1) In Jigsaw, students may be in heterogeneous home teams and homogeneous expert teams.

2) If there are sufficient numbers of students of each primary language, create heterogeneous/homogeneous teams. That is, to first divide the class by primary language,

but then assign heterogeneous teams within language groups. Thus, one team may have a high, two middle, and a low achieving student working together in English, and another team may have four language minority students with a range of achievement levels working together in their primary language.

3) For some activities, the teacher may allow random teamformation among all of the students who are to work in English and a second random teamformation for all the students who are to work in a native language.

4) Have homogeneous language pairs, who sometimes work only as a pair in their home language, but who sometimes pair up with another pair to form heterogeneous language teams.

In determining the extent to which groups should be homogeneous or heterogeneous with regard to language abilities, instructional objectives must be considered. In planning a lesson for a classroom with language minority students, perhaps the first question should be, "Is the primary objective of the lesson a language objective or a content objective?" In general, if the primary objective is content, then groups should be structured so that language is not a barrier to content acquisition. Unrestricted use of primary language may be appropriate. If language acquisition is the primary objective, groups might be structured so that English is used almost exclusively, but the level of language and number of contextual cues are appropriate for each group.

In a classroom which is part of a school-wide program which stresses primary language instruction and development, more use of homogeneous groups and inclusion of primary language experiences would be expected than in a classroom which is part of a school-wide program which contains only very early and limited access to primary language instruction. The classroom structures must articulate with the broader program objectives.

Parting Activities

The teams have been working together for five or six weeks. The teacher suddenly announces, "Tomorrow we will be forming new teams." The class is headed for trouble. Students are likely to spend the first couple of weeks in their new teams wishing they were in their old teams. Parting Activities allow students to express their feelings and prepare emotionally for ending the old team and beginning a new team. Some of my favorite parting activities follow:

1. Team Pictures. Take a snapshot of teams before they part and have them posted, or have the teams paste them in the class scrapbook.

2. Team Statements. Have the teammates make a final Team Statement to the class as a team. "Together we learned..."

3. Teammate Introductions. Have teammates introduce each other to the class as exciting potential new teammates. "What you can really learn from Johnny is...." "One thing you will like about working with Susan is...."

4. Parting Messages. Have students write a parting letter to each of their teammates; emphasis is on "What I have learned from you," and/or "What I have enjoyed about working with you." More sophisticated students can deal with regrets as well as appreciations. The following page may be used in a Simultaneous Roundtable as follows.

1. Students each write their name at the top of a copy of the Parting Message form from the following page.(Use colored paper when you zerox the form).

2. Students pass their Parting Message form to the person on their left within the team.

3. Each student writes a positive message to the person whose form they have.

4. Forms are passed and filled out until they return to the original sender.

We all have many partings throughout life; school can be a place where we learn to deal with them with dignity and grace.

Parting Messages for

_____

Name

I'll remember you ...

From: _____

I'll remember you ...

From: _____

I'll remember you ...

From: _____

Forming New Teams

Sheila Silversides (Edmund Partridge School, Winnipeg Manitoba Canada) developed the **Teamformation Wheel**, a clever method for forming new teams. The Teamformation Wheel is easy to make, easy to use, and assures that teams will consist of a high, two middle, and a low achiever each time teams are formed. See graphic.

Cut out four circles, of four sizes and place a brad in the center to allow free rotation of all circles. You may wish to laminate and write with a dry marker to reuse the wheel.

The names of the students are written on the outer ridge of four concentric circles; the high achievers on one, low achievers on another and the middle achievers on the remaining two, as indicated. For teams of three, leave a place blank; for teams of five, add another wheel. The circles are attached by a brad in the center which allows free rotation of all circles. A team consists of one student from each circle.

For the "extra" 1, 2, or 3 students, if your class does not divide evenly by four, I suggest the following: For three students, have one team of three which means on blank spot. For two or one students have two or one teams of five. You may wish to keep the names of one or two middle achievers off the wheel to fill in to complete the one or two teams of five, of you may wish to make a fifth wheel which can be rotated.

When it is time to form new teams, the circles are rotated. The inside circle stays, the next circle is rotated one space, the next circle is rotated two, and the outside circle is rotated three. The wheel allows the teacher to keep track of previous team assignments and to form new ones in a few minutes. Thanks, Shelia!

Teamformation Wheel

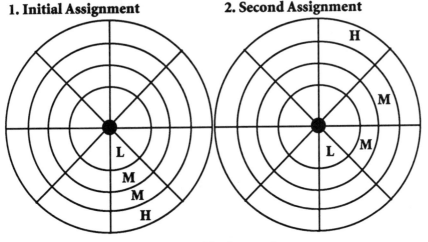

1. Initial Assignment   **2. Second Assignment**

L = Low achieving student
M = Middle achieving student
H = High achieving student

When new teams are to be formed, keep the inside wheel fixed, rotate the next wheel one ahead, the next wheel two ahead, and the outside wheel three ahead. Because high achievers are on the outside ring, middle achievers are on middle rings, and low achievers are on the inside, the teams remain heterogeneous after the rotation.

Team Reunions

Michael L. Bettino, (Rolling Hills High School, Palos Verdes Peninsula Unified School District) has a class with the following ethnic makeup: eight Anglo American, four Persian, four Japanese, three Chinese, two Indian (from India), one French, one Canadian, and one South American student. They instituted **Team Reunions**, as follows:

"After six weeks of heterogeneous groups in an 11th grade regular English III class (American Literature and Composition), it was time to make new groups. I made the changes and found a certain amount of hostility to the new

Spencer Kagan: *Cooperative Learning*©
Publisher: Resources for Teachers , Inc. • 1(800) Wee Co-op

groups. A student asked if they could have a five minute 'Group Reunion'.

I let them do this -- and then they returned to their new groups. Now the new groups are rolling along very smoothly.

A new group Reunion will take place in two weeks and will be a regular part of the program."

The **Team Reunion** well might be used in any class to have an old team become an on-going support group for students. As students discuss with their old teammates how things are going in their new teams, they might gain support as well as insights not otherwise possible. ❧

Chapter 7

Management

tional classroom. Cooperative classroom management differs radically from classroom management in the traditional classroom. In the traditional classroom, students do little talking and interacting so managing student behavior is relatively simple. Some system is instituted to keep students from talking or interacting. In contrast, in the cooperative classroom student-student interaction is encouraged and so management involves different skills. Some of the management concerns introduced along with the introduction of teams include seating arrangement, noise level, giving directions, distribution and storage of team materials, and methods of shaping the behavior of groups.

To give directions to a group, instructing them how to do a complex project involves a totally different set of management skills than those involved in telling students to open a workbook to page 293 and do problems 1 through 40.

Instructing teams how to do a complex project involves a totally different set of management skills than those involved in telling students to each open a workbook to page 293 and do problems 1 through 40. One cooperative learning lesson may include a number of structures, each of which can have many steps. The teacher must convey very complex sets of instructions very briefly in order to maximize time for student-student interaction. A well-managed cooperative learning lesson may take as little as one-fifth the teacher talk as does a poorly managed lesson, saving precious time for student interaction and learning.

Many teachers report that their management problems decrease dramatically once they switch to cooperative learning. The reason is that in the traditional classroom there is a mismatch between the needs of the students and the structure of the classroom. The nature of a student is active and interactive: Students want to "do" and to talk. And the traditional classroom demands that students be passive and isolated. Naturally, the students do not give up their basic needs without a struggle. And so a great deal of energy is spent keeping the students in their seats, "not bothering their neighbors," and quiet.

The cooperative classroom, in contrast, is better aligned with the needs of students. It is based on the assumption that learning occurs through doing and interacting. Students are encouraged to interact, move, create, and do. Feeling their basic needs met, students are no longer "management problems."

Nevertheless, there are a number of management skills necessary in the cooperative classroom, not involved in managing a tradi-

One of my favorite examples of the difference management techniques can make occurred one morning while I was observing some teachers after an initial workshop in cooperative learning, as they first moved their students into teams. In the first class I observed, the teacher read the team assignments to the students as they sat in their seats. She read from the class list, in alphabetical order: "Susan Aragon, you will be on team 4; Peter Birtch, you will be on team 7...." When she got done reading the list, predictably, there were a number of questions. "What is my team number? Where do I sit?..."

Management

Spencer Kagan: *Cooperative Learning*©
Publisher: Resources for Teachers , Inc. • 1(800) Wee Co-op

Somewhat irritated, she again read the list, admonishing the students to listen carefully. Nevertheless, there were again some questions when she finished reading the list the second time, and she ended up almost physically moving some of the students into their team assignments.

By the time she finally had the students in teams, about twelve minutes had elapsed.

When I observed the next classroom, the teacher was in exactly the same spot. She was about to move the students from rows into teams. She said the following, "Boys and girls, on your tables are some index cards, face down. Don't turn them over until I say. When you turn them over you will find four names on each card. You are then to quietly collect your books, and move to the table which has your name. We will see how quickly and quietly you can find your new team and sit down ready to learn about teambuilding."

The students were in their new teams and ready to work in about two minutes!

One teacher had attempted to manage a cooperative classroom using a sequential structure (reading the names one at a time) while the other teacher use a simultaneous structure (everyone up and moving at once). The simultaneous management technique was clearly superior.

THE QUIET SIGNAL

Teachers spend an enormous amount of time and energy trying to get their classrooms quiet, and trying to get the attention of all their students. "May I get your attention, please?" "Quiet please!" are phrases oft repeated, with inadequate response.

There is a simple solution: A quiet signal. Entire schools have adopted the quiet signal, a raised hand. It works well in the school bus, cafeteria, assembly, or classroom. When a teacher raises his/her hand, the students are to do the same, and to give full attention to the teacher.

A bit of explanation to students may be helpful when the quiet signal is introduced: After the groups are formed, the teacher explains that there is a natural tendency for a classroom of teams to become too noisy: As one team talks, a nearby team needs to talk a bit louder to be heard, which forces the first team to talk even louder. So noise levels can escalate. The teacher does not want to shout over the student talk to get the attention of the class. The teacher indicates that the class can solve this problem if it can learn to respond quickly to a quiet signal.

The Quiet Signal

1. **Hand Up, Stop Talking, Stop Doing**
2. **Signal Others**
3. **Look**
4. **Listen**

The Quiet Signal:

A Gift From the Cubs

I have been asked how I first developed the quiet signal. Here is the answer:
When I was doing my first cooperative learning demonstration lesson, it was the first time I had ever taught a class -- I was a University Professor trying to apply the principles of cooperation to classrooms. As the students began to get involved in their learning task and the talk escalated, without any thought I told them, "When I raise my hand, that will be our 'Zero-Noise-Level-Signal.' To make sure everyone sees the signal, when I raise my hand, you all do the same, until I lower my hand." It worked. Without knowing where the idea had come from, for several years I shared with many teachers the "Zero Noise Level Signal." It became popular. (Later I changed the name to "Quiet Signal" because talk in the cooperative classroom is not noise, but productive work.)

One day I was in the middle of lunch, and for for no apparent reason, I had a very vivid memory of an early experience as a Cub Scout: When the Troop Leader wanted our attention, he had us all raise our hand and give the Cub Scout salute. Without realizing it, during my first experience as a classroom teacher, I automatically turned to that early experience to help me manage the classroom.

Could it be that the extreme prevalence of the traditional classroom structure results from teachers unconsciously modeling themselves after the way they have been taught? If so, perhaps cooperative learning will become the way of the future as the students of today's cooperative learning classrooms become the teachers of tomorrow!

Spencer Kagan: *Cooperative Learning*©
Publisher: Resources for Teachers, Inc. • 1(800) Wee Co-op

Class Norms

1. Individual Responsibility: *"I am responsible for...:*

Trying: Improvement counts.

Asking: Ask for help from teammates.

Helping: Offer help to teammates.

Courtesy: Make polite requests and show appreciation.

Support: Give praisers, encouragers, and build ups (no put downs).

Filling Roles

Checker: Check for understanding and agreement.

Praiser/Encourager: Praise effort and ideas.

Recorder: Record ideas and decisions.

Taskmaster: Bring your team back to the task.

Gatekeeper: Make sure all participate (no bully; no loafer).

Reporter: Share with other teams, the class, the teacher.

2. Team Responsibility: *"We are responsible for...:*

Solving: We try to solve our own problems.

Asking Team Questions: We ask teammates before asking the teacher.

Helping: We help other teams, classmates, and the teacher.

Inner Voice: We use a voice heard by teammates, but not other teams.

The quiet signal is a signal to students to stop talking, to give their full attention to the teacher, and to have their hands and bodies still. Teachers choose different signals for their students. Some may simply ask for attention by saying "May I have your attention please." Others may flip the lights on and off. Others ring a bell.

The signal I like best is for the teacher to raise one hand. That signal is convenient because the teacher does not have to talk over the group noise level, and because he or she does not have to walk over to the bell or light switch. An additional nice feature of the raised hand signal is that the teacher can indicate that when students see the teacher's raised hand, they too should raise their hands. Thus, when the teacher needs the attention of the class, she or he raises a hand. This is quickly followed by students nearby raising their hands, which leads to yet other

students doing so. The raised hand of the teacher is like the pebble dropped in the pond: Quiet attention spreads from the teacher across the class like a ripple.

Some Variations on the Quiet Signal:

1. Different Signals. Have different signals, one to simply bring the noise level down (palm horizontal lowering slowly), another to bring the noise level down and focus students' attention on the teacher (arm up, index finger up).

2. Stoplight Cards. Teacher places a green card on the desk of teams if they are doing fine; a yellow card, if they need to tone it down a bit; a red card, if they need to become completely silent and count to ten before resuming interaction.

3. Quiet Captain. Each team has a Quiet Captain whose job is to remind students if they have become too loud. The Quiet Captain may use stoplight cards or a unique signal.

4. Mechanical Noise Monitor. One teacher has told me he has a noise monitor which sets off a buzz in the classroom when the noise gets above a certain number of decibels. Students automatically quiet down when the buzz goes off, so he does not need to manage noise level.

5. Random Timer. Use a random timer to bring noise levels down. The random timer goes off at teacher determined intervals and students are to become silent and reflect on how well they are using their inner voices.

6. Timed. A teacher could not get his class to respond well to the quiet signal until he told them they were going to do "sophisticated time management." He used a timer and told the class he would count and post seconds it took them to become quiet and to give him full attention. Seconds were time lost from a Friday ten minute free talk period. Students began to manage themselves because they did not want to lose the free time.

Spencer Kagan: *Cooperative Learning*©
Publisher: Resources for Teachers , Inc. • 1(800) Wee Co-op

CLASS RULES

Class rules can be very helpful. I like it best if rules are derived by students, rather than imposed on them. Having a rule such as, "Treat others with respect" which students themselves have created or at least agreed upon is much more powerful than having it come down as a rule imposed by the teacher. Often the way to have students generate rules is to have them reflect on their own group interaction. As students honestly look at how they feel when they receive a put-down as opposed to a praiser, they are more likely to endorse a rule to treat others with respect. A list of cooperative classroom norms appears in the box on the previous page.

An important element in a successful cooperative learning management system is communicating clearly your expectations. The teacher defines in advance those behaviors which are necessary for successful classroom functioning, and those behaviors which are appreciated. Necessary behaviors include quickly coming to full, quiet attention whenever the teacher asks. Appreciated behaviors include extra peer helping, peer validation, and attention to the needs, opinions, and desires of others.

Guidelines for Class Rules

1. **Make them positive.** (State: "We support classmates;" rather than "No put downs."
2. **Make them realistic.**
3. **Use simple wording.**
4. **Limit the number of rules to five.**

SEATING ARRANGEMENT

Principles of room arrangement: Arrange students so each student can 1) easily see the front (teacher, blackboard); 2) easily see his/her teammates; and 3) have equal and close proximity to each teammate. Teams can be close to each other without disturbing each other, opening up free space elsewhere in the classroom.

Co-op Seating Arrangements

Sometimes it is necessary to work around existing furniture to do cooperative learning. See graphic. If you have a large horseshoe table, students can work in teams at the corners (1). Similarly, they can work at the corners of long tables (2). Students sit at one side of lab tables for lab work (4a), but turn around to use both sides of the table when it is time for cooperative interaction (4b). If you generally use a horseshoe arrangement (3), carpet patches (4), or a traditional arrangement of rows (6), seat the teammates next to each other to make moving easy as they move into co-op clusters (7).

If students are to sit at individual armchair desks facing forward in co-op clusters (7), the best arrangement is a horseshoe with the two students furthest back facing forward and the other two facing sideways (8). This arrangement has two advantages: View of the front is less impeded, and only one student rather than two are trapped in the arm chairs.

My favorite arrangement for both workshops and classrooms is the simple co-op table arrangement (8). Teammembers sit two on each side of a table which is perpendicular to the blackboard. The arrangement allows easy viewing of the front, equal and easy contact among teammates, and a comfortable workspace.

It is probably best if furniture has been arranged with four chairs around each table or workspace. If the only chairs available are chair/desks, chairs with built-on desk tops, then those can be arranged so the desk tops form a common workspace. See graphic. If, worse yet, chairs/desks are nailed down in rows, first choice would be a crowbar. That not possible, students can be assigned to groups of four adjacent chair/desks. The arrangement of desks and chairs should be so that students can easily all touch one piece of paper, orient easily toward each other, and without strain orient also to the front of the room. Most often this means two students on one side of a table and two on another, seated sideways to the front of the room.

GIVING DIRECTIONS

Giving directions to groups is an art. Several principles help.

Verbal and Written

Some students are better auditory learners and others are better visual learners. Thus, it is wise to talk through instructions and at the same time to post them on a chart paper, blackboard, or overhead.

Seating Arrangements

1. Horseshoe Table   3. Horseshoe Arrangement

2. Long Table

4. Lab Tables

        a. Lab Work   b. Team Work

5. Carpet Patches (N = 24)

6. Traditional (N = 24)

7. Co-op Clusters (N = 24)

8. Co-op Tables (N = 24)

Ⓕ = Front

8. Arm Chair Horseshoe

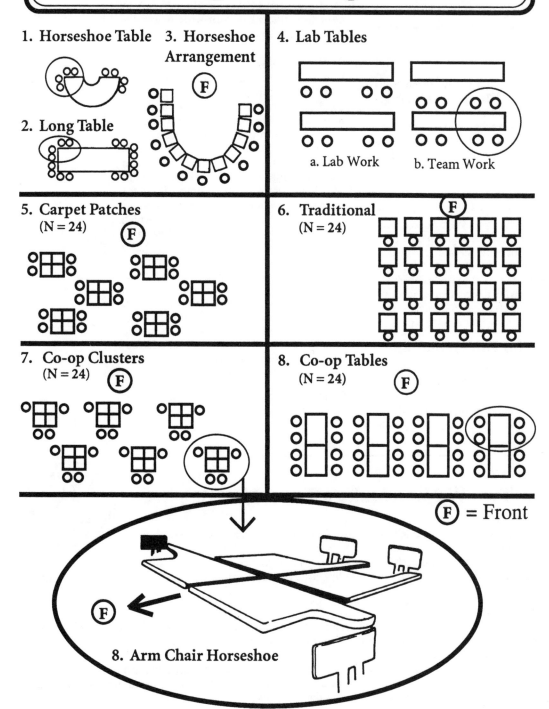

Spencer Kagan: *Cooperative Learning*©
Publisher: Resources for Teachers , Inc. • 1(800) Wee Co-op

Bite-Sized Bits

Give instructions a bit at a time; do not give more instructions at a time than all students can perform without asking for clarification. If you give a long sequence of instructions students will not complete the sequence without needing clarification.

Modeling

Too often teachers try to move through instructions by talk. The most efficient approach often is modeling. Students understand in a moment what to do if they have seen it done; they take a great deal of time to understand if they are only told. Sometimes I tell teachers to "Show-Don't-Tell" their instructions.

There are several ways to model: You can model the behavior yourself, you can pretend to be a member of a group and role-play the behavior with the group; you can work with a pair or group and then have them model for the class; or you can wait for the desired behavior to occur spontaneously and then ask the students to do again what they just did, for the whole class to see.

Checking for Understanding

After giving instructions, check for understanding. Make sure the students know what is desired as well as what is not desired. Some structures for checking include Choral Response, thumbs up or down on specific questions regarding the directions, having students explain the directions to a partner, and Numbered Heads Together. If the directions involve a sequence of steps you might use Roundtable or Roundrobin to have each student in turn write or say the steps, one per student.

Structuring

Within the steps of each structure, it is often useful to structure activities highly . For example, during the think time of a Think Pair Share the teacher might say something like "...I want you to imagine you were a settler and were about to go west in a covered wagon. What are all the things you would want to bring with you. Think about..." This high degree of structuring within the steps of a structure, determines the amount and quality of teamwork and helping which will result. If students are in five large groups in the classroom as when Similarity Grouping is used, and I say, "Talk over why you chose the group you did," then five assertive students in the class will talk. I can structure for participation by saying, "Turn to the person next to you so you are all in pairs, and then say why you choose the group you did." By adding this bit of structure, I have half the class expressing their values, rather than only five students.

Structuring can transform a lesson. See box, "Two ways to make a mural."

Structuring For Skill Acquisition
Two Ways to Make a Team Mural

Without Structuring
The teacher gives each team a piece of butcher paper, and lets students work as they please in making the mural.
Probable results: In many teams each student will take out his/her colors and work alone on some corner of the mural, with little if any cognitive or linguistic development, interaction, or development of conflict resolution skills.

With Structuring
1. Give students time to discuss in teams the pros and cons of two murals. Mural one has an all red rainbow, an all blue rainbow, an all yellow house, and all green tree. Mural two has a four color rainbow and a tree with green leaves, a red apple, and a brown trunk.
2. Announce that a team mural is to be made with only four colors, and each person is to use only one color;
3. Give the students time to create a team plan regarding what their mural will look like and who will do what. They must all agree on a team plan before they can take out their crayons.

POSITIVE ATTENTION

Most teachers are unaware of the tremendous power of positive attention. If tape recorders were randomly placed in classrooms and the ratio of positive to negative teacher attention ("Twenty seven students finished their homework" v. "Three students did not finish their homework") were recorded and calculated, we as a nation of teachers would score poorly. And it is positive teacher attention more than anything else which sets the tone of the classroom and paves the way to easy classroom management. Pay positive attention to what you want, and you will get more of it.

The most effective approach to classroom management for cooperative learning is to provide class- and group-based positive attention: If groups are not working well, the teacher gives his or her attention to the group which most approximates desired behavior, and holds up that group as a model. Other groups begin to model themselves after the group which is receiving the teacher's positive attention. When groups are working well, the teacher gives positive recognition to the whole class.

Studies demonstrate that in traditional classrooms, if teachers pay attention to undesired behaviors such as out-of-seat behavior or talking, the frequency of those behaviors increases. It does not matter if the type of attention is positive or negative. That is, even if the teacher severely scolds the students who get out of their seats without permission, other students will model themselves after the students who are receiving the attention.

So, too, is it in a cooperative classroom. If a teacher gives his or her attention to the team which is too noisy or not on task, other teams will follow the lead of the team which has managed to win the attention of the teacher, even if the attention is negative. Conversely, if the teacher ignores the teams who are least on task and gives attention and special recognition to those who are, soon most or all teams will be on task. This is especially so if the special recognition is immediate and public. The teacher does well to articulate to the whole class exactly why the model team is receiving positive attention.

TEACHER'S ROLE: OBSERVE AND CONSULT

As students work in teams, the teacher circulates, monitoring their progress. The teacher's

---

An Example:

The Power of Positive Attention

I cannot emphasize enough the power of praising groups for desired behaviors. One day I was in the classroom of a teacher first trying Jigsaw. She had been part of a one-day workshop with me, and had also seen me demonstrate Jigsaw with another class at her middle school.

She had all of the elements right. The class would come to full attention when she raised her hand. The student experts were standing as they presented their parts to their groups. One team had a missing expert, and the teacher handled that well by using the Teams Consult piece she had learned in the workshop.

But something was terribly wrong. The noise level was high. Over in one group the expert was using her new found authority to scold her teammates for being stupid. In another group as soon as the teacher was looking another way, the expert stuffed some paper in his nose which led to loud giggles and laughter. And the quiet signal was really not much help: The kids responded by quickly coming to attention, but right afterwards they would return to loud talking and off-task behaviors.

As I watched I became increasingly uncomfortable. What was wrong? What could be done? I remembered the theory of group-based positive reward and walked over to the teacher and said, "I am going to sit down again, but in a moment I want you to walk over to the best group in the class, give the quiet signal, and draw everyone's attention to the group, praising them for their good work, saying exactly what you like about their behavior. Don't give points; just say clearly what you like."

She did. And we were both surprised by the power of the praise. For about ten minutes after the positive attention, all the teams were markedly more on task. When they began to slip, I asked her to use group technique again. This time teams stayed on task longer.

By the end of the period, the class had turned around. We both saw Jigsaw working the way it should. The teacher was thrilled; she had a powerful tool for shaping the class.

Positive attention establishes the norms for the classroom; students learn which behaviors are valued; they receive a very clear message as to how to behave well in the new setting. Holding up as a model the groups which are behaving best is a clear way to give the message that you value certain behaviors. The students feel more secure when clear norms are established.

Spencer Kagan: *Cooperative Learning* ©
Publisher: Resources for Teachers , Inc. • 1(800) Wee Co-op

role is one of consultant and observer, not evaluator or director. Responsibility for the task and the learning remains with the students. Occasionally, if the students are moving down a blind alley with no possibility of discovering and correcting their error on their own, the teacher may intervene, but the intervention is usually to make them aware of a contradiction or of some additional resources. The responsibility for correcting or enhancing the work remains with the students. If a request from the students is made for an answer, the teacher attempts to make students aware of their own resources, and provides an answer only if the students could not obtain one on their own.

In contrast to what some other facilitators say, I do not prefer an attitude of distance between the teacher and students. Although the teacher attempts to not interrupt or interfere with the work of the students, at the same time, the teacher is seen as friendly and approachable rather than distant. This attitude is captured by the teacher who finds in the students' work something interesting and so comments on that, perhaps even sharing a personal reaction to the work. But the reaction is shared as a person-to-person, not an authority-to-pupil, and the students know they, on their own, are responsible for the direction and quality of their work.

TEAM QUESTIONS

When first assigned to teams, students will raise their hands and expect individual attention. They thus force the class back into a whole-class structure with only one student at a time participating. A neat way out of this is to have a rule: Team questions only. If a student has a question, he or she must try first to get it answered within the team. If no one on the team knows the answer, the team can consult with another team. If both do not know, then four hands, rather than

one, go up, signaling a need to consult with the teacher.

SIMULTANEOUS MANAGEMENT

Distributing Materials. An example of efficient versus inefficient management in a cooperative classroom is the contrast between sequential and simultaneous approaches to distributing materials. Some teachers walk around and hand out a worksheet to each team; others say, "Material Monitors, get one yellow worksheet for your team from the materials table." In the sequential mode there is dead time while the teacher walks the room; in the simultaneous approach, materials are distributed quickly and students are active rather than passive.

Answering Questions. The traditional approach to answering questions in a classroom is for the teacher to have all students wait while the question of one student is answered. Because questions are relevant to

Simultaneous Management

Goal	Sequential	Simultaneous
1. Teams Formed	Student names are called one at a time.	At once all students look for names on cards.
2. Materials Distributed	Teacher or student hands out materials one at a time.	Team Materials Monitors all go to materials center and retrieve materials for teammates.
3. Teacher to Answer Student Question	All teams wait while teacher talks.	Teams work while teacher consults.
4. Students to Share Answers	One student at a time is called upon.	All at once a student from each team go to the blackboard to write.
5. Students to Present Projects	One team at a time present.	Teams present to partner team.

only a few students, the traditional approach means dead time for most students. For them, in-depth answers are not likely, as the teacher knows to answer the question at length means increased down time for most students.

A management technique which increases cooperative learning time and allows for more in-depth answers and consulting to teams is for the teacher to wait to answer questions until all the other teams are actively involved in a learning task. This practice side-steps the problem of creating dead time for other teams, and avoids the pressure of other teams waiting which leads to superficial answers. While all the teams are productive, the teacher can walk over to the team with the question and consult with them in depth.

Whenever possible, a simultaneous rather than sequential management style is better, as when distributing materials, answering questions, forming teams, sharing answers, and presenting projects. See box: Simultaneous Management.

RECOGNITION SYSTEMS

Perhaps the most effective recognition system is for teachers to walk around while groups work, making positive comments. Occasionally the teacher may stop the class and point out to the class something positive a team has done. This approach is especially powerful when directed toward a specific "Skill-of-the-Week".

~ See Chapter 14: Social Skills Development. ~

Another way to give special recognition in the classroom setting is to use a chart or poster to record special recognition points. Whereas a positive comment is valued in the moment, if it is recorded it has additional power to motivate students toward desired behaviors. The recorded recognition points may be turned in for a team reward, make progress toward a class reward, or may simply stand on their own as recorded special recognition. In either case, teammates will work hard, encouraging each other toward desired behaviors, if they know their efforts are recognized.

~ See Chapter 15: Recognition ~

INDIVIDUAL CHALLENGES

There are a variety of individual problems which create management challenges. Students may be too bossy or shy. Others may refuse to work in a group. Others yet are made outcasts by group or class members. These problems are addressed in Chapter 14: Social Skills.

Discipline problems arise usually for one of four reasons: Students want attention, power, revenge, or they fear failure. (Alpert, 1989). Identifying the basis for the problem allows a more intelligent and differentiated response. For example, a student who wishes to control others or the teacher needs to feel in control, but that control must not be purchased at the expense of diminishing the feeling of power among others. Positive ways can be found to meet students' need for attention, even for those in whom the need is very strong.

Initial Resistance to Team Assignments

There are two ways of overcoming initial resistance to team assignments. First is teambuilding. Among the teambuilding techniques, the most effective for overcoming resistance are those which promote team identity and acceptance of individual differences. The second approach to overcoming resistance to team assignments is patience; allowing the power of group dynamics to take over. Team learning should not be attempted if there is active hostility among students; if there is hostility, additional teambuilding is necessary. But once that is overcome, the structure of the team learning experiences and group rewards are almost always strong enough to convert tolerance into active acceptance and liking.

As teachers, we need to control seat assignments and methods of grading. We assign students to teams and inform them that they will receive a team score based on the sum of their individual efforts. We need, then, to allow group processes to take over. We cannot force any members to interact, and we should not try. If a power struggle is avoided, resistant students most often will be drawn into the team effort. The power of group dynamics in situations of positive interdependence is remarkable. Teachers report that students who were once actively hostile toward each other have become best friends as a result of their experience of working together toward the team goal.

Individual Learning Problems

Once students have learned to work as teams, the teacher is free to consult either with teams which need help, or with individuals who need help. Teachers may organize pull-out programs for individuals with similar learning problems, so they may receive special tutoring as a group.

THE GOAL OF CLASSROOM MANAGEMENT

Management is critical. It frees teachers to teach and students to learn. The techniques outlined in this chapter are powerful tools for shaping group processes and classroom behaviors.

Some teachers resist the techniques because they view them as a form of manipulation or control. Others welcome the techniques. I have seen teachers and student teachers gain more from the cooperative learning management techniques than from any other aspect of cooperative learning -- for the first time they gain a sense of control of their classroom.

Management, however, is not an end. It is a means. We use management techniques in order to set the proper environment for learning. A fully developed approach to classroom management -- like good therapy -- has, as an aim, to eliminate the need for itself. That is, in the very well managed classroom, students learn to manage themselves. As that goal is approached, the need for extrinsic rewards for desired behaviors vanishes. Students in a well-managed classroom find it intrinsically rewarding to take responsibility for their own learning and prosocial development.

References:

Alpert, Linda. *A Teachers Guide to Cooperative Discipline.* Circle Pines, MN: American Guidance Service, 1989.

Collis, M. & Dalton, J. *Becoming Responsible Learners: Strategies for positive classroom management.* Devon Hills, Tasmania, Australia: Teamlinks, 1990.

Cummings, Carol. *Managing to Teach.* Edmond, WA: Teaching, Inc., 1989.

Charles, C.M. *Elementary Classroom Management.* White Plains, NY: Longman, Inc., 1983.

Emmer, Edmund T. *Classroom Management for Secondary Teachers.* Englewood Cliffs, NJ: 1984.

Evertson, Carolyn. *Classroom Management for Elementary Teachers.* Englewood Cliffs, NJ: 1984.

Nelson, Jane. *Positive Discipline.* New York, NY. Ballantine Books, 1981.

Chapter 8

Teambuilding

Our Team!!!

It is a sad comment on traditional classrooms, that more years in school result in poorer social relations and an increased need for teambuilding.

The amount, type, and timing of teambuilding you will do in your classroom depends on the needs and characteristics of your students and your own values. There are trainers in cooperative learning who do little or no teambuilding. There are others of us who emphasize teambuilding, especially when teams are first formed. Repeatedly, I have teachers tell me that when they have done extensive teambuilding, the 'time off' academic tasks resulted in greater, rather than less, academic achievement. This apparent paradox has a ready explanation: Teambuilding creates enthusiasm, trust, and mutual support which, in the long run, lead to more efficient academic work.

If there are racial or other tensions among students, teambuilding is a must. To go on with cooperative learning without dealing with such tensions, is to run a race with large pebbles in your sneakers. Remember, if you have used the heterogeneous teamformation method, you have placed students together with those they would least likely choose as teammates...and so some teambuilding may well be necessary.

Not all teambuilding is 'time off' academic work. There are many content-related teambuilding activities which serve the dual purposes of uniting the team and providing an anticipatory set and/or distributed practice in a lesson. For example, when I was asked to do a lesson on Greek History with some students who had never worked in teams, I first asked them to use Roundtable to list as many sports as they could. Next, followed a Roundtable listing of television programs. I then introduced the terms "comedy" and "tragedy," asked the teams to discuss which programs were happy and which were sad. They were to draw a happy face by those which were mostly happy, a sad face by those which were mostly sad, and both faces by those which were both. These simple teambuilding activities were a bridge into the lesson as we discussed how the sports they listed related to sport forms in the Greek Olympics, and how the television programs of today have their roots in the tragedies and comedies first developed as an art form in Greek theater.

If the cooperative learning lesson is simple and fun, as with the Flashcard Game or Numbered Heads Together, usually little or no teambuilding is necessary. If, on the other hand, the lesson involves activities in which conflicts might arise (choosing a team name, or the topic or format for a project) it is important that a strong positive team identity is developed prior to the lesson. For success in complex cooperative lesson designs, such as Co-op Co-op, students must develop communication skills and group processes which allow them to work well together.

If there is racial tension in the classroom, or if there is a wide discrepancy among the achievement-levels of students, then exten-

Spencer Kagan: *Cooperative Learning*©
Publisher: Resources for Teachers , Inc. • 1(800) Wee Co-op

sive teambuilding is necessary. Generally, primary students show little hesitancy toward working together. It is a sad comment on traditional classroom structures, that increased years in school result in an increased need for teambuilding.

Five aims of:

Teambuilding

1. **Getting Acquainted**
2. **Team Identity**
3. **Mutual Support**
4. **Valuing Differences**
5. **Developing Synergy**

---

1. Getting Acquainted

Getting acquainted activities are anything which helps teammates get to know each other, helps build a sense of comfort among teammates and a sense of belonging. It is important to feel one is known and accepted by one's peers.

Team Interview:

During a Team Interview, each teammate is interviewed in turn for a predetermined time, often while standing. A Team Interview is a natural structure for getting acquainted. Topics such as the following are suggested:

1. What's in a Name? Students interview each other regarding their names. How did they get their name? Is there an interesting family history associated with their name? Do they like their name? What would they be called if they could have another name? Do they have a nickname? What interesting experiences have they had associated with their name?

2. Where Have You Been? Interviews about where students have traveled, and where they would like to travel.

3. What Will You Be? Interviews about career and life goals.

4. Who Would You Be? If you could be someone from a story/novel, who would it be? Why?

Team Interviews are very useful in cooperative learning, and may be used for getting acquainted, but also are used at various places in the cooperative learning lesson, such as establishing an anticipatory set, checking for understanding, processing content and feelings following a lesson.

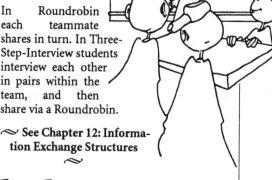

Two additional structures are also very well-suited for sharing getting acquainted information within a team: Roundrobin and Three-Step Interview.

In Roundrobin each teammate shares in turn. In Three-Step-Interview students interview each other in pairs within the team, and then share via a Roundrobin.

~ See Chapter 12: Information Exchange Structures ~

Turn Toss:

Name Learning. There are dozens of ways to have students learn names. Turn toss is one of my favorites. Here are the steps of Turn Toss, a perfect structure for name learning:

Step 1. Teammates Learn Names. One teammember wads up a piece of paper, catches the eye of another student, and tosses the paper to him/her, saying, "Hi, my name is Spencer, what's yours?" The student catches the paper ball, and and then says, "Hi, my name is Shlomo, what's yours?" as he tosses the paper to yet a third student. This proceeds for several tosses by each student.

Step 2. Teammates Begin Using Names. After all students have introduced themselves several times in Step 1, they begin using the names. A student says, "Glad to meet you Spencer," catches Spencer's eye, and tosses him the paper ball. That student then says, "Happy to be on a team with you Shlomo." and so on.

Step 3. Teammates Ask Each Other Questions. In the third round the students use the names to ask questions, such as, "Spencer, do you like school?" "Shlomo, how long have you been in this country?" and so on. *A possible rule:* If you don't like a question, answer with a question you wish someone had asked.

Turn Toss may be used as an information exchange structure which can be used as students quiz each other or share ideas.

∽ See Chapter 12: Information Exchange Structures ∽

Roundrobin:

1. This is my friend. (For primary students.) Teammates sit in a circle. One child introduces a person to the rest of the group by saying, "This is my friend *John*," raising his friend's hand as he does so. The friend introduces the person on the left, and around they go. The person who began is the last to be introduced, and at that point everyone is holding everyone's hand up. They stand and applaud.

2. Dream Car. Students in turn name their dream car and one reason why.

3. Ideal Vacation. Students say how they would spend a one week vacation, all expenses paid.

4. I Am... Students each introduce themselves to the group. They use I Am...

5. I Would Be... Students say whom they would be if they had to be an animal with a tail, a type of bird, a vehicle.

6. Quality Initials. Students can develop a rhythm to chant information which will help them remember their names. My favorite format is Quality Initials, which has four steps:

Step 1. Teammates Create New Names. Teammembers work together to create new names using their initials and adjectives (**S**pencer **K**agan becomes **S**pecially **K**ind).

Step 2. Teammates Use New Names in Chant. Teammembers practice these as a chant, initials first, then names, in a Roundrobin (Everyone would say "Specially Kind Spencer Kagan, Daringly Jovial David Johnson, Tremendously Great Ted Graves, Bountifully Smart Bob Slavin...").

Step 3. Add Rhythm. Rhythm is added as students chant the name and put it to a beat or a clap.

Step 4. Add Movements. Kinesthetic movements may be added according to favorite hobbies. Students make swimming motions for Spencer, Tai Chi movements for Ted, book reading movements for Bob.

Flashcard Game:

Fact Learning. Each team uses flashcards to learn the names and background information (favorite hobby, most unusual experience) of their teammates. The flashcards have a students' name one one side and facts about the student on the other.

The Flashcard Game may be used as a mastery structure, excellent for memorization.

∽ See Chapter 10: Mastery Structures ∽

Team Project:

Uncommon Commonalities. Students list as many uncommon commonalities as they can. Uncommon commonalities are things which teammembers have in common which make them unlike other teams. If all teammembers like ice cream, that is a common commonality; if they all like escargot, that is an uncommon commonality.

Have students look for uncommon commonalities along a number of dimensions -- **Favorites** (foods, subjects, sports, hobbies); **Places** (they have been, they have not been); **Family** (number of members, kind of house); **Cars, Pets...**

The search for uncommon commonalities serves not only to help students get acquainted, but also serves to build a team identity: "We are the team where everyone loves pineapple/coconut Ice Cream and we all want to visit Fiji."

My favorite format for having teams find their uncommon commonalities is to use Windows.

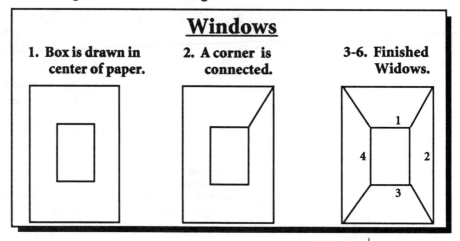

Structured Sort:

Windows. Windows are one of many ways to have student teams sort information.

The steps of Windows are as follows:

Step 1. Student Draws a Rectangle. A student draws a rectangle in the center of a paper and passes the paper to the person on his/her left.

Step 2. Corner is Connected. The next student draws a line from the corner of the rectangle to the corresponding corner of the paper (see box) and passes the paper.

Step 3-5. All Corners are Connected. The process is continued until all four corners of the window are connected to all four corners of the paper.

Step 6. Sections are Numbered. The four sections are numbered, 1, 2, 3, & 4.

Step 7. Students Record Commenalities. Student One suggests something all students might have in common such as "Do we all like chocolate ice cream?" If all students do, Student One writes "Chocolate Ice Cream" in section 4, if only two do, student one records it in section 2. Next, Student Two suggests a possible commonality and records it in the appropriate window. The Roundtable is continued and students discover qualities they have in common and those that are unique. Students search for things they all have in common, especially qualities which might make them distinct from other teams, called "uncommon commonalities." Later, teams build a team name based on their commonalities, and the center segment of the window is used to record the team name.

Windows is one of many possible structured sorts covered in detail in the chapter on thinking skills structures.

～ **See Chapter 11: Thinking Skills Structures** ～

Guess-the-Fib:

Life Facts. To play Guess-the-Fib, students state two true facts and one fib. In turn they each announce the three statements to their teammates, trying to fool them. Teammates come to consensus as to which one they believe is the fib. If the teammates are fooled, they guess among the two remaining possibilities.

Guess-the-Fib can be used as a review structure, on an occasional basis to spice up a review.

～ **See Chapter 10: Mastery Structures**

Fact-or-Fiction:

Life Facts. Students tell either a believable lie about themselves or reveal an unbelievable truth. It is up to their teammates to state whether they are hearing fact or fiction.

Fact-or-Fiction is a variation on Guess-the-Fib, also used on an occasional basis to spice up a review.

～ **See Chapter 10: Mastery Structures**

Individual Projects:

1. Affirmative Passport. At the beginning of the school year students make up a passport, including vital information about themselves such as date and place of birth, number of siblings, hobbies, favorite foods, likes, dislikes, places they have traveled to, times they have moved, taste in music, and a photo. These passports are available to share via Roundrobin, and for other students to browse through during free periods.

2. My Favorites. Students fill out a questionnaire which describes themselves. The information can then be shared via a number of structures, such as Roundtable, Team Interview, and Team Discussion. See "My Favorites" handout.

2. Team Identity

A team forms an identity by defining itself in a unique way, such as creating its own name, cheer, or solution to a problem. Successful completion of any team project can enhance the sense of team identity, if the team is allowed to complete the project in its own unique way.

Who Are We?

Team Projects:

1. Team Names. When teams are first formed they are asked to make up a team mural. Three simple rules for the group process are stated: (1) Each teammember must have a say; (2) No decision can be reached unless everyone consents; (3) No member consents to the group decision if he/she has a serious objection. These rules set the tone for future group processes which must include participation, consensus, and respect for individual rights.

The basis for the team name may be content (each team choosing the name of a planet, because they are working on an astronomy unit), or may be personal preferences. Team names are much easier following Uncommon Commonalities, see above. "We are the Fiji Pineapple Coconuts."

2. Team Hats. Paint stores sell inexpensive caps which are perfect to decorate with the team colors. Alternatively, allow teams to make their own hats from assorted scrap material (styrofoam, corrugated cardboard, paper, newspaper, poster board, sequins, feathers, buttons) and fasteners (glue, staplers, tape, brads, clips).

Hats from one team are not necessarily all identical, but something distinguishes them from the hats of another team.

A fun twist is to tell students that they must connect the four team hats so they are all worn at once because four heads together are better than one and we must practice putting our heads together!

3. Team Handshakes. Students can develop a team handshake which symbolizes their team name. Consensus rules apply here also: We don't have a team logo or cheer or handshake, unless we all agree.

4. Team Cheers. A simple, but effective team cheer is to have teams pick two adjectives and then repeat one three times and end with the other. For example, "Incredible...Incredible...Incredible...Great!"

The handshake and cheer often are extensions of the team name.

5. Collage Cubes. Team collage cubes are made from an empty cardboard box, magazines (to cut up pictures and words) and colored paper. The box is covered with paper and then a collage of pictures and words which teammates paste on the cube to tell who they are.

My Favorites!

Sport to Play: _____   School Subject: _____

Sport to Watch: _____   Color to Wear: _____

Hobby: _____   Type of Clothing: _____

Holiday: _____   Color: _____

Place to Be: _____   Person to Visit: _____

Time of the Day: _____   Dream Car: _____

Season: _____   Dream Career: _____

Flower: _____   Dream Vacation: _____

Tree: _____   Dream Future: _____

Song: _____   Food: _____

Group: _____   Drink: _____

Book: _____   Candy Bar: _____

Movie: _____   Author: _____

TV Program _____   Animal: _____

Spencer Kagan: *Cooperative Learning*©
Publisher: Resources for Teachers , Inc. • 1(800) Wee Co-op

TeamBoggle

Rules for TeamBoggle: Each Teammember in turn contributes a word. To count, the letters must each connect to the previous letter by a side or a corner. For example "Fit" and Finite" count, but "Few" does not.

Scoring for TeamBoggle: Each word is worth the square of the number of letters it contains. A one letter word is worth one point (1 x 1), but a 4 letter word is worth 16 points (4 x 4). For example "Fit" is worth 9 points (3x3) but "Finite" is worth 36.

Goals for TeamBoggle: Make as many points as possible in 4 minutes. Work to make a list of hints for another team such as "Find a 36 point word that begins with the letter 'F' and means the opposite of un-ending."

TEAMBOGGLE				
F	I	N	E	I
J	T	I	E	O
D	E	S	E	L
W	L	T	F	I
I	D	U	E	N

Spencer Kagan: *Cooperative Learning*©
Publisher: Resources for Teachers , Inc. • 1(800) Wee Co-op

6. Team Scrapbooks. The team scrapbook is a place for teammates to record memories, draw pictures about team activities, and store rewards and team essays.

Additional Possibilities:

7. **Team Banners**

8. **Team Logos**

9. **Team Mottos**

10. **Team Monuments**

11. **Team Greetings**

12. **Team Colors**

13. **Team Puff-mobiles** (Made with drinking straws and beads for rolling)

14. **Team Pipe Cleaners Inventions**

15. **Team Spaghetti Gum Drop Space Stations**

16. **Team Body Murals**

17. **Team T-Shirts, and**

18. **Team Murals...**

Team Puzzles and Projects

Team Projects:

1. TeamBoggle. Students find as many words as they can from a letter grid -- large words are worth more points. See handout on previous page.

2. Magic Number 11. In a circle, students hold out a clenched hand. They shake up and down three times and chant "One, two, three." On the count of three each puts out a number of fingers. The object: Make the fingers add to 11. No talking allowed. If teams finish early they try another number. After each success, teammates give each other a pat on the back.

3. Scrambled Sentences. Write one word on a card, and place words in envelopes as follows:

Envelope 1: **Spring begun eager me**

Envelope 2: **here blinded The dogs reading**

Envelope 3: **start The to have**

Envelope 4: **sunlight barking I'm is**

Instruct the students that each person in the group must form a meaningful sentence. People may exchange cards if they wish, but no member may speak. You may not ask for a card that another player has, you must wait until that players offers it to you. You may offer your own cards to any other player at any time.

Point out that the first words in the sentences have been capitalized as a clue. Some possible unscrambled sentences are:

Spring is here.

The sunlight blinded me.

The dogs have begun barking.

I'm eager to start reading.

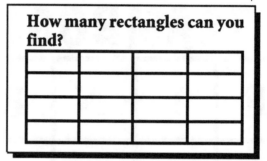

How many rectangles can you find?

4. Rectangles. Have the students figure out how many rectangles there are in a three by three square. If they solve that one, let them work on a four by four square.

5. Team Shelters. Each team makes its own shelter from newspapers and masking tape. The shelter must be big enough for all members to keep dry in an imaginary rainstorm. Hint: tent-like structures are relatively easy if poles are made from rolled-up newspapers.

6. Team Towers. Teams are told to make any kind of tower they wish from just two pieces of construction paper, scissors, and ten paper clips or brads. All teams celebrate the uniqueness of each team tower. Assigning social roles can help: One person checks for agreement before any cuts are made, another does the cutting, another is the only one to touch the clips or brads, and a fourth is the cheerleader responsible to make sure the team stops occasionally to celebrate its progress to that point. Have them build a structure of any size or shape using one piece of paper, scissors, and 10 paper clips.

7. Tinker Toy Structures. No one is too old for tinker toys -- have the students build and later describe a space station using tinker toys.

8. Rhymes Riddles. Have students create as many two word rhymes as possible and to turn them into riddles. Some examples:

>**A flexible sapling** is **Limber Timber** or a **Wee Tree**
>
>**An immobile large vehicle** is a **Stuck Truck**
>
>**A bee** is a **Nectar Collector**
>
>**Butter** is a **Bread Spread**

<u>Possible sequence:</u>

Step 1. List Nouns. Have students first list about eight nouns. (Cup...)

Step 2. List Rhyming Words. They list as many rhyming words as they can associated with each noun. (Cup: pup, sup, yup, up)

Step 3. Create Riddles. They create Riddles around their favorite two word rhymes. (A dish for a young dog --Pup Cup)

Step 4. Share Riddles. Teams list their favorite riddle/rhyme on the board for other teams to solve.

Roundtable and Roundrobin:

Like Three-Step Interview, Roundtable and Roundrobin are extremely important cooperative learning structures. In essence, students take turns contributing to the group -- in an oral form for Roundrobin and in a written form for Roundtable.

For Roundtable there is usually one piece of paper and one pen for the team. One student makes a contribution and then passes the paper and pen to the student on his or her left. The paper or pen literally goes around the table, thus the name: Roundtable. If the contributions are oral rather than written, it is called Roundrobin -- or, for the older students, a Sharearound.

Roundtable can be used repeatedly in many subject areas, at a variety of places in the lesson plan. Roundtable can be used to create an anticipatory set for a lesson, to check for acquisition of information, or liven up drill and practice.

If the content of Roundtable is to be teambuilding, have students:

1. Make Words. Make as many words as they can from the word "TEAMWORK."

2. Name Foods. Think of as many foods as they can in alphabetical order (first person writes Apple, second person Banana, Next comes Chile con carne.

3. Change-A-Letter. Change one letter at a time in a core word and see how far they can go (first person writes FUN, next writes FAN, next FAT, next SAT...).

4. Use a Belt. List as many ways as they can of using a belt if they were stranded on an island.

5. List Flavors. List ice cream flavors, cars, four legged animals, equivalent fractions, synonyms....

Roundtable is a robust structure and is used also for mastery.

⁓ **See Chapter 10: Mastery Structures** ⁓

Spencer Kagan: *Cooperative Learning*©
Publisher: Resources for Teachers , Inc. • 1(800) Wee Co-op

Brainstorming:

Any task which has many possible solutions may be set up for Brainstorming. Some possible topics: What are all the ways we could improve this school? This class? This world? How many ways could you use a belt if you were stranded on a desert island? What would you put in a time capsule for the next generation of students your age?

Brainstorming is far more effective if it follows the principles of 4S Brainstorming.

~ **See Chapter 11: Thinking Skills Structures** ~

Send-A-Problem:

Puzzles. Each team makes a picture or writes a message. They rip the paper with curved rips (by turning the paper as they rip) into about eight pieces. They send the paper to the next team as a jigsaw puzzle to solve. When they are done they send it to another team so the puzzles are sent around the room.

Send-A-Problem is a multi-functional structure used also for practice and for concept development.

~ **See Chapter 10: Mastery Structures** ~

3. Mutual Support

It is not enough for students to know each other and to feel they are part of a team. The team gains strength as the members feel they can count on each other for support. Any situation of positive interdependence creates the feeling of mutual support as students know they are on the same side. Many cooperative sport and game activities provide a feeling of mutual support, see support games such as Row Row Freeze, Build Maze, and Willow in the Wind in Chapter 22, Co-op Play. Some other teambuilders for mutual support are:

Team Activities:

1. Clapping Game. The clapping game is an all-time favorite.

Step 1. A Person Steps Out. One person from each team steps out.

Step 2. Teammates Pick Object. The teammates agree on an object somewhere in the room that the teammate could touch.

Step 3. Search Begins. The teammates all return and begin simultaneously searching; each one searches for the object their teammates have chosen.

Step 4. Support Provided. The teammates clap, clapping louder as their teammember approaches the object they have selected.

Step 5. Teammate Cheered. When the teammember touches the object, the team stands up, gives a cheer and invites the teammate back to the team.

2. Blind Caterpillar. Teammates stand in a line, each with their hands on the hips of the person in front of them. The leader has his or her eyes open, and leads the others who keep their eyes closed. The leader talks to his or her teammates while leading them around the room, telling them where they are in the room, providing support. At intervals, the teacher calls "change" and the person in front goes to the back. This activity produces feelings of trust. After each student has been a leader, teammates return to their seats and reflect on how they felt as the leader and as a follower.

3. Blind Walk. One student closes his or her eyes while a teammate takes them on a tour of the room. The student "shows" them the room through the sense of touch -- placing their hand on objects while describing the objects. After several minutes, students shift roles. Afterwards, teammates discuss how they felt giving and receiving care.

4. Care Lift. Teammates take turns receiving the care lift. The recipient lays down in the center of the group on his or her back, with eyes shut. Teammembers gently lift the individual, rock him or her, and return him or her to the ground. On this one you need five persons to lift one, and one must take care of the head. It is easily accomplished by having two teams pair up.

It is very important to emphasize that the care lift is a very gentle exercise. The person is lifted so gently and gradually that he or she cannot tell when they have left the ground, how high they are, and when they are about to touch the ground again.

For safety, pillows on the ground are probably a good idea. Or better yet, especially for young participants, students can be on their knees around the person on the pillows and the care lift can be only one or two feet high.

Team Formations:

Letters, Shapes, Actions. There are many possible formations. Ask students to shape letters or numbers by holding hands. They can become a common kitchen appliance, a silent jazz band with all the motions, or express a feeling.

4. Valuing Differences

Value clarification activities are designed to accomplish three things: First, to clarify for teammembers their own values; second, to clarify for them the values of their teammates; third, to have teammembers come to a realization that there is no right and wrong to values -- that values are to be accepted as enduring individual differences with which the team must work. There are numerous value clarification activities.

Value Lines:

1. Where Do I Stand? Students mark their position on a set of value lines indicating their preferences. See, "I am" and "I Prefer" handouts on the next page. Later, students discuss their responses with their teams to discover and appreciate individual differences.

2. What Values are Most Important? Teammates rank terminal values from most to least important. The values include the following: a world at peace, family security, happiness, an exciting life, wisdom, self-respect, salvation, inner harmony. In a second half of the exercise teammates rank instrumental values, such as honest, loving,

cheerful, forgiving, ambitious, intellectual, obedient, imaginative, independent, logical, and responsible. See handout on page 8:13.

After working with the values, students share and celebrate their uniqueness as revealed by their differences.

Team Project:

You Have to Have a Heart. The team must make a crucial decision. They must assign priority numbers to five patients on a waiting list for an artificial heart A brief description of each prospective patient is included. See handout on page 8:19.

To reach the decision, first each student must rank the potential recipients. Next, students discuss their rankings and attempt to come to consensus. The rule is before a student can express his/her opinion, he/she must validate the thoughts or feelings of a teammate, even if they differ in opinions.

5. Developing Synergy

Synergy refers to the increased energy released when individuals are working in co-operation. Because of the synergetic effect, the group product can be better than the product of even the best individual working alone. The sum of the parts interacting is greater than the sum of the parts alone. There are various ways of demonstrating synergy. Any task in which interaction causes stimulation and refinement of ideas will do.

Roundtable:

1. Squiggle Art. Each student draws one line on a piece of paper and then passes the paper to the person on the right within the team. The papers go around and students build on what each other have drawn to create a picture.

2. Blind Art. Students try to build pictures while blindfolded. Each student has a piece of paper and with eyes closed draws the frame of a house. They all pass the paper to the person on the left within the team. Next, they draw a window, still with eyes closed. (Most, of course draw the window in

I Am

Instructions: Mark line closest to the word that best describes you.

Fast ←————————————————→ **Slow**

Thinker ←————————————————→ **Doer**

Morning Person ←————————→ **Night Person**

Listener ←————————————————→ **Talker**

Leader ←————————————————→ **Follower**

Indoor Person ←————————→ **Outdoor Person**

I Prefer:

Instructions: Mark line closest to the word that best describes you.

Adventure Movie ←————————→ **Comedy**

Ice Cream ←————————————————→ **Cake**

Airplanes ←————————————————→ **Boats**

Sports Car ←————————————————→ **Luxury Car**

Beach ←————————————————→ **Mountains**

Dogs ←————————————————→ **Cats**

Spencer Kagan: *Cooperative Learning*©
Publisher: Resources for Teachers , Inc. • 1(800) Wee Co-op

odd places, and this is the fun of it). The paper is passed and a door is drawn. Finally, the chimney is placed on the house. When students open their eyes they have a good laugh.

Team Projects:

1. Team Juggling. Three paper balls are created by crumpling three 8x11 inch sheets of bond paper.

Step 1: Establish a Pattern. Student One passes to Student Three who sends it to one of the other two who sends it to the remaining student who sends it back to Student One.

Step 2. Three Rolling. Get all three going at once on the table. Remind students they can always go slower and that they should not send a ball until they are sure the receiver is ready.

Step 3. Three in the Air. Get all three in the air by underhand tosses. Optional additional steps: Stand up and get further apart. Use one hand. Get more than three balls going.

2. Survival in the Desert. Details of a plane crash in the desert are provided. See handout on pages 8:15-16.

Step 1: Individual Ranking. Teammembers are asked to individually rank the worth in this situation of 15 items.

Step 2: Team Rankings. Using a team discussion students rank the items as a team.

Step 3: Ranking Compared. Average score of individuals in the group is compared to the group score (U.S. Air Force ratings are used to determine scores).

Almost always the group does better than the average of the individuals. Often the group does better even than the highest scoring member alone -- demonstrating synergy. Synergy is the notion that the sum of the parts interacting is superior to the parts taken individually. Group members realize that as a group they can accomplish more than working individually.

3. Lost on the Moon. Details of this survival activity are provided on the following pages. Students experience synergy as in "Survival in the Desert." See pages 8:17-18.

What Do You Value?

World Peace	1	2	3	4	5	6	7	8	9	10
Family Security	1	2	3	4	5	6	7	8	9	10
Individual Wealth	1	2	3	4	5	6	7	8	9	10
Personal Happiness	1	2	3	4	5	6	7	8	9	10
An Exciting Life	1	2	3	4	5	6	7	8	9	10
Wisdom	1	2	3	4	5	6	7	8	9	10
Self-Respect	1	2	3	4	5	6	7	8	9	10
Salvation	1	2	3	4	5	6	7	8	9	10
Inner Harmony	1	2	3	4	5	6	7	8	9	10
Helping Others	1	2	3	4	5	6	7	8	9	10

How Do You Most Want to Be?

Honest	1	2	3	4	5	6	7	8	9	10
Loving	1	2	3	4	5	6	7	8	9	10
Adventuresome	1	2	3	4	5	6	7	8	9	10
Ambitious	1	2	3	4	5	6	7	8	9	10
Imaginative	1	2	3	4	5	6	7	8	9	10
Independent	1	2	3	4	5	6	7	8	9	10
Logical	1	2	3	4	5	6	7	8	9	10
Responsible	1	2	3	4	5	6	7	8	9	10
Cooperative	1	2	3	4	5	6	7	8	9	10
Playful	1	2	3	4	5	6	7	8	9	10

References:

Farnette, C., Forte, I., Loss, B. *I've Got Me and I'm Glad.* Nashville, TN: Incentive Publications, Inc. 1989.

Gregson, Bob. *Take Part Art.* Carthage, IL: Fearon Teacher Aids, 1991.

Johnson, D.W. & Johnson, F.P. *Joining Together: group theory and group skills.* Englewood Cliffs, NJ: Prentice Hall, 1975.

Macmillan, Mary. *Good Endings Make Good Beginnings.* Carthage, IL: Good Apple, Inc. 1989.

Schwartz, Linda. *Month to Month Me.* Santa Barbara, CA: The Learning Works, 1976.

Schwartz, Linda. *Think On Your Feet.* Santa Barbara, CA: The Learning Works, Inc., 1989.

Shaw, Vanston. *Communitybuilding.* San Juan Capistrano, CA: Resources for Teachers, Inc. 1991.

Stanish, Bob. *The Ambidextrous Mind.* Carthage, IL: Good Apple, 1989.

Trend Enterprises. *Story Starters: We Need Friends.* St.Paul, MN: Trend Enterprises, 1990.

Trovato, Charlene. *Teaching Kids to Care.* Cleveland, OH: Instructor Books, 1987.

Survival In The Desert

It is approximately 10:00 a.m. in mid July and you have just crash landed in the Sonora Desert in southwestern United States. The light twin engine plane, containing the bodies of the pilot and the co-pilot, has completely burned. Only the air frame remains. None of the rest of you have been injured.

The pilot was unable to notify anyone of your position before the crash. However, ground sightings, taken before you crashed, indicate that you are 65 miles off the course that was filed in your VFR Flight Plan. The pilot had indicated before you crashed that you were approximately 70 miles south-southwest from a mining camp which is the nearest known habitation.

The immediate area is quite flat and except for occasional barrel and saguaros cacti appears to be rather barren. The last weather report indicated that temperatures would reach 110 -- which means that the temperature within a foot of the surface will hit 130 . You are dressed in light-weight clothing--short sleeved shirts, pants, socks and street shoes. Everyone has a handkerchief. Collectively, your pockets contain $2.83 in change, $85.00 in bills, a pack of cigarettes, and a ballpoint pen.

The Problem:

Before the plane caught fire your group was able to salvage the 15 items listed below. Your task is to rank these items according to their importance for your survival, starting with "1" the most important, to "15" the least important.

You may assume that the number of survivors is the same as the number on your team and the team has agreed to stick together.

Step 1: Stop or Go. Teams decide if they are to stay at crash site or go for help.

Step 2: Individual ranking. Each member of the team is to individually rank each item. Do not discuss the situation or problem until each member has finished the individual ranking. Once discussion begins do not change your individual ranking.

Step 3: Team ranking. After everyone has finished the individual ranking, rank in order the 15 items *as a team*.

.45 Caliber Pistole (loaded)	1	2	3	4	5	6	7	8	9	10	11	12	13	14	15
Book: "Edible Animals of the Desert"	1	2	3	4	5	6	7	8	9	10	11	12	13	14	15
Bottle of Salt Tablets (1000)	1	2	3	4	5	6	7	8	9	10	11	12	13	14	15
1 Quart of Water per Person	1	2	3	4	5	6	7	8	9	10	11	12	13	14	15
Red and White Parachute	1	2	3	4	5	6	7	8	9	10	11	12	13	14	15
Compress Kit with Gauze	1	2	3	4	5	6	7	8	9	10	11	12	13	14	15
2 Quarts of 180 Proof Vodka	1	2	3	4	5	6	7	8	9	10	11	12	13	14	15
Sectional Air Map for Area	1	2	3	4	5	6	7	8	9	10	11	12	13	14	15
Flashlight	1	2	3	4	5	6	7	8	9	10	11	12	13	14	15
Jack knife	1	2	3	4	5	6	7	8	9	10	11	12	13	14	15
1 Topcoat per Person	1	2	3	4	5	6	7	8	9	10	11	12	13	14	15
Plastic Raincoat	1	2	3	4	5	6	7	8	9	10	11	12	13	14	15
Two Pair of Sunglasses	1	2	3	4	5	6	7	8	9	10	11	12	13	14	15
A Cosmetic Mirror	1	2	3	4	5	6	7	8	9	10	11	12	13	14	15
Magnetic Compass	1	2	3	4	5	6	7	8	9	10	11	12	13	14	15

Spencer Kagan: *Cooperative Learning*©
Publisher: Resources for Teachers , Inc. • 1(800) Wee Co-op

Survival Expert's Ranking

Source: Air Force Survival Training Manual
Teams should decide to stay at crash site.

1. **A Cosmetic Mirror**--In the sun, the mirror can produce bright light and be seen for several miles.
2. **1 Topcoat per Person**--Best thing to do is attempt to restrict the air flow around your body to decrease the amount of water evaporation that results in dehydration and death.
3. **1 Quart of Water per Person**--Will keep you "comfortable" for a while, however, there is a relatively short survival time with the water.
4. **Flashlight**--Helpful to aid searchers after dusk. Also with batteries removed the case can be used as a container for the plastic still.
5. **Red and White Parachute**--To produce shade by spreading parachute over the air frame of the plane.
6. **Jack knife**--Since cactus is available, you can use the knife to cut the cactus and use it in a homemade still to obtain moisture from the barrel and saguaros cacti.
7. **Plastic Raincoat**--Knife and raincoat go together to develop plastic still.
8. **.45 Caliber Pistol (loaded)**--Dangerous item to have because of physical and emotional stress of the group.
9. **Two Pair of Sunglasses**
10. **Compress Kit with Gauze**--Not needed since no one is injured and you should not be leaving the crash site.
11. **Magnetic Compass**--Not needed since you should not attempt to walk from the crash site.
12. **Sectional Air Map for Area**--Not needed since you should not attempt to walk from the crash site.
13. **Book: "Edible Animals of the Desert"**--Should not expend your energy attempting to leave the crash site to hunt.
14. **2 Quarts of 180 Proof Vodka**--Little value since the effects of alcohol on your system is to draw water in order to absorb the alcohol into your system.
15. **Bottle of Salt Tablets (1000)**--Will actually rob your body of moisture.

Rank Order of Items:

Item	1	2	3	4	5	6	7	8	9	10	11	12	13	14	15
.45 Caliber Pistol (loaded)	1	2	3	4	5	6	7	**⑧**	9	10	11	12	13	14	15
Book: "Edible Animals of the Desert"	1	2	3	4	5	6	7	8	9	10	11	12	**⑬**	14	15
Bottle of Salt Tablets (1000)	1	2	3	4	5	6	7	8	9	10	11	12	13	14	**⑮**
1 Quart of Water per Person	1	2	**③**	4	5	6	7	8	9	10	11	12	13	14	15
Red and White Parachute	1	2	3	4	**⑤**	6	7	8	9	10	11	12	13	14	15
Compress Kit with Gauze	1	2	3	4	5	6	7	8	9	**⑩**	11	12	13	14	15
2 Quarts of 180 Proof Vodka	1	2	3	4	5	6	7	8	9	10	11	12	13	**⑭**	15
Sectional Air Map for Area	1	2	3	4	5	6	7	8	9	10	11	**⑫**	13	14	15
Flashlight	1	2	3	**④**	5	6	7	8	9	10	11	12	13	14	15
Jack knife	1	2	3	4	5	**⑥**	7	8	9	10	11	12	13	14	15
1 Topcoat per Person	1	**②**	3	4	5	6	7	8	9	10	11	12	13	14	15
Plastic Raincoat	1	2	3	4	5	6	**⑦**	8	9	10	11	12	13	14	15
Two Pair of Sunglasses	1	2	3	4	5	6	7	8	**⑨**	10	11	12	13	14	15
A Cosmetic Mirror	**①**	2	3	4	5	6	7	8	9	10	11	12	13	14	15
Magnetic Compass	1	2	3	4	5	6	7	8	9	10	**⑪**	12	13	14	15

Spencer Kagan: *Cooperative Learning*©
Publisher: Resources for Teachers, Inc. • 1(800) Wee Co-op

Lost on the Moon

You are in a space crew originally scheduled to rendezvous with a mother ship on the lighted surface of the moon. Mechanical difficulties, however, have forced your ship to crash-land at a spot some 200 miles from the rendezvous point. The rough landing damaged much of the equipment aboard. Since survival depends on reaching the mother ship, the most critical items available must be chosen for the 200 mile trip. Below are listed 15 items left intact after landing. Your task is to rank them in terms of their importance to your crew in its attempt to reach the rendezvous point. Place number 1 by the most important item; number 2 by the second most important, and so on through number 15, the least important.

Step 1: Individual ranking. Each member of the team is to individually rank each item. Do not discuss the situation or problem until each member has finished the individual ranking. Once discussion begins do not change your individual ranking.

Step 2: Team ranking. After everyone has finished the individual ranking, rank in order the 15 items *as a team.*

Box of matches	1 2 3 4 5 6 7 8 9 10 11 12 13 14 15
Food concentrate	1 2 3 4 5 6 7 8 9 10 11 12 13 14 15
50 feet of nylon rope	1 2 3 4 5 6 7 8 9 10 11 12 13 14 15
Parachute silk	1 2 3 4 5 6 7 8 9 10 11 12 13 14 15
Portable heating unit	1 2 3 4 5 6 7 8 9 10 11 12 13 14 15
Two .45 caliber pistols	1 2 3 4 5 6 7 8 9 10 11 12 13 14 15
One case dehydrated milk	1 2 3 4 5 6 7 8 9 10 11 12 13 14 15
Two 100-pound tanks of oxygen	1 2 3 4 5 6 7 8 9 10 11 12 13 14 15
Stellar map (moon's constellation)	1 2 3 4 5 6 7 8 9 10 11 12 13 14 15
Life raft	1 2 3 4 5 6 7 8 9 10 11 12 13 14 15
Magnetic compass	1 2 3 4 5 6 7 8 9 10 11 12 13 14 15
5 gallons of water	1 2 3 4 5 6 7 8 9 10 11 12 13 14 15
Signal flares	1 2 3 4 5 6 7 8 9 10 11 12 13 14 15
First-aid kit containing injection needles	1 2 3 4 5 6 7 8 9 10 11 12 13 14 15
Solar-powered FM receiver-transmitter	1 2 3 4 5 6 7 8 9 10 11 12 13 14 15

Spencer Kagan: *Cooperative Learning*©
Publisher: Resources for Teachers , Inc. • 1(800) Wee Co-op

Lost on the Moon Scoring

Rank Order of Items:

Item	1	2	3	4	5	6	7	8	9	10	11	12	13	14	15
Box of matches															**(15)**
Food concentrate				**(4)**											
50 feet of nylon rope						**(6)**									
Parachute silk								**(8)**							
Portable heating unit													**(13)**		
Two .45 caliber pistols											**(11)**				
One case dehydrated milk												**(12)**			
Two 100-pound tanks of oxygen	**(1)**														
Stellar map (moon's constellation)			**(3)**												
Life raft									**(9)**						
Magnetic compass														**(14)**	
5 gallons of water		**(2)**													
Signal flares										**(10)**					
First-aid kit containing injection needles							**(7)**								
Solar-powered FM receiver-transmitter					**(5)**										

Scoring:

For each item, find the difference between your ranking and NASA's ranking number. Add these differences. The smaller your difference, the closer you are to the experts. Also do this for the team rankings. Compare accuracy of the individual predictions and group prediction.

Example:	Your Ranking	NASA's	Difference
Box of matches	8	15	7
Signal Flares	14	10	4

Explanation:

These are the answers supplied by the NASA scientists. The answers are split into groups--physical survival and traveling to the rendezvous.

The first two items are air and water without which you cannot survive at all. After that comes the map for locating position and figuring out how to get to the rendezvous. Food comes next for strength on the trip. It is not as necessary for survival as air and water.

The FM transceiver is for keeping in touch with earth. In a vacuum, without the ionosphere, radio transmission travels only in line of sight and would be limited on the moon to destination of approximately ten miles. On earth powerful receivers could pick up messages which would then be relayed to the mother ship. The next item would be the rope for lunar mountain climbing and traversing crevasses on the trip. The next item would be first aid for injuries. Parachute silk would offer excellent protection from sunlight and heat buildup.

The life raft is a carry all for supplies, (the moon's gravity permits heavy loads to be carried), as a shelter, and a possible stretcher for the injured. It also offers protection from micro-meteorite showers.

Flares cannot burn in a vacuum, but they, and the pistols, can be shot. Flares and guns would therefore be excellent propulsive devices for flying over obstructions. The milk is heavy and relatively less valuable.

On the moon overheating is a problem and not cold. Thus the heating unit is useless.

The magnetic compass is useless without a map of the moon's magnetic field.

The box of matches is the most useless item.

You Have to Have a Heart

You are one of the members of the City Hospital's Judicial Board and must make a crucial decision. Individually, you must assign priority numbers to 5 patients on a waiting list for an artificial heart. The Judicial Board (the team) must achieve consensus. (1 = first in line; 5= last in line)

Step 1: Individual Ranking. Working alone you must make a priority ranking of the 5 patients waiting for an artificial heart.

Step 2: Board Meeting. After you and the remainder of the Judicial Board (your teammates) have completed your own priority ranking, you must have a meeting. You must work together to finalize the priority ranking. The rule is before you can express your opinion, you must validate the thoughts or feelings of another member, even if they differ from your own.

&. George Mutti
- **Age:** 61   • **Occupation:** suspected of underworld involvement (mafia)
- **Description:** married, 7 children, extremely wealthy, will donate a very large sum to the hospital following the operation

1 2 3 4 5

&. Peter Santos
- **Age:** 23   • **Occupation:** "B" average student
- **Description:** single, studies hard, helps support poor family, aspires to be a policeman when he graduates

1 2 3 4 5

&. Ann Doyle
- **Age:** 45   • **Occupation:** housewife
- **Description:** Widow, supports 3 children, small income, no savings

1 2 3 4 5

&. Johnny Jaberg
- **Age:** 35   • **Occupation:** Famous Actor
- **Description:** divorced, wife has custody of both children, donates to create shelters for the homeless

1 2 3 4 5

&. Howard Wilkinson
- **Age:** 55   • **Occupation:** California State Senator
- **Description:** married, 1 child, recently elected, financially well-to-do

1 2 3 4 5

Spencer Kagan: *Cooperative Learning*©
Publisher: Resources for Teachers , Inc. • 1(800) Wee Co-op

Our Class!!!

Approach 1:
Class Restructuring
CLASS MEETINGS

How can we possibly prepare our students for full participation in a democracy by structuring our classroom autocratically? It is an amazing feature of our democratic educational system that we have settled so universally on an autocratic social organization of our classrooms. The teacher is the Congress, (making the laws), the President, (carrying them out), as well as the Judge, the Jury, and too often, the Executioner. Is it any wonder that teachers feel tired at the end of the day?

How can we possibly prepare our students for full participation in a democracy if we structure our classrooms autocratically? It is an amazing feature of our democratic educational system that we have settled so universally on an autocratic social organization of our classrooms. Thus arises the need for democratic class meetings.

Regularly scheduled class meetings are one of the most powerful tools we have for teaching mutual respect, responsibility, caring, social awareness, cooperative attitudes, and democratic principles. The class meeting can also be a major source of support for the teacher as students actively strive to improve the class, find solutions to problems, and suggest consequences for behaviors.

Whenever a problem comes up which does not need to be solved immediately, it can be placed on the agenda for the next class meet-

Classbuilding provides networking among all of the students in a class and creates a positive context within which teams can learn. Although students spend most of their time in teams, in the cooperative classroom, it is important that students see themselves as part of a larger supportive group -- the class -- not just as members of one small team.

There are a number of ways to improve class climate. The two primary approaches to classbuilding are Class Restructuring and Classbuilding Activities. Both approaches provide greater student empowerment and ownership and result in a feeling that this is "our class."

Functions of Class Meetings
1. Announcements
2. Mutual Support
3. Solve Problems
4. Improve Class
5. Plan Events

Spencer Kagan: *Cooperative Learning*©
Publisher: Resources for Teachers , Inc. • 1(800) Wee Co-op

ing. In the moment this provides a cooling-off period and satisfies the students that something is being done about their problem. Often the problem is solved by the students before the class meeting, and when that item comes up on the agenda, students are asked to share their own creative solutions.

Problems are not just conflicts. At one class meeting the students worked on how a blind boy could participate in kickball. When the students hit on a solution, it was used for the remaining years of that child's elementary education.

Unexpected, creative, student-generated solutions to problems can occur at the class meetings because many heads are better than one, students are less tied to traditions, and because students are closer to many of the problems for which they ask help.

Some guidelines for class meetings include:

Function. Meetings are used to make announcements, plan events, solve problems, improve class functioning, and provide mutual support.

Structure. Regular meetings rather than meetings just to put out fires are preferable. When possible, time is allowed to each of the five major functions at each meeting. In this way students know, for example, there will some time for students to compliment or support each other at each meeting, setting a positive tone, and putting the problem solving in a larger positive perspective.

Agenda. Usually the rule is, an item must be placed on the agenda prior to the meeting. Nothing is placed on the agenda unless the teacher feels comfortable with it, and no decision can be made unless the teacher agrees.

Student Planning. Students can be in charge of certain aspects of the meeting. For example, the class support committee, with a rotating membership, is in charge of finding creative ways to recognize and celebrate individual learning gains and positive attitudes and behaviors among students. It can set a positive tone to both begin and end class meeting with time for students to praise or compliment each other.

Schedule. It is best to begin by announcements and then to set a positive tone with compliments, both teacher and student generated. Problem solving might follow. Time is left for planning events and improving class functions. Finally, it is a good idea to end with a mutual support activity such as a classbuilder, described in this chapter.

Student Input. While problem solving, use a structure that ensures that each student's input can be seen be all the students. One such structure is a team discussion with a simultaneous blackboard share; a member from each team can write on the board or chart paper as the team comes up with a possible solution. Luci Bowers (Frank Jewett School, Bonny Eagle School District, W. Buxton, Main) gift waped a shoe box. All week students deposit postive items. During the Friday class meetings there is time to "Read the Box." Students praise each other and provide inspirational quotes such as, "To have a friend is to be one."

Teacher Modeling. The teacher models desired behavior during the meeting. For example, during the support time, the teacher may begin by modeling support phrases like, "One thing I really appreciate in our class is how Frank takes time to give compliments. Yesterday I heard him give Pete a great compliment. He said...."

CLASS GOALS

If the success of each team contributes to a higher level class goal, then all of the teams feel themselves to be on the same side -- success of one is success of all. This positive interdependence among teams can be created through the task structure -- if each team project is one aspect of a larger class project. It can be created also through the reward structure -- if the points earned by each team are summed, and contribute to a class goal. The importance of setting class goals becomes clear when we visit a classroom in which there has been only team-level recognition and no class projects or class level recognition. If students identify only at the team level, the classroom becomes a "civil war of teams" - each team rooting for the failure of the other teams. The climate changes radi-

---

Structure:

Spend-A-Buck

The steps of Spend-A-Buck:

Step 1: The class brainstorms as many alternatives as possible as when the class is going to come up with a class name. These alternatives are posted.

Step 2: Each student has three tokens to spend, often 50¢, 35¢, and 15¢,

Step 3: They each spend each token on a different alternative.

Step 4: The amount spent on each alternative is summed and the class decision is announced.

Note: Ties are broken by a new vote among the two or three top alternatives.

---

cally if there are class goals; the success of each team contributes to a higher level class goal and all students in the class support each other.

CLASS EMPOWERMENT

There are a variety of ways to have the class members feel they make important input to important class outcomes. If the teacher makes all of the decisions, the students are powerless; they feel like puppets at the mercy of a force beyond themselves. Student decision making can occur in a variety of areas.

Class Decisions. A vote often polarizes the class - some win and some lose. Thus, when the class is to make a decision, instead of a vote, it is usually better to use consensus seeking or Spend-A-Buck. Consensus seeking or Spend-A-Buck (See Box) are prefera-

ble to voting which can polarize the class. In the long run, consensus seeking is a far more powerful than voting as a way of decision making. Consensus seeking places a powerful value on minority rights. If we use consensus, we do not have a class decision until we are all comfortable with the decision. If we use voting, we might make a decision that almost half the class hates. Consensus seeking will work only if class members are flexible, they must realize that in the consensus process the goal is not to get their very favorite outcome each time but rather to get an outcome that everyone can live with.

Student Bulletin Boards. A student bulletin board or collage is perhaps the simplest. There can be a class decision as to how to use the space, and provision that all students have an opportunity to contribute.

Student Input into Room Arrangement. If students are asked how they would feel comfortable and have an opportunity to contribute to room arrangement, they get the feeling that this is "our class."

Student Input into Rewards and Celebrations. If there is a class goal, students can decide how to celebrate progress toward the goal. For example, in teams students can brainstorm and prioritize possible class celebrations (free-time music, snacks, class picnic, cooperative game) and the teacher can say which celebrations are possible.

STUDENT EVALUATIONS

Students can make a very valuable input into the classroom environment and become important coaches for teachers if a very simple procedure is followed. On a weekly basis students fill out a very simple questionnaire which allows them to reflect on what is helping them learn and what could help them learn more. The teacher uses the answers to determine which teaching practices are most helpful and

---

Student Evaluation:

How are We Doing?

1. **Three things which have helped me learn:**

    1. _____
    2. _____
    3. _____

2. **One thing the teacher could do to help me learn more.**

    1. _____

3. **One thing I could do to help me learn more.**

    1. _____

which might be even more helpful. Because students are asked to reflect on what they could do to learn more, they take responsibility for their own learning. Because they are asked to reflect on what the teacher could do to help them learn more, they assume the role of coach or helper to the teacher, and become more identified with reaching the goals of learning. The positive tone puts teachers and students all on the same side in an attempt to improve "our class."

Approach 2:
Classbuilding Activities

Another approach to classbuilding is represented by classbuilding activities and structures, like those described in the remainder of this chapter. Some of the activities are exactly like teambuilding activities, except occur at the class level. The blind walk for mutual support, a teambuilding activity, can be transformed into a classbuilding activity by having students from different teams group. So too, with having a *class* name, *class* logo, *class* song.

Some classbuilding activities, though, do not have their counterpart in teambuilding. Graphing the number of students with certain characteristics by forming a Person Bar Graph can be done with a whole class, but not within a team. Geography Placement (pretending the room is a map and having students place themselves where their home is) is another classbuilding activity which

---

Five aims of:
Classbuilding

1. **Getting Acquainted**
2. **Class Identity**
3. **Mutual Identity**
4. **Valuing Differences**
5. **Developing Synergy**

---

does not have a counterpart in teambuilding.

Classbuilding, like teambuilding, can serve a variety of functions: Creating a positive climate in the whole class, allowing classmates to get to know each other well, having a positive class identity, valuing individual differences, and experiencing mutual support and synergy.

1. Getting Acquainted

An essential part of classbuilding is for students to feel they know the others in their classroom and that the others know them. Many of the getting acquainted activities which are done within teams can be adapted to the class. But getting acquainted with 36 others can be quite different -- and a lot of fun.

Find Someone Who...:

People Hunt. Students search for people who have certain characteristics. Possible characteristics: Favorite television program, type of family car, favorite food.

In one version students fill out a form describing themselves and then go on a people hunt to find others with the same characteristics. See the People Hunt form.

The structure, Find Someone Who.... was developed by *Laurie Robertson* (Consultant, Resources for Teachers). It can be used for a range of objectives: to practice skills, recall information, and even share concepts. If the worksheet has low consensus material (What kind of job do you imagine Tom Sawer will have when he grows up?) students "Find Someone Who..." has the same or similar answer as themselves to sign their worksheet.

~See Chapter 10: Mastery Structures and

Chapter 11: Thinking Skills Structures~

Similarity Grouping:

Student Characteristics. The teacher announces a dimension such as color of hair or birthday months. Everyone with the same answer forms a group. They then discuss positive and negative aspects of that

People Hunt

Instructions:

Fill in answers for yourself. Then circulate throughout the class and find another person and ask him/her a question for a match. If you get a yes, sign each other's People Hunt sheets. If you get a no, that person asks you a question looking for a match. Continue alternating asking questions until you find a match, then form new pairs. Try to get all your boxes filled in.

*Adapted from a People Hunt provided by Laural Robertson.

	Self	Friend
1. Favorite Color		
2. Favorite School Subject		
3. Favorite Ice Cream		
4. Astrological Sign		
5. Favorite TV Show		
6. Dream Car		
7. Favorite Singing Group		
8. Favorite Dessert		
9. Favorite Season of the Year		
10. Miles from Home to School		
11. Favorite Sport		
12. Dream Vacation		
13. Favorite Hobby		
14. I Am an (Only, Oldest, Youngest, Middle) Child		
15. Eye Color		
16. (Fill In)		
17. (Fill In)		

Spencer Kagan: *Cooperative Learning*©
Publisher: Resources for Teachers , Inc. • 1(800) Wee Co-op

characteristic. It can include paraphrasing across groups. Some dimensions: pets owned, favorite sport or hobby, favorite type restaurant, dream vacation. Similarity Grouping like Line-Ups and Class Bar Graphs can be followed by frequency graphs which provide a good visual description of the class.

Inside-Outside Circle:

Who are We? Students stand in two concentric circles, with the inside circle facing out and the outside circle facing in. They make a quarter right turn. Teacher tells them how many to rotate, they face a partner and share information about themselves, such as name, where born, favorite book.

Inside-Outside Circle is also a mastery structure, excellent for practicing skills and facts.

~See Chapter 10: Mastery Structures~

Roundrobin:

Gesture-Name-Game. Form circles of about ten students. One at a time, each student says his name, by breaking it into syllables, and adding a movement or gesture to go with each syllable. In unison, the group repeats the name and imitates the movements. If first names get too easy, use first and last names.

Class Line-ups:

Inside-Outside Circle

Student Characteristics. Students line up in order of height, birthdays, alphabetical order, number of blocks from school. Line-Ups and Similarity Groups are often followed by graphing.

Line-ups can be used in a variety of ways to promote communication and to develop certain concepts.

~ See Chapter 12: Communication Building Structures ~

Formations:

Class Living Bar Graph. Students form a bar graph on some getting acquainted topic, such as number of: rooms in their house, blocks they live from school, times they have moved, pets they have owned. Later, they may make team or individual bar graphs of the data and the data may be posted, analyzed, and become part of a survey or math lesson.

Linkages:

Student Preferences. One student states something about himself or herself, such as "I'm Susan, and I like chocolate ice cream." Any in the class can link on by holding

Line-Ups

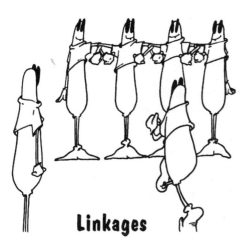

Linkages

hands or linking arms and saying, "I'm Simon, and I'm glad you like chocolate ice cream Susan, because I do too! And I like to go to the movies." A student who likes to go to the movies can link on by saying, "I'm Carlos, and I'm glad you like to go to the movies Simon, because I do too. And I like to go fishing." And so on.

When the last student links on he or she completes the circle by walking around and also linking on to the first person. When the students are in a circle they might say, "We are 'class name' and we are glad." and then give the class cheer.

Class Project:

Class Calendar. Include not only birthdays but at least one other important event from each student's life on the class calendar, so as a class we can celebrate birthday's and the anniversary of important events. One format I like particularly is to have a class norm about birthday celebrations: The person whose birthday it just was chooses someone else in the classroom to help plan a celebration of the next birthday. Celebration formats go beyond just the traditional singing of "Happy Birthday." Rather, students are interviewed by the celebration planners, they have choice of a favorite cooperative game for the class, may be allowed to play their favorite song, remember for the class their proudest moment, and are made to feel special in ways decided by the celebration planners.

Fact-or-Fiction:

Who am I? Students state either a believable lie or an unlikely truth about themselves. Classmates attempt to guess which it is.

Guess-the-Fib:

Who am I? Students say three facts about themselves. One is a fib. Classmates try to guess the fib. Guess-the-Fib may be used to review information from science, math, social studies, and literature.

Structures like Guess-the-Fib and Fact-or-Fiction may be used to review information.

~See Chapter 10: Mastery Structures~

Fact Bingo:

Who are We? A bingo type card is made up with little known facts about students filling the cells. Students circulate and try to fill the card or get bingo by locating classmates who fit the description. Classmates sign the cell when they are correctly identified.

Mix-Freeze-Pair:

Getting to Know You. Students circulate through the classroom. When the teacher calls "Freeze", they stop. When the teacher calls "Pair", they form pairs, turn to the person closest to them, and interview each other on the theme announced by the teacher. Some suggested themes:
1. **Fun Vacations.**
2. **Places I Have Lived.**
3. **Pets I Have Had.**

2. *Class Identity Building*

A positive class identity can be built, like a team identity, through class names, banners, songs, and so on. A deeper sense of identity is built through what the class creates. A positive class identity is created by a successful class project which the class shares with other classes. Choice is an important element of building class identity. If students are involved in room arrangement or in decorating a bulletin board, it becomes "our classroom." Other projects include an acceptable graffiti board, monthly mural, a class tree planting, adopting a child or elder, making a class party to honor a special school person, creating a class charity....

Class Projects:

1. Class Books. A Class Scrapbook or Memory Book is a great way to create a positive class identity. If our class has a Visitor Book, then with pride we can ask visitors to sign in. The scrapbook can have separate sections for happy, sad, fun, exciting, silly, and difficult events. Teams can rotate making contributions. The class can create a book about a field trip -- each team making a chapter and each individual on the team making a page of the chapter. When we are done, we "publish" by sending it to other classrooms, with some pages in the back for them to give us some comments. Some other books: class cookbook, monster book, shape books, and Book of Books (a page of drawing or writing for each of our favorite books).

2. Chain of Friendship. Ask the children to start noticing kind and helpful things that other children do at school. During the day a child may come and tell the teacher about the 'good deed' they saw. That child will receive a colored "link" to glue or staple onto the chain. The friendship chain can grow and be a growing, visible measure of kind and helpful deeds.

3. Class Names
4. Class Motto
5. Class Songs
6. Class Cheers
7. Class Banners
8. Class Logos

3. Valuing Differences

Students need to know, not only that they are known by others in the classroom but also that they are valued or appreciated. The norm in a strong class is that "We accept and appreciate those with values and characteristics different from our own." Through activities in which differences are understood and appreciated, we come to "celebrate diversity." Our class is richer because we have students taking different stances during corners or line-ups.

We would be less, if we all were the same.

Corners:

Preferences. This structure is designed to allow students to know and accept themselves and others more. Any individual difference dimension can be the focus, such as favorite season, intended profession, or even type of shoe you would like to be. Students go to the corner of the room representing their choice; so, for example, all the tennis shoe people go to one corner, the hiking boot people go to another. Students then share reasons for their choice with a partner in their corner. Finally students play a paraphrase game in which they must listen carefully to the reasons of the other groups (high heels, hiking boots, loafers) in order to be able to correctly paraphrase them.

Typical Corners Sequence:

Step 1. Announce Corners. Announce the corners, with a number in each corner and with visuals posted in each corner, if possible. Usually there are four corners, but sometimes three or more corners would be appropriate, depending on the curriculum.

Corners

Corners Content:

1. **Favorite seasons:**
   Fall Winter, Spring, Summer
2. **Type of bird you would be:**
   Falcon, Flamingo, Hummingbird, Seagull
3. **Professions:**
   Teacher, Doctor, Scientist, Artist
4. **Cars:**
   Jeep, Cadillac, Volkswagen, Porsche
5. **Characters from a novel**
6. **Characters from history**
7. **Metaphors:**
   • The future is a great roller coaster ride on a moonless night.
   • The future is a mighty river flowing inexorably along its course, carrying us with it.
   • The future is a great ocean with many destinations which can be navigated well.
   • The future is a random, colossal dice game.

might do Corners on students beliefs about which of four was the most important reason for the war.

Values Lines:

Taking a Stance. A statement is announced and students take a stand on an imaginary line which stretches from one end of the classroom to another.

The strongest agree student in the class stand at one end of the line; the strongest disagree student stand at the other and the remaining students stand between, closer to one end or the other, depending on how much they agree or disagree with the statement.

Students listen carefully to those with a similar point of view (those standing next to them in the value line), the value line is folded, and then they play Paraphrase Passport to make sure they understand a point of view different from their own.

Alternative Version: Teams get consensus first using team value lines, and then, as a group, take a stand on an agree-disagree class value line.

Step 2. Think & Write Time. Give students a bit of silent think time to clarify for themselves their preference. Have them write the number of their preferred corner on a slip of paper. (This way they will clarify their own values, not just go to the corner Johnny prefers).

Step 3. Students Group in Corners. Students go to their corners and pair up to express the reasons for their preferences. They then form groups of four within the corner, and students in the group paraphrase their partner from the paired listening. The teacher calls on students from one corner to announce to the class reasons for that choice.

Step 4. Students Paraphrase. Students in pairs in the corners paraphrase the reason. This last sharing and paraphrasing is repeated for each corner.

Step 5. Teams Review. When students are back in their teams, they make sure everyone can name reasons supporting each choice.

Corners is a useful structure to begin and end a lesson. For example, before a unit on the Civil War, I might ask the students who they would rather be (Soldier from the North, Plantation Owner, Abolitionist, or Southern General). Following the lesson I

Value Lines Content:

1. **Agree or Disagree:**
   • Capital punishment should be abolished.
   • Parents should never divorce.
   • The money we now spend on space exploration should be spent instead on feeding the world's hungry.
2. **Which would you rather be:**
   • A dandelion or an orchid?
   • A patchwork quilt or an electric blanket?
   • A Rolls Royce or a Volkswagen?

Spencer Kagan: *Cooperative Learning* ©
Publisher: Resources for Teachers , Inc. • 1(800) Wee Co-op

4. *Mutual Support*

Through mutual support activities students come to feel they can depend on their classmates. Our class has gained a sense of mutual support when members feel the classroom is a caring community.

Pairs:

Hidden Helpers. Each student is assigned a secret pal. Their job is to do something nice for their secret pal each week without letting the secret pal discover who is their hidden helper. Guidelines may be necessary, for example, gifts may be limited to compliments or favors, not material gifts.

Special Roles:

Ticket Agents. This exercise emphasizes looking for positive things in other's behavior. Every day, assign one or two students to hand out 'tickets' to those who are being very helpful, considerate, or cooperative during the day.

Mix-Pair-Discuss:

Who Am I? Students brainstorm the names of familiar people or characters, often from books just read. Each name is written on a piece of construction paper. the paper is punched with two holes in the upper corners

Who-Am-I?

and a string of about two feet of yarn is placed through the holes and tied to the corners. The paper is worn on the back of each class member so that they cannot see who they are. Classmates then wander the room attempting to find out who they are. They seek help from their classmates by asking up to three questions which can be answered with a "yes" or a "no."

Once a student discovers who they are, they wear their identity on their chest, and they then can circulate giving hints to the classmates who have not yet discovered who they are.

As an aid to those who might not otherwise figure out their identity, a list of all the characters may be posted, and once students discover who they are, they are to put a check mark by that character.

Mix-Freeze-Group:

Number Puzzles. Students "Mill and Mingle" around the room until the teacher calls "Freeze." The Teacher then poses a problem which has a number for an answer, such as, "What is (teacher claps twice) plus (teacher claps three times)?" Students then rush to huddle and hold each other in

Mix-Freeze-Group Content:

1. **How many blind mice chased the farmer's wife?** (3)
2. **How many dwarfs in the story of Snow White?** (7)
3. **How many balls plus strikes in a full count?** (5)
4. **How many feet in a yard?** (3)
5. **How many inches in foot?** (12)

groups of five. Those who are left over go to a designated spot by the teacher, called "lost and found." Rule: You cannot go to lost and found twice in a row, so students must look to hold lost and found students first.

Similarity Groups:

Puzzled People. A drawing is made. The drawing is cut into four parts, like parts of a jigsaw puzzle. Each team member has a part. Students circulate, trading parts with other students in the class. At a signal students attempt to find those who have the

Formations Content:

1. **Letters of the alphabet**
2. **Numbers** (numbers, solutions to problems, number sentences)
3. **Shapes** (Square, Triangle, Our Room)
4. **Solar System** (With all rotations)
5. **Pictures** (House, Tree)
6. **Words** ("at," "cat," "catatonic")
7. **Symbols** (Shape of Molecule, H_2O)

corresponding parts, to solve the puzzle.

Animal Sounds.
The students are randomly grouped. The students of each group make up an animal sound unique to their group. They practice the sound until they can recognize it. They mix and mingle until they are away from their zoo animal team. They then close their eyes and are to find each other again by just making their animal calls.

5. Synergy

Synergy is the energy released through synthesis. All of us interacting produce far more that the sum of what we can produce working alone. Students need to feel the power of synergy if they are to enter fully into the cooperative process.

Formations

Formations:

1. Geometric Forms. The teacher draws a geometric figure such as two concentric circles, a square, or a triangle. Students are to form the figure with their bodies by holding hands. Sometimes they are not allowed to talk.

Math problems: For example, Teams form specific parts. For example one team may be a 2, another the 7, a third the plus sign, a fourth the line underneath in the problem 2+7=. The remainder of the class must figure out the answer and quickly get into formation. Then the teacher announces that the 7 must become a 5 and the answer must change.

2. Objects. *Laurie Robertson* (Consultant, Resources for Teachers) was doing a unit on the Westward Movement. She had students become a covered wagon which actually traveled as the wheels rotated. I like to have students become a happy face, sad face, and melting ice cream cone. Other favorites are to have students spell words, make number sentences, and to act out the solar system, including the moon traveling around the earth which is traveling around the sun.

3. Imaginary Machine. Teacher describes a machine as having various parts and movements. One student plays the part of a crank by bending arm at elbow. Another student adds on by placing hands on waist of first student and doing deep knee bends in time to the cranking motion. A third connects and moves her head in a circle, etc., until the whole class becomes a "Class Living Machine." ∿

References:

Co-operative College of Canada. *Co-operative Outlooks.* Saskatoon, Saskatchewan: Co-operative college of Canada, 1980.

Canfield, J. & Wells, H.C. *100 Ways to Enhance Self-Concept in the Classroom: A handbook for teachers and parents.* Englewood, Cliffs, NJ: Prentice Hall, 1976.

Chase, Larry. *The Other Side of the Report Card: A how-to-do-it program for affective education.* Glenview, IL: Goodyear Books, Scott, Foresman & Co., 1975.

Gibbs, Joan. *Tribes: a process for peer involvement.* Santa Rosa, CA: CenterSource Publications, 1987.

Glassman, M., Kisiow, E., Good, L., O'Connor, M., Alderson, I., & Kutz, S. *Cooperation and Community Life.* Saskatoon, Saskatchewan: Cooperative College of Canada, 1980.

Graves, Nan & Ted. *Getting There Together. A sourcebook and desk-top guide for creating a cooperative classroom.* Santa Cruz, CA: Cooperative College of California, 1988.

McCabe, M. E. & Rhoades, J. *The Nurturing Classroom. Developing self-esteem, thinking skills, and responsibility through simple cooperation.* Willits, CA: ITA Publications, 1988.

Moorman, C. & Dishon, D. *Our Classroom: We can learn together.* Englewood Cliffs, NJ: Prentice Hall, 1983.

Prutzman, P. *The Friendly Classroom for a Small Planet.* Wayne, NJ: Avery Publishing Group, Inc., 1978.

Raths, L.E., Harmin, M. & Simon, S.B. *Values and Teaching: Working with values.* Columbus, OH: Charles E. Merrill, 1966.

Saskatchewan Department of Co-operation and Co-operative Development. *Working Together, Learning Together.* Saskatoon, Saskatchewan: The Stewart Resources Center, 1983.

Schmuck, R.A. & Schmuck, P.A. *Group Processes in the Classroom.* Dubuque, IO: Wm. C. Brown Co., 1988.

Schniedwind, N., Davidson, E. *Cooperative Learning, Cooperative Lives.* Duboque, IA: Wm.C. Brown Co. Publishers, 1987.

Simon, S.B., Howe, L.W. & Kirschenbaum, H. *Values Clarification: A handbook of practical strategies for teachers and students.* New York: Hart Publishing Co., Inc., 1972.

Spizman, Robyn. *Bulletin Boards Plus.* Carthage, IL: Good Apple Inc., 1989

Stanford, G. *Developing Effective Classroom Groups.* New York: Hart Publishing, 1977.

Stanford, G. *Learning Discussion Skills through Games.* New York: Citation Press, 1969.

Vacha, E.F. *Improving Classroom Social Climate.* Orcutt, CA: Orcutt Union School District, Orcutt, California, 1979.

Vacha, E.F. *Project Class.* Orcutt, CA: Orcutt Union School District, Orcutt, California, 1982.

Wenc, Charlene. *Cooperation: Learning Through Laughter.* Chicago, IL: The American Institute of Adlerian Studies, LTD.

A distressing number of our students leave school unable to correctly identify the century in which the Civil War took place, unable to give an answer to simple problems like one half divided by one eighth, and unable to locate Spain on a map of the world. The structures described in this chapter are designed to remedy that situation.

As a nation, we have not been successful in producing a population with a generally high level of basic skills and information. This has been made painfully clear through a number of publications and surveys examining what our high school seniors know. A distressing number of our students leave school unable to correctly identify the century in which the civil war took place, unable to give an answer to simple problems like one half divided by one eighth, and unable to locate Spain on a map of the world.

The structures described in this chapter are designed to remedy that

situation. For example, the Flashcard Game applies what we know about memory to create a structure which increases rather dramatically the efficiency of students in recalling basic facts. Numbered Heads Together is used to have students review information and make sure all students can solve problems. Pairs Check is a tremendous aid in skill acquisition, designed to replace the boring isolation of worksheet work. All of these structures include peer support and tutoring, simultaneous interaction among all students, frequent correction opportunities, and immediate feedback lacking in traditional structures. In addition there are a host of structures which can be useful in practice and review of information of skills.

It is important to note that these mastery structures can be used to master a broad range of content. Pairs Check can be used with traditional worksheet problems and can be used with creative manipulatives. In one case the students are coaching each other as they do written problems; in the other case they are coaching each other as they construct solutions with manipulatives. In both cases, however, they follow the same eight steps of the structure. Similarly, the problem posed by the teacher in Numbered Heads Together might call for a verbal response, a finger response, or an elaborate, unique response by each student, using manipulatives. In all cases, however, the same four steps of Number Heads Together are followed.

The structures covered in this chapter are effective in producing mastery of academic content and skills. Although these structures are useful in dealing with the high consensus materials, such as knowledge and comprehension, many are also useful for other purposes. They are multi-functional. Depending on the content used, these structures can be used for teambuilding, communication building, and the development of concepts and thinking skills.

Spencer Kagan: *Cooperative Learning*©
Publisher: Resources for Teachers , Inc. • 1(800) Wee Co-op

For example, Roundtable is a simple structure in which students pass a paper around the table each in turn contributing one answer or idea. Roundtable may be used for teambuilding if the directive is, "Each time the paper comes around to you, write down one way your team might spend a hundred dollars to have fun." For communication skill building, the directive might be, "Roundtable all the possible polite phrases you might use to tell someone they are not listening to the ideas of others." For Mastery, the directive might be, "Roundtable as many constitutional amendments as you can as a team." For concept development and thinking skills, it might be, "Roundtable as many possible causes for the Civil War as you can imagine."

When I first worked out the steps of Numbered Heads Together, gave it a name, and began training teachers in the structure, I thought it had a relatively limited domain of usefulness -- good only for knowledge and comprehension questions. After all, if the directive is to "Make sure everyone on your team knows..." it seemed logical that there must be high consensus materials, something everyone can agree on.

Later, as we began to explore the limits of Numbered Heads Together, we realized that the directive can be "Make sure everyone on your team can give one good idea for..." and each member of the team might have a very different answer -- even though they have worked together. We discovered that Numbered Heads Together had a much broader Domain of Usefulness than we thought originally. Thus, although Number Heads Together is described as a mastery structure in this chapter, it is multi-functional, used to reach a range of objectives.

Numbered Heads Together

When the traditional teacher wants to check for understanding or do a quick review or wake students up after talking at them for a prolonged period, she/he uses Whole-Class-Question-Answer. That is, the teacher asks a question and then calls on a student who raises a hand.

Let's examine this structure closely. It is terrible. When the teacher first asks the question about ten of the thirty students raise a hand. So at that point the teacher has lost about two-thirds of the class who became comatose or semi-interested. Now the teacher calls on one student. The other nine who had their hands up lower their hands and their sense of involvement. Often they register a subvocal protest - they have lost in the competition for the teacher's attention.

If the student who is called on does not immediately meet with the teacher's approval, he or she may begin to struggle. Some will begin saying anything that comes to mind as they grasp at straws in a desperate situation. The other nine, begin to wake up. Like sharks in the water sensing blood, they raise their hands. Some may even say "Teacher, teacher, call on me." They are excited, happy. The failure of a classmate has increased their chances to win the teacher's recognition.

Thus traditional Whole-Class Question-Answer is a situation of negative interdependence. It sets the students against each other. The failure of one student increases the chances of success of another, and students, therefore, begin to hope not for their peers to do well, but to do poorly. The antidote is Numbered Heads Together.

Sequential Numbered Heads Together

One day when I walked into the classroom of *Russ Frank*, (Chaparral Middle School, Diamond Bar, CA) Russ was teaching a grammar lesson. He put a sentence on the overhead projector, and then questioned, "Where should the comma go? Put your heads together and consult with your team." The students literally put their heads together, and talked it over. There was a buzz of animated chatter. After a short time, Russ flipped off the lights. Total silence. Then he touched his ear and called out a number. The hand of one student in each team quickly grabbed an ear. Russ called the student who grabbed his ear first. A correct answer led to points for that team. The next time students had to put a hand on their head to signal they knew the answer, and the first to do so, was called upon. Teams were in intense competition for points and for recognition.

Each student on a team had a number and the students knew that only one student would be called on each time to represent the team. The buzz of animated discussion was the attempt by the students to share the information so that everyone knew the answer and was ready to respond with the unusual signals Russ indicated. They knew that if they shared information their team would receive a point no matter which number was called.

As I analyzed the video tape of Russ' classroom, I realized he was using a very powerful structure. I took the liberty to give it a name: Numbered Heads Together. I took out the between-team competition by dropping points and the race to be recognized,

and found the structure is a marvelous way to produce positive interdependence, simultaneous interaction, and individual accountability. By having only one student represent the group but not informing the students in advance who the group representative will be, each student knows he/she may be held individually accountable. In Numbered Heads Together, students cannot depend on the high achiever to do the work for them; they all have to know the answer or how to get it if they are to be assured of recognition.

Numbered Heads Together is a marvelous antidote to Whole-Class Question-Answer which often boils down to a conversation between the teacher and the high achievers in the classroom with the rest of the class between semi-interested and comatose.

STEPS OF NUMBERED HEADS TOGETHER

Numbered Heads Together is a simple structure, consisting of four steps: (1) Students Number Off; (2) Teacher Announces a Question and a Time Limit; (3) Students Put their Heads Together; and (4) Teacher Calls a Number.

Step 1. Students Number Off. Each student on the team has a different number. For teams of three, Number Three may answer when either Number Three or Number Four are called. For teams of five, Number Five or Number Four may answer when Number Four is called.

Step 2. Teacher Asks a Question. The question asked of students during Step 2 is formulated as a directive. Instead of saying, "What is the meter in the poem?" the teacher says, "Make sure everyone on the team can describe the meter in the poem."

Steps of:

Numbered Heads Together

1. Students Number Off

2. Teacher Poses Question

3. Heads Together

4. Teacher Calls a Number

Spencer Kagan: *Cooperative Learning*©
Publisher: Resources for Teachers , Inc. • 1(800) Wee Co-op

The question may be either high or low consensus, but is phrased accordingly. For example, for a low consensus question, the teacher might say, "Put your heads together and name the chemical which combines with chlorine to form table salt." For a higher level thinking question, the teacher might say, "Make sure you can all make several predications about the future behavior of the American Economy based on the paper shortage and the law of supply and demand."

To quicken the pace, the teacher may sometimes provide a time frame for students. So, for example, the teacher might say, "How many pounds are in a ton; you have thirty seconds to make sure everyone on your team knows."

Step 3. Heads Together. Students literally put their heads together and make sure everyone knows the answer. The role of the Checker may be added here.

Step 4. Teacher Calls a Number. The teacher will call a number at random and students with that number raise their hands to be called upon, as in the traditional classroom. A Numbered Heads Together spinner for the overhead is available which makes the structure more game-like. The spinner is handy also because teachers do not have to remember which numbers they have called.

If the answer is within the capacity of most teams, but only one or two students raise their hands, the the teacher might say, "Not enough Number Twos have their hands up; I'll give you one more minute, make sure all your Number Twos know the answer."

If the answer has several parts, such as, being able to name four parts of an atom, then the teacher will get fuller participation by asking for the number ones to name one part, the number twos to name another, and so on.

If a student gives a partially correct response, the teacher might ask, "Is there a Number Three who can add to that response?"

Variations:

Think-Heads Together

One of the best ways to improve Numbered Heads Together is to add Think Time after posing the question and before allowing the

groups to put their heads together. Think Time does several important things. For the weaker or slower student, there is time to put some thoughts together. Without Think Time, the lower achiever may simply give up trying and wait to hear the answer from a high achiever. For the stronger student, Think Time allows deeper thinking. There is greater participation, more equal participation, and deeper thought if we take five slow seconds to allow students to formulate their responses on their own before sharing them in Heads Together.

Simultaneous Numbered Heads Together

As teachers and I worked with Numbered Heads Together, several powerful variations evolved. *Becky Nehan* (Coachella Unified School District, Coachella, CA) developed what I have come to call Simultaneous Numbered Heads Together. Becky recognized that there are two structural weaknesses in the sequential form of Numbered Heads which Russ had developed: (1) There is minimal participation of students when only one is called upon to report; and (2) When a number is called and a member reports the correct answer, the teacher has no way of determining if the other teams knew the right answer or not -- once an answer is given, other teams are not called upon.

What Becky did is provide ways for all of the students with a given number to answer at once by allowing each student with the number called to respond, all at once. Consider these forms of Simultaneous Numbered Heads Together Becky and others have developed:

1. Blackboard Responses

Following practice on a type of math problem, if number three is called, all of the Number Three's might come up to the board at once to do a problem of that type.

Some teachers have a place for each team to write and then students can record a point on the board by their team name if they have a correct answer.

2. Thumbs Up or Down

If the question is a true-false question, and number two is called, all the twos who think true is the right answer, put thumbs up while all those who believe false is the right answer, put thumbs down. Thumbs up and down are not as easy to see as colored strips of paper, so each team might have a red and a green flag to wave. The rule is that no one can touch the flag until the number is called, and once a number is called, there is no more talking or helping. If the question can be answered by a number from one to ten, fingers might be used.

Some teachers use a thumbs up or down to indicate agreement or disagreement by "all the other Three's" after calling on one to respond.

3. Team Slates

If the question is a short answer, students might have slates to hold up.

4. Response Cards

A set of response cards can be provided. For example, if drill is to be on certain vocabu-lary and those words are to be used as responses, the students might make response cards. For young students, pictures, letters of the alphabet, numbers, or shapes might be the content of the response cards. The question might be something like, "Make sure everyone knows which shape has three corners." The response would be for students to hold up the triangle card if their number is called.

APPLICATIONS:

Numbered Heads is most often used to master basic facts and information which have been presented through direct instruction or written material. Numbered Heads may be used to review before a test. The method is also useful to create an anticipatory set for a lesson: Before a unit on electricity, the teacher might say, "Make sure everyone on your team can name three reasons electricity is important."

Numbered Heads Together can be used with a very wide range of educational objectives. For example, with math manipulatives such as Fraction Bras and Base 10 Kits, the teams might be directed to "Make sure everyone on you team can build...." In that case, in the last step of the structure, all the students with the number called would be on their own to build the answer using manipulatives.

The video, *Numbered Heads Together: Exploring the Structure in Depth*, demonstrates the steps and many variations of the structure, showing how manipulatives are used.

Pairs-Check

When it is time to practice a new skill, careful structuring of a worksheet and the process of working on the worksheet can lead to a dramatic difference in the mastery which results. If I give very little structure, say for example, give each student on the team a worksheet, and

Steps of:

Pairs Check

1. Individual Work **2. Coach Checks** **3. Coach Praises**

4. Individual Work **5. Coach Checks** **6. Coach Praises**

7. Pairs Check **8. Team Celebrates**

Spencer Kagan: *Cooperative Learning*©
Publisher: Resources for Teachers , Inc. • 1(800) Wee Co-op

casually tell the students to cooperate and help each other as they do their practice, very little cooperation is likely to result. When I check back after half an hour, the high-achiever is done, the middle achievers are half done, and the low achiever is either stuck on the first problem, practicing the wrong method of solving the problems, or perhaps has given up, and has begun to try to distract the other students.

One way of ensuring that there will be helping among students and that all students will stay on task is a simple structure to be used with mastery oriented worksheets. The structure is Pairs Check. The instructions on the worksheet might read like those in the box to the right.

The worksheet itself might be set up with problems placed in pairs, and with reminders when to stop and check with partners. I like to include exaggerated praisers, to liven up worksheet work, and to make it more game-like.

Using the Pairs-Check format, all of the students stay on task and work together to master the worksheet skill.

Teams will finish at different rates, so an attractive content-related sponge activity built into the worksheet is usually a good idea.

STEPS OF PAIRS CHECK

Step 1. Pair Work. Teams break into two sets of pairs. Partners work on a worksheet. One student works on the problem while the other, the coach, watches, and helps, if necessary.

Pairs Check Worksheet

Instructions: You are to work in pairs in your teams. Person one in the pair is to do the first problem, while person two acts as a coach. Coaches, if you agree that person one has done the first problem correctly, give him or her some praise, and then switch roles.

When you have both finished the first two problems, do not continue. You need first to check with the other pair. If you don't agree on the first two problems, figure out what went wrong. When both pairs agree on the first two problems, give a team handshake, and then proceed to the next two problems.

Remember to switch roles after each problem. Person one does the odd numbered problems; person two, the even numbered problems. After every two problems check with the other pair.

	Topic: Math Addition Date: Name:	Topic: Math Addition Date: Name:	
1	25 37 22	28 38 22	✔ ✔
2	72 37 22	68 67 22	
3	69 37 22 85	68 77 23 85	✔
4	69 67 62 85	86 89 62 84	✔

Sponge: If your pair finishes early, practice Polite Waiting. Take out your Base 10 Kit and build your answer.

Step 2. Coach Checks. The coach checks his/her partners work for agreement. If the partners don't agree on the answer, they may ask the other pair on the team. If the team as a whole cannot agree on an answer, each teammate raises a hand. The teacher knows four hands up is a team question.

Step 3. Coach Praises. If the partners agree on the answer, the coach offers his or her partner a praiser.

Pairs Check ✓

Name: _____   Name: _____

Date: _____   Date: _____

		✓
		✓
		✓
		✓
		✓
Sponge:	Sponge:	

Spencer Kagan: *Cooperative Learning*©
Publisher: Resources for Teachers , Inc. • 1(800) Wee Co-op

Steps 4-6. Partners Switch Roles. The partners switch roles and repeat steps 1-3. The student who had been the coach now becomes the problem solver, while the other student becomes the coach.

Step 7. Pairs Check. The team reunites; pairs compare answers. If they disagree and are unable to figure why, four hands go up.

Step 8. Team Celebrates. If the team agrees on the answer, they do a team handshake.

A PAIRS CHECK WORKSHEET

In the box on the previous page is an example of a Pairs Check Worksheet. Notice, after the first two problems there is a line with a check mark. This is a reminder to the pair to check with the other pair before going on. When both pairs agree on the answers to the first two problems, they circle the check mark and proceed to the next two problems. Notice also that the worksheet can be cut in half to bring home or to finish as homework. If it is completed as homework, then there is someone to check with the next day. The person in pair one with the left side of the worksheet checks with the person in pair two with the left side of the worksheet -- as do the other two teammates for the right side.

This worksheet might be modified by having the first two problems finished for the students as examples.

Pairs check is a particularly good structure for practicing new skills.

Pairs Check Advantages

Pairs Check v. Traditional

	Pairs Check	Traditional
Reinforcement	Immediate Frequent Peer's Praise	Delayed Infrequent Teacher's Mark
Teacher's Role	Facilitate	Evalute
Peer Relations	Coaching Encouragement Social Comparison	Isolation Negative Social Comparison
Correction Opportunities	Many Immediate Success-Oriented	Few or None Delayed Failure Oriented
Metacommunication	Value on Learning Value on Helping	Value on Grades Value on Winning

---

APPLICATIONS:

Grammar: Circle the noun. Correct the sentence. Diagram the sentence. Change to past tense. Substitute a new preposition.

Math: Reduce the fraction. Solve the word problem. Find the area. Calculate the angle. Determine the remainder. Write the time (from the clock pictured). Divide by fractions using fraction bars. Add, subtract, multiply or divide using Base 10 Manipulatives.

Social Studies: Which event came first? Match the person and accomplishment. Locate the city from the longitude and latitude.

Science: Calculate the velocity. Write the outcome of combining two chemicals. Calculate the stopping distance. Prove the angles are equal. Perform an experiment.

The video, *Pairs Check: Exploring the Structure in Depth,* provides details of how to implement Pairs Check, and illustrates many applications.

The Flashcard Game

The Flashcard Game is designed to facilitate the memorization of facts. Content can vary depending on grade and subject, ranging from knowledge of letter sounds to memorization of chemistry valences. Prior to playing the Flashcard Game, students make up flashcards, usually on items missed on a pre-test. The flashcard can take many forms:

A picture of an apple on one side of a card and the letter "A" on the back (used to aid in remembering initial letter sounds)

The Flashcard Game

A vocabulary word on one side and a definition on the other.

A name of a math formula on one side and the formula on the other.

A math problem on one side (2 x 3) and the answer on the other (6).

ROUNDS OF THE FLASH-CARD GAME

Round 1. Maximum Cues. Once the cards are made up, students sit in pairs. One student hands five or so of his or her cards to the other. The tutor holds up one card, shows and reads the tutee the front of the card (question or cue) and then shows and reads the back (answer). For young children and kinesthetic learners, the tutee may trace the answer or write the answer. The tutor then turns the card around again, showing the front, and asks for the answer from short term memory. The tutee attempts an answer. If the answer is correct, the tutor gives an exaggerated praise, such as, "You are a fabulous learner," "Super fantastic job," and the card is "won back" (returned to) the tutee. At this point, 90% or more of all answers should be correct, because the student has been told and shown the answer immediately before being asked for it. If, however, the tutee fails to answer correctly, he or she receives a "helper" rather than a "praiser." Helpers might be hints, showing and telling the card again, an opportunity to trace or write the right answer, reminders, and the joint creation by tutor and tutee of fantastic visual images which are difficult to forget. If a "helper" is given, the card is not won back, but rather placed back in the stack of cards the tutor holds, so that it will be repeated. Note: this method insures time-on-needed-task, as the easy items are quickly returned to the tutee and the more difficult items are repeated as needed. When the tutee wins back all of his or her cards, the tutor and tutee switch roles.

Round 2. Few Cues. After both students have won back all of their cards on round 1, they progress to round 2. In round 2 the same basic procedure is followed, but this time fewer cues are given, and students move from short to long-term memory.

Thus, for example, the tutor shows the tutee the front and asks for the back from memory. Not having just seen the back, the student must produce the information on the back from long-term memory. The same rules prevail, a correct answer produces an exaggerated praise and the card is returned to its maker; a slow or false answer produces a helper, and the card is placed back in the stack of items to master. To keep the game fresh, for both the tutor and tutee, each time a card is won the tutor must make a different, unexpected praise. Students are encouraged to be creative about the praises, so as the teacher circulates he/she might hear things like, "Ronald Reagan loves you for being so bright.", "Our team will always be a winner with you.", "You are extraordinarily intelligent."

Round 3. No Cues. Again, after *both* students win back their set of cards, they move up a round. On the third round, no cues are allowed. So, for example, the tutor might call out the multiplication question or say the vocabulary word without even showing the tutee the card. As in the other rounds, a correct response receives the card as a token of success accompanied by a praiser; a hesitant or false response receives help and repeated work.

The Flashcard Game can stand alone as a mastery structure, but it is most often used as one structure within a lesson design called Color-Coded Co-op Cards. The Color-Coded Co-op Card design includes tests, improvement scoring, and recognition at the individual, team, and class levels.

∼ See Chapter 17: Mastery Designs ∼

Notes on:

The Flashcard Game

1. Rounds Can Differ in Format.
The exact form of each round will be different depending on the level of students and the content. For example, if the content is foreign language vocabulary or English as a second language, on one side of a card might be a picture of a telephone and on the others side the printed word, "telephone." Round 1, in this case might consist of having the tutor spread all the pictures face up, say the word "telephone," and have the tutee point to the correct picture. Round 2 might be having the tutee say the word telephone when shown the picture. Round 3 might include correct spelling and the use of the word in a sentence.

2. Equal Time and Status -- the "Five Alive" Rule.
At the pretest, some students may get all the items right whereas others may miss all the items. It is important that both the high and low achiever experience both roles -- tutor and tutee. The high achiever needs to continue learning, and to have the opportunity to contribute to the team achievement points; the lower achiever needs to be presented the work in bite sized chunks so he or she is not overwhelmed. Thus the "Five Alive" rule: All students need to have five items to work on each time they begin the Flashcard game. The high achievers have bonus items to draw from (all of us can increase our vocabulary; it would not hurt to know the 12 times tables); the low achiever is never to work on more than five items at a time.

3. Distributed Practice: Storing the Cards.
Practice is distributed over time not only by having the three rounds, but also by having students store their cards and take them up on different days. Storage is facilitated by students having two small and one large envelope. The large envelope has the student's name; one small envelope is marked "mine" and the other is marked "not yet mine" to separate items which have been won back three times from those which need more work. One nice format for keeping the Co-op Cards is to use a 3 ring binder and cut the paper in thirds so each card is held by one ring of the binder. In this way students can keep separate those they have mastered, those they are working on, and those to work on later. Section dividers in the binder separate cards from different units. The binders lend themselves to unit reviews.

4. Change Partners.
If students A and B have been tutor-tutee partners on Monday, let students A and C work together on Tuesday. This will provide a richer variety of "praisers" and "helpers" as well as creating more of a sense of team identity.

Inside-Outside Circle

Inside-Outside Circle is an excellent mastery structure -- not used often enough. The way to structure Inside-Outside Circle, is described in Chapter 9: Classbuilding. For Mastery, I/O Circle can be used in two forms:

Variations:

Teacher-Directed Inside/Outside Circle

Students stand in two circles. The inside circle faces out, and the outside circle faces in. Each student has a partner. See diagram. Once students each have a partner, the teacher poses a review question. The rule is, "Make sure you and your partner know the answer. If the two of you get stuck, consult with the pair on either side. Use all your resources, so we can make sure everyone in the class knows."

Occasionally, the teacher may call for a response from students in the inside circle, sometimes from the outside circle, but often from the whole class with finger responses or choral responses.

Flashcard-Directed Inside/Outside Circle

Either the students or the teacher have made up flashcards on the topic for review. The flashcards have a question on one side and

an answer on the other. Each time the students rotate in Inside-Outside Circle, they practice with a new partner. The norm is, give a praiser if the answer is correct, and a helper if it is not.

"Give a good praiser if your partner gets the answer correct, if not, praise the effort, and give a helper. Show him or her the back right away. Don't give hints. Go to work together to figure out how your partner might remember next time."

Partners trade cards before rotating, to double the amount of practice.

Send-A-Problem
STEPS OF
SEND-A-PROBLEM

Step 1. Students Author Review Questions. Each student on a team makes up a review problem and writes it down on a flashcard. Encourage high-consensus problems which have a right or wrong answer, verifiable by the text. For younger students the format might be standardized (true-false, missing word, multiple choice).

The author of each question asks it of his or her teammates. If there is total consensus, the author writes the answer on the back of the card. If not, the question is revised so that it produces consensus. The side of the card with the question is marked with a Q; the side of the card with the answer is marked with an A.

Step 2. Teams Send-A-Problem. Teams pass their stack of review questions to another team.

Step 3. Teams Respond. Student 1 reads the first question. The team attempts to answer it. If they have consensus, they turn the card over to see if they agreed with the sending team. If not, they write their answer as an alternative answer. Student 2 reads the next one, and the procedure is repeated. The stacks of cards can be sent to a third and fourth team, and so on. Upon return of the cards to the senders, there is opportunity to discuss and clarify any questions indicated on the back of the cards.

Variation:

Trade-A-Problem

In Trade-A-Problem, teams simply trade a problem with another team. If there is going to be discussion, Trade-A-Problem is better than Send-A-Problem because teams won't have to wait as teams finish at different rates. Send-A-Problem is better if the review involves many high consensus, quick answers, because the problems can be rotated again and again to new teams.

Team Test Taking for Practice

It is the day before the test. Give the students a copy of the test. Tell them, "Tomorrow you will get this test as individuals, and there will be no helping tomorrow. You can help each other all you want today. Make sure all of your teammates can score a perfect score tomorrow."

When I first started suggesting this, a cry went up from some teachers. And a similar cry went up from students when some of the teachers were brave enough to try it. The cry: That is not fair!

Why not? All of the students learn. In some classrooms everyone gets 100%! If our goal is learning, not ranking students, why not set things up so everyone gets all the material perfectly?

I admit that some of the objection to team test taking for practice is legitimate. If the practice results in low-level memorization of materials without understanding, it is not serving us well. On the other hand, there are some things we want our students to master which are memorizations. For examples, certain geography facts, math facts, and recognition of certain types of sentences.

If the test is seen as a sample of material to be learned, and something to motivate students to learn everything in a unit, telling students just what is on the test might lead them not to master other material. This problem can be addressed. For example, on the first two times have the quiz and the practice worksheet be identical. By the third time, when all students are motivated to help

Send-A-Problem

each other on the worksheet, announce, "About half of the items on the worksheet will be on the quiz tomorrow, the other half will be taken from pages x to y in your book. If you finish the worksheet and everyone on your team knows how to answer all of the questions perfectly, turn to pages x to y and try to guess what I will ask, and begin tutoring each other on that material."

Variation:

Pair Test Taking

Pairs can work together to take the test on Thursday before they take it alone on Friday.

Roundtable

Roundtable is a simple cooperative learning structure which can be used with any subject matter. Roundtable is most often used at the beginning of a lesson to provide a content-related teambuilding activity.

Step 1. The Problem. The teacher asks a question with many possible answers, such as, name all the sports you can, all the possible pairs of numbers which add up to 11, all of the items in your home which were not invented fifty years ago.

Step 2. Students Contribute. Students make a list on one piece of paper, each writing one answer and then passing the paper to the person on his or her left. The paper literally goes round the table, thus the name -- Roundtable.

Roundtable

#1 Contributes

#2 Contributes

#3 Contributes

#4 Contributes

Variations:

The structure can be used in a variety of ways. Roundtable can be used with little or no time pressure or may be structured in a race-like format, with recognition given to teams which get the most answers, or with recognition toward a class goal which is a sum of team contributions. It may be well

Origin of Roundtable

A Gift From Millard

When I was in the doctoral program at UCLA, my thesis advisor was Professor Millard Madsen. Millard had developed the Madsen Cooperation Board. The board was designed to measure cooperation and competition. Essentially, goals were set up and children attempted to reach the goals by pulling strings attached to a marker. If the children cooperated they developed a strategy of moving the marker around the board by alternatively pulling and releasing the strings. Children who competed exhausted their efforts pulling against each other, receiving nothing. It was watching the non-adaptive competitiveness of American children, so dramatically demonstrated by Millard's Cooperation Board, that led me to dedicate my work to making sure children knew a cooperative alternative.

When I first began to apply the principles of cooperation to the classroom, I borrowed from Millard's concept to develop Roundtable. Instead of having students move a marker around a board, I had them pass a paper, with each one contributing in turn.

Through his patience, understanding, and brilliance, Millard gave direction to my life work. It has always been a pleasure for me, when introducing Roundtable, to know that I am passing along a gift from my mentor.

to use Roundtable in a variety of ways. If it has been used as a race, it might be well to counterbalance the competitive tone created by that format by using it with little or no time pressure. The effectiveness of the Roundtable and Roundrobin often is in the processes they create, rather than in the products.

Simultaneous Roundtable

Sometimes for long answers or where production is a goal, two, three, or even four papers may be sent around simultaneously. For example, a Roundtable on the Food Groups might have one paper representing each of the food groups.

Rallytable

Students work in pairs in groups of four. They pass a paper up and back writing down answers to a problem which has many answers. When time is called they compare their answers with those of the other pair in the team. They conclude two pairs are better than one. Note: Rallytable doubles the participation compared to Sequential Roundtable. Rallytable lends itself to the use of a Venn diagram to categorize responses into three categories: unique to one pair, unique to the other pair, or shared.

Roundrobin is the oral counterpart of Roundtable.

~ See Chapter 12: Information Exchange Structures ~

Toss-A-Question

Toss-A-Question can be used as students within teams to review information and practice skills. They make a ball by wadding up a piece of paper, and then take turns tossing review questions. For example, each time the paper ball is tossed to a student, he or she answers a math question (What is 2 x 4?), and then the student tosses another question to someone else on the team.

Variation:

Rallytoss

The students divide into pairs, each pair with a ball. The pairs then attempt to recite the alphabet as they pass the ball back and forth. As a child passes the ball to his partner, he calls out the next letter. The same procedure can be followed to spell each other's names, animal names, colors, review facts, answer questions which are tossed, and to state synonyms or antonyms. Have the pairs seated on the floor, facing each other. Use a small or lightweight ball.

Guess-the-Fib

Guess-the-Fib can be played either within teams or within the class. When played within teams, students try to fool their teammates; when played within the class, teams try to fool other teams.

The idea is simple. In Guess-the-Fib students state two rather unbelievable facts and one believable fib. They announce all three as facts, and it is the job of the teammates, or other teams to guess which one is the fib.

Finger responses can be used with Guess-the-Fib. Students simply hold up one, two, or three fingers, depending on which statement they believe is the fib.

Variation:

Fact-or-Fiction

In Fact-or-Fiction, students try to find a believable fib or an unbelievable fact, and announce it. The job is to guess if the statement is fact or fiction.

For example, a student might state, "George Washington had wooden teeth which he had trouble controlling."

If students are playing within teams, the other three students think for a moment, consult, and then each one puts a thumb up or down. Students may earn points for how many teammates they have fooled.

If the game is played within the class as a whole, a team announces the statement and allows time for other teams to consult. The team which came up with the statement then announces, "Show your thumbs." Individuals vote with their thumbs --thumbs up for Fact; thumbs down for Fiction. Teams get points based on how many individuals they fooled. Fact-or-Fiction can be played with the rule that teams must vote as a block -- which forces consensus procedures and makes counting easier.

Find-Someone-Who...

Students each receive a worksheet. They mill about the room until the teacher announces, "Find Someone Who Knows." They are to find someone in the class who knows an answer to a question on the worksheet. After interviewing that person, they are to write the answer in their own words. The person must sign off on the worksheet, and the pair part, looking for another person who knows an answer they have not yet written in. They cannot write an answer on their worksheet unless they have "Found Someone Who Knows," interviewed that person, and had the person sign indicating that the answer is correct.

One very nice feature of this structure is that a very weak student who initially knew none of the answers, after filling in one or two answers may assume high status as they become the Someone Who Knows. We owe this structure to *Laurie Robertson* (Consultant, Resources for Teachers.)

Mix-Freeze-Group

This structure is good for review questions only if they have a number for an answer. Students mill about the room. The teacher calls "Freeze." The teacher then asks a question, such as "How many players are there on a baseball team?" Students are to quickly group according to the answer -- in this case they would form groups of nine. If the class does not divide evenly by the answer, the students left over are to go to "Lost and Found," which is by the teacher. The rule is that you cannot go to Lost and Found two times in a row, so on the next question, classmates group first with those from Lost and Found.

Q-Materials

Mix-Freeze-Group is good for review of math facts. Variations in how the questions are asked keep the game interesting. For example, the teacher may ask, "How many are (She claps twice) times (she claps three times) minus (she holds up one finger.)"

With a bit of structuring, Mix-Freeze-Group can be used to practice division and remainders.

For example, have only twenty-one students play while others watch, and then ask a division problem, like, divide by five. Before the students form groups of five, there is a think time and they try to guess what the remainder will be. All the students watching are to state their prediction to a partner.

9. Q-Review

The Q-Matrix, Q-Materials, and Q-Structures include a great many ways of reviewing information. Students can spin dials, roll dice and use dozens of Q-Structures to produce question prompts which are then used as the basis of structured review sessions. The rule is that when students are using the Q-Trix for review, they must make up a question to which they know the answer. See Wiederhold (1991).

Team-Directed Numbered Heads

Students work together to make up questions for the whole class to review. If they are working from a text, team one might take its questions from the first section of the chapter, team two from the second, and so on. They must be instructed on the nature of high consensus questions. For example, the teacher might say the answer must be in the text.

After each team has several questions, the teams, each in turn, lead the class in a round of Numbered Heads Together. For example, Person One on the team gives the quiet signal, gets full attention, and announces the question and the time limit. Person Two gives the quiet signal after the time limit and calls a number. Person Three evaluates the answer. Person Four adds any additional information the team had.

The game can be played for points, but students enjoy it just as a fun review without extrinsic points.

Variation: Students may bring in the questions as part of homework assignment and teams receive points for bringing in questions.

I particularly like Team-Directed Numbered Heads because it has a broad domain of usefulness. As the students make up the questions they are forced toward higher levels of thought: Application, Analysis, Evaluation, Synthesis. As they play the game, they get a good review, usually at the knowledge and comprehension level.

Rotating Review

Topics are written at the top of chart papers which are posted about the room. There are as many topics as teams. (If you have fewer topics, some teams can pair up.) Teams each stand by a topic chart. They have one minute to write as many facts as they can on the topic. The teacher or class timer calls stop and the teams are to rotate to the next topic. They have two minutes to read and discuss what the previous team has written. They can put a question mark by any item with which they disagree or if they have a question. Then they have one minute to write additional information. They then rotate to the next topic.

The procedure is continued until each team rotates back to its initial topic. Individuals are given some time to take notes on the information on the charts.

Choral Response

Choral Response is a traditional structure which can be effective for memory work. At a cue from the teacher, all students say a response aloud, in unison. Often the response is the answer to a question. Sometimes it is just a repeat of what the teacher says. The best part of the structure is the 100% simultaneous participation.

Turn-4-Review

Turn-4-Review makes otherwise boring review material game-like. This structure can be used for any high consensus questions on the overhead, in a textbook, or on a worksheet.

Steps of Turn-4-Review

Step 1. Number Off. Teammates number off, 1 through 4.

Step 2. Turn Over Question Card. Students turn over a Question Card. The card reads: "Teammember 2, Read Question 6." Teammember Two reads Question 6. Students then take a little time for everyone to think about the question, with no talking.

Step 3. Turn Over Answer Card. Students turn over an Answer Card. The card dictates which student will answer the question:

"Teammember 4, Answer the Question." Teammate Four attempts to answer Question 6. Students then take time to think over what was said.

Step 4. Turn Over Check Card. Students turn over a Check Card. This card says which student is to lead the group in checking the validity of the answer of the student who just answered the question: "Teammember 2, Lead the Team in Checking." The checker does not do all the checking. Rather, he or she leads the group in checking. Students as a team consider the answer and decide if it is correct. They may have an answer sheet or text to work with.

Step 5. Turn Over Praise or Help Card.

Students flip over the Praise/Help Card. This card picks a student to either praise the answer if it was correct, or to help the student, if the answer was not correct: "Teammember 1: Lead the team in Praising or Helping." Work with your students when you introduce this skill so they have examples of good praisers and helpers.

If the Check Card or the Praise/Help Card picks the student who has answered, that student praises himself, or picks another student to lead the group in checking the answer.

Step 6. Repeat 2-5. After the first round of Turn-4-Review, students play another round. Steps 2-5 are repeated for each round until all questions are answered.

Turn Leader. On each round, a "Turn Leader" is chosen who turns over the cards and who directs the students in the think time before each card is turned over.

Variation:

Turn-2-Review

To play a fast game, use just two sets of cards: Question Cards and Answer Cards.

Recommendation:

For both Turn-4-Thought and Turn-4-Review, choose one student to be the "Think Time Monitor." The job of this student is to make sure there is at least five good seconds of think time before each card is drawn. This leads to far deeper thinking and more equal participation. ∾

References:

Books:

Wiederhold, Chuck. *Cooperative Learning and Critical Thinking: The Question Matrix.* San Juan Capistrano, CA: Resources for Teachers, Inc., 1991.

Videos:

Numbered Heads Together - Exploring the Structure in Depth. Resources for Teachers, Inc. 1991.

Pairs Check - Exploring the Structure in Depth. Resources for Teachers, Inc. 1991.

Manipulatives:

Turn-4-Learning - bright colored, heavy card stock gameboards and gamepieces for 9 teams, (18 gameboards and 864 gamepieces). Resources for Teachers, Inc. 1991.

Answer Key for Sample Geography Questions:
(See Page 10:19)

1. **True**
2. **a - Florida**
3. **Utah, Colorado, Arizona, New Mexico**
4. **c - Salt Lake City**
5. **Alaska, Hawaii**
6. **False**
7. **Florida, Texas**
8. **Wyoming**
9. **Eastern**
10. **Utah, Colorado, Kansas**
11. **Nevada**
12. **True**
13. **North Dakota, South Dakota, Nebraska**
14. **Alaska**
15. **Missouri, Oklahoma, Texas, Louisiana, Mississippi, Tennessee**
16. **c - Michigan**

Turn-4-Review Gameboard

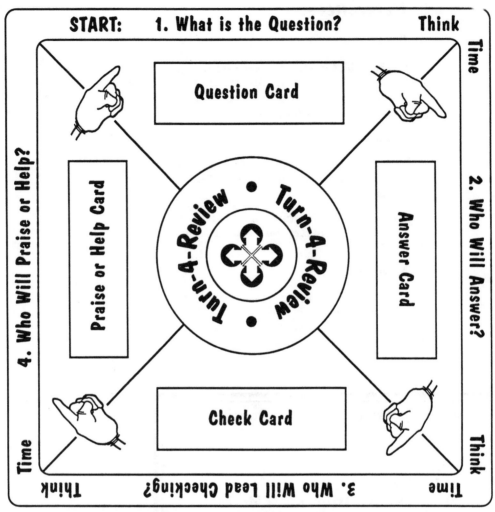

START: 1. What is the Question?   Think

Time

Question Card

2. Who Will Answer?

Answer Card

Think

Time

Check Card

3. Who Will Lead Checking?

Think   Time

4. Who Will Praise or Help?

Praise or Help Card

Turn-4-Review   Turn-4-Review

Start: What is the question?
1. Draw a **Question Card**
2. Read and follow card directions

What is your answer?
1. Have teammates think:
   How would they answer?
2. Draw an **Answer Card**
3. Read and follow card directions

Is the answer correct?
1. Have teammates think:
   Was the answer correct?
2. Draw a **Check Card**
3. Read and follow card directions

How would you praise or help?
1. Have teammates think:
   How would you praise or help?
2. Draw a **Praise or Help Card**
3. Read and follow card cirections. **Start Again!**

Sample Cards

Front:	Question Card	Answer Card	Check Card	Praise or Help Card
Back:	Teammember #1, Read Question #1	Teammember #1, AnswersQuestion #1	Teammember #1, Lead Team in Checking Answer	Teammember #1, Lead Team in Praising or Helping

Spencer Kagan: *Cooperative Learning*©
Publisher: Resources for Teachers , Inc. • 1(800) Wee Co-op

Turn-4-Review: Geography

These are 16 questions on geography to use with Turn-4-Review. The questions may be used while students view the map, and for advanced groups, may be used after students have studied the map.

1. **True or False?** Alaska is the largest state in the United States.

2. The Atlantic Ocean and Gulf of Mexico both border on what state?
   a. Florida
   b. Michigan
   c. Maine

3. Which four states come together to a point?

4. What is the capital of Utah?
   a. Provo
   b. St. George
   c. Salt Lake City

5. What two states are not on the continental United States?

6. **True or False?** Delaware is the smallest state.

7. Which two states span the furthest south of any state in the United States?

8. You are in the Texas Panhandle, and are traveling north. You drive through two states without getting out of your car. You take a rest stop in the next state. In what state are you?

9. The Appalachian Mountain Range expands north and south. In which part of the United States is it - - Eastern or Western?

10. Name three states which have a southern border in a continuous line?

11. Which state is further north - - North Carolina or Nevada?

12. **True or False?** Maine is the only state which borders only one other state.

13. Name the three states which have a continuous western border.

14. Name the state which is furthest west of all the other states.

15. Name the six states which border Arkansas.

16. Lake Michigan, Lake Huron and Lake Erie all surround which state?
    a. Wisconsin
    b. Ohio
    c. Michigan

Sample Content

Turn-4-Review: Geography

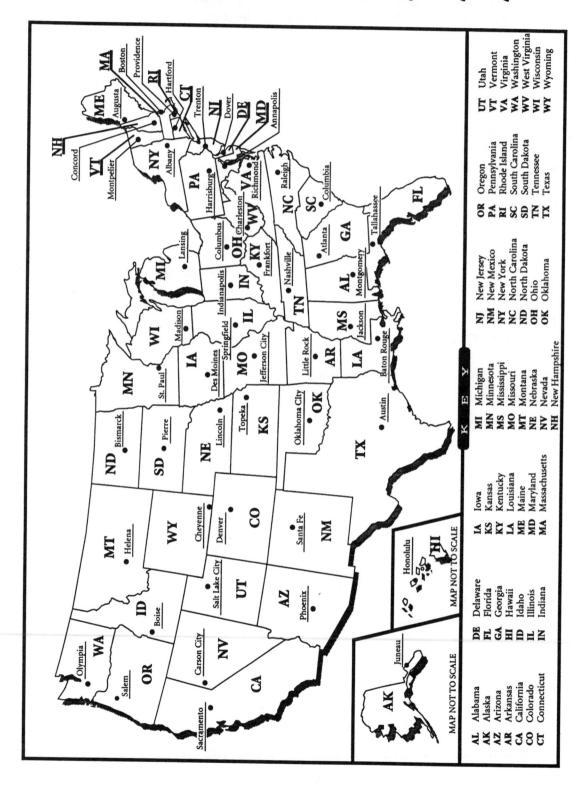

which will ask questions never asked by people. If a question has been asked of a data base similar to a new data base being generated, without being asked, in its free time the computer will ask the question of the new data base. The answer will be stored, ready for some future time when a human thinks of the question and needs the answer!

The sum of our technological information doubles every few years, and the rate at which information doubles is itself quickening logarithmically. The information explosion will continue to expand. In the face of these transformations, memorizing one new fact is of little relative value compared to the ability to question and categorize information and think up new applications for existing information.

Increasingly we will move away from defining educational success exclusively in terms of the quantity of information mastered. Instead, to a large extent, we will define educational success as the ability among students to generate, question, combine, categorize, recategorize, evaluate, and apply information. Secondary will be the content of the information; primary will be thinking skills.

Increasingly we will move away from defining educational success exclusively in terms of the quantity of information mastered. Instead, we will define success as the ability among students to generate, question, combine, categorize, recategorize, evaluate, and apply information. Ability to categorize information becomes a survival tool in the information age. The content of the information will become secondary; primary will be thinking skills — thus, the need for thinking skills structures in our classrooms.

Two forces are converging to make us redefine what we mean by educational success. Ours has become an information-based, high-tech economy. More people are employed in the information segment of our economy than any other, and it is the fastest growing segment of our economy. These two forces, the movement into a high technology and the movement into an information based economy, combine to augment each other: Computers are increasing dramatically our capacity to collect, store, categorize, and analyze information, pushing us to ever higher levels of need with regard to technology. The increased technology, in turn, creates a demand for ever greater sophistication with regard to the use of computers. Computers are on line

The mastery structures are designed to maximize the chances that all students will produce the same answer when asked certain high consensus questions like "How do you spell 'consensus'?" "When was the Civil War fought?" "How many are six sevens?" The thinking skills structures, in contrast are designed to reach the opposite objective: To have students be able to create and exchange novel, unique, set-breaking ideas to low consensus questions such as, "How might our present shift in moral standards be related to economics?" "What might we do as a class to keep the school yard clean?" "Are there ways to apply the laws of supply and demand to make our classroom a happier and more efficient environment?"

Spencer Kagan: *Cooperative Learning*©
Publisher: Resources for Teachers , Inc. • 1(800) Wee Co-op

There are many types of thinking skills. For ease, the thinking skills structures have been divided into six types. See box.

Types of Thinking Skills Structures
I. Generative, Reflective
Structures which promote thought and reflection.
II. Relational Thinking
Structures which have students explore the relation of one piece of information to another.
III. Analytical Thinking
Structures which have students take apart a complex whole, examine its components.
IV. Concept Attainment, Application
Structures which have students induce a general rule or concept from specific examples and/or apply a general rule to specific instances.
V. Categorizing
Structures which have students apply or create categories to sort specific examples.
VI. Question Generation & Response
Structures which have students generate or respond to questions at a range of levels of thought.

I. Generative, Reflective
Pair Discussion

The simplest of all cooperative learning structures is a Pair Discussion. Students may be in traditional rows, or on the rug, or at a learning center, or within their cooperative teams. You simple say, "With a partner, talk over...."

A pair discussion over any low consensus topic is usually better than a team discussion because it produces twice the amount of active participation. (In a group of four, on the average one out of four are talking at a given moment. In groups for two, the ratio is twice as good: one in two are producing language and ideas at any one moment.

The topic for a Pair Discussion can be anything, from contrasting ways of solving math problems, to the reason a science experiment failed to produce the predicted results.

Often following a Pair Discussion, I like to use a Pairs Compare, in which pairs discuss with another pair which ideas they came up with in common and which were unique to each pair. This can be formalized with a Venn Diagram for the group to record ideas.

Team Discussion

A Team Discussion, just like a Pair Discussion, is an unstructured discussion within a group. The only difference is that in a Pair Discussion the group size is two, whereas in a Team Discussion, the group size usually is four.

If students are sitting in groups, it is simple to ask at various times during a lecture or presentation for the students to discuss the topic. For example, before an experiment, the teacher might ask, "What do you think might happen? Talk it over." Following the experiment, "Why do you think the water turned blue? Talk it over." Other introductions to Team Discussion, "What would our world be like today if we had all sources of power but not electricity?" "What do you think cars will be like in twenty years?" Following the Team Discussion, students share their ideas. Thus, Team Discussion is a simple, two step structure: Talk it over; share your ideas.

Think-Pair-Share

Professor *Frank Lyman* and his associates (University of Maryland Howard County Southern Teacher Education Center, MD) have developed a simple but very powerful thinking skills structure, Think-Pair-Share.

In Think-Pair-Share, a problem is posed, students think alone about the question for a specified amount of time, then form pairs to discuss the question with someone in the class, usually a teammate. During Share time, students are called upon to share the answer with the class as a whole.

Think-Pair-Share

1. Problem Posed

2. Think Time

3. Pair Work

4. Share with Class

the topic within their teams rather than one student at a time sharing with the class, there is eight times as much participation. Further, positive interdependence is created among students as students hope others have a correct answer to share. Whenever only one student at a time is to be called upon, there is a high probability of negative interdependence because each student knows that if another student gives and full and correct answer, it decreases the chances of their own opportunity to be recognized.

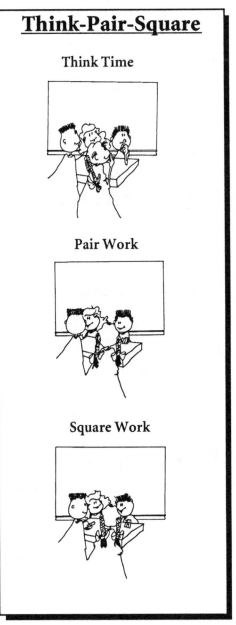

Think-Pair-Square

Think Time

Pair Work

Square Work

Sometimes students are held accountable for listening to their partner because during share time they are called upon to share the answer they heard from their partner.

The Think time may be unstructured, or may be accompanied by guided imagery ("Imagine it was a hot, humid day and you were very thirsty....") or focusing directives ("Be able to come up with at least three ways you could....").

Variations:

By combining different elements, it is possible to create a large number of variations on the basic Think-Pair-Share structure. Some of my favorites include:

Think-Pair-Square

By substituting a Team Discussion for the last step of a Think-Pair-Share, a very different structure is created. If students discuss

There are times when a Think-Pair-Share is the structure of choice, as when you want all students to hear a unique responses of one student, or when you wish to be able to comment on the responses of students or direct the thinking of students. There are more times, however, when the increased active participation and positive interdependence of a Think-Pair-Square makes it the structure of choice.[1]

As with all structures, each member of the Think-Pair- family of structures has its domain of usefulness, and knowing exactly when to choose which comes with extensive practice.

Think-Write-Pair-Compare

There is little individual accountability in a Think-Pair-Share. If students take a moment to jot down their thoughts before sharing them with a partner, and then if pairs take some time to compare with other pairs afterwards, there is more individual and pair accountability.

Think-Build-Square

If students are working with manipulatives, it is powerful to have them work individually to build a solution to a problem before sharing their responses with the group.

Think-Roundrobin

There is greater individual accountability if students are each in turn required to share their thoughts with the group as opposed to a Team Discussion. In a Team Discussion there is usually very unequal participation and some students may not contribute at all. Even a Pair Discussion without structuring can become one student telling the other an answer without equal participation. A Roundrobin ensures participation by all.

Teammates Consult

If you pass out four worksheets per each four-person cooperative team, and tell the students to work cooperatively as they fill out the worksheets, little or no cooperative work will result. Each student will begin work on his or her worksheet, with little or no interaction. It does not matter that you have told the students to work together, the situation created by individual worksheets speaks more powerfully than your words.

And students working alone will not produce as much higher-level thinking as an animated Team Discussion. Individualistic work, each student working at his or her pace, with little or no stimulating interaction over subject matter is how students have been conditioned by the traditional system. They will fall back into that pattern unless it is very clear that they are in a different structure.

One relatively simple, but powerful way of restructuring worksheet work is Teammates Consult.

STEPS OF TEAMMATES CONSULT

Step 1. Pens Down. All teammates put their pens in a pencil holder (tin can, cup, supply basket).

Step 2. Team Discussion. A student reads the first question and students seek the answer from the book and/or by Team Discussion.

Step 3. Check for Agreement. The student on the left of the Reader checks to see that teammates all understand and agree with the answer.

Step 4. Individuals Write. When there is agreement, then all students pick up their own pens and write their answers in their own words.

Step 5. Roles. Students progress to question two. The Checker becomes the new Reader; the person on her left becomes the Checker.

Without the pencil cup and the separate, structured times for Discussion and Writing, the teamwork can degenerate into low-level dictation by the high achiever to the rest of

---

1. The "Square" of a Think-Pair-Square is a Team Discussion, as is the "Heads Together," of Numbered Heads Together. Some teachers like the term "Huddle" rather than "Team Discussion."

the group. Thus, the insistence that the students discuss until everyone knows what he or she wants to write, and then each student writes his/her responses in his/her own words.

Team Statements

Team Statements produce a powerful higher-level synthesis and often produce a depth of thinking which surprises everyone involved.

At first, each person makes an individual statement on a topic, and then the team reaches consensus on one statement which captures the essence from which the individual statements sprang.

My favorite example was a Valentine's Day activity. The teacher passed out little hearts and each student wrote his/her own sentence, beginning, "Love is..." After reading and discussing their individual statements, the teams received a large Valentine and wrote their Team Statement. Students need to be reminded that writing a team statement is not like stringing beads -- it is not one long run-on sentence which combines all four of the individual sentences. Rather it is one sentence which captures the underlying essence.

Many topics are good candidates for Team Statements. Consider the following:
• World War II resulted in...
• Shakespeare's genius was that ...
• Tom Sawyer was...
• Existentialism is...
• Dogs are...

My favorite Team Statement was one produced by a team of teachers during a workshop. They were given the topic: "Cooperative Learning is...." Their statement was,

$$\text{Cooperative Learning} = \text{Learning}^4$$

Note, their Team Statement, which they read as "Cooperative learning is learning, to the fourth power," was shorter than any of their individual statements and did not resemble any of the individual statements. It is the power of the interaction which led the team to settle on a statement which each endorsed more fully than his/her individual statement. We each have a part of the truth; together we can grasp more.

When I do Team Statements, typically I use the following steps:

Step 1. Think Time. Teacher announces the topic and allows at least 20 seconds of Think Time.

Step 2. Pair Discussion. Students pair and discuss their thoughts.

Step 3. Individual Write. Students individually write one sentence on the topic.

Step 4. Roundrobin. Students read their individual sentences, Roundrobin, with no comments.

Step 5. Team Discussion. Teammates discuss the individual sentences, seeking the underlying source from which they sprang.

Step 6. Consensus & Share. Teammates come to consensus on a Team Statement and share that with the class, usually via a simultaneous sharing structure such as Blackboard Share.

Step 7. Team Discussion: Compare Statements. Teammates discuss their statement in relation to the other Team Statements.

Step 8. Team Discussion: Synergy. Teammates discuss the concept of synergy. Was there a release of energy through synthesis? Was the group smarter than any one of us alone?

4S Brainstorming

One of the most effective ways of getting groups to open the doors to creativity is brainstorming. We are all at root creative (look at our dreams); the problem is not in becoming creative, but rather, in getting rid of the blocks. Brainstorming, by setting the censor aside, releases creativity.

An effective format for Brainstorming includes roles. In 4S Brainstorming, each student is assigned a role and corresponding gambits.

"Speed Captain:" The Speed Captain says things like, "Let's get more," "Let's hurry." The Speed Captain puts on the time pressure.

"Super Supporter:" Another student makes sure all ideas are encouraged with no evaluation of ideas. The Super Supporter says things like, "All ideas are great." "Another fantastic idea."[2]

"Chief of Silly:" Having a good percent of silly ideas is very helpful in the flow of ideas, in keeping the tone creative, and in increasing the range of ideas. The silly idea may not be part of a final solution, but may well lead to an idea which is. The Chief of Silly says things like, "Let's have a crazy idea."

"Synergy Guru:" The Synergy Guru encourages the teammates to build on each others ideas, saying things like, "Let's combine those two," or "Let's change that one to...."

Recording Ideas. If each idea is recorded on a separate slip of paper and placed on the table for all to see, it facilitates having students build on each other's ideas, and later categorization and recategorization of ideas. (See Unstructured Sorts).

One student is usually chosen as a Recorder, but a Roundtable works well also so everyone participates in recording the ideas.

II. Relational Thinking

Sequencing
1-Dimensional Puzzles

A comic strip is cut out of the Sunday paper. My favorites for this purpose are Peanuts and Calvin & Hobbs. The comic strip is then Xeroxed, and the copies are cut up into separate panels and placed in an envelope, one per team.

---

2. To make positive statements during brainstorming is contrary to the classical literature on the topic which prohibits evaluative statements. It is my experience, though, after watching hundreds of Brainstorming sessions, that having lots of unconditional positive statements promotes the flow of ideas and increases the range of ideas for more than just having a rule excluding evaluation. This is why, in my recent work, I have changed one of the 4S Brainstorming roles from "Suspend Judgment" to "Super Supporter."

4S Brainstorming

Teammates open the envelope, place the panels of the comic strip face down without examining them, and shuffle them around the table. In turn they then each draw a panel, going around until they have all the panels in their hand, usually one or two each.

Blind Hand

Teammates are allowed to describe their own panels as fully as they can, but they are not allowed to look at the panels of their teammates. When they have agreed on which panel is first in the cartoon, they place it face down on the table. When they have placed them all face down in order, and have

reached consensus, they turn over the cartoon to see if they have sequenced it properly.

Applications:

This simple sequencing structure can be used with a wide range of content -- almost anything which has an ordinal sequence. Some of the many examples are listed in the box.

Content For Sequencing

Science:
Life Cycles
Steps of Mitosis
Steps of Lab Experiment
Seasons

Math:
Steps of a Proof
Size of Unreduced Fractions
Steps of Algorithm (Subtracting Mixed numbers with borrowing)

Social Studies:
Time Line

Language Arts:
Events from Story
Words in Sentence
Sentences in Paragraph
(Topic Sentence, Supporting Sentences, Conclusion)
Paragraphs in Essay
Parts of a Letter
Alphabetize
Dialogue

Other:
Procedures for Shop Class
Recipes
Steps of Dance Routine

2-Dimensional puzzles

When moving to two dimensional sequencing, I drop the blind hand procedure and move to the traditional jigsaw puzzle format with all pieces face up and all hands busy at once.

Any picture can be Xeroxed and cut up into as few or many pieces as you wish, depending on the level of your students. One simple procedure is to mark a four by four grid over one picture and cut it into sixteen pieces. Arrange then the sixteen pieces in random order and tape them down into a square. Xerox the scrambled picture and hand a copy to each team. The teammates are to cut up the pieces and rearrange them in order. See next page for a 4X4 puzzle.

3-Dimensional Puzzles

To get students to work on the relation of parts in three dimensions, I like to use Build-What-I-Write and Formations.

Build-What-I-Write

Begin with two sets of legos, lincoln logs, blocks, or spaghetti and gumdrops for each student. If you used gum drops or jelly beans and spaghetti (my favorite for this activity) make sure the student has two of each color gum drop, so the two sets of construction material is truly identical. Each student needs also one large shopping bags, and a paper and pencil.

Students are to spread out, away from their teammates, at tables or on the floor. They are to work with one set of building materials and to leave an identical set in their paper bag. They have about five to ten minutes to construct something such as a space station, home, playground, or car.

When students have made their masterpieces, time is called and they are not allowed to touch them. They then have about ten to twenty minutes to describe the construction as fully as they can in writing. They are to describe color, shape, and position so fully that someone can replicate the construction identically from just the writing.

When the writing is done, they take the identical set of construction materials out of the bag, set them by the construction, set their written description of what is under the bag by the materials, cover their construction with the paper bag, leaving the second set of building materials and the writing uncovered.

They then trade places with a teammate. They are then each to play Build-What-I-Write. Afterwards they discuss how the writing could be improved so that the contractor could not go wrong!

There is a family of structures like Build-What-I-Write.

~ See Chapter 13: Communication Skills Structures ~

Formations

Another structure which can promote thinking about the relation of parts in three dimensions is formations, which is described in Chapter 9: Classbuilding. One of my favorite Formations is to have students become the solar system:

Spencer Kagan: *Cooperative Learning* ©
Publisher: Resources for Teachers , Inc. • 1(800) Wee Co-op

4X4 Puzzle

Instructions: 1. In your teams cut the picture below into four strips so that each strip has four boxes. 2. Give one strip to each teammate. 3. Take out eight different colored crayons and give two to each teammate. 4. Teammates color the pictures in your strip, using your two colors only. Then cut your strip along the lines to make four boxes. 5. Everyone place your four boxes on the table so everyone can see them all. 6. Each of you can touch only the boxes you colored. You can suggest to teammates where they might move their boxes, but be careful, touch only your own.

Your job, working as a team, is to solve the puzzle!

Picture the earth as four students with backs toward each other, holding hands, walking in a large circle around the sun which is perhaps twenty students holding hands in a circle facing out. Meanwhile the moon -- one student -- is rotating around the earth. Other planets are added until we have a class living solar system. (At first, when students are grasping the idea of the solar system they are informed that what they have done is not to scale. Later they calculate how far the earth would have to be from the sun and how many students they would need to be the sun, earth, and moon if they were to do a formation which was to scale.)

III. Analytical Thinking

The simple generative structures like Think-Pair-Square are used to foster analytic thinking by asking questions which demand analysis. For example, ask students to Think-Write-Pair-Compare all the parts of the body.

Some communication building structures are especially powerful in producing analytic thinking. I debated repeatedly in organizing this book as to whether Same-Different belonged in this section on analytic thinking, or was better placed in the communication skills chapter. Although it is placed among the communication skills structures, it is probably the most powerful structure we have for fostering analytic thinking (See Chapter 13: Communication Skills Structures). To solve Same-Different problems, students must analyze the pictures into their components. The whole family of Draw-What-I-Write structures is very strong also in fostering analytic thinking. The concept attainment structures are powerful also in promoting analytic thinking.

IV. Concept Attainment, Application

The essence of concept attainment approaches is inductive reasoning. Students are given many examples which follow a rule and then are to figure out -- induce -- the rule. This approach is in contrast to a more traditional approach which attempts to teach the rule first. Inductive approaches are generally more powerful because the rule has a meaningful referent in the student's experience and because it is discovered by the learner.

Two-Box Induction

Stage 1. Inducing a Rule. The teacher places items one at a time on the blackboard, in one of two boxes. The items placed in Box 1 differ from the items in Box 2 because the teacher is following a rule. The job of the students is to figure out the rule.

You can use a variety of thinking skills structures as you do Two-Box Induction. For example, place two items on the board like so:

Box 1	Box 2
Tree Branch	*Fork*

Then do a Think-Pair-Share with the students on all possible rules which you are following to distinguish Box 1 and 2 items..

Next add an item to Box 2, like so:

Box 1	Box 2
Tree Branch	*Fork*
	Knife

and ask students to Think for about 10 seconds about all the possible things Box 2 items have in common which make them different from the item in Box 1, and then to have a Team Discussion.

Next I would add an item to Box 1, like so:

Box 1	Box 2
Tree Branch	*Fork*
Block of Wood	*Knife*

and ask students to Think-Write-Share their hypotheses. The Share might be a simultaneous Blackboard Share. The goal would be to get students to generate and explore all possibilities. At this point some hypotheses among students might be:

Hypotheses

Box 1	Box 2
wood	metal
non-utensils	utensils
dull	shiny
more than 1 word	1 word

Each time you add more items to Box 1 and Box 2, use a different cooperative structure or element to promote inductive thought among students. Be sure to have some give-away items at the end so you don't have to tell the students the rule, but rather have them discover the rule. By the end the blackboard might look like:

Box 1	Box 2
Tree Branch	Fork
Block of Wood	Knife
Oil	Titanic
Leaf	Anchor
Boat	Rock
Cork	Brick

And the students will be able to tell you with some certainty that you are dealing with things that float versus those that sink.

Stage 2. Testing the Rule. At that point, go into the second stage of Two-Box Induction. Having induced a rule, the students need to test it. Ask them in their teams to come up with new items to add to Box 1 and Box 2.

Stage 3. Class Consensus. Once the class could generate with ease new predications based on the rule, have them reach consensus on a statement of the rule being followed.

Stage 4. Apply Rule to New Items. Finally, use a structure like Numbered Heads Together to check for understanding at the application level, providing the class new items and asking them to be able to place them.

Variations:

On-the-Line

Items are placed on a line and the nature of the line is induced. (See Box.) With On-the-Line it is usually best to place items in the middle first, and work out to the ends gradually, using a variety of thinking skills structures in the process.

Application

The inductive structures can be used across the curriculum. Some examples:

Math:
Functions (Box 2 numbers = Box 1 number plus 3)
Odd -- Even
Prime -- NonPrime

Language Arts:
Fiction -- NonFiction
Tell -- Show (writing samples)
Adverbs -- Adjectives
Regular Spelling -- Irregular

Science:
Chemical -- Physical Changes
Vertebrates -- Invertebrates
Fact -- Opinion
Conductors -- Nonconductors

Social Studies:
Modern -- Traditional
Western States -- Eastern

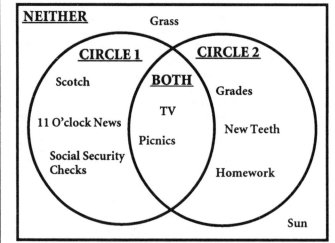

Venn Diagram

NEITHER — Grass

CIRCLE 1 — Scotch, 11 O'clock News, Social Security Checks

BOTH — TV, Picnics

CIRCLE 2 — Grades, New Teeth, Homework

Sun

Venn Diagrams

Items are placed one at a time within a Venn Diagram until the labels for Circle 1 and 2 are induced. See Venn Diagram for Adults (Circle 1) and Kids (Circle 2), in box.

Fire	Blood	School	Ocean	Stream	Ice

Match Mind

Match Mind, designed by *Laurie Robertson* and illustrated by *Celso Rodriguez* (Resources for Teachers, Inc.) is an application of the Match Mine structure to enhance thinking skills. See Match Mine, Chapter 13: Communication Skill Structures.

Match Mind is played by students in grades K to 12, but is used primarily in the elementary grades to develop concepts such as "above, below, beside," "inside, outside," "upper left, lower right," and "Shape Discrimination." On the following pages are the Match Mind Gameboards and Game Pieces for Zim·Zam·Zip, one of the ten Match Mind games included in the Match Mind Kit.

Some individuals will say, "Oh, that is obvious, the boy and dog go together because they both have one limb in the air." Others will say, "The woman and boy go together because she is the mother and has baked a cake for her son." Yet others will say, "The woman and boy go together because they are both humans."

The three types of sorts represent cognitive styles. One person is sorting on the basis of a detail in the picture (limb raised) and is said to have an analytic style. A second person is sorting on the basis of a relationship (mother to son), and is said to have a relational style. The third person is applying a category system to make the sort (human v. non-human) and is said to have a categorical style. All three styles are valuable and students need to have cognitive flexibility enough to see the information in a variety of ways.

Zim • Zam • Zip

Concept: describing "left, right, front" orientation of shapes and rows versus columns

Materials:
1 game board per person
9 pieces per person (cut out rectangle size)

Directions: Duplicate the gameboard twice and the pieces once for each pair who is to play. Both students start with blank gameboards and set of Zim • Zam • Zip game pieces. The *sender* places his/her 9 pieces in the 9 empty boxes on his/her gameboard. The sender selects 1 piece, describes it's characteristics. The *receiver* picks up that piece. Next, the sender describes where it is placed on the gameboard, (3rd row, 2nd column) and the receiver places it where it belongs. The game continues until all 9 pieces have been placed by the receiver. Students check gameboards and celebrate successes.

Zim·Zam·Zip. To play, the pieces and gameboard are duplicated and then students follow the directions provided. See direction card.

V. Categorizing

A great deal of research has investigated the cognitive styles of children and adults, and it turns out that there are a number of dimensions along which people differ. For example, which two of the following three pictures go together?

1. A boy with one hand raised.

2. A dog with paw outstretched.

3. A woman, with an apron on, holding a cake bowl.

Students differ dramatically in their styles. Imagine this: You raid your kitchen drawers and garage cubby holes and come to class with a bag full of objects including can openers, bottle caps, screws, bolts, nuts, old pliers, and small scraps of metal. You then dump the objects all on a table and ask your students to come in one at a time to sort them any way they wish. You would find something remarkable. With some students when you came back after 20 minutes they would be busy at the task. They would take endless time making their category system, because they know that screws must be separated from bolts and among the screws the phillips screws must be separated from standard screws, and within each of those categories the brass and steel screws must be separated....

Two Sets of Zim • Zam • Zip Game Pieces

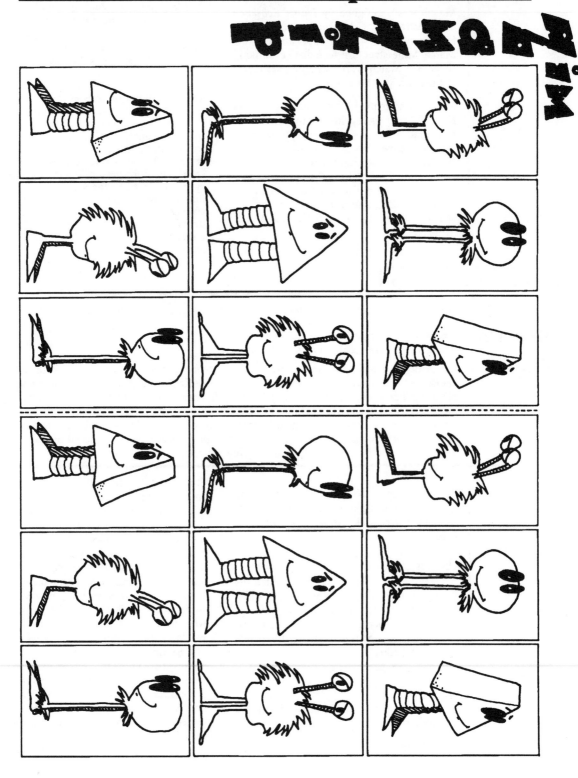

Zim • Zam • Zip Game Board

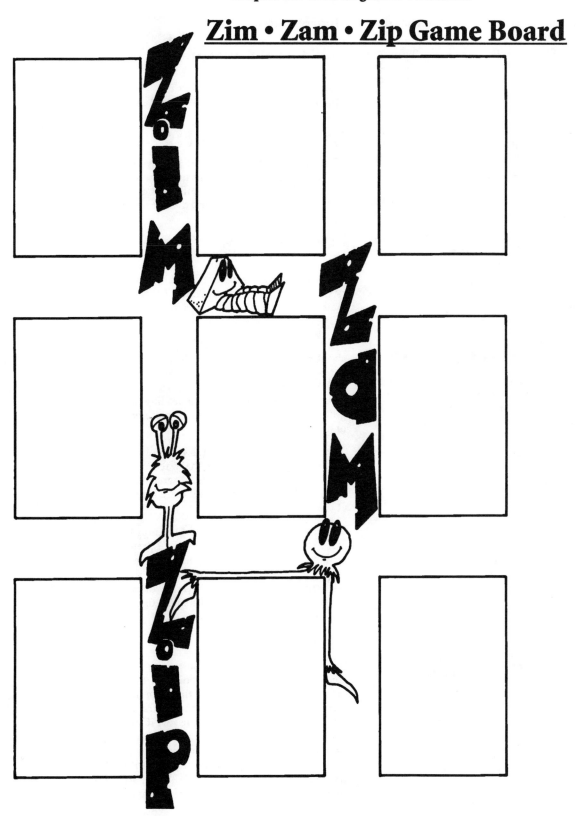

Spencer Kagan: *Cooperative Learning*©
Publisher: Resources for Teachers , Inc. • 1(800) Wee Co-op

With other students the picture is quite different. If you checked one minute after they began you would find the student done. A glance at the table or a question to the student would reveal why: To that student there are two categories, big things and little things.

The former student in our example has a differentiated, analytic style and the latter student has an undifferentiated, global style. It turns out that students who are analytic generally score better on standard tests of intelligence, perform better in school, and have more career success.

We can move students from an undifferentiated, global style if they interact with those who are more differentiated. And in general, by having students interact through categorization structures we can create greater cognitive flexibility which is important to the range of higher-level thinking skills.

Unstructured Sorts

During 4S Brainstorming have students write down each item they generate on a separate slip of paper. Afterwards, have them lay out all the items so they can read them all. Now tell them, "Working together as a team, sort these items into two categories."

Have the students share their category systems through a simultaneous Blackboard Share. Now tell them, "Working as a team, come up with a new category system, one that has not been used by the class yet. Sort so that items which fell together are now separate and items which were separate are in the same category."

Repeat this procedure several times, each time listing all the category systems generated, and instructing the teams to come up with yet new ones.

Result: Students get a cognitive stretch. No matter what their cognitive style, students are pushed to see the world differently and end up more flexible and differentiated.

The content for Unstructured Sorts can be anything, including:
• Events from a story
• Vocabulary or Spelling Words
• History events
• Classmates
• Historical or Fictional Characters
• Books
• Animals
• Pictures from magazines

Structured Sorts

Structured sorts provide the category system and ask students to place items using the system. For example, the students may draw and label a Venn Diagram, and then be given a list of items to sort.

I like the following way to implement a Structured Sort:

Students either draw or are given the category system such as a Venn Diagram, Tree Diagram, 2 x 2 matrix, agree -- disagree line, or a One & All window.

They are then given a sheet of paper with about sixteen items to sort, in boxes. They cut out the items and distribute them, four to a teammate. They then do four rounds of Roundtable, each one in turn leading the group in a discussion of where to place one of his/her items.

The students know no item is to be placed unless all agree, and if more that a few minutes is spent on one item without agreement, it is set aside to be dealt with if there is time at the end.

Rather than just using direct instruction to teach students the category systems, I prefer an inductive approach. Categorizing an example of an inductive lesson to have students acquire the concept of a variety of category systems is provided in Chapter 20: Co-op Lesson Planning.

People Sorts

One variation of Structured Sorts is to give students cards representing items and then have them place themselves in the room in a giant Venn diagram or other sorting frame. Corners can be used as a People sort if students are assigned attributes, such as being words, historical characters, art masterpieces, and so on. Once they are familiar with who they are in their new role, they sort themselves according to teacher determined category system, and sorting and resorting according to new category systems can be the stepping off place for a discussion.

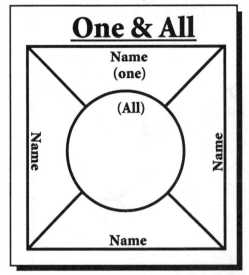

One & All

One & All is a simple framework for discovering similarities and differences, developed by *Wayne* and *Karen Trainor*. As a teambuilder, students would place items which are true of all of them in the center and items which are true of one, but not all of them in the outside segments. One & All can be used also for comparing and contrasting books, characters in books, animals, plants, countries, and math factors. See box.

Team Word Webbing

Word-Webbing, Semantic Maps, Clustering, Chains, Spider Maps, and Concept Maps, are a powerful set of tools in concept development and exchange.

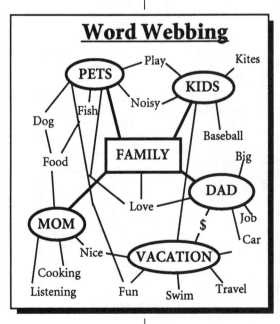

Give each student a different color pen or marker. Give the team one larger poster sized piece of butcher paper. Have them write the topic in the center, not too large (in a rectangle), let them do a round of Roundtable on the Core Concepts (in ovals), and then let them free-for-all -- each adding Core Concepts, Supporting Elements, as they feel the impulse.

The completed Word-Web provides a natural tool for assessing group functioning. Because each student has written in only one color and the color code is placed at the bottom of the Word Web, it is easy to see the type of contribution made by each team member.

For example, if you observed a core concept written in one color, and all the supporting details also in that one color, and no bridges are made from that concept or it's supporting elements to other concepts, and the color is not found anywhere else on the Word Web, there is a pretty good chance you are dealing with a cognitive and perhaps social isolate. On the other hand, if you find the four colors all over the Word Web, you can bet you have a team whose members relate to each other's ideas. The completed Word Web is also a natural tool for assessing cognitive style. You may find some students who contribute only bridges (Relational Thinkers), others who contribute only core concepts (Global Thinkers), and yet others who write in mostly supporting elements (Analytic Thinkers). You can give all the students a cognitive stretch by having them make up four role cards (Core Concept Captain, Supporting Element Engineer 1, Supporting Element Engineer 2, and Bridge Builder), assigning the roles within teams randomly, and then rotating the roles periodically while the students make the Word Web.

The Core Concept Captain is not allowed to contribute a new core concept unless the team reaches consensus that it truly is a core concept rather than just a supporting element. For example, if we were to do a Word Web on "Cooperative Learning," as a team we would be in trouble if we wrote down "Think-Pair-Share" as a core concept -- we would have to make dozens of core concepts. "Think-Pair-Share" is a supporting element in a core concept called "Structures."

Maps and Chains

Semantic Maps, Spider Maps, Chains, and Concept maps all differ from Word Webbs. For more details on various kinds of mapping see (Basin, 1974, Alexander eat ad, 1983, Stahl & Venezuela,1986). Wiederhold (1991) provides discussion of Spider Maps, Chains, and Concept maps.

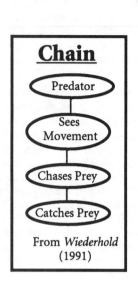

Chain

- Predator
- Sees Movement
- Chases Prey
- Catches Prey

From *Wiederhold* (1991)

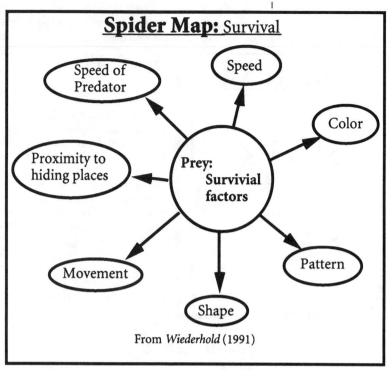

Spider Map: Survival

Prey: Survivial factors

- Speed of Predator
- Speed
- Color
- Proximity to hiding places
- Movement
- Shape
- Pattern

From *Wiederhold* (1991)

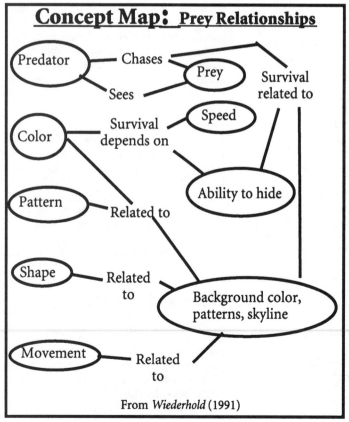

Concept Map: Prey Relationships

Predator — Chases — Prey
Sees
Survival related to
Survival depends on — Speed
Color
Pattern — Related to
Ability to hide
Shape — Related to
Background color, patterns, skyline
Movement — Related to

From *Wiederhold* (1991)

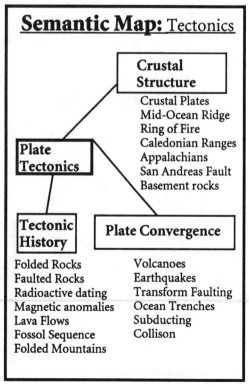

Semantic Map: Tectonics

Crustal Structure
Crustal Plates
Mid-Ocean Ridge
Ring of Fire
Caledonian Ranges
Appalachians
San Andreas Fault
Basement rocks

Plate Tectonics

Tectonic History
Folded Rocks
Faulted Rocks
Radioactive dating
Magnetic anomalies
Lava Flows
Fossol Sequence
Folded Mountains

Plate Convergence
Volcanoes
Earthquakes
Transform Faulting
Ocean Trenches
Subducting
Collison

	EVENT	SITUATION	CHOICE	PERSON	REASON	MEANS
PRESENT	1. What Is?	2. Where/ When Is?	3. Which Is?	4. Who Is?	5. Why Is?	6. How Is?
PAST	7. What Did?	8. Where/ When Did?	9. Which Did?	10. Who Did?	11. Why Did?	12. How Did?
POSSIBILITY	13. What Can?	14. Where/ When Can?	15. Which Can?	16. Who Can?	17. Why Can?	18. How Can?
PROBABILITY	19. What Would?	20. Where/ When Would?	21. Which Would?	22. Who Would?	23. Why Would?	24. How Would?
PREDICTION	25. What Will?	26. Where/ When Will?	27. Which Will?	28. Who Will?	29. Why Will?	30. How Will?
IMAGINATION	31. What Might?	32. Where/ When Might?	33. Which Might?	34. Who Might?	35. Why Might?	36. How Might?

VI. Question Generation & Response

Q-Trix

A remarkable set of set of structures, materials, and student checklists have been developed to empower students to generate and answer questions at the full range of cognitive processing. This approach to student question generation is based on the Question Matrix, from which come a variety of Q-Materials, including, Q-Dice, Q-Spinners, Q-Strips, Q-Chips, and Quadrant Cards. By the roll of the dice or the spin of a spinner, question prompts are produced and students generate questions to ask of fellow students. These Q-Materials are given to students to use within specially designed cooperative learning structures, called the Q-Struc-

tures. Chuck Wiederhold (1991) details over two dozen "Q-Structures," including Tic-Tac-Q, Roundtable Question, and Quad-Question. Many of the structures are adaptations of the simple cooperative learning structures provided in this book. Along with the structures are Student Checklists so students can run themselves through the structures.

Let's look at an example, "Two-Way Q-Interview. Students are in pairs and each pair is provided question generation material such as the Q-Dice, and a checklist for Two-Way Q-Interview.

Students roll the dice and generate either a True Question (one for which they do not have an answer) or a Review Question (one for which they have an answer.) Following the checklist, they then write their question, ask a partner, wait for an answer, paraphrase the partner's answer, praise

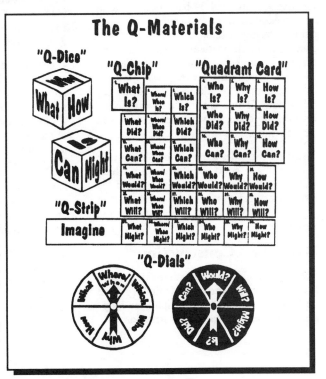

The Q-Materials

Spencer Kagan: *Cooperative Learning*©
Publisher: Resources for Teachers , Inc. • 1(800) Wee Co-op

the partner's answer, augment the answer, and then reverse roles.

The teacher can determine the level of thought of students by deciding on which materials are to be used, or how the materials are to be used. For example, if the students are to explore the characters of a book, the teacher might say, "Take out the Person Q-Strip to generate your questions." Student questioning would then be limited to: Who Is? Who Did? Who Can? Who Would? Who Will? and Who Might? Or if the teacher wanted to focus on developing imagination, he/she might say, "Set one of your Q-Dice to 'Might.' To generate the questions, we will spin only the other die." The questions which students would ask each other then would be: What might? Where might? When might? Which might? Who might? Why might? and How might?

Blooming Worksheets

Worksheet work has gotten a bad name. And rightly so, at least the way it is usually structured in classrooms. Hours of boring worksheets -- students working alone on question after question at the knowledge and comprehension level -- have done a great deal to extinguish the excitement with which students come to school. Blooming Worksheets are an alternative. After working on them a few times, students show excitement when they are told their team will have another Blooming Worksheet. Students say things like, "Those are the fun worksheets," or "Oh, those are the worksheets where you have to think."

There are two sides to good worksheet work: (1) creating a good worksheet, one which will stimulate thought and learning, and (2) structuring good worksheet work within teams. Let's look first at how to make good worksheets.

Worksheet Construction

Teachers are not familiar with making worksheets for groups, and on their first try often go wrong. Here are six principles for cooperative learning worksheet construction:

1. Clarity. If there is any lack of clarity in a question, the group will spend its time debating what is being asked rather than in determining the best answer. Be specific. If the text lists five reasons for an event, ask in the question, "What were five reasons for...?" If you don't, you may have some groups stopping after one answer, and other groups debating the merits of additional answers.

2. Group Language. Don't forget the worksheet is answered and studied by groups. Questions like, "What is the most important...?" and "How do you explain...?" are out. There is no one "you" in a group and members will not always agree. Questions like, "List three important..." and "List three explanations of..." are in. Otherwise team discussion, evaluation, and information seeking can degenerate into debate, disagreement, and power plays.

3. Difficulty Ordering. Easiest questions come first. Otherwise a group can get hung-up on a tough question and not finish. Begin the worksheet with search and find type questions that the lowest level students should answer correctly given time to search the text. Key words here are Find, Name, When, List, etc. Move from knowledge and comprehension to application and analysis. Key words are Compare, Contrast, Use, Divide, etc. Finally move to Synthesis and Evaluation with questions beginning with Formulate, Create, Criticize, and Prioritize.

4. Open-Ended Last Questions. As a management device, it is important that quick groups have something to work on while slower groups finish up. So make the last worksheet question something like, "Name as many reasons for ..." "List all the advantages and disadvantages of ..." or "Try to perfect a plan for ..."

5. Format for Thought. How a worksheet is formatted determines the amount and kind of thought it will produce. Contrast the two worksheets in the box below.

In the worksheet without the formatting, students might answer, "It was smaller," or "There were Indians in it." With the formatting, and the open ended last question, a rich response is pulled.

Formatting a Worksheet for Thought

Worksheet: 1   (Weak Format)
How was an Indian Village different from Huron?

_____

_____

Worksheet: 2   (Stronger Format)
How was an Indian Village different from Huron?

Indian Village   **Huron**

| Size |

- - - - - - - - - - - - - - -   - - - - - - - - - - - - - - - -

- - - - - - - - - - - - - - -   - - - - - - - - - - - - - - - -

| Houses |

- - - - - - - - - - - - - - -   - - - - - - - - - - - - - - - -

- - - - - - - - - - - - - - -   - - - - - - - - - - - - - - - -

| Family Life |

- - - - - - - - - - - - - - -   - - - - - - - - - - - - - - - -

- - - - - - - - - - - - - - -   - - - - - - - - - - - - - - - -

Fill in other differences below. Consider foods, religion, cooking....
(use back to write more)

[   ]

- - - - - - - - - - - - - - -   - - - - - - - - - - - - - - - -

- - - - - - - - - - - - - - -   - - - - - - - - - - - - - - - -

[   ]

- - - - - - - - - - - - - - -   - - - - - - - - - - - - - - - -

- - - - - - - - - - - - - - -   - - - - - - - - - - - - - - - -

6. Blooming Worksheets. Use Bloom's Taxonomy to insure that your worksheet questions cover the range of cognitive complexity. A good worksheet will have something for everyone: Questions even the lowest achiever can answer on his or her own, and questions which will stimulate the highest achiever.

USING BLOOM'S TAXONOMY FOR WORKSHEET CONSTRUCTION

Worksheet questions should stimulate the range of cognitive skills. Choosing questions from each of the levels of Bloom's Taxonomy makes for a stimulating worksheet. Here are the levels:

1. Knowledge. Recall or recognize information. *Recall, define, recognize, identify... • Who was...? What was?*

2. Comprehension. Organize learned material, rephrase it, describe it in his/her own words. *Describe, compare, illustrate, rephrase, explain, contrast...... • Why was...? What was the main idea of....?*

3. Application. Use previously learned material to solve a problem. *Apply, classify, choose, use, select, solve... • Use the principle of supply and demand to explain........? • Which of the following statements is an over-generalization....?*

Application questions make particularly good worksheet questions. For example, the text may give an example of Pavlov conditioning dogs with meat powder associated with the sound of a bell. Your worksheet may refer students to that portion of the text, but ask them to explain why a puff of air to the eye following a touch on their tails will lead cats to blink when their tails are touched. Having students **apply** the text information to solve new problems is one of the best ways to lead them to a deep and useful learning.

4. Analysis. Identify reasons, causes, and motives; consider available evidence to reach a conclusion, inference, or generalization; analyze a conclusion, inference, or generalization to find supporting evidence. *Analyze, identify cause, infer, deduce, detect.... • Which was the cause of....? What can be concluded from...? • Provide evidence for...*

5. Synthesis. Combine ideas or related information; produce original communications, make predictions based on several bits of information, solve a problem using several sources. *Write, design, plan, construct, combine, develop..... • Construct a plan to satisfy the needs of all three .... • Combine the ideas of Locke and Hobbs in an expanded view of...*

6. Evaluation. Judge the merits of an idea, solution, or esthetic work. *Judge, argue, appraise, criticize...... • How good, beautiful, wise.....? Which is better........?*

Note: Evaluation questions are important but difficult to adopt to group language. Instead of asking, "Which is better," ask, "List the positive and negative aspects of the two alternatives." That way input from students, who have both positive and negative evaluations, can be incorporated.

BLOOM'S TAXONOMY

Knowledge statements ask the student to recite the pledge.
Example: "Say the pledge."

Comprehension statements ask the student to explain the meaning of words contained in the pledge.
Example: "Explain what indivisible, liberty, and justice mean."

Application statements ask the student to apply understandings.
Example: "Create your own pledge to something you believe in."

Analysis statements ask the student to interpret word meanings in relation to context.
Example: "Discuss the meaning of 'and to the Republic for which it stands' in terms of its importance to the pledge."

Synthesis statements ask the student to apply concepts in a new setting.
Example: "Write a contract between yourself and a friend that includes an allegiance to a symbol that stands for something you both believe in."

Evaluation statements ask the student to judge the relative merits of the content and concepts contained in the subject.
Example: "Describe the purpose of the pledge and assess how well it achieves that purpose. Suggest improvements."

From *Wiederhold* (1991)

Sample Blooming Worksheet

On the Taxonomy -- for Adults

1. Name the six levels of Bloom's Taxonomy.

2. Write a sample question for each of the six levels. Use cooperative learning theory for content.

3. Label each of these six questions as to primary level of the taxonomy.

4. Which levels of thought are involved in question 3 besides application?

5. Create a question on Bloom's taxonomy which combines all six levels of thought.

6. Which of the six levels of thought is most important to stimulate? List reasons or write an essay to defend your position.

On Patterns -- for K

(Children work in pairs on the worksheets; one child has a blue and yellow crayon, the other has a red and green crayon. Each child works with his own crayons only. For a sponge, when done, children work on an Indian bead necklace on a pattern of their choice.)

Finish the Pattern:

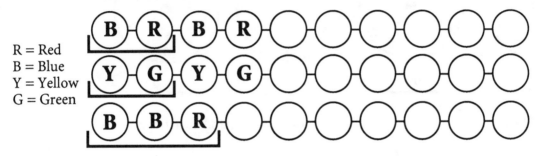

R = Red
B = Blue
Y = Yellow
G = Green

Make the Pattern:

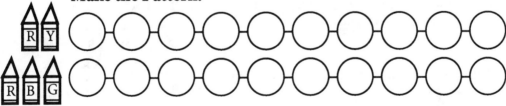

Is It a Pattern:

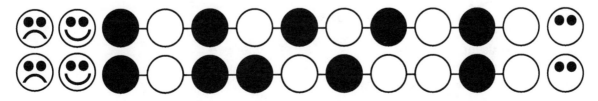

Spencer Kagan: *Cooperative Learning* ©
Publisher: Resources for Teachers , Inc. • 1(800) Wee Co-op

Just In Time

Knowledge: (Please circle one)

How many minutes in one hour?	30	40	50	60
How many minutes in a half hour?	30	40	50	60
The big hand points to the	minutes	hours	seconds	
The small hand points to the	minutes	hours	seconds	

Comprehension: (Please write the time)

_____   _____   _____

Application: (Please make the clock show the time)

9:00   1:00   7:00   11:00

Analysis: (Please circle one)

There are 24 hours in one day, how many times does the hour hand have to go all the way around the clock in one day?

24   12   2   6

Synthesis:

Juan went to Tony's house at 1:00. He stayed for 2 hours. Make a clock to show when Juan returned home.

Evaluation: Which clock is easier to read? Color it green.

   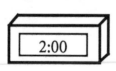

2:00

Sponge: Discuss what time your team members:
Go to bed
Wake up
Eat dinner
What is your favorite time of the day? Why?

Spencer Kagan: *Cooperative Learning*©
Publisher: Resources for Teachers , Inc. • 1(800) Wee Co-op

Turn-4-Thought

Turn-4-Thought

Turn-4-Thought is one of the two learning games which come in the Turn-4-Learning Kit (Kagan, 1991).

Turn-4-Thought can be used to stimulate thinking about any sixteen low consensus questions.

Step 1. Number Off. Teammates number off, 1 through 4.

Step 2. Turn Over Question Card. Students turn over a Question Card. The card reads: "Teammember 2, Read Question 6." Teammember Two reads Question 6. Students then take a little time for everyone to think about the question, with no talking.

Step 3. Turn Over Answer Card. Students turn over an Answer Card. The card dictates which student will answer the question: "Teammember 4, Answer the Question." Teammate Four attempts to answer Question 6. Students then take time to think over what was said.

Step 4. Turn Over Paraphrase & Praise Card. Students turn over a Paraphrase & Praise card. This card says which student is to paraphrase and praise the student who just answered the question: "Teammember 2, Paraphrase & Praise."

After the paraphrase and praise, students consider the answer and decide if they can augment the answer.

Step 5. Turn Over Augment Card. Students turn over an Augment Card. This card picks a student to add to the question, if possible: "Teammember 1: Add if you can." After the student has augmented if they can, any other student can augment if they wish, and students are encouraged to engage in a discussion of the question.

As in Turn-4-Review, if a card tells a student to praise or augment himself, the student is encouraged to do so, praising or augmenting their own answer!

Turn Leader. On each round, a "Turn Leader" is chosen who turns over the cards and who directs the students in the think time before each card is turned over.

Variation:

Turn-2-Think

To play a fast game, use just two sets of cards: Question Cards and Answer Cards.

References:

Alexander, C., Cowell, J., Maestre, T., Zimmerman, N. *Mapping Insights.* Alameda, CA: Learning Insights, 1983.

Buzan, Tony. *Use Both Sides of Your Brain.* NY: E.P. Dutton, 1974.

Davidson, N., Worsham, T. *Enhancing Thinking Through Cooperative Learning.* Sacramento, NY: Columbia University, Teachers College Press, 1992.

Stahl, S., Vancil, S. *The Reading Teacher.* Oct., 1986, p. 63.

Wiederhold, Chuck. *Cooperative Learning and Critical Thinking: The Question Matrix.* San Juan Capistrano, CA: Resources for Teachers, Inc., 1991.

Materials:

Kagan, Spencer *Turn-4-Learning.* San Juan Capistrano, CA: Resources for Teachers, Inc., 1991.

Robertson, L., Rodriguez, C. *Match Mind.* San Juan Capistrano, CA: Resources for Teachers, Inc., 1991.

Wiederhold, Chuck. *The Q Materials Packet.* San Juan Capistrano, CA: Resources for Teachers, Inc., 1991. ᗧ

Turn-4-Thought Gameboard

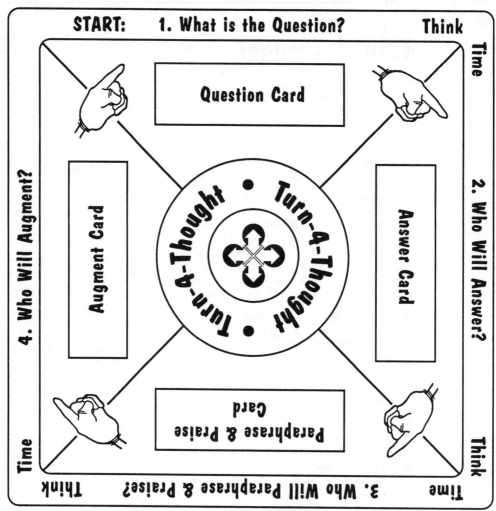

Start: **What is the question?**
1. Draw a **Question Card**
2. Read and follow card directions

What is your answer?
1. Have teams think:
   What is their answer?
2. Draw an **Answer Card**
3. Read and follow card directions

How would you paraphrase & praise?
1. Have teammates think:
   How would they paraphrase & praise?
2. Draw a **Paraphrase and Praise Card**
3. Read and follow card directions

What can you add?
1. Have teammates think:
   What can they add?
2. Draw an **Augment Card**
3. Read and follow card directions
4. Lead teammates in discussing the question. **Start Again!**

Sample Cards

Front: **Question Card**	**Answer Card**	**Paraphrase & Praise Card**	**Augment Card**
Back: Teammember #1, Read Question #1	Teammember #1, AnswerQuestion #1	Teammember #1, Paraphrase & Praise	Teammember #1, Add if You Can

Spencer Kagan: *Cooperative Learning*©
Publisher: Resources for Teachers , Inc. • 1(800) Wee Co-op

Sample Content for Turn-4-Thought:

Story Character

These are 16 generic questions on character(s) to use after reading any piece of literature. They were generated using the Q-Matrix and were written by Christina Chapman, Arthur Lopez, and Kim Vincent (LA County Unified School District, Los Angeles, CA).

1. What Did the main character do to make you like or dislike him/her?

2. What Is one color that describes the main character and why?

3. What Can you say about the main character's family life?

4. Where Can you find an example of a problem the character had that you also have faced in your life?

5. How Is the role of the supporting character(s) important to the story?

6. How Did the character change/grow from the beginning to the end?

7. Why Is the main character like or unlike you?

8. Who Did the character go to for support and understanding?

9. What Would happen if the main character was of the opposite sex or another species?

10. What Might the main character have done in the beginning to change the outcome of the story?

11. What Will happen to the character in a sequel to the book?

12. Where Will the main character be 20 years from now?

13. Who Might be able to replace the main character from your favorite animated show?

14. How Might you describe the character to a blind person?

15. Why Would you want to be or not be the character's friend?

16. How Would the character(s) be different if the type of literature was fiction or nonfiction?

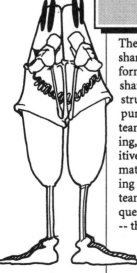

There are two main types of information sharing structures: Structures for sharing information within teams, and structures for sharing information among teams. These structures serve a number of instructional purposes. Sharing information among teammates is central to teambuilding, tutoring, concept development, and creating positive peer response groups. Sharing information among teams is central to classbuilding as well as higher level thinking. As each team shares a different answer to a thought question, their answer challenges -- stretches -- the thinking within other teams.

More people are employed today in the the information segment of our economy than any other. That is, they spend their time, generating, analyzing, and communicating information. And it is the fastest growing segment of our economy. As students in cooperative learning experience the range of ways to share information, they are preparing for the world of the future.

The traditional approach to sharing information has been to call on one student at a time to speak. This approach violates the simultaneity principle. To have each student in the class share for two minutes in this approach would take an hour. Simultaneous sharing structures can accomplish the same goal in two or three minutes.

Sharing Among Teammates
Roundrobin

Roundrobin is the oral counterpart of Roundtable: Students simply take turns stating answers or ideas, without recording them. Roundrobin can be used with children too young to write or when participation rather than a product is the goal. Roundrobin for older students sometimes is called a Sharearound.

Variation:
Rallyrobin

Students form pairs within the team and take turns with their partner sharing ideas back and forth. Afterwards, the pairs discuss which ideas came up in both pairs and which ideas were unique to one or the other pair.

APPLICATIONS:

Informally, Roundtable or Roundrobin often can be used as one-time activities to introduce or provide an anticipatory set for a lesson. For practice and mastery, students take turns contributing to a worksheet. At very young ages this may amount to each child marking one letter among many distracter letters, or placing one item in a basket which is passed around the table.

The structures can be used in just about any subject at any grade level. Some examples follow:

Social Studies: For a unit on the western movement, the teacher might have students do a Roundtable listing all the items settlers would need for the trip.

Math: Students might Roundtable possible ways of dividing ten items, list prime numbers, equivalent fractions, or complementary angles.

Grammar: Students can Roundtable nouns, past tense verbs, or exclamatory sentences.

Writing: Roundrobin is an excellent pre-writing structure -- give each team a story starter and let them Roundrobin a story.

Teambuilding: Form 3 letter words from "TEAMWORK," make new words from "FUN" by changing one word at a time. List

Spencer Kagan: *Cooperative Learning* ©
Publisher: Resources for Teachers , Inc. • 1(800) Wee Co-op

foods beginning with an A food, like Apple; B food, like Banana; C food like........

Social Skill: List praisers (and then place a check mark by those you use during discussion today); Roundtable gambits to use to encourage participation from the shy student.

Review: Roundtable facts we learned in yesterday's lesson.

OUTCOMES:

Teams pull together when doing Roundtable; helping increases. Following Roundtable and Roundrobin, students are more likely to seek participation of all members, even in situations in which full participation is not structured. Roundtable and Roundrobin are very effective in creating a positive team identity and a willingness to work in teams. They can be used to overcome initial resistance to working in teams which is often found in desegregated classrooms, especially at the secondary level.

Team Interview

A Team Interview is like a Roundrobin, with one exception: Each student has an allotted amount of time, and teammates ask that student questions. Often the student who is "up" stands. Team Interviews are excellent for getting acquainted and for having students identify with a character from history or literature as they are interviewed in role.

I like the rule that "If you get a question you prefer not to answer, answer a question you wish you had gotten."

Team Interview was developed by *Jeanne Stone* (Consultant, Resources for Teachers, Inc.).

Three-Step Interview

Three Step Interview is another simple information sharing structure. It consists of three steps and works best in groups of four, but can be adapted for larger or smaller groups. In Step 1, students are in pairs; one is the interviewer, the other the interviewee. In Step 2, the students reverse roles. In Step

3, students do a Roundrobin, each one in turn sharing with the team what they learned in the interview.

The content of the interview can be anything. Often interview is used to have students relate personal experiences on a topic related to the learning unit; it is thus an excellent method of creating a strong anticipatory set for learning more about something of interest.

Where in the Lesson?

For Anticipatory Set: "What do you most want to learn about this topic?" "What experience have you had with...?" "When in your life would you find it useful to...?"

For Closure: Interviews are often good near the end of a lesson to get closure. Topics: "What did you learn from the lesson?" "What would you like to know more about?" "How will you use what you have learned?"

To Reinforce Homework: Interviews on the night's reading. What did you find most interesting? Difficult?

APPLICATIONS:

For Social Studies: If the topic is the western movement, the interview topic one day might be "Have you moved, and what was it like?" The next day students might interview each other regarding what they would bring if they were pioneers about to make the western trip. Interviews on current events might include, interviews about articles students have read and interviews on their opinions about current events. Each student on the team may be assigned a different type of current event -- local news, state, national, and international.

For Math: Interviews on how problems were solved, how children divide their day (before a division unit); how adults use a certain kind of math skill (preceded by a homework assignment of students interviewing adults); "Which homework problem did you find most difficult...?"

For Literature: Interviews on favorite characters, books, stories. Interviews in role, like, "How do you feel Huck Finn as you are drifting on the raft?" "Have you ever been away from home?" Interviews on topics re-

3-Step Interview

Variation

For Groups of Three

For groups of three, at each of the three steps of Three-Step Interview, two teammembers interview a third.

lated to the theme of the literature; if the theme were death, several days of interview might be in order. Day 1: "Something important you have lost." Day 2: "Where were you when the Challenger exploded?" Day 3. "Have you ever had a pet die?" Day 3. "How does your family deal with death?"

For Grammar: Practice the past, or future tense by directing the interview toward past or future events. Practice exclamations, or questions.

For Science: Interviews on personal hypothesis. On revision of hypothesis. On what/how the student might test a hypothesis. Interviews in role: "How do you feel, Einstein?"

Associated Social Skills

Interview might well be associated with lessons on elements of active listening such as non-verbal and verbal modes of communicating interest, how to ask open-ended questions, and how to follow the lead of the interviewee. One effective way of introducing those skills is for the teacher to role-play good and poor listening skills as she/he interviews a student, and then to have students in groups answer questions like, "How was the interviewee feeling each time? How much information was shared each time?" For example, to introduce the importance of open ended questions, the teacher would first interview a student by asking closed questions like, "Did you go to the beach this weekend? Did your family go on a trip this weekend? Did you have any friends stay at your house this weekend?" Following this "yes/no" session, the teacher might say, "That was Interview 1. Now I am going to do something different, watch and listen

Three Step-Interview

Step 1: One Way Interview

Step 2: The Reverse

Step 3: Roundrobin

#1 Shares

#2 Shares

#3 Shares

#4 Shares

carefully so you can discuss the difference between Interview 1 and Interview 2." The teacher would then ask open-ended questions, following the lead of the student: "How did your weekend go?" (Student says something about what they did for fun, for example, fishing). "Oh, that's interesting, "Tell me more about fishing -- what do you like best and least about it?" After several open-ended questions which follow the lead of the student, the teacher would turn the discussion over to the groups, asking, "What was different about Interview 1 and 2? How did the student feel each time? How much information was shared each time?"

Variations:
Six Step Interview

Six-Step Interview is a variation on Three-Step Interview for shy and limited English proficient students. Shy students and those just beginning to acquire English find it impossible to talk to a whole class and difficult to talk to three others. Many of these students become quite fluent if allowed to talk to just one other. A variation of Interview which allows that is Six-Step Interview.

In the first two steps of Six-Step Interview, A interviews B, while C interviews D and then the students switch roles so the interviewer in each pair is interviewed. Next the students turn to a new partner and each in turn shares what they have learned, steps I call Gossip and Gossip. In the final two steps, the new partners interview each other. Six-Step Interview boils down to Interview, Interview, Gossip, Gossip, Interview Interview, as pictured.

Six-Step Interview is good if the objective is language acquisition. Six-Step Interview allows practice of expressive skills. In the last step, students are interviewed on the same topic a second time, allowing a practice opportunity not possible in Three-Step Interview. Also, they never have to speak to more than one person at a time.

Four-Step Interview

Four-Step Interview is a variation for the very young. Young children have a hard time remembering what their partners have told them especially if they are interviewed about themselves before they have a chance to share what they have just heard. A variation which solves this problem is Four-Step Interview:

Step 1. One Way Interview. In pairs, one student interviews the other.

Step 2. Two Share. The two interviewers tell the group what they have just learned.

Step 3. The Reverse. Pairs reform and the interviewer becomes the interviewee.

Step 4. Two Share. The two new interviewers tell the group what they have just learned.

Six-Step Interview

Step 1: Interview	**Step 2: Interview**
Step 3: Gossip	**Step 4: Gossip**
Step 5: Interview	**Step 6: Interview**

Spencer Kagan: *Cooperative Learning*©
Publisher: Resources for Teachers , Inc. • 1(800) Wee Co-op

Sharing Among Teams
Simultaneous Sharing

1. Share & Compare

Ask for teams to share their best answer with the team next to them. Thus, all teams are active at once during sharing.

2. Team Notebooks

Have students record their ideas in a team notebook to be looked at by the teacher and/or other teams.

3. Class Notebook

Each team records their ideas or product on a sheet of three ring binder paper. The sheets are kept in the Class Notebook which has labeled dividers. The notebook is available for other teams to use.

4. Blackboard Share

Have one representative from each team go to the board or chart paper and all teams can simultaneously post their best answers. This one is my favorite. It allows teams to continue working while the ideas are posted, and for the ideas of one team to impact on the discussions of others.

5. Carbon Sharing

As teams record their answer, they are producing two or more copies via carbon paper.

These copies are given to other teams to examine and/or comment on. "Carbon booklets" facilitate carbon sharing. A four copy booklet is simply four pieces of paper with a carbon sheet face down under the first three; a staple or paper clip holds the booklet together before it is taken apart for sharing. Carbon booklets are also a powerful aid in the writing process: They allow simultaneous peer responses to individual writing.

6. Stand & Share

Stand & Share is a technique introduced to me by *Donna Klarin*, (John Kelly School, Coachella Valley Unified School District, CA. who got it from *Catherine Foster*). In Stand & Share, teams discuss an issue until each individual on the team feels he or she could share an important idea with the whole class, at which time they stand up. When all the teams are standing, the teacher asks one student to share his or her idea. After the student shares, all students with that idea or a very similar one sit down. A second student is then called upon to share, following which again all students with that idea sit down. The process is repeated until all students are seated. The methods is attractive because all students feel their idea got represented, but the process does not take a long time.

7. Roam The Room

At a signal, students move about the room as individuals to view the products of other teams or individuals. When the signal to return is given they do a Roundrobin to share what they have learned.

8. Gallery Tour

Students move about the room as a team to look over, discuss, and give feedback on the products of other teams. The products may all be posted, as when they are paintings or writing samples. Or they may be displayed at the team desks. Often a blank feedback sheet is placed by the product so teams can give each other feedback. Sometimes teammates may be asked to split up, each going to a different station so that they can inform each other about different products when they return to their teams.

Spencer Kagan: *Cooperative Learning*©
Publisher: Resources for Teachers , Inc. • 1(800) Wee Co-op

9. Three Stray, One Stay

If it is a product to be shared, three members of the team rotate to the table of the next team while Student One stays back to explain the product to the visiting team. After the students return, Student Two stays back while the other three rotate two teams. Then Students Three and Four each stay back while the teams rotate three and four teams ahead.

This structure is also called Teams Tour. When Teams Tour is done, each student has seen three team products, and has explained his/her own once. At that point, students discuss the differences among the products they have seen, and use the information to improve their own. For example, if the students have seen three or four ways of categorizing material, they make sure they all understand all of the ways, and then select the one they want for their own team display. If the visiting teams had input, the student who remained can share with the returning teammates.

10. One Stray, Three Stay

If the goal is to give students experiences in reporting back to the team, like an independent consultant, then turn things around and have "One Stray, and Three Stay." After visiting another team, the reporter explains what he or she has seen. This structure also is done with rounds, so on round one, each the reporter moves one ahead to another team. On round two a different reporter is chosen, and this time the reporter advances two ahead to another team, and so on.

11. Roving Reporters

While students are working on projects, one student from each team may for a certain amount of time be a "Roving Reporter," wandering the room gathering information such as discoveries of other teams which might be useful.

12. Carousel

Carousel allows each student to share with several teams. It goes like this: In step one, Student One in each team remains seated while his/her teammates rotate to occupy the seats of first team seated clockwise. Student One then shares. In step two, the teams rotate again, so Student One has a second opportunity to share. Several rotations may occur.

One of the best applications of Carousel is the sharing time in kindergarten. One fourth of the students share each day. The students designated to share stay put while the other three rotate to hear someone from another team share. After the second or third rotation, the students who are sharing begin to polish their presentations and develop communication skills usually reserved for speech makers.

Carousel is well-suited also for classrooms with Limited English Proficient students, or for any Foreign Language acquisition.

13. Rotating Review

Following a unit, chart paper is posted. At the top of each sheet, is a topic covered in the unit. There is one sheet per team. (If only four topics are to be reviewed, then there are two sheets per topic so that each team has its own sheet).

Teams have their own color marker. They each stand by one sheet and for one minute write down all the information they can about the topic.

The teacher then has teams rotate to the next topic. A minute is spent reading what has been written by the previous team. A new recorder is chosen for the team, and they then spend one minute adding information to the sheet.

Teams continue rotating, each time first reading what has been written by previous teams, and then adding information. If a team disagrees with previous information, they are to use their color marker to place a question mark by the questionable information for later discussion.

14. Team Inside/Outside Circle

When students are to do team presentations, a Team I/O Circle has a number of important advantages over the traditional approach of having each team take a turn at the front of the class. Let's analyze the two.

Spencer Kagan: *Cooperative Learning* ©
Publisher: Resources for Teachers , Inc. • 1(800) Wee Co-op

Team Reports: Traditional

Presentations:	8 x 5min	=	40 minutes
Transitions:	8 x 1 min	=	8 minutes
Q-A:	8 x 2 min	=	16 minutes
Total		**=**	**64 minutes**

Let's say we have an hour to devote to the team presentations. With the traditional approach, each team would stand in front of the class for about five minutes. They would take at least one minute of transition time -- to take their place in front of the class before the presentation and then to sit down after the presentation. Further we would probably want to devote at least two minutes per team to questions-answer time, or to express appreciations. And, with eight teams -- that would be all we could fit into an hour:

Applying the simultaneity principle, we can get a great deal more from our hour. First we form the students into a Team Inside/Outside Circle, with each team facing another team. Next we give the Inside Circle teams five minutes to give their presentation to their partner team on the Outside Circle. Following that we have a Roundrobin of specific appreciations by the partner team. They are to each say what they liked about the presentation and what they learned. Next the Outside Circle Teams present and their partner teams give a Roundrobin of specific appreciations. At that point, our time looks like so:

Using a Team Inside Outside Circle have accomplished in 14 minutes what it would have taken 64 minutes with the traditional approach!

So now we have time for some learning! We have the teams pull apart and spend five minutes working on their presentations to improve them. They have just gotten specific feedback and have just experienced giving the presentation so they are motivated to improve.

Following their Improvement Session, the teams reform into the Team Inside/Outside Circle and the teacher calls, "Right face, rotate two ahead to another team." When the teams have their new partner teams, they each give their presentations again. Students learn that by working on their presentations, they improve them. At this point, the time schedule looks like so:

Team Reports: I/O Circle with Two Rounds

Inside Circle Teams Present:	5 minutes
Roundrobin Appreciations:	2 minutes
Outside Circle Teams Present:	5 minutes
Roundrobin Appreciations:	2 minutes
Improvement Session:	6 minutes
Rotate:	1 minute
Inside Circle Teams Present:	5 minutes
Roundrobin Appreciations:	2 minutes
Outside Circle Teams Present:	5 minutes
Roundrobin Appreciations:	2 minutes
Total	**35 minutes**

Applying the simultaneity principle, we have accomplished far more than twice as much in half the time!

And let's examine how students have spent their time. In the traditional approach, they have spent about seven minutes as active participants and the the remainder of the hour as passive observers. With Team Inside/Outside Circle, the students have been active participants for almost the full hour because even when they were not presenting, they were the direct recipients of a presentation following which they would each be held accountable for giving specific reactions.

If the teams do not give their best presentation in their first try, they are left in the traditional approach to conclude that they are not very good at team presentations. In contrast, with Team I/O Circle, they have an opportunity to improve and are likely to conclude that with practice they can give great presentations. ❧

Team Reports: Inside/Outside Circle

Inside Circle Teams Present:	=	5 minutes
Roundrobin Appreciations:	=	2 minutes
Outside Circle Teams Present:	=	5 minutes
Roundrobin Appreciations:	=	2 minutes
Total		**= 14 minutes**

Success in life is more a function of one set of skills than any other: Communication Skills. Progress which has set the mankind apart from the other species has been built on the ability of one generation to communicate its learnings to the next. Whether workers will build upon or wastefully duplicate efforts of fellow company employees is a function of communication skills. The extent to which a marriage will flourish or falter is a function of communication skills. Communication skills are learned. Given these realities, improving communication skills should be one of education's highest priorities.

The success of cooperative learning teams as well as the success of their members throughout life is a function of their skills in communication. In the information age, in which the communication of information is the basis of our economic success, the acquisition of communication skills is necessary for job as well as life success.

A number of communication building structures have been developed. They are classified in this chapter as:

Communication Regulators: Structures which help equalize communication among team members and which help promote positive communication patterns.

Decision Makers: Structures which help groups make decisions while respecting individual opinions.

Communication Builders: Structures which build specific communication skills.

Communication Regulators

Talking Chips

Some cooperative skills can be learned by "tacking-on" skill related structures to regular learning tasks. For example, one of my favorites is Talking Chips. If Talking Chips are used during discussions, each person on a team is given a marker (their pen does fine). Instructions are simple: "If you want to talk, place your chip in the center of the table. You cannot talk again until everyone has placed his or her chip in the center of the table. When all the chips have been used, the chips are retrieved, and anyone can talk again if they place their chip in the center again."

The reason I like the Talking Chip game so much is that it takes care of the free-rider and bully problems all at once. It ensures that everyone will talk, but also that no one will do all the talking. After using the approach for some time, students internalize the principles of universal and equal participation.

Variations:

Colored Chips

If each person is given a number of colored chips, it facilitates reflection. For example, after five minutes there might be seven red chips, five blue chips, but only three green chips and no yellow chips used. Students are then asked not to touch the chips, but to dis-

Spencer Kagan: *Cooperative Learning*©
Publisher: Resources for Teachers , Inc. • 1(800) Wee Co-op

Chapter 13. Communication Skills Structures

cuss: "How equal was your participation, and what do you need to do to ensure that it is about equal?" The chips serve as a visual reminder of the number of turns each member took.

Timed Turns

No one can talk for more than a minute and there is a Timekeeper on each team.

Freebies

You can briefly respond to yes/no questions without giving up a chip.

The Yarn Yarn

This structure provides record of interaction patterns designed for young children. Each time they want to talk they must ask for the ball of yarn and make a wrap around their wrist. After the conversation they have a visual marker indicating who did most and least of the talking. For reflection, simply ask students to discuss how it happened that some children had many wraps and some had few or none.

Affirmation Chips

Students are given a certain number of Affirmation Chips and are instructed to use them up during a Team Discussion. They use up an Affirmation Chip by affirming or validating a teammate. For example, teammembers listen to a teammate describe an attempt to deal with a difficult life problem. To use an Affirmation Chip they say things like, "You are trying as hard as you can to solve that problem." "You really want to do what is right for both yourself and for your friend." Teammembers learn to listen and validate each other without suggesting and evaluating. Affirmation chips are also called validation chips. Initially, to introduce the idea of using Affirmation Chips, use a Roundrobin, each student in turn practicing affirmations. Students are instructed to interview each other on a theme. After listening to an individual they attempt to affirm the individual, using one of the affirmation gambits they have brainstormed. For example they might say "You did a great job," "You really helped your team," or "You took good care of your little brother."

Gambit Chips

Students working on one Social Skill have a variety of Gambit Chips representing the gambits for that response. For example, if the skill is paraphrasing, some Gambit chips might be, "You believe..." "If I hear you right..." In your opinion..." "Tell me if I have it right..." "Let me see if I hear you..." The Social Roles packet has two gambits written for each of the twelve social roles, and a place to write in four more. When first introducing a desired Social Role, students Brainstorm gambits associated with that role and the gambits are posted on a Gambit Chart. (See Social Skill: Chapter 12) Gambit Chips may be made from the Gambit Chart.

Paraphrase Passport

In Paraphrase Passport, the ticket to talking is not giving up a chip -- rather it is correctly paraphrasing the person who has just spoken. After someone has contributed an idea, another person must correctly restate that idea before contributing his/her own idea. There are two positive outcomes of the Paraphrase Passport. First, it makes sure that the group is not one in which "everyone is talking and no one is listening." Second, it lets individuals know how their ideas are heard by others, and can give them cues regarding their communication skills.

Paraphrasing Game. Students are instructed to interview each other on a theme. After listening to an individual, they attempt to paraphrase the individual, reflecting the full meaning of the disclosure. Either a third individual or the speaker gives feedback with regard to the completeness and accuracy of the paraphrase.

Response Mode Chips

Materials, Instructions: Xerox the sheet of response mode chips on different colored papers, so that each teammate has one sheet and each teammate has a different color.

Communication Regulators

Talking Chips

Affirmation Chips

Paraphrase Chips

Gambit Chips

| Social Skill: _____ |
| Gambit: _____ |
| _____ |

| Social Skill: _____ |
| Gambit: _____ |
| _____ |

| Social Skill: _____ |
| Gambit: _____ |
| _____ |

| Social Skill: _____ |
| Gambit: _____ |
| _____ |

Spencer Kagan: *Cooperative Learning*©
Publisher: Resources for Teachers , Inc. • 1(800) Wee Co-op

Response Mode Chips

Teammembers cut them up. Provide each team with an envelope for repeated use.

Rules: If a student wishes to speak he/she places a chip in the center of the table, representing the response mode used

Outcomes: Students and teachers can easily reflect on which response modes are used; metalinguistic understanding is fostered; and students use up their most common response modes so are pushed to use less dominant response modes with resulting social and linguistic stretching

Decision Makers

There are times when teams must make a decision, such as when choosing a team name, deciding on the topic for the team report, deciding on how to make present a project to the class, deciding how best to proceed on an investigation. Cooperative decision making structures can help resolve conflicts.

Voting

Voting is the worst way for a team to make a decision. Voting leads to winners and losers. The result is to undermine spirit of team unity. Losers are less committed to any team decision based on voting.

Consensus Seeking

When there is sufficient time and no need for an immediate decision, Consensus Seeking is the decision making structure of choice. Students are simply instructed to find the best solution to which they can all agree. They are told that, they are not each trying to get their own way but rather to find a solution which they can live with. Perhaps no one person will get his/her favorite outcome, but all teammates will have input. Critical in the consensus process is the rule that "We do not have a decision until we all agree. If anyone does not feel good about our decision, we do not have a decision."

An example of the power of consensus seeking occurred while I was giving one of my very first demonstration lessons. It was a first grade class and the students were trying to come up with a team name. There were quite a few teachers and the principal in the back of the room watching, and this university professor teaching first grade was just a bit nervous.

I thought all the teams had their names, and began to list them on the the board. When I got to Team 3, I discovered they had not agreed on a name. I responded, "That is ok, You will be 'Team 3' for now; later when you agree on a name, tell me and I will put you new name on the board." It was more than half way through the hour and I had forgotten that Team 3 had not made up a name. At that point, one girl on Team 3 raised her hand. In a very soft voice she said, something I could not hear. Not understanding the nature of a first grader, I asked her to speak up. She repeated herself, again in a voice too soft for me to hear. This time I took a few steps forward and asked her to say it again. Again too soft. After several more rounds of this, with me more than a bit nervous in from of the principal and teachers, I ended up with my ear a few inches from the girl's mouth as she said it again. What I heard, was for me quite memorable. That very soft voice was saying, "We decided, we are the Care Bears."

As I erased "Team 3" from the board where I had recorded the team names and replaced it with "Care Bears." I felt also that the team had experienced a much more powerful teambuilding event than if I had forced them to choose a team name by any other method than consensus seeking.

Spend-A-Buck

When students must reach a decision quickly, Spend-A-Buck can be used. Each student is given four quarters to spend any way they wish on the choice alternatives. Each student must spend his/her quarters on more than one item. The team then tallies the results to determine the team decision. Spend-A-Buck, unlike voting, does not produce clear winners and losers.

To make the decision even less polarized, have the teams spend ten dimes. With this version each member is obliged to spend something on at least three items.

Value Lines

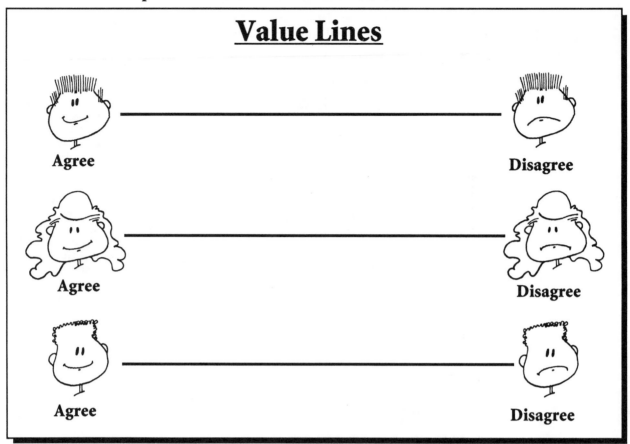

Agree — Disagree

Agree — Disagree

Agree — Disagree

Proactive Prioritizing

If teams have a bit more time, Proactive Prioritizing may be used to further evaluative thinking. Each student is instructed to defend as strongly as possible his/her preferences, and to be open to the point-of-view of others. Students are allowed to make proactive statements only: Students can say why they like what they like, but cannot comment on or evaluate other people's preferences. For example, in trying to decide possible team names, students would be allowed to say, "I like 'Foxy Four' because..." They would not be allowed to say things like, "I don't agree..." "That's not a good idea..."

If the team, by weight of the discussion, reaches consensus on its favorite item, it tries to reach consensus on item 2, and so on. This approach pushes students to defend their own point of view, and to look for a variety of dimensions with which to evaluate. From the teacher's point of view, the object is not so much a quick decision or even consensus, but rather higher-level evaluative thinking.

Communication Builders

Values Lines

Team Value Lines

Students place their mark on an agree-disagree line. After taking a stance, they must listen to why each person took his/her stance. Usually Paraphrase Passport is included.

Spencer Kagan: *Cooperative Learning*©
Publisher: Resources for Teachers , Inc. • 1(800) Wee Co-op

A positive climate is fostered within teams by allowing students to clarify their own values and to understand and accept value differences among their teammates. Value lines allow the clarification of one's own values and provide the basis for a Team Discussion or a Three-Step Interview which will promote acceptance of value differences.

Step 1. Statement of the Value Issue. The teacher provides a value judgment with which students agree or disagree. Examples of such statements are:

a. Modern art is more creative than traditional art.

b. Capital punishment should be abolished.

c. Happiness is more a function of luck than hard work.

d. Students should receive monetary rewards for good grades.

e. Including a teacher in the Challenger spacecraft was a good idea.

Step 2. Taking a Stand. At the count of three each student on the team simultaneously places his or her mark on a value line, indicating strong agreement, strong disagreement, or something between.

Step 3. Uncovering Differences. Students use a Three-Step Interview or a Team Discussion (often with Paraphrase Passport or Talking Chips) to determine the basis for the value differences.

Optional Steps:

Step 4. Taking a New Stand. Students may repeat Step 1 to discover if there has been any movement as a result of their discussion.

Step 5. Discovering Underlying Principles & Seeking Higher Synthesis. Students may seek and prepare to state the core values underlying their stances. For example, teachers differ strongly on the issue of merit pay. Beneath their disagreement they often agree on two values which in this case come into conflict: They want to work in environments which are not marked by status hierarchies, and they would like extra compensation for extra work. Having discovered the underlying core values, they might seek an alternative plan which could allow both sets of values to be realized.

Value line activities are successful if the team comes to feel that divergence provides the basis for mutually enriching discussions and creativity, and if each student feels accepted and validated for his/her own opinions and values. If the proper attitude is adopted, students will "celebrate diversity." That is, they will feel we are a richer team because our teammates differ.

Class Value Lines

Class Value Lines offer a chance for students to interact with others beyond their team, and the learning potential is increased dramatically. The steps are as follows:

Step 1. Statement of the Value Issue. Just as in Team Value Lines, an issue is stated. Choose an issue which is likely to produce a range of opinions, including strong agreement and strong disagreement.

Step 2. Students Mark a Value Line. Just as in Team Value Lines, students mark a value line, but they each mark their own on a slip of paper. They are told to mark the ends of the Agree ... Disagree Value Line only if they agree or disagree very, very strongly; otherwise they are to mark a position somewhere between the ends.

Step 3. Take a Stance. Students get up and literally take a stand on an imaginary line which stretches from one side of the room to the other. They are to stand in the spot along the line which corresponds to where they have marked their own value line.

Step 4. Similarity Pairs. Students pair up with a person next to them in the Value Line, discussing why they took the stand they did.

Step 5. Folded Value Lines. Students on the agree end walk to the disagree end to find a new partner with an opposing position. See box on next page. When this step is concluded, the strongest agree person is standing across from the strongest disagree person, the second strongest at each end are facing each other, and so on.

Spencer Kagan: *Cooperative Learning*©
Publisher: Resources for Teachers , Inc. • 1(800) Wee Co-op

Step 6. Paraphrase Passport. Students play paraphrase with their new partner.

Split Value Lines

Split value lines are like folded value lines up to the point of folding the line. At that point, the line is split rather than folded. See box.

When the line is split, the person in the center who has either no opinion or who can see the issue either way, is facing a person with the strongest opinion in the class. Learning occurs at the ends of the split value lines as the person who can see both sides of the issue interacts with the person who sees things in only black-and-white terms. Or the person who does not take strong stances interacts with the person who has very strong opinions.

Estimate Lines

Estimate lines are just like value lines except students line up based on their estimates. A wide range of content is possible such as:

• How many days until we reach the fourth goal on the Class Thermometer?

• How many marbles will fit in this jar?

• How many pockets are there in the clothes of the people in class?

• How many people were killed in the last war?

• How many points will be scored in the school basketball game this Friday?

• If we fill in 100 squares on a piece of paper, how many pieces of paper will it take to make a million?

• If we laid out the papers end to end on the playground, how far would they stretch?

• How many drops of water will fit on the head of a penny? (See Surface Tension Experiment, Chapter 15: Cooperative Projects)

• How many states will vote Democratic?

After students have folded and split the estimate lines to discuss their estimates and the reasons for their estimates, a new line up is made so students can express how much they have changed their estimate and why.

Folded Value Lines

Step 1. Students Line Up. Students line up on a value line.

Step 2. Fold Value Line. Agree and Disagree walks to fold line so opposing opinions meet.

Split Value Lines

Step 1. Students Line Up. Students line up on a value line.

Step 2. Split the Value Line.

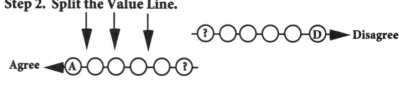

Step 3. Slide the Value Line.

Spencer Kagan: *Cooperative Learning* ©
Publisher: Resources for Teachers , Inc. • 1(800) Wee Co-op

Variations:

Pin A Place

Students use clothes pins to pin their estimate or stance on a value line on a long piece of yarn. They simply place their name on a slip of paper and use the clothes pin to clip their name on the yarn which has been stretched from one end of the room to the other. These estimates or stances on a value line are stored.

Heterogeneous groups are formed to discuss and/or investigate the topic for estimation or value issue. The groups are formed by folding a folded value line, see Topic-Specific Teams, page 6:9, in Chapter 6: Teams. After the discussion and/or investigation in these topic-specific heterogeneous groups, the students make new estimates on a new piece of yarn. Then the original yarn is produced and the before and after estimate lines are compared. Students discuss how much they have changed as individuals and why, as well as how much and in what direction the class changed, and why.

Draw-What-I-Say

Students working in pairs make a picture. They don't let the other pair on the team see the picture. They return to the team and attempt to communicate their picture with the other pair so well that the other pair can draw it.

Variations:

1. Students take turns giving one command at a time to the others who attempt to draw it.

2. For beginners, restrict the drawing to the use of squares and circles.

3. For advanced students, the senders cannot see what the receivers have done until they are finished.

Draw-What-I-Write

To develop written communication skills. Each student on a team of four makes a picture. For the first time, keep it simple. (I like to have the picture be a robot made of eight figures, using only circles, squares, and triangles). Students work alone so no teammate can see their figure. They take about ten minutes to describe their figure in writing as clearly as possible. To facilitate the later editing process, have the students write leaving a wide margin and skipping lines. When they return to their teams they work in pairs, exchanging written descriptions without showing the original drawings. Teammates attempt to produce the figure from the description. Afterwards the pairs compare the originals with the attempts. Still working in pairs students choose the attempt which is furthest from the original and edit the writing sample which produced it. Pairs within teams then exchange edited writing samples. Working from these improved writing samples, pairs attempt to draw what is described. Following this, students compare original, attempt 1, and attempt 2. Students thus can demonstrate for themselves the power of the editing.

The reason I am very fond of this structure is that a great deal of learning about writing can result with no direct instruction; it takes a functional, communication-based approach to writing.

Variations:

The family of Draw-What-I-Write structures is quite large and continues to be expanded as teacher experiment with the structure. Build-What-I-Write has been described in Chapter 11: Thinking Skills. Other structures in the family include:

Arrange-What-I-Write

Start with four pieces of construction paper (two of one color and two of another), a glue stick, a pencil, and a sheet of lined paper per student. Students pair up with another student whose pieces of construction paper are a different color.

Once the students know who their partner is, the partners go to different areas in the room so they cannot see what the other one is doing.

Now students are instructed to set two identical pieces of construction paper in front of them (called mats) and to hold the other two, making sure the two pieces in their hands are one on top of the other overlapping perfectly.

Students are now instructed in how to make duplicate sets of tear art pieces. They are to rip off an irregular shaped piece from the two pieces of construction paper they are holding. Two identical pieces result. One piece is placed on one of the mats in front of them and the other piece is placed on the other mat. They repeat this process until they have about a dozen pieces of construction paper on each mat.

One mat with its pieces is set aside: that mat and pieces will be for their partner. Working on the other mat students now arrange and rearrange the pieces until they have an arrangement they like.

They use the glue stick to glue down the pieces. They write instructions to their partner telling them how to make an identical art project. Finally, they trade instructions and provide for their partner the mat and pieces they will need so their partner can attempt to arrange what has been written.

These art projects may be around a holiday theme such as Halloween, in which case the contrasting colors might be black and orange.

Arrange-What-I-Say

For young children only two pieces are used the first time, and instead of having them tear random pieces, they are given a stylus to trace and cut, so the two pieces might be a square and a circle (if you are working on shapes) or a snowman and a Christmas Tree (for a holiday). Young students do not write about what they have arranged, but rather give oral instructions to their partners. They know they must tell, not show, although they can be looking at their own picture when they are telling their partner what to do. They also know they cannot point or touch their partners pieces so they develop oral communication skills.

Color-What-I-Say

Rather than using cut-art or tear-art, students may simply color a simple picture and describe it to their partners in words. Again they would be working on direction giving.

Find-What-I-Write

Students hide an object in the room, and then give written instructions to their partners as to how to find the object. The instructions are not to say, "I have hidden a red crayon under a book on my desk." Rather, the instructions are to say, "Stand by the flag. Face the blackboard. Walk to the corner of Ms. Smith's desk. Turn right. Walk to... ...You will find a book on the desk. Pick up the book and you will find the hidden object!"

Act-What-I-Write

Older students might try to give some stage directions in written form. This version is best carried out team to team, as teams develop and write a script for another team.

Same-Different

Students each see (or hear, or smell, or touch, or taste) something which is in some ways the same and some ways different. Without seeing what the other sees, they attempt to find what is the same and what is different in the two pictures. Communication skills are built. See the sample Same-Different materials in this chapter and the Same-Different books on the order form.

There are a number of variations on the Same-Different structure, a number of ways of fostering development of communication skills among students through the structure, and various recognition systems which can be used with Same-Different.

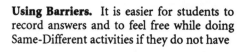

Using Barriers. It is easier for students to record answers and to feel free while doing Same-Different activities if they do not have to hold the pictures. A simple barrier of books can be used. Self-supporting cardboard barriers can be used. They are easy to make with two manila folders paper clipped together.

Pair Work

Pairs of students chosen randomly or from within cooperative teams work together. They are given different colored copies of the Same Different pictures, and are told to find as many differences and similarities as they can without looking at each others' copy. Usually students have one recording sheet and may either alternate recording differences they find, or may select one student as a recorder.

General Hint

To ensure success and a challenge for all, include in each Same-Different activity some differences which will be obvious for the slowest achievers and some which will be difficult for the highest achievers. The remaining differences should be distributed between the extremes.

Communication skills are fostered if teachers interrupt the process and ask students to reflect on what roles and strategies they are using, and if students are encouraged to experiment with alternative roles and strategies.

Team Work

One picture is provided each pair of students on a team of four. The pairs sit opposite each other. After some unstructured interaction time, the teams are asked to reflect on and change their process. For example, usually in a pair, one student does more of the talking. Students are asked to discover who that is, and to switch roles.

Split Class Work

Half the class is to be given copies of one picture and the other half is given copies of the other. Before they are given the pictures, they develop a class strategy to find as many differences as they can within a limited time. Successful strategies can include divisions of labor: One pair looking for shading differences, one pair looking for facial expression differences, a pair each looking for differences in one quadrant only (upper right, lower left, etc.).

Cooperative Format

The number of differences found by pairs or teams are summed, adding toward a class goal. Each team or pair is appreciated for its contribution to the class goal.

Competitive Format

Pairs or teams are given a limited amount of time and are encouraged to find as many differences as they can. Those who find the most are recognized. Those with successful strategies are encouraged to explain their strategies with others.

Memory Only

Students are each given five minutes to look at their pictures. The pictures are set aside. They see how many differences they can discover from memory only. Alternatively, they can be given the written list of differences to view for one minute before doing the task. This latter memory format ensures some success for all students.

Writing Only

Students are give about 10 minutes to write as full a description of their pictures as they can. They write using carbon paper so they keep a copy of their own writing. They give their partner a written description of their picture, but are not allowed to speak. They each find as many differences as they can by comparing their own writing with that of their partner.

Students are encouraged to process their attempts, and to develop and record strategies which might help them be more successful on a future attempt. They can produce edited versions to try on another receiver to view the effects of editing.

Communication Experiments

Half the class is instructed to use one communication strategy, for example to ask only "Yes-No" questions. The other half is encouraged to use another strategy, say, to spend a full minute each way describing the picture before asking any questions. The outcomes of the two strategies are contrasted as well as the feelings of the team members using each method. Principles about communication are inferred.

Creating Same-Different Curriculum

DESIGNING SAME-DIFFERENT ACTIVITIES

For those teachers who may be interested in developing their own Same-Different Activities, suggested procedures follow. You may wish to adapt your own curriculum so that students will be learning communication skills while working on whatever curriculum content you are teaching. In the process you may develop materials and ideas which have usefulness beyond your own classroom.

Procedures for Making Materials

It is extremely easy to make same-different materials.

White-Out Method. Take a drawing, map, photo, or written material. Make two Xerox copies. Use white-out and a black line marker to add and subtract content to one copy. Add and subtract different content to the other copy. Use the two altered copies as originals and Xerox copies for your class. Use a different color paper for each original to keep everyone straight.

Photo Method. Arrange objects in a scene. Take a picture. Rearrange the objects in the scene. Take a second picture. Use the enlarging Xerox on resulting photos to create two master copies and then Xerox copies of each for classroom use.

Photo Hint: Place your camera on a tripod and keep the outside margins of the photo the same to make only the objects and not the perspective change.

Answer Key: Same-Different

Christmas

1. Doll's Face
2. Santa's Bag
3. Elve's Bracelet
4. Glue Bottle
5. Fire Truck
6. Christmas Tree Pot
7. Present Wrapping
8. Calendar
9. Color of Elve's Hat
10. Mistletoe on Elve's Hat
11. Can of Nails
12. Elve's Boot
13. Elve's Socks
14. Number of Tree Ornaments
15. Number of Items in Bag
16. Doll's Face
17. Elve's Face
18. Santa's Face
19. Light
20. Accessories on Wall

Student Handout:

Answer Sheet: Same-Different

Same	Different
1._____	1._____
2._____	2._____
3._____	3._____
4._____	4._____
5._____	5._____
6._____	6._____
7._____	7._____
8._____	8._____
9._____	9._____
10._____	10._____
11._____	11._____
12._____	12._____
13._____	13._____
14._____	14._____
15._____	15._____
16._____	16._____
17._____	17._____
18._____	18._____
19._____	19._____
20._____	20._____

Same-Different Picture #1

Spencer Kagan: *Cooperative Learning* ©
Publisher: Resources for Teachers , Inc. • 1(800) Wee Co-op

Same Different Picture #2

Spencer Kagan: *Cooperative Learning*©
Publisher: Resources for Teachers, Inc. • 1(800) Wee Co-op

Match Mine

To increase accuracy of verbal communication, students can play Match Mine. Each student has an identical set of figures. A barrier is set up as in Same-Different, or the students simply sit back to back. One is the sender and the other is the receiver. The sender sets his figures in a pattern. She then describes the pattern as clearly as possible. The receiver attempts to match the pattern. The teacher stops the action to point out and label the use of helpful communication patterns such as requests for clarification, checking for understanding, use of clear descriptors.

On the following two pages a simple Match Mine activity is provided: Just Xerox two copies of the figures and the grid, let the students cut out the figures, have them turn their backs to each other and they are ready to play a challenging game which develops communication skills and a sense of interdependence.

Variations:

Match Mine can take many forms, depending on the content objectives.

Match Mind

A variation of Match Mine, Match Mind, was developed by *Laurie Robertson* (Resources for Teachers) to promote concept development through play. Because of how the gameboards and pieces are arranged, students learn concepts such as

• top, bottom, right, left
• inside - outside
• in front of - in back of

    ⌇ **See Chapter 11: Thinking Skills Structures** ⌇

Teachers can make their own Match Mind sets to help reach specific learning objectives through play. Some examples:

Specific vocabulary:

• Food: The grid is replaced by a plate and the objects are food objects.

• Shapes: The objects are squares, circles, triangles, and the job is to build a house and garden.

Geography skills:

• The grid is replaced by a map, and the object to be placed are cities, or natural resources.

Spatial relations:

• The grid has at its center a compass, and instructions are given in terms of compass points such as North, North East.

Kiddie Versions. For young students start with only two pieces, for example, a red circle and a black square. When the students have gotten proficient at the task, change it only very slightly. If the goal is to facilitate the learning of shapes, you might have a black circle and a black square, so they cannot use color as a descriptor. If the goal is to facilitate the learning of colors, you might have a red circle and a blue circle, so they cannot use shape as a descriptor. Structure for success by starting with very simple tasks, and then work up.

Fixed Content. A Xerox copy of the the arrangement to be communicated may be provided so all students are trying to communicate the same thing.

Teacher Role-Play. In initially teaching the concept of Match Mine the teacher may provide the students a copy of the arrangement to be communicated and then role-play being the receiver, working at the overhead or on a felt board. As the students give directions the teacher "plays dumb," purposefully misinterpreting ambiguous instructions in order to force students to develop more precise communication patterns. For example, if the students say "Place the hat on top," the teacher places the piece on top of her own head, forcing the students to be more precise.

A Fight Forgotten

While I was dreaming up Match Mine, two of my sons, Carlos and Miguel, were fighting. I finished making the figures and then told them in a stern voice they they had to do something before they could do anything else. I then set them to playing the newly created Match Mine. After watching them get involved and seeing the power of positive interdependence take over, I left them playing and returned upstairs to the computer. After considerable time -- I forgot all about them -- they finished on their own. When I came downstairs again, two sets of figures were perfectly matched on the table. The fight was forgotten and they had gone on to play. Later, when I asked them about Match Mine, with broad smiles they bragged: "We did it perfectly."

Match Mine Figures

Spencer Kagan: *Cooperative Learning*©
Publisher: Resources for Teachers , Inc. • 1(800) Wee Co-op

Match Mine Grid

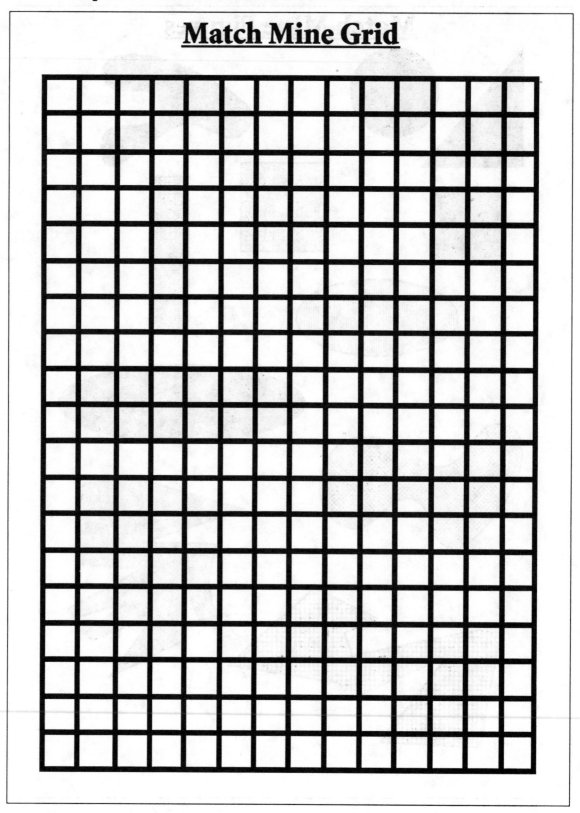

Spencer Kagan: *Cooperative Learning*©
Publisher: Resources for Teachers , Inc. • 1(800) Wee Co-op

Broken Squares

Teammembers are each given several pieces of a broken square. See graphic on next page. The pieces belong to different squares. They must create the whole square by taking turns giving each other one piece. They cannot ask for what they need. The activity promotes an awareness of the needs of others, a looking out for what one can give rather than receive.

The object of Broken squares is not to complete squares, it is to learn sensitivity to the needs of others. I have seen teachers announcing to teams how many squares they have completed, setting up a between-team competitive atmosphere, completely defeating the kind of learning which is the object of this game. If a team completes the squares quickly, congratulate them, mix up the squares, and have them do it again. Remind them that the object is to learn to see what others need.

References:

Cihak, M., Heron, B. *Games Children Should Play.* Goodyear Books, Scott, Foresman, & Co, Glenview, Il:1980.

Feshbach, N., Feshbach, S., Fauvre, M., Ballard-Campbell, M. *Learning to Care.* Goodyear Books, Scott, Foresman, & Co, Glenview, Il:1983.

Gordon, Thomas. *T.E.T.: Teacher Effectiveness Training.* Addison-Wesley/Longman, Inc. Reading, MA: 1974.

Johnson, David. *Reaching Out.* Interaction Book Company, Edina, MN: 1986.

Johnson, D., Johnson, F. *Joining Together.* Interaction Book Company, Edina, MN: 1982.

Kagan, Spencer. *Same-Different: Holidays Edition.* Resources for Teachers, Inc., San Juan Capistrano, CA: 1990.

Shaw, Vanston. *Community Building.* Resources for Teachers, San Juan Capistrano, CA:. 1992

Smith, A., Helming, E., Mabrey, J. *Team Up: Activities for Cooperative Learning.* National Educational Service, Bloomington, IN: 1990.

Solomon, R., Solomon, E. *The Handbook for the Fourth R: Relationship Skills.* National Institute for Relationship Building, Columbia, MD: 1987.

Solomon, R., Solomon, E. *The Student's Handbook for the Fourth R: Relating.* National Institute for Relationship Building, Columbia, MD: 1987.

Solomon, R., Solomon, E. *The Relationship Book.* National Institute for Relationship Building, Columbia, MD: 1988.

Broken Squares

Instructions:

1. Cut up copies of the squares above, placing them in four envelopes. Color one piece in each envelope, as follows:

Envelope	Contains Pieces	Colored Piece
1	a,a,c	c
2	j,e	j
3	d,f,a,i	f
4	b,f,k	b

2. Distribute a set of the four envelopes to each team. Teammates each choose one envelope.
3. Tell students: "Your task is to form a square for each individual, using these rules:
   1. You may not speak.
   2. You may not use nonverbal signs to ask anyone for a part.
   3. You can give parts to others, but keep the colored piece.
   4. If your team finishes before other teams, mix the pieces, each draw three, and try it again.
   Each individual must end up with one square the same size as everyone else."

Note: *For more advanced groups, a more difficult game is created if you do not color any piece.*

Trainers in cooperative learning differ dramatically in their approaches to cooperative skill development. At one extreme there are those who provide almost no instruction in social skills, with the belief that skills will be acquired naturally in the process of social interaction. They feel that if students are in situations of positive interdependence they will discover ways of keeping each other on task, supporting each other's work, and so on. At the other extreme there are those who emphasize social skills as a defining component of a cooperative learning lesson, and recommend including, with each lesson, formal instruction in a social skill. These trainers include formal processing forms on the skills, formal assignment of roles corresponding to the skills, and systematic teacher and student observation and evaluation of the use of the skill.

With the Structured Natural Approach a middle-ground is taken: A Skill-of-the-Week is adopted. Some lessons may have no focus

For years, our traditional approaches to the acquisition of social skills failed. Students memorized the eight major approaches to conflict resolution. They then passed the test on the topic. The bell rang for recess and they went out on the playground. They got into a conflict and they beat each other up! Learning about social skills is not the same as acquiring social skills. Cooperative learning is a natural arena within which to acquire social skills.

on social skills, but others may include social skills. During each week, an important part of a very differentiated social skills curriculum is delivered. This social skills curriculum is delivered with little time off academic tasks and little teacher preparation time.

Formal and Natural Approaches to Skill Development

Two very different approaches to social skill development can be distinguished: *The Natural Approach* an d *The Formal Approach.* Each approach has its domain of usefulness. Both approaches have some value at all grade levels, but social skills are probably best fostered by a heavy use of a formal approach for the first few years of schooling, with a transition after second grade, away from the formal approach, toward the natural approach.

The analogy of the learning of social skills and the learning of language is useful. One of the greatest failures of the American educational system has been its inability to produce second language acquisition. Somewhere around 85% of the students who pass our foreign language classes never become fluent in the language they have studied. This has been the consequence of relatively exclusive reliance on a formal approach to language acquisition. The students memorize vocabulary words, conjugations of verbs, and grammar structures. They pass the tests. And then, one unhappy day, they get in a situation in which they actually have to speak the language. At that point, they find that learning about the language in a formal approach was very little help in actually acquiring the language. The human brain cannot possibly stop in the middle of a sentence, go back and recall the proper word or conjugation, plug the word or phrase into the sentence, and keep on talking fluently. Learning to speak the language just does not work that way. *Learning about* language is not the same as *acquiring* language.

Spencer Kagan: *Cooperative Learning*©
Publisher: Resources for Teachers , Inc. • 1(800) Wee Co-op

In contrast, young children learn to speak languages very easily. They do not memorize words in a formal way. Rather they learn to speak by speaking. They learn in the natural approach -- in the context of negotiating meaning during meaningful interactions.

The analogy between language acquisition and the acquisition of social skills is strong. For years our traditional approaches to the acquisition of social skills has failed. Students memorize the eight major approaches to conflict resolution. For example, one day they pass the test on the topic, the next day they get into a conflict, and beat each other up! *Learning about* social skills is not the same as *acquiring* social skills.

Cooperative learning provides a golden opportunity for students to acquire social skills in the natural approach. As the students interact in their cooperative groups, they become skillful in listening, paraphrasing, taking the role of the other, managing group processes, and dealing with the dominant, shy, hostile, and withdrawn group members. They *acquire* skills, not just learn about skills.

The reason the natural approach is more successful that the formal approach in acquiring language and social skills is that the formal approach is based on a false assumption. It is based on the assumption of easy transference -- that skills learned in one context easily transfer to another. In fact, social skills are often situation-specific and difficult to transfer. For example, if a student learns how to keep one group on task, she may not be able to keep another group on task. To become expert in that skill, the student will have to use it in a number of groups. With each new setting in which the student has practiced the skill, it becomes easier to transfer the skill to the next new setting. This is one of the reasons it is important to have students work in a variety of groups or teams.

When Groups or Teams Fail?

When cooperative learning teams fail, it is almost always for one of two reasons. First,

the students don't want to work together, or the students don't know how to work together. Cooperative learning teams have problems either because the students lack the *will* to work together or the *skill* to work together.

Will to Work Together

A lack of desire to work together, resistance to being part of a team, is usually overcome by teambuilding. See Chapter 8: Teambuilding. When we first assign students to groups, we have intentionally assigned them to work with others they would be least likely to choose on their own. If the students could group themselves, they would have self-segregated themselves along the lines of race, achievement, interest, and, at certain grade levels, gender. We avoid having teams of high achievers and teams of low, teams of one race and teams of another. Through heterogeneous teams, we improve cross-race relations, tutoring, and management.

But our good intentions can create some strong resistance among some students -- they would rather have other teammates. This is where teambuilding comes to the rescue. Having enjoyed the process of building team shelters together, designing team T-Shirts, flying the team airplane, and supporting each other through a blind walk, resistance is overcome. At some point the students "Team." They feel a strong sense of belonging and identity: a desire to be with and work with their teammates. I can say with confidence that teambuilding works, having seen it overcome the resistance to working together even with members of different gangs. Teambuilding on an occasional basis throughout the time the team stays together renews and strengthens the *will* to work together.

Skill to Work Together

Having established the will to work together, the teams begin a cooperative project. They want to work together and want to do well.

Social Skill Problems

Teams are:
- Too noisy
- Off-task
- Without clear goals
- In conflict
- Bogged Down

Students:
- Give put-downs
- Tell answers
- Talk all at once
- Don't ask for help
- Don't offer help
- Don't listen to others
- Grab papers
- Don't express appreciations
- Don't respect opinions

One Student:
- Does it all
- Does little
- Is too shy
- Refuses to work
- Is Bossy
- Is Hostile

We soon observe though, that the *will* to work together is no substitute for the *skill* to work together. In one team, with all good intentions, Susie, the high achiever, is telling everyone what to do. Resentments are building up and the will to work together is quickly eroding. In another team, Sam has decided not to participate. Sam's three teammates all want to include Sam, but they are not quite sure how to do it. They wish he would be part of the group, but they don't know how to make that happen. In yet another group, a high achiever is telling a low achiever all the answers. "Write down eighty-eight for question seven." The high achiever wants to help, but does not know how. He never learned "Telling an answer hurts a teammate; showing how to get an answer helps a teammate." He lacks good helping skills. Students are getting too noisy; they give each other put-downs; they get off task; they do not listen well to the ideas of others. Further, they don't know how to deal with difficult teammates such as students who are dominant, shy, hostile, rejected, or who would simply rather work alone. The list of problems is long. The students do not know how to overcome these problems because nothing in the traditional curriculum gave them cooperative skills. The will to work together is no substitute for the skill to work together.

Problems as Curriculum in Disguise

All of the social skill problems the students are having are educational opportunities. Every social skill problem is an important piece of curriculum not yet acquired. The problems tell us what the students need to learn. If students are off-task, it is because they need to learn how to monitor their behavior, checking to see if it is on-task, and adjusting accordingly. Staying on task is a social skill which can be learned, just as any skill. In fact, all of the social skill problems in a classroom indicate only that there is some part of the social skills curriculum yet to be been learned.

Why Social Skills Instruction?

Including a social skills curriculum is necessary, not only to make our cooperative learning groups function well, but also to prepare our students with essential tools for success in work and life. For every student who loses his/her first job for lack of technical skills, there are two students who have lost their first job because of lack of social skills. Because of the breakdown in traditional socialization practices, for many students school is the only opportunity to acquire social skills. And acquisition of social skills is critical for success in today's world. There is hardly a job that does not involve working with others. As we move into greater technological complexity in the workplace, interdependence and teams become the norm, and success increasingly depends on social skills. We can no longer prepare our students for a life on the frontier in which the ability to solve all problems on your own defines success. Today, social skills define success.

Social Skill Problems Define Social Skill Curriculum

Problems	Curriculum Needed
Teams are	
• Too noisy	Inner Voices
• Off-task	Taskmastering
• Without clear goals	Setting, Revising Agendas
• In conflicts	Conflict Resolution Skills
• Bogged down	Cheerleading, Brainstorming
Students	
• Give put-downs	Praising
• Tell answers	Helping Skills
• Talk all at once	Gatekeeping
• Don't ask for help	Questioning Skills
• Don't offer help	Helping Skills
• Don't listen to others	Listening Skills
• Grab papers	Requesting
• Don't express appreciations	Appreciating
• Don't respect opinions	Paraphrasing
One Student	
• Does it all	Gatekeeping
• Does little	Encouraging, Gatekeeping
• Is too shy	Encouraging, Praising
• Refuses to work	Encouraging, Praising
• Is bossy	Gatekeeping
• Is hostile	Conflict Resolution Skills

The Structured Natural Approach

> **Four Tools of The Structural Natural Approach**
> **Tool 1: Roles & Gambits**
> **Tool 2: Structures & Structuring**
> **Tool 3: Modeling & Reinforcement**
> **Tool 4: Reflection & Planning**

> *Seven Steps Of:*
> **The Structured Natural Approach**
> 1. Set up a Social Skills Center
> 2. Select a Skill Each Week
> 3. Introduce the "Skill-of-the-Week"
> 4. Assign Rotating Roles & Develop Gambits
> 5. Structure for Skill
> 6. Model and Reinforce Skill
> 7. Reflect on Skill

If we had to teach a unit on each social skill in addition to our regular academic curriculum, it would be overwhelming. The alternative is a Structured Natural Approach in which students acquire social skills while they are doing their math, or science, or social studies with little time off the regular curriculum. Teachers using the approach actually cover more of the academic curriculum than those who do not, because their classes function smoothly: There is little time lost as students keep themselves on task, give efficient helpers to each other, and monitor and adjust their own noise levels.

Research reveals that with no social skills instruction at all, students in cooperative teams become more caring, helpful, and understanding of each other. Nevertheless, if we really wish to deliver a differentiated social skills curriculum, and to have our teams and classrooms run as efficiently as possible, we cannot depend entirely on the natural acquisition of social skills. Thus, we use a *Structured* Natural Approach to structure for social skills acquisition using four tools: 1) Roles & Gambits, 2) Modeling & Reinforcement, 3) Structures & Structuring, and 4) Reflection & Planning Time. Most importantly, we use these four tools in an integrated approach.

In the Structured Natural Approach there are four tools. To understand this integrated, Structured Natural Approach, and how to use the four tools, let's follow the seven steps to the approach:

Step 1. Set Up a Social Skills Center

The Social Skills Center consists of a place to record and post the name of Skill-of-the-Week, the name of the Role-of-the-Week, and the gambits associated with the Skill. See Graphic. The gambit charts should be in a form that will allow add-ons, storage, and reuse.

The Social Skills Center is at the heart of the Structured Natural Approach. The center allows the four tools to be integrated toward one objective: Acquisition of one new social skill each week. We refer students' attention to the Social Skills Center each time we use one of the four tools. The center is an ongoing physical reminder as to which social skill we are working on -- a reminder both to students and to ourselves. Once the skill has been posted in the Social Skill Center, the Center is used repeatedly as we use our four tools to develop the Skill-of-the-Week.

Step 2. Choose a Skill-of-the-Week

To choose a Skill-of-the-Week, you examine the functioning of teams in your classroom and select the one social skill they are most in need of acquiring. If it is early in the school year and students have had little previous cooperative learning, it is a difficult choice. There is a long list to choose from!

The wise teacher knows, however, that good learning is focused learning. When the initial assessment on the math skills shows students lack skills in the areas of dividing by fractions, interpreting graphs, column addition, and long division, we would not dream of teaching all those skills at once. We choose to work first on column addition, knowing that when that is mastered, students can move on to long division. We structure for success by choosing one skill at a time.

It is the same in structuring for success in the acquisition of social skills. When we see that the students are getting off task, putting each other down, telling answers, and getting too noisy, we would not dream of trying to teach all the lacking social skills at once. So we choose a Skill-of-the-Week. The first week we will work on Praising; week two, Inner Voices; week three, Staying On Task; week four, Giving Good Helpers, and so on. If by week five the students are not using many praisers, we will work on that skill again, posting again the old gambit charts. Just as recycling and review is an integral part of learning academic content, so too is it an integral part of learning social skills.

Step 3. Introduce Skill-of-the-Week

There are a number of ways to introduce the Skill-of-the-Week to the students, including the following:

Teacher Talk. You might simply say to students that you are not comfortable with the noise level in the classroom and so you have decided to make talking with "Inner voices" the next Skill-of-the-Week. If paraphrasing is the skill, you might provide a more elaborate rationale, such as:

> "In your life you will be in many relationships -- relationships with teammates, loved ones, friends, and in the workplace. One thing which will determine the success of all those relationships is how much you show the other person that you know and understand what they are communicating. This is true whether or not you agree with the other person.
>
> Paraphrasing is one of the main ways we have of letting others know that we are listening, and that we know and understand their thoughts and ideas. Paraphrasing communicates a basic respect for the other person. To increase everyone's skill in paraphrasing, we will make that our next Skill-of-the-Week."

Ask "What if?" Ask students to think about what would happen if the skill were never used. For examples, "I have been noticing that you have been working hard in your groups, but we seldom stop to appreciate each other's efforts. *What* would happen *if* we never got appreciation for our efforts?"

If the skill is Inner Voice, the "What if" question would be: "One team in the classroom is talking, so the team next to them talks louder to hear themselves. This makes the first team talk louder yet. *What* would happen *if* we never did anything to break this cycle?"

Our Skill-of-the-Week this week will be Cheerleading: Getting your team to stop and celebrate its accomplishments. Let's start by asking a *what if* question: "*What if* there were no cheerleaders at football games?" Talk that over in your teams.

Students Discuss & Share. Have students talk over the importance of the skill in their teams, sharing their conclusions with other teams or with the class as a whole. Have teams share via one of the information sharing structures such as Blackboard Share or Teams Compare.

Simulations. One of my favorite ways of introducing a role is through simulations. For example, when I was introducing the importance of having a Taskmaster, I gave all the teams a difficult puzzle to solve. I then told them they would have "Secret Roles." All the Number 1 students came up and I handed them their role cards. Then the number two students received their role, and so on. They were instructed to keep their role assignments secret and not to discuss their roles with anyone. What the students did not know was that in all of the teams one student was assigned the role of Off-Task Captain, but in only half the teams was there a Taskmaster!

Their role cards looked like this:

Off-Task Captain

Off-Task Captain: "Try to get the group off the task. Without getting wild or obnoxious, attempt to distract the group by talking about interesting things other than the puzzle. Do not let anyone on your team know your role, and try to act in a way they do not discover your assignment.

Taskmaster

Taskmaster. Your job is to keep the group on task. If anyone distracts the group, simply get everyone to pay attention to the task by saying things like, "This puzzle is really interesting." "Do you think we will be able to solve the puzzle before the time is up?" Keep your role secret so no one on the team knows you have been assigned the role of Taskmaster.

Later as we reflected on what happened in the teams, it was clear that those teams with a taskmaster spent much more time on task. The simulation worked also to generate a variety of successful Taskmaster Gambits which the students shared with the class.

Having introduced the skill, we are ready to use the first of our four tools to ensure skill acquisition.

Step 4. Assign Rotating Role & Develop Gambits

Tool 1: Roles & Gambits

Note: Although many techniques are presented along with each of the four tools, in practice, each teacher will use but a few of these techniques. With only a few techniques used with each tool each week, a very powerful impact on social skill development results.

Social Skills and Corresponding Social Roles

Social Skill	Corresponding Role
1. Encouraging Others	Encourager
2. Praising Others	Praiser
3. Celebrating Accomplishments	Cheerleader
4. Equalizing Participation	Gatekeeper
5. Helping	Coach
6. Asking for Help	Question Commander
7. Checking for Understanding	Checker
8. Staying on Task	Taskmaster
9. Recording Ideas	Recorder
10. Reflecting of Group Progress	Reflector
11. Not Disturbing Others	Quiet Captain
12. Efficiently Distributing Materials	Materials Monitor

Assign Rotating Role-of-the-Week. Assign a Role-of-the-Week associated with the Skill-of-the-Week. Each student will get a turn at the role because it rotates each day: Monday, the role is given to Student 1, Tuesday, Student 2, Wednesday, Student 3, and Thursday, Student 4.

If the Skill-of-the-Week is Staying On Task, the Role-of-the-Week will be Taskmaster. If the skill is Showing Appreciating, the role will be Praiser.

The Role of the Week is posted in the Social Skills Center, along with the gambits associated with the role.

Generate and Record Gambits. Students will not know how to fulfill their role unless they have positive models of what to do and say. Students need to know what it **"Sounds Like"** and **"Looks Like"** to fill the role well -- the gambits for the role. Gambits are the verbal and non-verbal behaviors which allow role fulfillment. It is not the job of the teach-er to generate these gambits, but rather to lead students in generating and recording the gambits.

Through gambit development students learn how to solve social skill problems and how to fulfill roles. For example, if the skill is Staying on Task, the Role would be Taskmaster, and the students and teacher would post those gambits which would facilitate being a good Taskmaster. Students learn that a good Taskmaster does not say, "Stop talking about the big game." Rather, they learn to say, "The big game is really interesting, but if we are going to complete our project in time, we need to...." Students learn that one of the best gambits for a Taskmaster is to simply talk about the task in an interesting way. Rather than saying, "We are off task," they say, "Problem three really looks interesting. Do you think the answer could be related to ...?" Some of the techniques for generating and recording gambits follow:

Post Gambit Chart: Once the gambits have been generated, the teacher posts them on the gambit chart in the Social Skills Center. As new gambits are generated during the week, the teacher adds them to those initially posted when the skill was first introduced.

Teacher Models Gambits: You may model the role for the class. A strong strategy is to model the role correctly, then incorrectly, and have students in teams discuss the difference. For ex-ample, you might contrast weak versus strong Gatekeeper gambits, e.g., Weak: "John, you are talking too much; Susan, talk more." Strong: "That's in-teresting John; Susan, do you agree?" It is probably a good idea to finish your modeling on a positive note: End by modeling strong, positive gambits.

A Team Models Gambits: Get one team "up on the role" by working with them while the other teams are busy on another task. The selected team then can serve as a model to demon-strate the role. For example, you might have one teammember pretend not to know how to solve a problem, and have the "Coach" model how to help a student solve a problem without doing it for him. Choose one of the weakest teams to model for the class and they will gain in status and will acquire the role at a level they might not otherwise.

Teacher Plays dumb: Tell students,

"I have been noticing that we have been getting off-task while working on our projects, so 'Staying on Task' will be our next skill of the week. But I am not so sure what you would say or do in your teams if you saw someone off task. Put your heads together and discuss what you might say or do to get the team or a teammate back on track. What could we put on our Gambit Charts?"

Class and Teams Brainstorm Gambits: Use 4S Brainstorming or one of the other concept generating structures in Chapter 11: Thinking Skills Structures. Have students generate gambits for the Gambit Chart.

The topic is Gatekeeping and a team suggests that you tell Susan to "Shut-up." Ask how she is likely to feel and what that will do to relations in the group. Pose it to the class as a problem to come up with gambits which will get Johnny participating without making Susan feel put-down. They come up with things like, "Susan, that is interesting; do you agree Johnny?"

If allowed freedom, students can generate very creative gambits. Some student-generated gambits include:

1. Drawing a happy face on one side of a slip of paper and a sad face on the other side, and keeping one or the other side of the paper turned up, depending on whether the team is on-task. (Developed by eleven year old Emmanuel Lloyd, Hedges Elementary School, Mansfield, Ohio.)

2. Giving a "thumbs-up" signal when the group is using quiet, inner voices, and a steady, soft knocking on the table when the group has gotten too noisy.

3. Making slips of paper with question marks on them, and then handing one to any student who has not been participating. The

Encourager who developed those gambit chips informed his group that they meant, "What do you think?"

Develop Gambit Chips: Students brainstorm things they can say or do and write down the gambits on slips of paper or Gambit Chips. Later they use the gambit chips during their teamwork. Premade Gambit Chips can be found in Chapter 13: Communication Skills Structures.

```
Social Skill: _____

Gambit: _____

_____
```

Develop A Gambit Exchange Bank: Students deposit the Gambit Chips in the "Gambit Exchange Bank." Later, students can exchange old gambits for new. Any time a team comes up with a new gambit for the skill of the week, it writes a new Gambit Chip and uses the chip for awhile. When the gambit grows old, the team trades it in for a new one from the Gambit Exchange Bank.

Simulations. Have one student play the role of a problem student, and then have the teammates see what kinds of gambits they can develop to deal with the problem. Later have teams share their favorite gambits, or write them up for the Gambit Bank.

Unstructured Role Plays: Role-play, as its name suggests, is a very natural mode of learning. It is a chance to play with behaviors, to try them on, practice. Close observations of play reveals it is often practice of roles for later use. Unstructured role-play in the classroom is the same thing: the teacher provides students with a situation to role-play, allows them to experiment with possible solutions, and then to share and discuss their solutions with other teams.

For example, the teacher might say, "In your teams, role-play this situation and see if you can find a solution you like."

Sample Role Play Situations

• Jennifer borrowed some crayons from her friend Stacy. Jennifer accidentally broke one of the crayons. What should Jennifer do?
• Bill grabbed the ball away from John during recess. What should John do?
• Tom sees Pete hit Jim. What should Tom do?
• Sally and Monica find a wallet on the playground. It has money in it, but does not have the owner's name. What should they do?

helpful or cooperative behaviors as a model for other groups to see.

Structured Role Plays: One of the most powerful ways of learning new behavior or changing old behavior is to practice the desired behavior in a context similar to the one in which the behavior actually will be used. In China, teachers make extensive use of structured, teacher-written and directed role-plays to help students recognize and learn appropriate helping and cooperating behaviors. Through structured role-play students practice the proper response to various situations, such as returning a lost object, or asking permission to borrow something.

As a team role-plays the desired behavior, the other teams may be given observation forms, to ensure that the behavior is being observed, and to give the group feedback.

Use Role Cards: By simply cutting a piece of paper and then folding it in half the long ways, a role card is made. On one side of the role card the name of the role is written so all can see, on the other side there is room for gambits. Below is a reduced version of a role card from the Role Card Packet.

The Role Cards Packet (Kagan, 1991) offers 108 role cards: Twelve role cards for each of nine teams. The role cards are color coded so each of the nine teams can have its unique set of twelve role cards.

Whether they are homemade or commercial, sets of role cards have several advantages. They stack perfectly for easy storage; they can be turned inside out so twelve additional roles can be assigned; they can be laminated so students can write in their own gambits with a dry marker and then easily wipe them clean when the role rotates.

Having a set of twelve role cards at their disposal is empowering for students. For example, if the students are working on a project, you may ask them to take out all twelve role cards and discuss which of the roles they are using, and which they might wish to adopt.

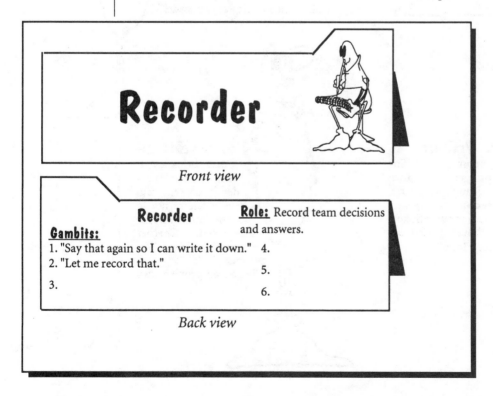

Recorder

Front view

Recorder

Role: Record team decisions and answers.

Gambits:
1. "Say that again so I can write it down."
2. "Let me record that."
3.

4.

5.

6.

Back view

Spencer Kagan: *Cooperative Learning*©
Publisher: Resources for Teachers , Inc. • 1(800) Wee Co-op

The twelve most common roles and some associated gambits are as follows:

Brief Overview of 12 Social Roles

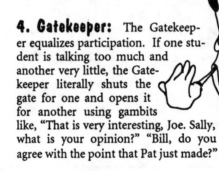

1.   Encourager: The Encourager "brings out" the reluctant student, and attempts to motivate the team if it gets bogged down. The Encourager goes to work before a student has spoken, with gambits such as, "Let's listen to Pete."

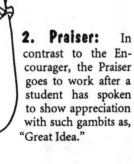

2.   Praiser: In contrast to the Encourager, the Praiser goes to work after a student has spoken to show appreciation with such gambits as, "Great Idea."

3.   Cheerleader: The cheerleader, unlike the praiser, does not say things like, "Fantastic Job." Rather he or she gets the team to show appreciation for the accomplishments of one teammate or the team as a whole. The cheerleader literally leads the group in a cheer with gambits like, "Let's all give Pedro a pat on the back."

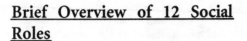

One of my favorite cheerleader gambits is to have students pick two positive adjectives or phrases and then chant the first phrase three times and the second one once. For example; students would chant, "Great! Great! Great! Fantastic!"

4.   Gatekeeper: The Gatekeeper equalizes participation. If one student is talking too much and another very little, the Gatekeeper literally shuts the gate for one and opens it for another using gambits like, "That is very interesting, Joe. Sally, what is your opinion?" "Bill, do you agree with the point that Pat just made?"

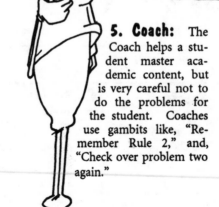

5.   Coach: The Coach helps a student master academic content, but is very careful not to do the problems for the student. Coaches use gambits like, "Remember Rule 2," and, "Check over problem two again."

6. Question Commander: The Question Commander occasionally checks to see if anyone in the group has any questions and, if so, makes sure they are asked and the the group attempts to answer them. The rule is that the team attempts to answer all questions first. If the team cannot, then the team has a "Team Question," and the Question Commander uses a signal to let the teacher know that the team has exhausted its resources. My favorite signal for a team question is simply to have all four students on the team raise their hands. Alternatively, the Question Commander can have a red flag (slip of paper) to hold up.

7. Checker: The Checker makes sure everyone has mastered the material. The team knows that each person is on their own during the quiz or exam so the team must check to see each person is prepared. The Checker leads the team in this with gambits like, "Let's do one problem each while the team watches to make sure we all have it."

Sometimes the teacher assigns other job definitions to the checker, so the checker may be asked to check for understanding, check for agreement, check for completeness, or check to see if the team is following a specific rule.

8. Taskmaster: The Taskmaster keeps the group on task. It is important to distinguish positive and negative gambits for the taskmaster; they are to say things like, "We have not done problem three yet," but not to say things like, "Stop fooling around."

9. Recorder: The Recorder writes down group decisions and answers. Sometimes the role of the Recorder may be modified so that he or she is simply responsible for making sure things get recorded.

10. Reflector: The Reflector leads the group in looking back. Group process is improved if the Reflector occasionally summarizes group process. Also, most importantly, the Reflector has the team reflect on how well it is using the Skill-of-the-Week, using gambits like, "How well did we all stay on task?"

Spencer Kagan: *Cooperative Learning*©
Publisher: Resources for Teachers , Inc. • 1(800) Wee Co-op

11. Quiet Captain:

The Quiet Captain makes sure the team does not talk loudly enough to be overheard by other teams. A teacher may wish to distinguish "loud voices," "12 inch voices," and "6 inch voices." It is the job of the Quiet Captain to make sure teammates huddle and whisper if the teacher has called for 6 inch voices.

12. Materials Monitor:

The Materials Monitor obtains and returns supplies and makes sure the team cleans up.

When Not to Use Roles

Most Structures: Most simple cooperative learning structures, like Numbered Heads Together, Three-Step Interview, Roundtable, and Roundrobin, do not need roles. In fact, role assignment would detract from the effectiveness of these structures.

When to Use Roles

Team Projects: Whenever teams work on projects, roles are important. For example, with no roles, given an interesting or challenging task, it is probable that the highest achieving students will "take over" and do the task for the team. It is the job of the Gatekeeper to make sure all participate. If each student has his or her role, such as Checker, Recorder, Taskmaster, and Cheerleader, there is a much greater probability that all will participate and each

will feel he or she has made a unique contribution to the project.

Team Discussions: Team discussions without roles often consist of one or two students talking most or all of the time. As a remedy, you might assign some of the following roles: Gatekeeper (who makes sure all participate), Taskmaster (who makes sure the team stays on the topic), Reflector (who makes sure the team occasionally reflects on its progress and on its use of any particular social skill which is the focus), and a Cheerleader (who makes sure the group stops and celebrates its accomplishments).

Step 5. Structure for Skill

Tool 2: Structures & Structuring

The second set of tools in the Structured Natural Approach is to choose structures and structuring which will foster the development of the Skill-of-the-Week.

Structures. Quite a number of structures are useful for skill development. For example, if students are working on the skill of Equal Participation, the structure of choice would be Talking Chips. For Praising, use Affirmation Chips. See Communication Skill Structures. See the box: Structures for Promoting Social Skills for some suggested structures.

I have seen Kindergarten students given the task of making a team picture by tracing around a stylus. Without any special instructions from their teacher, each student worked for a little while and then passed the paper to a teammate to continue the work. These students had used Roundtable a great deal in previous cooperative work, and so

Structures for Promoting Social Skills

had internalized the structure. When no structure was provided, they naturally assumed that Roundtable was the way to work when working with others.

Structuring. Structuring is the myriad things we do to determine how an activity is carried out. If the skill of the week were Listening, a structure I might choose during the week would be Team Interviews. Structuring is not just choosing a structure, it is telling students how carry out a task. During the week, to use structuring I might say things like, "Remember attentive listening is our skill of the week." While we work on our projects remember to show your teammates you are listening by using some of the non-verbal gambits we have listed on our Gambit Chart."

Structuring for skill acquisition includes simply telling the students to use a skill. One of the surest ways to structure for the acquisition of a skill is to hold students accountable for the skill. For example, I might say, "Listen to each other's ideas carefully today, because at the end of the day I will have you take out a piece of paper, write down two ideas you heard from someone else, sign it, and turn it in."

Structures themselves can be used with little structuring or a great deal of structuring. For example, if the students are to do a Team Interview, I can give very different instructions depending on how much structuring I do. See box: High v. Low Structuring.

Notice, with high structuring the teacher has structured the Team Interview so that each teammate will have equal time, both in interviewing and in being interviewed. This equal participation, however, is bought at the high price of spontaneity and student empowerment. A teacher uses either high or low structuring depending on the goals at hand.

Many times it is possible to structure a cooperative learning task so that the acquisition of social skills is an integral part of the learning experience, or necessary for task completion.

For an example of structuring for social skill acquisition, see Box: "Two Ways to Make a Mural" (Chapter 7: Classroom Management).

Structuring for a Skill: Let's say the skill is listening. To structure for increased listening, if the task is an essay or report about fun vacation activities, the teacher might require that each student write about the fun activities of someone else on the team. This structuring of the task ensures that interviewing and listening skills are developed.

Destructuring for Internalization. If a teacher always structures every step of behavior, she/he will rob students of learning opportunities.

High v. Low Structuring

Low Structuring: "In your teams take turns, asking each person questions."

High Structuring: "Teammate Number 1, stand up. You have exactly three minutes to be interviewed by your teammates. If you are doing the interviewing, you may ask one question, but you many not ask a second question until each of your teammates has asked their question."

Spencer Kagan: *Cooperative Learning* ©
Publisher: Resources for Teachers , Inc. • 1(800) Wee Co-op

Clearly, we would like to get to a point where we do not have to use structuring, or assign structures and roles because our students know them so well that they use them when it is appropriate. My belief, though, is that we will get to that point faster by early experiences with formal assignment of roles and structures than by using unstructured collaborative work and just hoping that students discover cooperative skills.

We can structure for early acquisition of social skills through structuring and structures, so all students experience a positive model of social interaction, but then as the skills are acquired, we can destructure in a paced way for internalization of the social skills. If there is a high degree of structure and little interaction among students; fewer management and social relations problems arise among students, but there is less opportunity for development of higher level thinking skills as well as internalization of social skills and roles.

It is generally a good idea to move from high to low structuring as students acquire the social, cognitive, and linguistic skills necessary to cooperate in situations with low structuring. Systematically destructuring for internationalization allows students to internalize cooperative skills and to become cooperative rather than just to behave cooperatively.

Thus, in a paced way, the teacher provides less and less structure, allowing the students to structure their interaction for themselves. As a teacher destructures, however, he/she must include more reflection time. For example, if the structure does ensure that all students are participating, students need time to reflect on that question, and make a plan as to how they can ensure everyone has an opportunity to participate.

Step 6. Model and Reinforce Skill

Tool 3: Modeling & Reinforcement

The Skill-of-the-Week is modeled and reinforced in a variety of ways during the week.

By Teacher. The Social Skills Center is a reminder, not just for the students, but for the teacher as well. If the Skill-of-the-Week is praising, the teacher is sure to model many forms of praising during the week. If the skill is Equal Participation, the teacher him/herself will use good Gatekeeping Gambits while working with the students.

To model a skill for a team or for the whole class, the teacher may briefly join a team to model the behavior.

Model Groups. If a desired behavior is not being used, a teacher may wish to work with a group on the behavior until they are proficient, and then have the team model the behavior for the whole class.

Spontaneous Models. During the week the teacher is looking for good use of the skill. Without formal observations, the teacher simply notes when a skill has been used well. At that time the teacher would say something like, "Class, I would all like you to hear what I just heard -- Johnny just used a wonderful gambit to paraphrase. He said, 'It seems to me you are saying....' Let's add that gambit to our Gambit Chart."

If you have a Social-Skill-of-the-Week, you are looking for examples of the use of that skill to hold up as a model for the rest of the class. So, for example, if the Skill-of-the-Week is Staying on Task, you might get the attention of the class somewhere during the lesson and then say something like, "I have been watching the Astronauts for awhile, and I am really impressed how well they have been staying on task. At one point they started to talk about recess, but than got right back on task. Nice job, Astronauts! You are doing a great job at our new skill for this week." See Box, "The Power of Positive Attention," Chapter 7.

If the skill were praising and encouraging, the teacher might say, "I just heard and saw a great praiser. Susan would you please let the whole class hear what you just told Sally and show them the silent round of applause you just gave?" "Notice how Susan smiled and looked right at Sally as she told her what a great job she was doing."

Holding students' focus on desired behavior creates positive class norms and produces more of the behavior modeled. Reinforcement for the behavior comes primarily from the positive attention paid the behavior by the teacher, but points, chips, tokens, and certificates are possible as well. Some teachers have a specific skill of the week token to give individuals and teams when they are using the skill well. See Chapter 16: Scoring and Recognition.

Role plays and Simulations. Role plays and simulations are useful ways to model and reinforce a skill, not just when a skill is being introduced, but also during the week. For example, see the Helping Behavior Role Play Lesson included later in this chapter.

Step 7. Reflect on Skill

Tool 4: Reflection & Planning

Students need time to reflect on how well they are using the Skill-of-the-Week. There are a variety of ways of promoting reflection.

Reflection Questions. At various times during the week, the teacher takes a little time off the academic task to ask a reflection question designed to have students reflect on the social skill of the week. For example, "Our skill of the week is Staying On Task. How well is your group staying on task as you are playing Turn-4-Review? If you have gotten off task, it is time now to make a plan to stay on task."

Notice, the teacher does not wait until the end of the class period to have students reflect on the skill. If she did, some groups during reflection

time would discover they had not used the skill all class period. Rather, the reflection time comes rather early in the lesson (about one third of the way through) so that students have time to change their behavior and benefit from the reflection.

Integration with the Social Skills Center. During the reflection time, a link is made to the Social Skills Center by asking questions like,

"Look at the Gambit Chart. Did you hear or see any of those gambits so far today?"

"Have you heard any new gambits today which we can add to our Gambit Charts?"

Structures for Reflection. Reflection can be facilitated by using information sharing structures such as Roundrobin (each one says one Gambit they heard or wished they had heard); Think-Pair-Share ("How much encouragement have we shown each other?); Three-Step Interview (students are interviewed on how they feel the team is doing on the Skill of the Week); and Brainstorming (students come up with ideas about how they could use the skill more).

Student Self-Monitoring. Without a doubt one of the most effective ways of producing change is through self-evaluation. Having family members view themselves interact, and rate their own individual interactions on video tape is a powerful technique in family therapy -- it leads to improvement of family dynamics.

Although not many teachers have the resources to video tape individual students and teams act and interact, and then to allow them to rate their own interactions, self-monitoring and evaluation forms may be the next best thing. See sample Self-Evaluation Form.

The Teammate Observer. One student on each team has the role of observer. His/her job for the day is to focus on a specific social skill such as encouragement among teammates. The observer that day may use an observation form to mark down each instance of encouragement and its source, so that good use of that skill is recognized among teammates. See sample Social Skills Observation Form.

Reflection Questions

For Helping
> Did I give help when asked?
> Did I ask for help if I needed it?
> What help was most helpful?

For Praising
> What praise did I give?
> What praise did I receive?
> What praise felt good?

Spencer Kagan: *Cooperative Learning*©
Publisher: Resources for Teachers , Inc. • 1(800) Wee Co-op

Class observers. Individuals may be selected to observe the good use of gambits and skills, with the aim of fostering thoughtful reflection based on the information they provide. Sometimes you may choose individuals low on a particular skill to observe that skill, providing them useful modeling experiences.

Team Observers. Occasionally a teacher may want teams as a whole to serve as observers for each other. A team may be asked to stand around another team in a fishbowl format, with observation sheets. When the team is finished with the learning activity, the observing team can give them input regarding the social skills under observation.

Teacher Observations. Reflection time can be facilitated by the teacher sharing an observation or observations regarding how well the Skill-of-the-Week is being used. Often it is best for teachers to simply share an observation and leave the teams take responsibility for what is to be done about it. For example, the teacher may simply say, "One person in this group seems to be doing most of the talking, take a moment to talk over how well you are using your skill of Gatekeeping, and what you need to do." or, "Today, in some teams I saw people raising their hands to state the team opinion before checking for consensus with all their teammates."

Teacher Time Samples. If a teacher stands by each team for one minute and records each instance of the use of a skill, after two rounds, there will be a pretty good sample of how much the skill is being used and by which groups. Time Sample forms are simple to make. See sample Skills Observation Form.

Formal Reflection Forms. Although the informal reflection question focused on the skill of the week is probably the most powerful way to promote reflection, various observation and reflection forms can help as well. The students may fill out the forms individually and then compare answers with their teammates, or they may attempt to reach consensus as a group filling out one form for the team. Samples of typical reflection forms for various skills at various grade levels follow. Notice, the best reflection forms do not have students reflect on more than one skill at a time. Popular Reflection Forms which have students answer questions about staying on task, use of quiet voices, mutual support, equal participation, and help giving all on one form are probably of very limited value. These forms are like having students work on their addition, subtraction, multiplication, division, and logic skills all at once! The power of reflection is revealed when it is an integral part of the plan to deliver one Skill-of-the-Week.

Social Skills Observation Sheet

	Skill 1	Skill 2	Skill 3	Skill 4
Team 1				
Team 2				
Team 3				
Team 4				
Team 5				
Team 6				
Team 7				
Team 8				

Observation Date _____

Instructions:

Stand by each group for one minute. Do not interact with group members. Record each use of each skill with a mark.

Spencer Kagan: *Cooperative Learning*©
Publisher: Resources for Teachers , Inc. • 1(800) Wee Co-op

Skills Observation Sheet

Skill _____ Date _____

	#	Comments
Team 1		
Team 2		
Team 3		
Team 4		
Team 5		
Team 6		
Team 7		
Team 8		

Instructions to Observer:

Stand by each group for one minute. Do not interact with the group. Record use of the skill with a mark in the "#" box. Under "Comments" record gambits for later sharing.

Spencer Kagan: *Cooperative Learning* ©
Publisher: Resources for Teachers , Inc. • 1(800) Wee Co-op

Reflection: Primary

Did We Take Turns?

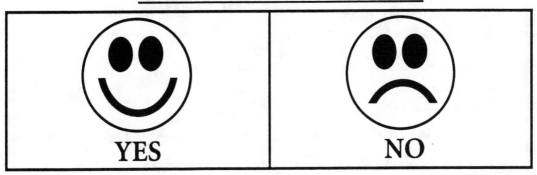

Did We Praise?

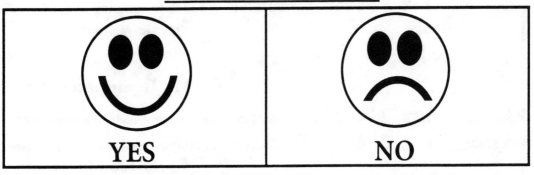

Did We   ?

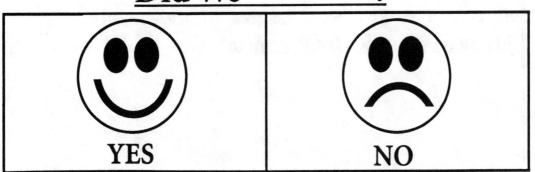

Spencer Kagan: *Cooperative Learning*©
Publisher: Resources for Teachers , Inc. • 1(800) Wee Co-op

 # Reflection: Elementary

USE THIS SCALE

① **Strongly Agree**
② **Agree**
③ **Somewhat Agree**
④ **Disagree**
⑤ **Strongly Disagree**

Name _____

Team Name _____

Date _____

Circle the number

My Team:

Agree	1 2 3 4 5	Disagree	1) Had clear goals
Agree	1 2 3 4 5	Disagree	2) Made progress toward the goals
Agree	1 2 3 4 5	Disagree	3) Stayed on task
Agree	1 2 3 4 5	Disagree	4) Made decisions based on views of all

My Teammates:

Agree	1 2 3 4 5	Disagree	1) Listened well to each other
Agree	1 2 3 4 5	Disagree	2) Helped each other by giving useful suggestions
Agree	1 2 3 4 5	Disagree	3) Were respectful of all points of view
Agree	1 2 3 4 5	Disagree	4) All Participated

My Suggestions for Improvement:

Reflection Form: Secondary

1. What one word would you use to describe how the group was today?

   _____

2. What one word would describe the way you would like the group to be?

   _____

3. Is everyone paricipating?

   Yes, always ____ Usually____ Occasionally ____ Rarely____ No, never ____

   If not, why not? _____

4. Are you (everyone in group) trying to make each other feel good?

   Yes, always ____Usually ____ Occasionally ____Rarely ____ No, never ____

5. Are you trying to help each other feel able to talk and say what you think?

   Yes, always ____Usually ____ Occasionally ____Rarely ____ No, never ____

6. Are you listening to each other?

   Yes, always ____ Usually____ Occasionally ____ Rarely____ No, never ____

7. Are you showing you are listening by nodding at each other?

   Yes, always ____Usually ____ Occasionally ____ Rarely____ No, never ____

8. Are you saying "That's good" to each other when you like something?

   Yes, always ____Usually ____ Occasionally ____ Rarely____ No, never ____

9. Are you asking each other questions?

   Yes, always ____Usually ____ Occasionally ____ Rarely____No, never ____

10. Are you listening and really trying to answer these questions?

    Yes, always ____ Usually____ Occasionally ____ Rarely____ No, never ____

11. Are you paying attention to each other?

    Yes, always ____Usually ____ Occasionally ____ Rarely____No, never ____

12. Is any one person talking most of the time?   Yes ____ No ____

Adapted from: Aronson E., Blaney, N., Stephan, C., Sikes, J. & Snapp, M. *The Jigsaw Classroom.* Beverly Hills, Ca: Sage, 1978.

Spencer Kagan: *Cooperative Learning*©

Publisher: Resources for Teachers , Inc. • 1(800) Wee Co-op

Variations:

SKILL-OF-THE-STRUCTURE

Certain structures have associated social skills. For example, the four social skills associated with Pairs Check are Helping, Praising, Celebrating, and Patient Waiting. Without some work on Patient Waiting, for example, when a pair finishes their two problems, they are likely to drum their fingers on the desk, stare at the slower pair, and in other ways communicate their impatience. Students need to know what to do if they finish early (check their work, ask if there is another way to solve the problem, work on the sponge activity). The mini-skills associated with each structure do not merit work as a Skill-of-the-Week, they are taught when the structure is introduced.

SKILL-OF-THE-LESSON

In contrast to the Skill-of-the-Week approach which is central to the Structured Natural Approach is the work of David and Roger Johnson, (1984), who advocate that each lesson have two objectives: a social skill objective and an academic objective. Personally I find it too difficult to write in a distinct social skill for every lesson, and I feel that one social skill per week provides a more focused learning agenda.

There is no reason, however, that a teacher cannot do both. That is, there can be an ongoing social skill of the week, and also a specific social skill associated with some or even all of the lessons. Often the Skill-of-the-Lesson approach includes formal instruction on the skill, as well as formal or informal assessment and feedback.

For the very youngest students there can be value in a very heavy use of a formal approach to social skill development to supplement the natural approach. Whereas beyond second grade a very sophisticated and powerful social skills curriculum can be delivered with very little use of the formal approach, for the youngest students "A Skill of the Lesson" is a powerful model. This is so because of the shorter attention spans of the youngest students, and the greater need to give detailed instructions to the students as to exactly how to carry out any given skill. Social skills are, to a large extent, core curriculum for the very youngest students. Thus a somewhat different model of social skill instructions is useful.

The distinction between Skill-of-the-Week and the Skill-of-the-Lesson approaches to social skills is reflected heavily in three books in the structural approach. In their books on cooperative learning and language arts and cooperative learning and mathematics Jeanne Stone (1991) and Beth Andrini (1991) include almost no social skill components to their very sophisticated lessons. The assumption they make is the while the content is being delivered the Structured Natural Approach is being used. The four tools of the natural approach --Roles & Gambits, Modeling & Reinforcement, Structures & Structuring, and Reflection & Planning -- can always be used, regardless of the lesson being taught.

Quite in contrast to the Andrini and Stone approach is Lorna Curran's (1991) approach in, *Lessons for Little Ones: Literature-Based Language Arts and Social Skills.* Each of the three dozen K-2 lessons provided in the book gives at least as much attention to social skills as to the language arts curriculum content. Lorna writes into each lesson how the skills will be modeled, processed, debriefed, and rewarded. The assumption is that for young students social skill acquisition to a very large extent is the curriculum, and that the students need formal instructions in the social skills necessary for each lesson.

A focus on Specific Skills

The most common social skill problems which can hinder cooperative learning all can be handled with the four tools of the Structured Natural Approach: Roles & Gambits, Modeling & Reinforcement, Structures & Structuring, and Reflection & Planning.

The four tools of the Structured Natural Approach provide the main tools for dealing with every social skill related

Most Common Social Skill Problems
Noise Level
The Refusenick
Rejected Student
Shy Student
Dominant Student
Hostile Student
Interpersonal Conflict
Poor Helping

problem. After setting up a Skill-of-the-Week, during the week we use the four tools to ensure acquisition of the skill. Here are some problem specific approaches which have been developed.

Problem 1.
NOISE LEVEL

It is very natural that the noise level in a co-operative classroom will escalate unless something is done. This is so because as one team talks, the team near them may talk louder to hear themselves, forcing the first team to talk louder yet, creating a vicious circle. The circle must be broken if noise is not to escalate to unacceptable levels. Students need to learn the skill of Inner Voice.

Skill-of-the-Week: Using Inner Voices.

When defining the skill of using inner voices, begin by stating that an inner voice is one which is heard within a team, but which does not interfere with other teams.

Seat students five feet apart and have students talk just loud enough so they can be heard. Tell them, that is a "Five Foot Voice." Then have them move to three feet, and define that level of talk as a "Three Foot Voice." Repeat the procedure at one foot and at six inches. You can then request at any point that students use only their Six Inch Voices (when you want only quiet co-operative learning), or their three foot voices (when you want to encourage very animated interaction).

Roles & Gambits. Assign a Quiet Captain and work to develop gambits. Students like non-verbal gambits for the Quiet Captain, such as a red Q-Chip (red piece of paper with a Q in a circle) which the Quiet Captain is to use whenever the noise level has escalated.

Modeling & Reinforcement. Go to the quietest group and comment to them and/or to the class on how they are contributing to a positive class tone by respecting the rule of inner voices.

Structures & Structuring. As you begin a task, call for the level of talk you wish such as "During your projects for the next half hour I want no voices above a one foot voice."

Reflection & Planning. Stop the work and have students reflect on their use of quiet voices. Have them make a plan as to how to use only inner voices.

Problem 2.
THE REFUSENICK

One day while watching *Doug Wilkinson* (Dana Point Elementary, Dana Point, CA) begin cooperative learning, I was surprised to see a young boy immediately pop out of his seat, walk over to Doug and in a loud voice say, "I don't want to work with anyone else." Wisely, Doug replied, "That's ok, if you want to work alone, you can. There is a desk in the back you can use."

The boy worked alone for almost the full hour, and just as the hour was ending, he walked over and peeked at the work of the other students who were working in teams.

Within a few months, when Doug would call for cooperative work, the picture was quite different. The boy would walk over to Doug and in a quiet voice say, "I don't want to work with anyone." Doug would say that was ok, and the boy would begin working alone. Within about five minutes he would join his group.

Doug reported that there had been a steady decline in how much time the boy worked alone and a steady increases in cooperative work. As a psychologist I recognized a classic situation of desensitization. For whatever reason, the boy had developed an aversion to working with others. And slowly, at his own pace, he was desensitizing himself to working with others, finding it rewarding.

The boy had learned the most important lesson possible that school year. And it was made possible because Doug wisely side-stepped the power play. If, when the boy had said he did not want to work with others, Doug had replied, "You have to," they would have gotten stuck in a power play, each trying to control the other.

Although you might want to control seating and ask students to sit with their teammates, cooperative learning should be an opportunity rather than an assignment. If students are not ready for teamwork, that is fine. The modern think tank is a nice model for the classroom. Sometimes people work alone, sometimes in groups, and there are individual differences in how much time each person prefers team versus individual work.

One way of increasing the probability that all students will participate is to make the positive interdependence of the cooperative learning task more salient. If all students know that the gain of one is a gain for all, teammates will be more likely to encourage participation of all members. Further, if the the refusenick is a good student who does well on his or her own, when that student realizes that helping others will lead to gains for him/herself, the student will be more likely to participate.

Assigning attractive roles is another approach. For example, if the Refusenick is Student 3 on a team, I might say, "Today all the Student 3's will have a very special role. They will be in charge of carefully cutting out the materials we will use in building our team space stations. Be very careful, all Number 3's, the success of you teams depends on you. Your teammates are counting on you." Later in the lesson, I might structure for encouragement or praise by saying, "Teammates, take a moment and let all the Number 3's know how much you appreciate the careful job they are doing."

Skill-of-the-Week: Encouraging Participation, Polite Requests, Accepting Individual Differences, Helping.

Roles & Gambits. Encouragers learn how to "bring in" a student without getting into a power play. Demands (You have to do more") are weak gambits. Polite requests ("Would you be willing to...") are strong gambits.

You may assign a special role to the refusenick. For example, a student may be assigned to the role of roving reporter to check for bright ideas coming from various groups. Given special status, the student might warm to participating.

Modeling & Reinforcement. The teacher compliments groups when all members are working together. She/he points out strong encouraging gambits.

Structures & Structuring. Roundtable, Roundrobin, Talking Chips, Three-Step Interview, Flashcard Game, Pairs Check, all often encourage involvement.

Reflection & Planning. Ask groups to talk about what they are doing to make all participants comfortable. How encouraging are they? What new encouraging gambits can we add to our Gambit Chart? How can we be sure to include everyone?

Problem 3.
THE REJECTED STUDENT

Some students begin the school year carrying heavy baggage from previous years. The rejected student may have been rejected far before you begin cooperative learning. As students first sit down to their teams, at one team there are comments like, "Oh yuck!" and "Look who we got stuck with."

Students can be incredibly cruel. They do not realize the hurt they are causing with their rejecting statements. They are not motivated to hurt, but to be part of the group. They need to stop and reflect on the effect they are having with their rejecting statements. One technique is to have them role play receiving rejecting statements and then the share with each other how they felt when they were rejected. This, of course, is done without specific reference to any person in the class. If successful, the technique leads to an enhanced empathy among students so they cannot reject a fellow student without sharing the pain because they know what it feels like to be on the receiving end of the rejection. At that point, they will not want to reject a fellow student.

If you know you have a rejected student, you may wish to use the sociometric approach to forming teams. See Chapter 6: Teams. By placing the student with three others who do not mind, you stack the cards dramatically in favor of a positive experience for the student.

Another powerful technique is to talk with one of the class leaders, preferably the most popular student in class and discuss the problem. Ask if the student would "adopt," the rejected student. If a student becomes friends with a very popular student, they are accepted by the other students.

Look also for special skills or distinguishing facts in the rejected student and then build a cooperative project which will bring those skills to bear. This approach can include giving the student some special reading or task in preparation for a team project, so the student will have a special contribution to make. The jigsaw approaches work well in this regard as well.

You may work with students to learn the skill of "Dignifying Errors," what to do or say to make someone feel good when they make a mistake, (appreciating the effort, Indicating you understand how easy it would be to make that error, showing how the answer is a correct response to a different question).

Skills-of-the-Week: Encouraging Participation, Equal Participation, Dignifying Errors.

Roles & Gambits. Encourager, "I would like to hear what you think, Stanford."

Modeling & Reinforcement. Pay positive attention to those teams who are including all students, saying things like, "I really appreciate how every member of the Mars Team is involved."

Structures & Structuring. Roundtable, Roundrobin, Talking Chips, Three-Step Interview, Flashcard Game, Pairs Check, all often encourage involvement.

Reflection & Planning. What are we doing to make all students feel included? How can we make sure everyone is included?

Problem 4.
THE SHY STUDENT

Shyness is a serious and common problem. Cooperative learning can help many students overcome what otherwise can become a crippling personality disorder.

The shy student finds it far easier to talk to one other person than to talk in a group of three, and infinitely more comfortable to do pair work than to speak in front of the whole class.

One of the most effective approaches with the shy student is to get the other three students to request, show interest in, and praise the contributions of the student. Teammates, when caring and motivated can "bring out" the shy student in remarkably short order.

Like with the rejected student, if you can engage the services of a student leader to befriend the shy student, you will have more than half the battle won.

Also, finding the special interests or talents of the shy student and making that area a project topic is a powerful approach.

You may try when forming groups to include the shy student in a team with at least one other quiet or less dominant student. The shy student needs "room" to make an entry and does not do well with all dominant others.

Skill-of-the-Week: Encouraging Participation.

Roles & Gambits. The Encourager learns how to provide inclusion opportunities without putting a student on the spot. Weak Gambit: "John, you haven't said a thing. What is your opinion." Stronger Gambit: "John, I would like to know what you think about that?"

Have students practice "starter gambits" -- gambits which begin a contribution. ("I have an idea..." "Let me add..." "Let me see, I think...")

You may wish to assign the shy student to the role of teammate observer, watching for a specific behavior, with the job of reporting back to the group about that behavior.

Modeling & Reinforcement. Let the student know you understand their difficulty and appreciate their contributions.

Structures & Structuring. Talking Chips, Turn Toss, Roundrobin, Roundtable, Pairs Check, Flashcard Game, Broken Squares.

Reflection & Planning. Have we made everyone on the team comfortable? Are we including everyone?

Spencer Kagan: *Cooperative Learning*©
Publisher: Resources for Teachers , Inc. • 1(800) Wee Co-op

Problem 5.
THE DOMINANT STUDENT

The dominant student is often a well-intentioned, high-achieving student who does not realize the alienating effect of their controlling efforts. Sometimes, by force of personality, a weaker student academically will get a team to go along with a poor approach to a problem or a false answer, while a meeker student has a superior solution.

The dominant student needs to learn their stimulus value for others. It can be helpful to have students take turns each playing the role of the "Team Boss," and then reflecting on how it felt to be the boss and to have a boss. Finally they discuss gambits for dealing with over-controlling behavior on the part of one teammate. It is helpful also if they recognize the good intentions which usually underlie the controlling behavior. This may increase the ability of teammates to label and deal with dominance gambits.

Skill-of-the-Week: Equal Participation.

Roles & Gambits. Gatekeeper, Question Commander, Encourager. Have students practice gambits for including everyone. Poor: John, you are doing all the talking. Stronger: Susan, what do you think about what John has been telling us?

Assign roles so that each person has a unique and important contribution to make to the task.

Modeling & Reinforcement. Let the class see good gatekeeping. Pay positive attention to groups in which there is equal participation.

Structures & Structuring. Talking Chips with Timer, Paraphrase Passport, Response Mode Chips, Roundtable, Roundrobin, Pair Work.

Reflection & Planning. How equal has our participation been so far today? How can we make it more equal?

Problem 6.
THE HOSTILE STUDENT

You assign Talking Chips, and Steven throws them at his teammates. Jane grabs the crayon out of Sandy's hand. Peter insults Jane, calling her an idiot. Verbal and physical hostility among students, unfortunately is common.

If there is reason to anticipate inappropriate behaviors, during an initial class discussion examples of desired and inappropriate behaviors are discussed and role-played. The class generates a list of inappropriate (put-downs, killer statements, grabbing) and desired behaviors (appreciations, encouragement, asking for). Groups are given time to discuss the potential consequences of each type of behavior. This will give them a reference point later in dealing with the bully, and will place their focus on behaviors, not individuals.

The first rule is that the classroom must be safe physically and emotionally for all students. Certain behavior is not permissible.

Hostile and aggressive behavior is often attention-seeking behavior, so it is important that it not be rewarded. If a student throws things or hits another, that should not be rewarded with special attention in the form of teacher talk. Rather, students who are hostile need to know ahead of time that their behavior will lose them attention.

If a student has been hostile, allow some time to transpire between the offending incident and the talk. Postponing dealing with the hostile incident until the class meeting is a good way of allowing a cooling off period and providing room for students to seek their own solutions.

If a student is hostile repeatedly, it is helpful to clearly state what you would appreciate from the student, and what you need. Clear consequences for the inappropriate behavior need be stated. Again, a power play is avoided. Rather than "Don't do X," it is better to say, "If You Do X, I will do Y." In an extreme case, some pull-out from the team may be necessary. This is a last resort and should be avoided if possible. If a pull-out is used, it should always be accompanied with a reentry program which includes a certain amount of time with the team during fun teambuilding activities, and an opportunity for more such time contingent on desired behavior.

Some teachers develop a warning system. Students who behave inappropriately receive a warning card. They know that if they receive a predetermined number of warning cards, they will be asked to sit apart from their group, in isolation. If the rules of the warning and isolation system are clearly stated for all before they are applied to any individual, the system can be carried out with almost no interruption of the class. Such a system, however, is necessary only with very unusual classes or individuals.

It is best whenever possible to avoid an individual teacher-student confrontation. Remember, responsibility remains with the team. Teammembers will gladly give the bully problem back to the teacher, but if the teacher takes over, he or she has given up the most powerful potential tool for dealing with a student -- peer influence. Over time, the teammates of the individual who is demonstrating inappropriate behavior will confront him or her with the fact that he or she is preventing them from reaching desired goals.

Immediately following a disruptive incident the teacher may give a quiet signal, draw attention to teams which are working well together, and give them positive recognition. This will increase the motivation of teammates to bring the bully in line. It will also increase their frustration at his or her disruptive behavior.

Some aggressive behavior occurs for lack of knowledge of alternatives. Students grab paper or materials because they have not practiced "Polite Requests."

Hostile and aggressive behavior is much more likely in situations in which there is low structuring than if there is high structuring. For example, hostile behavior will almost never occur during a quick paced Roundtable. During unstructured Team Discussion, the probability of hostile or aggressive behavior increases dramatically. Therefore, if there is some likelihood of hostile behavior, high structuring is preferable.

If a student is hostile very often, you may work with his/her three teammates to create a reinforcement schedule. Have the teammates make positive statements and attention to the student each time he/she goes for ten minutes with no hostility. They say things like, "I am really enjoying working with you today, Mike." This approach is extremely powerful, and may be applied with good success will full knowledge of all of the students, including the hostile students. In introducing the approach you might say something like, "Mike, you have had some trouble controlling yourself. I want you to be clear about the positive effect it has on others when you do show control. So, I am going to ask your teammates to share with you how good they feel about working with you any time you go for ten minutes without grabbing materials, hitting anyone, shouting at, or putting anyone down."

Some hostile behavior is simply a reflection of negative peer norms. For example, "Put downs" are very common -- so common that students give them to each other and themselves without reflection. Here, as with rejecting statements, there is value in having students practice receiving a put-down and sharing how they feel. Through this process they can come to an agreement on a class norm against put-downs. If the class is using many put-downs, the Skill-of-the-Week should be Praising.

Skill-of-the-Week: Praising, Polite Requests, Disagree Politely, Conflict Resolution

Roles & Gambits. Praiser, Helper, Gatekeeper. Develop gambits for disagreeing politely, and for resolving conflicts.

Modeling & Reinforcement. Model and reinforce creative responses to conflict.

Structures & Structuring. Affirmation Chips.

Reflection & Planning. Have we been showing respect and appreciation to each other? What can we do if there is a disagreement? What can we do if someone grabs something from us? Which polite request gambits have your heard today?

Problem 7.

INTERPERSONAL CONFLICT

Interpersonal conflict occurs primarily in situations of low structure, especially when there are not good models of decision making and conflict resolution. The decision making structures include Spend-A-Buck, Consensus, and Proactive Prioritizing. See Chapter 13: Communication Skills Structures.

To resolve conflicts students need to know a variety of approaches and to practice gambits associated with each.

Many teachers find it useful to share with the students the eight modes of conflict resolution and to teach the students the mnemonic: STOP HACC which stands for Share, Take Turns, Outside Help, Postpone, Humor, Avoid, Compromise and Chance.

After students learn the mnemonic, they practice gambits associated with each mode of conflict resolution. Simulations like "Truck Driver" can be designed to set students into a structured conflict to allow them to interact and reflect afterwards on the effectiveness of various approaches.

Problem 8.
POOR HELPING

Noreen Webb, (1985) and her associates at UCLA have documented the importance of helping skills for producing academic gains. If students do not ask for help, they do not receive it and do not show great gains. If they as for help but are ignored, they do not show gains. If they ask for help and are told answers, they do not show gains. If they ask for help, and are showed how to get answers, they show gains. Thus we must work on two sides of the helping issues: Asking for Help and Providing Good Helpers -- helpers which empower the learner.

In addition to the same four tools which can can be used with every social skill, specific tools were developed at UCLA, including, Helping Observation Forms, Helping Reflection Forms, and the Helping Role Play Lesson.

8 Modes of Conflict Resolution

Share
Take Turns
Outside Help
Postpone
Humor
Avoid
Compromise
Chance

Conflict Resolution Simulation

Adapted from Dr. Arthur Thayer, Assistant Executive Secretary, Association of California School Administrators.

TRUCK DRIVER

Purpose: To involve students in a simulated value problem concerning the individual's values in relation to a group of other individuals. The simulation focuses on self-interest and requires decision making and conflict management/resolution.

Objectives:

- To identify conflicts between individuals.

- To develop alternative strategies and processes for resolving conflicts.

- To involve individuals in a problem solving activity.

- To encourage use of decision-making skills.

- To analyze the process of decision making.

- To analyze the values that are demonstrated.

Related Concepts: Value conflict, conflict management and resolution consensus, compromise, problem solving, decision making.

Materials: Conflict Resolution Scenario, one copy for each teammember.

Time: 30 minutes to one hour, specified by the teacher in advance. Inform students that some may not reach a decision in the time allotted.

Grade Level: Upper elementary - adult

The Activity: Prior to playing the simulation, begin by asking the following questions:

"What is a conflict?"

"How can conflicts be managed and/or resolved?

"What are the alternatives?"

"What is a value? Upon what information (data) can values be determined and analyzed?"

Put all responses on chart or transparency and put it away until after the simulation. Divide participants into groups of seven or fewer. Ask each group to select a foreman (observers will note how the foreman was selected). Hand out the scenario to the groups and have them follow the directions.

Conflict Resolution Scenario

THE SCENARIO
Today the Resources Repair Company received a new service truck to add to the existing group of six other small service trucks owned by the company. As has been done in the past, the new truck is exchanged for an old truck. The company has to decide which of the five drivers should get the truck.

THE TASK
• Decide to whom the new truck is to be given.
• Be able to discuss how you arrived at your team decision.
• You have _____ minutes to make the decision.
• Each person in the group assumes one role. If you have fewer than seven people, leave out some employees, but do not leave out the observer or the foreman.

THE ROLES

1. Ben Taylor, Foreman: has a two-year old Ford truck. As the foreman, you have the problem of deciding to which of your crew you should give the new truck. Often there are hard feelings because each member of the crew seems to feel he/she is entitled to the new truck, so you have a tough time being fair. As a matter of fact, it usually turns out that whatever you decide, most of the crew consider it wrong. You now have to face the same issue again because a new truck has just been allocated to you for distribution. In order to handle this problem, you have decided to put the decision to the entire crew. You will tell them about the new truck and will put the problem in terms of what would be the fairest way to distribute the truck.

2. George: You have been with the company 17 years. You feel you deserve the truck because you have been with the company longer than any of the other workers. Your Ford truck is in excellent shape, and you want to receive the new truck. Seniority is the only way to determine who gets the new truck.

3. Leslie: 11 years with the company has a five-year old Dodge truck. You feel you deserve a new truck and it certainly is your turn. Your present truck is old and since the more senior member of the crew has a fairly new truck, you should get the next one. You have taken excellent care of your present Dodge, and have kept it looking like new. A person deserves to be rewarded if he/she treats a company truck like his/her own.

4. John: 10 years with the company has a four-year old Ford truck. You have to do more driving than most of the other members of the crew because you work in the suburbs. You have a fairly old truck and you feel you should have the new one because you do so much driving. Besides, Ben's wife is your cousin.

5. Carroll: 5 years with the company has a three-year old Ford truck. The heater in your present truck is inadequate. Since Lee backed into the door of your truck it has never been repaired to fit right. The door lets in too much cold air, and you attribute your frequent colds to this. You want to have a warm truck since you have a good deal of driving to do. As long as it has good tires, brakes and is comfortable, you don't care about its make.

6. Lee: 3 years with the company has a five-year old Chevrolet truck. You have the poorest truck in the crew. It is five years old, and before you got it, it had been in a bad wreck. It has never been good and you've put up with it for three years. It's about time you got a good truck to drive, and it seems only fair that the next one should be yours. You have a good accident record. The only accident you had was when you sprung the door of Carroll's truck when he opened it as you backed out of the garage.

7. Observer: Your task is to observe the activities of the members of your group. You should keep notes about what the group did. Some questions you might consider are:

1. Do you agree (or disagree) with the group on their decision and how it was reached?
2. What steps did the group take in deciding who was to get the truck?
3. How did the individuals react to one another in the decision-making process?
4. Was there a systematic (step-by-step) way of solving the problem?
5. When tentative decisions were posed, was there any agreement or consensus?
6. What conflicts were strongest? How were these conflicts managed or resolved?
7. Did Ben Taylor demonstrate leadership ability? Explain.
8. What insights (information) did you gain about individual values in the group?
9. Were there any unusual or important decisions made by any individuals in the group?. What learning seemed to take place by individuals or the group?
10. Which style of conflict resolution did each member adopt?

SUGGESTIONS FOR DEBRIEFING TRUCK DRIVER

Concerning the Simulation: Ask each group who received the truck and why they gave it to whom they did. (Ask foreman, then ask drivers to see if there is agreement or disagreement). Ask each group how they arrived at their decision. Ask the observer of each group for comments (agreement of disagreement) on why the group gave the truck to whom they did, and how they arrived at this decision.

Concerning the Process: Ask the observer to explain or comment on the process used to make the decision. Then ask the participants for their reactions to the observer's comments.

Concerning the Participants: Ask if any participants gained insights into what they value. If there are responses, ask them to explain what they learned about themselves. Ask how they felt while taking part in the simulation:

Closure Questions:

1. Can this problem happen in real life?

2. Has anything like this happened to you in real life?

3. How did you feel as a participant?

4. Would you do anything differently as a result of this activity?

5. How did you feel about the other drivers? anger? frustration? sympathy? empathy? etc. How did you deal with these feelings?

Concerning the Concept/Objectives: Take out the overhead or chart paper generated at the outset of the lesson. Have students discuss if then ideas changed about conflict, conflict management, and values.

Helping Behavior Role Play Lesson

Adapted from: Lee, K., et al, (1985).

Strategy: Role Play

Level: Lower Elementary and above

Step 1: Select an Activity. Demonstration of a helping behavior --The teacher gives a group a task to perform in front of the room. The group performs the task demonstrating the designated helping behavior. (Explaining a skill, concept, or rule; or asking a specific question about something not understood). Any of a variety of tasks may be used depending on the content or class. Example: punctuation rule to be used, a word problem to be solved, a science experiment to be explained, a passage from a text to be learned, a poem to be evaluated, a map or chart to be interpreted, vocabulary to be understood.

Step 2: Make Decisions

Group Size: 3 or 4 to perform, the rest of the class as an audience

Room arrangement: Class as audience sitting together with one group performing in the front

Time Allotment: 15-minute periods spread over several weeks

Materials Needed One set of materials for the group to use during the task and a chart with helping behaviors listed. Observation charts for audience (optional).

Step 3: Set the Lesson

a. Task Statement: "In your small group you need to role play how you would complete the task of _____." (Whatever task the class is doing). As you work, you need to have someone act as if she or he didn't understand. That person needs to ask questions that someone else in the group will answer. The helper will offer an explanation of the _____ (rule, concept, or skill being covered)."

To the audience: "You need to watch the group perform and be ready to identify questions that were asked and the explana-tions that were given. You also need to be ready to evaluate how effective the group members were at helping each other learn. You may assign points as follows:

Were specific questions asked? (1-3 points)

Were explanations given? (1-3 points)

Was every member involved? (1-3 points)

Step 4: Reflection After the role playing performance, the groups analyze and evaluate the role, perhaps using the checklist. They discuss how the behaviors shown could be applied in their own groups.

Step 5: Anticipate Possible Problems and Interventions

a. Possible Problem: Individuals in the role play group do not ask for help or give the help when asked.

b. Possible Interventions: 1) Stop the group and review what the checklist shows; 2) Encourage the students to ask for or give help; 3) Model for the students how to ask for or give help; 4) Bring to the students' attention who has asked for help and not been helped; 5) Ask the audience for suggestions.

Variations

1. The role playing format can also be used for solving problems that occur while groups are working: Using other words besides "You're wrong," to avoid win/lose situations; or saying something/offering help in a tone of voice or with words that peers can "hear".

Helping Gambits

Helping
Looks like: eye contact, leaning toward the other
Sounds like: "Do you understand?"
"Let me explain."
"You do it like this because .."

Asking for Help
Looks like: eye contact, leaning toward the other
Sounds like "I don't understand why . . ."
"Explain how . ." "Why is the answer .?"

(How to avoid-shouting, talking down to those that don't understand, etc.)

2. The role playing format can also be used for building a variety of group skills like encouraging, keeping to the task, taking turns, sharing materials, contributing ideas, praising.

3. One or two students are selected to use observation sheets to count the various kinds of helping behaviors that occurred.~

References

Andrini, Beth. *Cooperative Learning and Mathematics.* Resources for Teacher, Inc. San Juan Capistrano, CA: 1991

Curran, Lorna. *Cooperative Learning Lessons for Little Ones: Literature Based Language Arts and Social Skills.* Resources for Teachers, Inc. San Juan Capistrano, CA: 1990.

Gwilliam, J., Hughes, G. , Jenkins, D., Koczka, W. & Nicholis, L. *"Working together, learning together: The cooperatively structured classroom."* Regina: Department of Cooperation and Cooperative Development -- Education Unit, Saskatchewan Co-operation and Co-operative Development, 1983.

Johnson, D., Johnson, R. *Creative Conflict.* Interaction Book Company, Edina, MN: 1988.

Kreidler, William. *Creative Conflict Resolution.* Goodyear Books, Scott, Foresman & Co., Glenview, IL: 1984.

Lee, K., Oakes, J., Cohn, J., Webb, N. & Farivar, S. *"Helping Behaviors Handbook."* Los Angeles: Unpublished Manuscript, Graduate School of Education, University of California, Los Angeles, CA, 1985.

Lewin, K. *Resolving Social Conflicts.* New York: Harper & Row, 1948.

Shaw, Vanston. *Community Building.* Resources for Teachers, San Juan Capistrano, CA., 1992

Shure, Myrna. *Problem Solving in the Preschool.* Hahnemann University, Philadelphia, PA: 1989.

Stone, Jeanne. *Cooperative Learning & Language Arts: A Multi-Structural Approach.* Resources for Teachers, Inc. San Juan Capistrano, CA. 1989.

Sapon-Shevin, Mara. *Teaching Cooperation.* In G. Cartledge & J.F. Milburn .(Eds.) Teaching Social Skills to Children. New York: Pergamon Press, 1986.

Webb, Noreen M. *Student interaction and learning in small groups: A Research Summary.* **In R. Slavin, S. Sharan, S. Kagan, R. Hertz-Larowitz, C. Webb, & R. Schmuck** (Eds.) *Learning to cooperate, cooperating to learn.* New York: Plenum, 1985.

Materials:

Kagan, Spencer. *The Role Card Packet.* San Juan Capistrano: Resources for Teachers, Inc: 1991.

How Helpful Was I?

 1. When I knew an answer
or had an idea, I shared it.

 2. I encouraged others in my group.

3. I used names.

 4. I felt encouraged by people in my group.

5. When my answer was not the same as
my partner's, I tried to find out why.

 6. When I did not understand something, I asked my partner.

 7. When my partner did not understand, I helped him/her.

Goal Setting
What can you do to make your group better?

Did I Help?

Name _____   **Group Name** _____

Date _____

		Often	Sometimes	Never
1.	I checked to make sure everyone understood what I did.	☐	☐	☐
2.	I answered any questions that were asked.	☐	☐	☐
3.	I gave explanations whenever I could.	☐	☐	☐
4.	I asked specific questions about what I didn't understand.	☐	☐	☐
5.	When I had difficulty, I got extra practice or help.	☐	☐	☐
6.	I paraphrased what others said to be sure I understood.	☐	☐	☐

How can I be more helpful?

_____

_____

_____

_____

Adapted From: Lee,K., Oakes, J., Cohn,J., Webb, N. & Farivar, S. "Helping behaviors handbook." Los Angeles: Unpublished Manuscript, Graduate School Of Education, University of California, Los Angeles, Ca. 1985

Giving Help Observation Sheet

	Giving Explanations	Checking for Understanding	Modeling How To Get An Answer	Receiving Help
Team 1				
Team 2				
Team 3				
Team 4				
Team 5				
Team 6				
Team 7				
Team 8				

INSTRUCTIONS:
Stand by each group for one minute. Do not interact with group members. Record each use of each skill with a mark.

Observation Date _____

Observer Name _____

Adapted form: Lee,K., Oakes, J., Cohn, J., Webb, N. & Farivar, S. "Helping behaviors Handbook" Unpublished Manuscript, Graduate School of Education, UCLA, CA. 1985

Chapter 15

Cooperative Projects

Cooperative learning reaches its full power as all students work together, each making an important individual contribution toward a group goal. Perhaps the purest form of cooperative learning occurs as all students coordinate efforts to complete a cooperative project.

There are an infinite number of possible cooperative projects. Simple teambuilding and classbuilding projects such as Team Notebooks, Team Towers, Team Airplanes, Team Shelters, and Class Books have been described in Chapters 8 and 9. Structured Sorts and Team Word Webbs are also projects (See Chapter 11: Thinking Skills Structures). Cooperative projects involve a product which is a unique creation to which all team-members have contributed.

Cooperative projects range from highly-structured curriculum-driven lessons to very loosely structured activities. Let's distinguish three types of projects: Team Challenges, Teacher-Directed Multi-Structural Lessons, and Student-Directed Multi-Structural Lessons.

Team Challenges

A Team Challenge may be quite simple: "On your desk you will find ten pieces of spaghetti and ten gum drops. Your job as a team is to build a space station. You may break the spaghetti, but you may not cut the gum drops. You have fifteen minutes. Go." Or a Team Challenge may be more complex. In this chapter you will find two sample Team Challenges: "Haunted Hangers," a typical cooperative art project, and "Let's Make Squares," a project I designed to help students learn geometry through play.

Teacher-Directed Multi-Structural Lessons

A Teacher-Directed Multi-Structural Lesson has students complete a project by taking them through a series of structures. There are now several books on multi-structural lessons (Andrini, 1991; Curran, 1991; Stone, 1991; Wiederhold, 1991). In this chapter, you will find a sample Teacher-Directed Multi-Structural Lesson, "Fables," from Jeanne Stone's book *Cooperative Learning and Language Arts* (1991).

Student-Directed Multi-Structural Lessons

Finally, there are Student-Directed Multi-Structural Lessons. The science lesson, Surface Tension, is an example of a Student-Directed Multi-Structural Lesson developed by *Miguel Kagan* (Resources for Teachers). Instead of a teacher leading students through a class-paced series of structures, the team leads itself, at its own rate, through a series of structures which are designed to reach a predetermined set of learning objectives. Student-Directed Multi-Structural Lessons are ideal for Workstation Jigsaw (See Chapter 18) and Rotation Learning Centers (See Chapter 19).

Spencer Kagan: *Cooperative Learning*©
Publisher: Resources for Teachers , Inc. • 1(800) Wee Co-op

Project Principles

As students work on projects, they may need a block of time with no teacher intervention. The extent to which this time is productive depends in part on the amount and kind of structuring put in place before the students go to work. Unstructured group work can lead to unequal participation, time off task, power conflicts, and poor learning. To maximize efficient group work, we apply the basic principles of cooperative learning: Positive Interdependence, Individual Accountability, and Simultaneous Interaction.

~ See Chapter 4: Six Key Concepts ~

POSITIVE INTERDEPENDENCE

Structuring positive interdependence into cooperative projects is useful for a number of reasons. When students working together 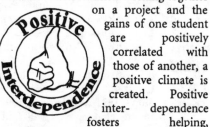 on a project and the gains of one student are positively correlated with those of another, a positive climate is created. Positive inter dependence fosters helping, encouraging, and tutoring. There are a number of ways to promote positive interdependence in project work. See box.

INDIVIDUAL ACCOUNTABILITY

Making each student individually account able for his/her contribution to the team project is another way to get all students to participate. Some students will put more ef 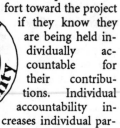 fort toward the project if they know they are being held individually ac countable for their contribu tions. Individual accountability increases individual participation and aids in equalizing participation, and eliminates the problems of the freeloader and the workhorse. The box "Structuring Individual Accountability"

Structuring

Positive Interdependence For Projects

1. Goals
We all have the same goal in doing this project.

2. Rewards
We will receive team recognition for our project.

3. Task
The task is structured so we can't do it alone. Everyone must contribute for our project to be successful.

4. Resources
We depend on Sue for work with the scissors, Jose for gluing, Veronica for writing, and Pete for drawing.

5. Roles
We each have an important role; Such as Materials Monitor, Reporter, Cheerleader, and Recorder .

---

gives a few suggestions for structuring a project to include individual accountability. Equal participation allows for a mutual feeling of ownership. Each student feels that this is "our project" and is more inclined to want work on the project. There are a few basic

---

Structuring

Individual Accountability

For Achievement
1. Color-code individual contributions.
2. Recognize teams based on individual performance.
3. Give teams time to reflect on individual contributions and role performance.
4. Assign and grade Mini-Topics, parts of the project for which students are individually accountable.

For Participation
1. Use Talking Chips.
2. Have students summarize their individual participation.
3. Have students take time to reflect on participation.
4. Give students their own parts (see color-coded strips of "Lets Make Squares").

For Listening
1. Use Paraphrase Passport and Three-Step Interview.
2. Have students share ideas heard from others.

Structuring

Equal Participation

1. Task Structure

The task is structured so that everyone involved must participate. Division of labor is effective to insure that everyone has an unique contribution to the project.

2. Reward Structure

Rewards are obtainable only if all participate.

3. Resources

Divide the resources among those involved in the project. Make each individual accountable for the way their own resources are used. Use a different color paper or ink per student.

4. Roles

Each student has a different, important role. Roles might be task specific, such as "Gum Drop Holder," "Spaghetti Pusher." Roles as Gatekeeper, Taskmaster, and Encourager are effective for encouraging equal participation.

---

ways to ensure that students will participate equally. See "Structuring Equal Participation."

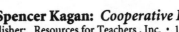

SIMULTANEOUS INTERACTION

Simultaneous interaction is very important in cooperative projects. The task should be structured so that interaction occurs simultaneously both within and among teams. Simultaneous interaction ensures that projects are more efficient, since all are working on the project concomitantly. Active involvement by all students decreases the probability of management problems and increases learning opportunities.

Simultaneous Sharing

There are a number of simultaneous sharing structures which allows for the sharing of cooperative projects. For example, using Team Inside Outside Circle, in ten minutes each team in a class can have five minutes to share their project, whereas it would take a full class period for all teams in a class to share their project if the traditional, one-at-a time, structure is used. ∾

∾ See Chapter 12: Information Sharing Structures ∾

References:

Cohen, Elizabeth. *Designing Groupwork.* New York, NY: Teacher College Press, 1986.

Johnson, D. & R., & Holubec, E. *Circles of Learning: Cooperation in the Classroom.* Edina, MN: Interaction Book Company, 1986.

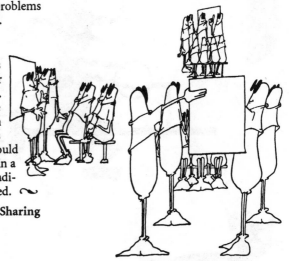

Team Inside-Outside Circle

Spencer Kagan: *Cooperative Learning*©
Publisher: Resources for Teachers , Inc. • 1(800) Wee Co-op

Student Handout:

Haunted Hangers
(A Halloween Cooperative Project)

Team Challenge: Your team is to design and create a wall hanging using construction paper shapes on the theme Halloween. Let's see how creative you can get!

Team Materials:
- 2 Scissors
- 1 Glue Bottle
- 4 Sheets of Colored Construction Paper

Team Roles:
- Gatekeeper
- Taskmaster
- Encourager
- Cheerleader

Possible Shapes:

Circles

Squares

Rectangles

Ovals

Semi-Circles

Triangles

Teacher Guide:

"Let's Make Squares"

Introduce the Materials and Game Rules

Duplicate and distribute the three student handouts, Instructions, Game Rules, and Game strips. Each team receives all three handouts. Have students in teams create the strips, experiment with them, discuss the rules, and attempt to master the rules on their own.

Check for Understanding of Game Rules

Check for understanding on the following:
1. **Recognizing "Stackers"**
2. **Recognizing "Touching"**
3. **Recognizing "Crossing"**
4. **Recognizing "Extras"**

Pairs Check, Numbered Heads Together, Send-A-Problem, and Trade-A-Problem work well to check for understanding on these. For example, to have students improve their counting, use Trade-A-Problem as follows:

1) Have teams draw some squares using twelve lines.

2) Students write the answer on the back of the paper.

3) Students then Trade-A-Problem with another team to check for understanding and agreement.

Assign Rotating Social Roles

1. **Chief Scribe:** Record all solutions with paper and pencil.

2. **Cheerleader:** Make sure your team stops to celebrate each time a solution is found.

3. **Taskmaster:** Keep the group focused. If you have found a one square solution, make sure the teammates all look for a two square solution, and so on.

4. **Executive Encourager:** If the group gets discouraged, find a way to increase optimism and effort.

Have the students make role cards and then tell them the roles will rotate each time they make a new number of squares. The easiest way to have the roles rotate is to simply have them Roundtable the role cards -- pass them one person to the left.

Play "Let's Make Squares"

1. Play Open and Closed Games. Have students make squares 1 to 12 playing a game. Later have them do it again, playing a game with "Extras allowed." Give them instructions each time, something like this:

"After you make one square from the twelve strips, try making two, then three, and so on. See how high your team can go. Be sure to record each solution."

You may try a simultaneous share as the solutions are collected in bins so later students can explore how many solutions they made for each number of squares.

2. Greatest Number. What is the *greatest* number of squares you can make with just twelve strips? With eight strips?

3. Ways to make___? How many ways can you find to make 5 squares? 11 squares?

4. Try Eight. Once your team has found a way to make every number of squares from 1 to 12 with 12 strips (this could take several sessions), see what you can do with only 8 strips -- two per teammate.

5. Roll and Race. Roll dice and give your team and another team a time limit, say 10 minutes, and see how many ways you can make the number of squares on the roll of dice. Work alone as teams, record your solutions, and when the time limit is up, compare your solutions. Use a Venn diagram to record how many solutions were unique to each team and how many you both found.

Spencer Kagan: *Cooperative Learning*©
Publisher: Resources for Teachers , Inc. • 1(800) Wee Co-op

"Let's Make Squares"

Game Strips

Instructions: Cut these strips and divide them so each person in the team has strips with a different pattern.

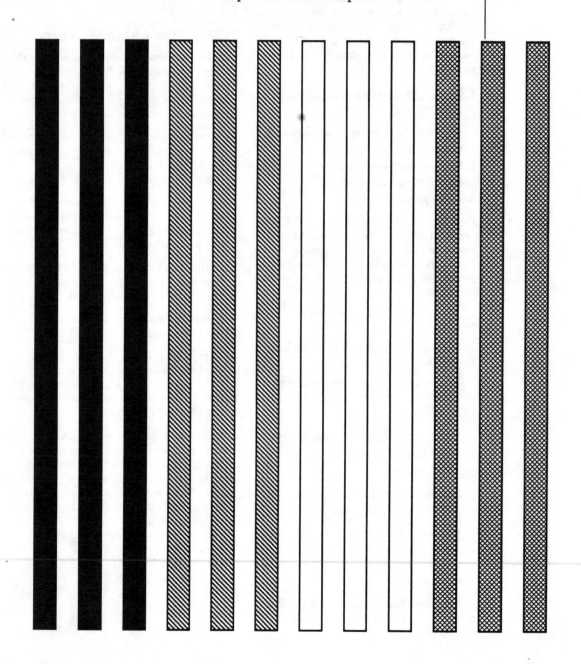

Spencer Kagan: *Cooperative Learning*©
Publisher: Resources for Teachers , Inc. • 1(800) Wee Co-op

Student Handout 2:

"Let's Make Squares"
Instructions

There are four members to a team. Cut out the game strips. Each of you takes three strips of one color. When you play "Let's Make Squares," each of you is allowed to handle your own color strips only. As a team your job is to "Make Squares."

The way you "Make Squares" is to lay down all of the strips and to count the number of squares you have made. For example, the twelve strips in Figure 1 make three squares. The same twelve strips rearranged in Figure 2 make four squares. It turns out that with the twelve strips you can make one square, two squares, three squares, four squares, five squares, and so on.

Figure 1: Three Squares

Figure 2: Four Squares

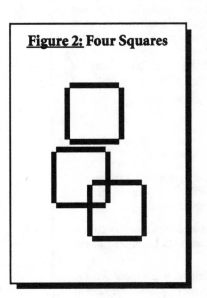

Spencer Kagan: *Cooperative Learning*©
Publisher: Resources for Teachers , Inc. • 1(800) Wee Co-op

Student Handout 3:

"Let's Make Squares"
Game Rules

Never Allowed

Stacking: Stacking is when a strip lays lengthwise on top of some part or all of another strip. Stacked strips face the same direction. *Stacking is never allowed.*

Touching: Touching strips lay side-by-side with edges touching. *Touching is never allowed.*

Always Allowed

Crossing: Two crossed strips touch at one point only; they face different directions. Crossing is *always* allowed. A strip can cross many other strips.

Sometimes Allowed

Extras: Extras are strips which have an open end or which do not contribute to making a square. Three strips alone in the shape of a triangle have no open ends, but are "extras" because they do not contribute to making a square. A strip which helps make a square, but which has an open end which does not touch another strip is also an "extra." Extras are allowed in a game if we say "Extras Allowed," but they are not allowed if we say "No Extras." Playing with "No Extras" is much harder, so you should play first with "Extras Allowed."

RULES

1. 12 Only: You must use all twelve strips each time you "make squares."

2. One Color: Each teammate can handle one color strip only, but your strips can cross the strips of teammates.

3. No Cuts or Bends: Strips must lay flat on the table; you cannot fold, bend, tear, or cut a strip.

4. No Stacking: Strips can cross any number of other strips, but they cannot lay on top of another strip lengthwise.

5. No Touching: Strips cannot lay side by side with edges touching.

6. Extras: If "No Extras" is the rule, all strips must contribute to making at least one square, and no strips can have open ends (an end which does not touch another strip).

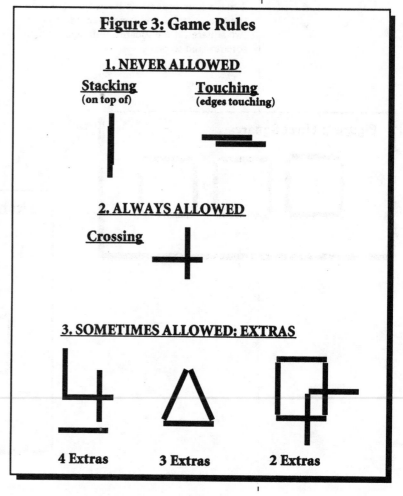

Figure 3: Game Rules

1. NEVER ALLOWED

Stacking (on top of)   **Touching** (edges touching)

2. ALWAYS ALLOWED

Crossing

3. SOMETIMES ALLOWED: EXTRAS

4 Extras   **3 Extras**   **2 Extras**

Spencer Kagan: *Cooperative Learning*©
Publisher: Resources for Teachers , Inc. • 1(800) Wee Co-op

Possible Solutions:

Let's Make Squares
Teacher's Guide

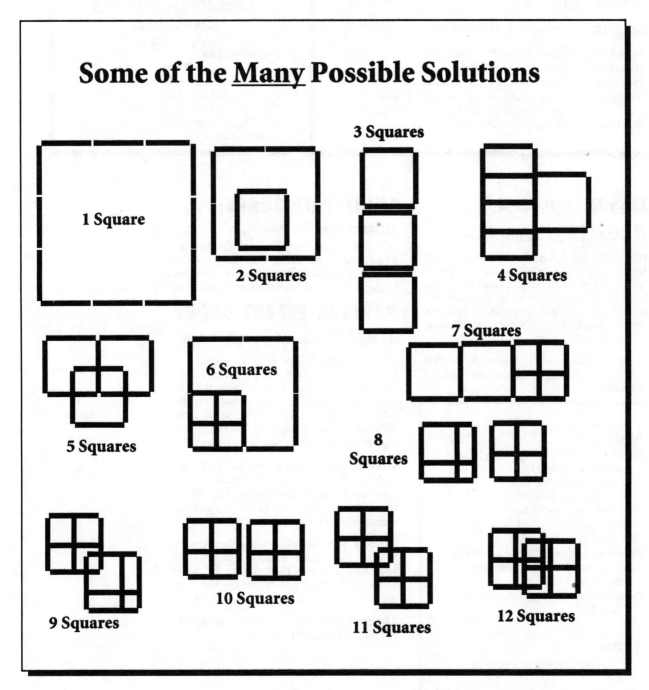

Some of the <u>Many</u> Possible Solutions

1 Square

2 Squares

3 Squares

4 Squares

5 Squares

6 Squares

7 Squares

8 Squares

9 Squares

10 Squares

11 Squares

12 Squares

Spencer Kagan: *Cooperative Learning*©
Publisher: Resources for Teachers , Inc. • 1(800) Wee Co-op

Sample Lesson From Jeanne Stone (1991) *Cooperative Learning and Language Arts*

FABLES

Grades: 4-8

Domain: Imaginative/Narrative

Academic Skills:

Listening: Listen to storytelling
Speaking:: Participate in a group discussion
Reading: Relate personal experiences to a fable
Read a variety of fables
Writing: Write a new fable (Extension)

Cooperative Learning Structures:

- Modeling
- Think-Pair-Share
- Partner-Expert Group Jigsaw
- Team Discussion
- Simple Projects
- Team Interview
- Fastwrite

LESSON SEQUENCE

MODELING: Telling a Fable

Introduce the lesson to the students by telling them that they will be learning about fables. Fables were said to have been first told by Aesop, a slave in sixth-century Greece. Fables are short stories that teach a moral. Usually animals are among the main characters.

Using "The Lion and the Mouse" or another common fable, <u>tell</u> (<u>not</u> read) the fable to the students.

Materials:

Four fables - One each per team (these or any other four)
"The Lion and the Mouse"
"The Fox and the Crow"
"The Crow and the Pitcher"
"Belling the Cat"
"The Donkey Carrying Salt"
Proverbs handout (extension activity)
Fable Outline handout (extension activity)
Compare/Contrast handout (extension activity)

Time:

Two to three language arts periods

THINK-PAIR-SHARE:

Determining the Moral

After listening to the fable, have the students Think-Pair-Share about the moral of the fable. After some class sharing, give the students the moral from the fable itself.

PARTNER-EXPERT GROUP JIGSAW: Learning a New Fable

Pass out a set of four fables to each team. Each team will use the same set of fables. Each student selects a fable from the set. The class forms new groups based on the fables chosen. All students with the same fable form a new group. Within each of the new groups, the students find a partner.

Working with a partner, the students read and learn the fable. If needed, they can take notes on the **Fable Outline** handout. They should be able to tell the basic story and the moral without referring to the Fable Outline.

Partners pair to make an expert group. Within the expert groups, the students review their fable. They discuss the fable, agree on the main points and the moral of the fable.

The partners return to partner groups to practice telling their fable.

Teacher's Note

This lesson will be strengthened if preceded by students having an opportunity to read fables or have fables read to them. Some sample books might be:
Aesop's Fables by Aesop (edited by Ann McGovern)
Three Aesop Fox Tales by Paul Galdone
Aesop's Fables selected and illustrated by Michael Hague
Frederick's Fables by Leo Lionni
Fables by Arnold Lobel
Mousekin's Fables by Edna Miller

The students meet back with their teams. Each student tells his or her fable to the rest of the team. The students should allow for some discussion before stating the moral to allow the team to figure out what the moral is.

TEAM DISCUSSION:
Choosing a Fable to Work With

Each team discusses the relevancy of the fables just heard. They need to discuss which of the fables and morals is most pertinent to their lives and come to consensus on one they will continue working with. After coming to consensus, the team should write the moral of the fable in their own words.

MODELING: Acting Out a Fable

Using "The Lion and the Mouse" have a team volunteer to act the fable out. One of the team members can be the lion. One (or two) can be the mouse. The remaining one or two team members can be animals who pass by without helping, or animals that observe what is happening from a distance. Have the students act out the fable using the dialogue from the actual fable or paraphrasing it in their own words.

SIMPLE PROJECTS:
Acting Out a Fable

Each team reads the fable they selected. This can be Paired Reading or a reader can be selected from the team. The team then assigns roles (all team members must participate in some way) and improvises the action and dialogue in the fable.

Option - Have the teams present their fables to the class or to other teams.

TEAM INTERVIEW:
Character Role Play

Starting with team member #2, each student sits in the center of their team. The other team members ask questions relating to their fable and the character being portrayed. For example, in "The Lion and the Mouse" some sample questions for the mouse might be:

How did you feel while you were chewing the lion's ropes?

Did you really expect to be able to pay the lion back for his good deed?

Some sample questions for the lion might be:

Why do you think no other animals came to help you?

Did you really think the mouse would be able to return the favor?

Repeat the process until all team members have been interviewed.

FASTWRITE:
Personally Relating to the Fable

Have the students fastwrite on how they personally relate to the fable they have been working with. They could write about a personal incident that matches the moral, rewrite the moral in their own words, or write to explain the fable to a younger brother or sister.

ROUNDROBIN:
Responding to Writing

Have the students Roundrobin to share their fastwrites (all or part).

SIMPLE PROJECTS:
Creating a Modern Day Fable

Using the fastwrites as a starting point, each team discusses the moral with its application to today. Using one of the fastwrites or an idea that has developed during the discussion, each team creates a real-life situation that teaches the same moral. The real-life situation becomes a mini-play. Each team member must have a role.

Encourage the use of dialogue and action. When all the groups are ready, the plays can be shared with the whole class.

EXTENSIONS:

INDEPENDENT WRITING

The students have now become familiar with one fable and have physically created a new fable. The next step is to write a fable. Pass out a **Proverb** handout to each student. Have them look over the handout and identify a proverb that could become a moral for their fable.   Decisions that students must make before creating a fable can be recorded on the **Fable Outline** hand-out.

Moral

     Characters (usually animals)

     Setting

     Problem

     Solution

COMPARE/CONTRAST

Students (or teams) can select a current day fable (Lobel or Lionni) and compare it to one written by Aesop or LaFontaine. A Venn diagram may be helpful when doing this.

COMPARE/CONTRAST
A Venn Diagram

Name _____

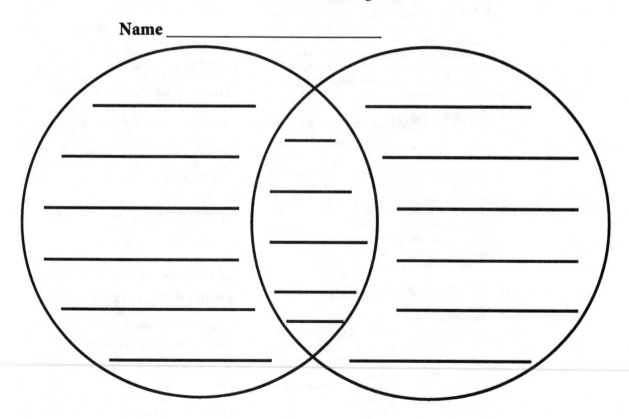

PROVERBS

1. Do not begrudge to others what you cannot use yourself.

2. One trick deserves another.

3. Little friends may prove to be great friends.

4. Don't count your chickens before they hatch.

5. He who is too greedy may end up with nothing.

6. Don't try what is impossible.

7. Money has no true value if it is not used.

8. Be warned by what happens to others.

9. Think twice before you leap.

10. If you try to please all, you will please none.

11. A noble soul never forgets a kindness.

12. If you want something to be surely done, do it yourself.

13. Prepare today for the needs of tomorrow.

14. Slow and sure is better than fast and careless.

15. Borrowed feathers do not make fine birds.

16. It is a poor friend who deserts you when you are in trouble.

17. Kindness works better than force.

18. One good turn deserves another.

19. A liar will not be believed even when he tells the truth.

20. The wicked will always find an excuse for doing what they like.

21. Half a loaf is better than none.

22. He who is hard to please may get very little in the end.

23. Do unto others as you would have them do unto you.

24. A kingdom divided against itself can't stand.

25. Stretch your arm no further than your sleeve will reach.

26. Think before you act.

27. Never trust a flatterer.

28. Biggest is not always best.

29. Look before you leap.

30. Necessity is the mother of invention.

31. Slow and steady wins the race.

32. Don't pretend to be something that you are not.

Spencer Kagan: *Cooperative Learning*©
Publisher: Resources for Teachers , Inc. • 1(800) Wee Co-op

FABLE OUTLINE

Moral: _____

_____

_____

_____

_____

Characters: _____

_____

_____

_____

Setting: _____

_____

_____

_____

Problem: _____

_____

_____

_____

Solution: _____

_____

_____

_____

_____

Student-Directed Science Experiment:

Surface Tension

Materials:
(Per Team)

- 1 Worksheet
- 1 Eyedropper
- 1 Cup of Water
- 1 Nickel
- 1 Penny
- 1 Pen
- 1 Piece of Chalk
- 1 Think Pad
- 1 Blue Crayon
- 1 Red Crayon
- Paper Towels

Step 1
Roundrobin: Number Off

Number off 1 through 4.

In this experiment, there are plenty of steps to read, so the team should share the job of reading. Whenever you see ❖, this means that it is time to switch readers.

Let's start with Student 1.

❖ *Student 1 Read*

Description. This is a team science experiment on surface tension. We will guess how many drops of water a coin will hold. Then, we will perform the experiment and see how close our guesses came to the outcome of the experiment.

❖ *Student 2 Read*

Step 2
Roundtable:
Pick Rotating Roles

For this experiment, four roles are necessary:

1. Representative. The Representative is in charge of going to the chalkboard and representing the team. The Representative must check to see everyone on the team agrees before writing on the chalkboard.
Tool of the Trade: Chalk.

2. Recorder. The Recorder is in charge of recording information for the team. The Recorder must check to see that everyone on the team agrees before anything is written down.
Tool of the Trade: Pen.

❖ *Student 3 Read*

3. Guess Grapher. The Guess Grapher is in charge of graphing the team's range of predictions of how many drops of water the coin will hold. The Guess Grapher must check to see everyone on the team agrees before he/she graphs the team's range.
Tool of the Trade: Blue Crayon.

4. Outcome Grapher. The Outcome Grapher is in charge of graphing the number of water drops the coin held in the experiment. The Outcome Grapher must check to see everyone on the team agrees before he/she graphs the outcome.
Tool of the Trade: Red Crayon.

❖ *Student 4 Read*

For Round 1, the roles are:
Student 1 is the *Representative*.
Student 2 is the *Recorder*.
Student 3 is the *Guess Grapher*.
Student 4 is the *Outcome Grapher*.

STOP Each teammember is to collect his/her tool of the trade now.

For the first round, we will use the Head of the Penny. So The Head of the Penny will be placed in the center of the workplace so we can all see and reach the penny.

Round 1:
Head of Penny
Step 3

❖ *Representative Read*

Think-Write-Roundrobin:
Take a Guess

Individual Thinks. Take a look at the cup of water. Then look at the face of the coin. If we drop drops of water onto the coin one at a time from an inch high, how many drops of water will the coin hold? Take ten seconds for everyone to think. There is no talking.

❖ *Recorder Read*

Individual Writes. Every person write down your guess on a slip of paper. A guess is also called a hypothesis. A hypothesis is what you will believe will happen. So let's write down our hypotheses. Write down your guess on a slip of paper now. No discussing.

❖ *Guess Grapher Read*

Roundrobin. One at a time, we will read to the team what our guess was. Read to the team what your guess was, starting with Student 1.

❖ *Outcome Grapher Read*

Step 4

Pair-Square-Write:
Discuss Guesses

Pair Discusses. The students with the highest and lowest guesses form a pair. The other two students also form a pair. Discuss

in pairs why you think that the coin will hold the number of drops you chose.

❖ *Representative Read*

Team Discusses. Now that we have met together as pairs, let's discuss our guesses as a team. Discuss your guesses as a team.

Individual Writes.

We have heard each others' different guesses and explanations for the guess. Maybe we may want to change our original guesses a bit. You can now change your hypothesis if you want. Give your new hypothesis to the Recorder.

❖ *Recorder Read*

Step 6

Teammate Writes:
Record and Graph

Teammates Record. The *Recorder* collects the team's guesses and writes the guess range under the first graph on the Record Sheet. The guess range is the lowest guess to the highest guess. For example, if our guesses were 5, 8, 6, and 10, our guess range would be from 5 to 10. You can write the range "5-10".[1]

Once the team's guess range is figured, the *Representative* goes to the chalkboard and writes the team name, and under the team name writes: "Guess Range_____" and the team's guess range in the blank space. This is so that your classmates can see your guess

---

1. To figure the size of the range, count all the numbers from the lowest to the highest guess, including the lowest and highest guess. For example, the size of the range from 6 to 10 is 5, because it includes 6, 7, 8, 9, and 10.

Spencer Kagan: *Cooperative Learning*©
Publisher: Resources for Teachers , Inc. • 1(800) Wee Co-op

range, and you can see theirs. With the blue crayon, the *Guess Grapher* graphs the guess range on the guess side of the first graph. See the sample Guess Graph on the next page. Recorder, Representative, and Guess Grapher, do your jobs now.

♣ *Guess Grapher Read*

Step 7
Roundtable:
Drop a Drop

The *Outcome Grapher* fills up the eyedropper with water from the cup. In a moment, Outcome Grapher will drop a drop of water on the coin. For dropping the water, you need a real steady hand. Balance your wrist, and don't drop the water from higher than one inch. After the first drop, the group counts out loud together, "One." After the second drop, "Two." We will count together until the water spills over the side of the coin. *Outcome Grapher*, fill up the eyedropper and start dropping now. Team: Don't forget to count out loud.

♣ *Outcome Grapher Read*

Step 8
Teammate Writes:
Record the Outcome

Teammates Record. On the Record Sheet, the *Recorder* writes down the number of drops the coin

held. With the red crayon, the *Outcome Grapher* graphs the outcome number. To graph the outcome, the graph is filled in from 0 to the number of drops the coin held. If, for example, the coin held 12 drops, the graph would look like the sample Outcome Graph on this page. At the same time, the *Representative* goes to the chalkboard again. Under the guess range, the *Representative* writes "Outcome ____" and the actual number in the blank. *Recorder, Representative,* and *Outcome Grapher*, do your jobs now.

♣ *Representative Read*

Step 9
Read-Think-Square-Write:
Answer Questions

Answer the question that follows each experiment in the Reflection Questions Box on the next page.

Teammate Reads. The *Representative* reads the question.

Individual Thinks. Take some time to think about the answer without talking.

Team Discusses. Discuss with your teammates what you think about the question.

Teammate Writes. After the team has reached an answer, the *Recorder* writes down the team answer.

Answer the question for this round now. The question is found on the Reflection Questions box.

Round 2: Tail of Penny
SWITCH ROLES AND TOOLS OF THE TRADE.

For Round 2, the roles will be:

Student 1 will be the *Recorder*,

Student 2 will be the *Guess Grapher*,

Student 3 will be the *Outcome Grapher*, and

Student 4 will be the *Representative*.

Sample:
Guess Graph

10

0

Guess | Outcome

Guess Range: 6-10

Sample:
Outcome Graph

10

0

Guess | Outcome

Guess Range: 6-10

Outcome: 12

Spencer Kagan: *Cooperative Learning*©
Publisher: Resources for Teachers, Inc. • 1(800) Wee Co-op

Each teammember is to collect his/her tool of the trade now.

Repeat Steps 3-9 using the tail of the penny.

Round 3:

Head of a Nickel

SWITCH ROLES AND TOOLS OF THE TRADE.

For Round 3, the roles will be:

Student 1 will be the *Guess Grapher*, Student 2 will be the *Outcome Grapher*, Student 3 will be the *Representative*, and Student 4 will be the *Recorder*.

Each teammember is to collect his/her tool of the trade now.

Repeat Steps 3-9 using the head of the nickel.

Round 4:

Tail of a Nickel

SWITCH ROLES AND TOOLS OF THE TRADE.

For Round 3, the roles will be:
Student 1 will be the *Outcome Grapher*,
Student 2 will be the *Representative*,
Student 3 will be the *Recorder*, and
Student 4 will be the *Guess Grapher*.

Each teammember is to collect his/her tool of the trade now.

Repeat Steps 3-9 using the tail of the nickel.

Step 10

The final step is to answer the questions on the Thinking Questions page.

Reflection Questions

Round 1 Question

1. Did the coin hold more or less than the team guess?

More _____ Less _____ Why do you think this is true?_____
_____
_____
_____

Round 2 Question

2. Did the coin hold more or less than the team guess?

More _____ Less _____ Why do you think this is true?_____
_____
_____
_____

Round 3 Question

3. Did the coin hold more or less than the team guess?

More _____ Less _____ Why do you think this is true?_____
_____
_____
_____

Round 4 Question

4. Did the coin hold more or less than the team guess?

More _____ Less _____ Why do you think this is true?_____
_____
_____
_____

Spencer Kagan: *Cooperative Learning* ©
Publisher: Resources for Teachers , Inc. • 1(800) Wee Co-op

Record Sheet:

Surface Tension

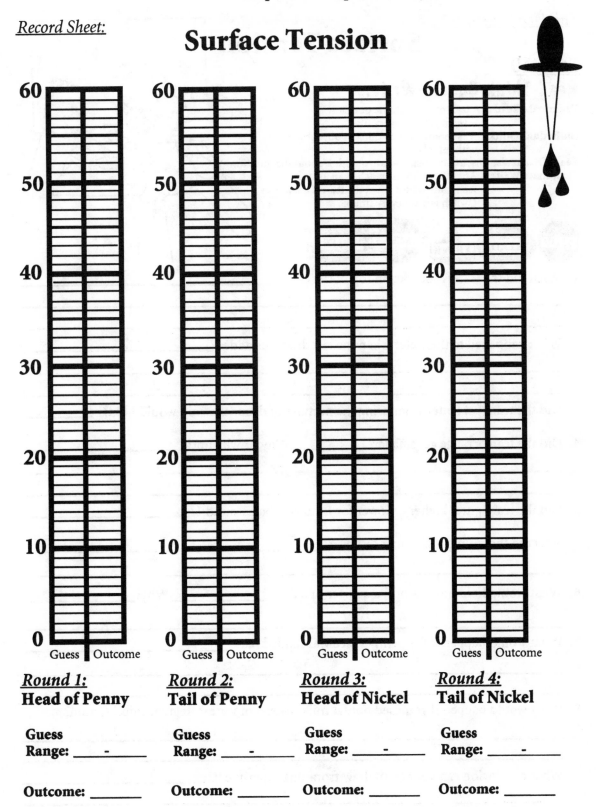

Round 1:
Head of Penny

Guess
Range: _____ - _____

Outcome: _____

Round 2:
Tail of Penny

Guess
Range: _____ - _____

Outcome: _____

Round 3:
Head of Nickel

Guess
Range: _____ - _____

Outcome: _____

Round 4:
Tail of Nickel

Guess
Range: _____ - _____

Outcome: _____

Spencer Kagan: *Cooperative Learning*©
Publisher: Resources for Teachers , Inc. • 1(800) Wee Co-op

Thinking Questions

Surface Tension

Step 10
Read-Think-Square-Write:

Teammate Reads. A teammate reads the question (switch readers every time).
Individual Thinks. Take some time to think about the answer without talking.
Team Discusses. Discuss as a team what you think about the question.
Teammate Writes. After the team has reached an answer, a teammate writes down the team's answer (switch writers every time).

STOP **READ** **THINK** **DISCUSS** **WRITE**

1. What did the water look like on top of the coins?_____
_____
_____

2. What happened to the water when the last drop was added?_____
_____
_____

3. Did the team get better at guessing the number of drops the coin would hold? _____

4. Did the team's range get smaller?_____Why or why not?_____
_____
_____

5. Did the team guess higher or lower for Round 2 than Round 1?_____

   Why did the team guess higher or lower? _____
_____

6. What would hold more drops, a quarter or a dime?_____ Why?_____
_____

7. What would happen if the penny's face was sanded flat? _____
_____
_____

8. What would happen if you used nonfat milk instead of water? Regular milk? Cream?
_____
_____

9. What conclusion can your team draw from this experiment?_____
_____

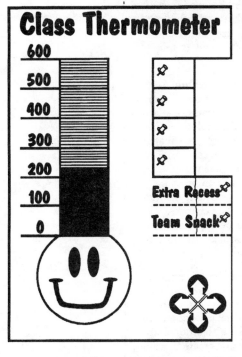

There is a tragedy created by our present classroom scoring and recognition systems: Every child comes to school a winner, but a great many end up losers. Ask students entering school how they are going to do. The response: I am going to do fine. Regardless of economic class and culture, we receive a class full of winners.

By the end of second grade, if you ask the same question, you get a slightly different answer. Some students know they are falling behind, but

As we watch students coming to school on the first day of kindergarten, it is easy to see that every parent sends us a winner. Students are dressed up with a new jacket and new lunch pail. Ask the students how they are going to do in school, and they will tell you, "Great!" Ask again after several years of traditional scoring and recognition, and they will tell you, "I don't do great in school, but I don't really care." At that point we have drop outs. We will have their bodies for a number of years to come, but we have lost them.

ped out. We may have their bodies for a number of years to come, but we have lost them. They need to believe that it does not matter to them that they are not doing well in school because it would be too painful to face the truth -- that they do care, but no matter how hard they try they cannot succeed. It is actually adaptive for the students to stop trying. To try and to fail is more painful than not to have tried.

The most fundamental problem with our recognition system is that some students consistently get positive recognition and others do not. If you compare the initial test scores in a classroom with final grades, there is a high correlation. To give the top students positive recognition all year and to give little or no positive recognition to the low students results in a class of winners and losers. The traditional system works well if the aim is to have schools function as a filter, sending some, but not other students, onto higher education and better jobs. The system works very poorly if the aim is to maximize the potential of each student.

This problem is clearer by example. Lets examine four students the fifth week of school. (See Figure 1). The students have taken a test which is scored on a percentile basis, 0 to 100. Student 1 has received a 95, and the teacher has given the student an "A." Students 2 and 3 scored 75s and received "C's." Student 4 scored 35 and received an "F."

most still feel they will do well. Students are resilient. When asked, they say, "I didn't do that well, but I'm going to do great next year." If you ask the same question of students by fifth or sixth grade, the picture has changed dramatically: Many will say, "I didn't do that great, but I don't care."

Students at that point have drop-

Figure 1:

Grades After Week 5 Quiz

Week	1	2	3	4	5	Grade
Student 1					95	A
Student 2					75	C
Student 3					75	C
Student 4					35	F

Spencer Kagan: *Cooperative Learning*©
Publisher: Resources for Teachers , Inc. • 1(800) Wee Co-op

Chapter 16. Scoring and Recognition

This is the traditional approach to grading. It is based on a competitive model: We have stacked the students up and given the top students the "As," the middle students the "Cs," and the low students the "Fs."

To realize the foolishness of this, let's look at the students developmentally, comparing their scores not with each other, but with their own usual level of performance. We will look at the same students horizontally rather than vertically. See figure 2.

To show the students that we care about their development, we have put in place an improvement scoring system developed by *Dr. Robert Slavin*, in which students will get either 0, 1, 2, or 3 points each week depending on how much they improve. Because we know it is difficult always to be perfect, and that we cannot punish a student who always gets 100, we have decided to add a twist at the top to our improvement scoring system. Students who get 100 will always get three points, and those who score between 95 and 99 always get at least 2 points.

Now let's score our students (See Figure 2). Student 1, is a brilliant student who has never gotten anything but 100. This student could get 100 by spending only a few minutes glancing at the text. The student got a 95, clearly not indicating improvement, but because we recognize very high performance, we give the student 2 points.

Student 2 is just like student 1, a brilliant student. When this student gets a 75, he has earned 0 improvement points. Student 3 also received a 75, but is a very different student. School work has come with difficulty for the student, but the student is working diligently, showing steady improvement, Starting at 35, the student has climbed to 75 by week 5. We celebrate the improvement with 3 Points.

Notice, students 2 and 3 who looked identical in the traditional approach suddenly look very different. We want a parent conference for student 2 to find out what has gone wrong and to get things back on track if possible. We want a parent conference for student 3 also, but for this student it is to share with the parents the fantastic improvement. Note: The traditional approach

does not distinguish these two students, giving them identical feedback!

Student 4, who in the traditional approach was a straight F student, also suddenly looks very different. The student has made steady, strong improvement. Taking a developmental perspective, we recognize improvement: The student earns 2 points and is told to keep up the great work!

The tragedy created by the traditional approach to scoring and recognition is exemplified by Student 4. In the traditional approach after a few weeks the student realizes that there is no reason to try. No matter how hard he may try, he will receive an F. It is actually adaptive for the student to give up trying! The student is in a position of helplessness. If improvement scoring is instituted, however, the whole picture changes. The student knows effort will be appreciated by the teacher and by those who count most for most students, peers.

Now let's look at the relation of improvement scoring to cooperative learning. The four hypothetical students in our example are members of a heterogeneous cooperative learning team. If we take a traditional approach to scoring we might create a team score by summing the percentile scores. The team score for week 5 would be 300 (95 + 95 + 75 + 35). The improvement of the low achiever would not be recognized. In contrast, if the improvement scores are used, the team score would be the sum of improvement points (7), and the contribution of the low achieving, but improving student is recognized. In fact that student is seen as a very valuable member of the team. Note also,

Figure 2:
Improvement Points After Week 5 Quiz

Week	1	2	3	4	5	Improvement Points
Student 1	100	100	100	100	95	2
Student 2	100	100	100	100	75	0
Student 3	35	45	55	65	75	3
Student 4	15	20	25	30	35	2

Team Score: 7

with traditional scoring the highest achiever has little reason to try harder; with improvement scoring they need to make extra effort to get 3 points.

If you have one high, one low, and two middle achievers on a team and create a team score based on the sum of the scores of the students, each week the lowest achieving student will contribute the fewest points to the team score and you will end up with three students wishing they were not stuck with the fourth. "Give us a new teammate, please!" Students will recognize that no matter how hard they work with and encourage the lowest achiever, he/she is not going to contribute much to the team score. And the low achiever realizes that there is no sense in trying -- even if he or she makes good improvement, it will probably still be the lowest score on the team. Why try? The most adaptive thing a low achiever can do when faced with a competitive scoring system is to make ego-preserving attributions -- "I don't really care about grades," and then to act accordingly, putting no effort into school work. The traditional system which compares students with each other is a prescription for helplessness, depression, and drop-out for a substantial number of students.

In contrast, if team scores are created based on how much each student improves, then each student, regardless of initial ability level, can bring in a top score, and students will be pleased to work with and encourage the lowest achievers. In fact, the lowest achievers can easily bring in maximum points, if improvement is what is valued.

There are obvious advantages to providing each student feedback each week about how he or she is performing compared to his or her usual level of performance. An improvement scoring system allows weak students as much chance to receive top scores as strong students. It is motivating for the top students as well, because they must strive to beat their own usual performance (which is difficult) rather than trying only to beat other students (which for them is easy).

Why we need an improvement scoring system. We could provide for each student an improvement score each week which is the simple difference between this week's performance and last week's performance, but there would be problems: Would you want to give a 0 to the student who scores a perfect score each week? Would you want to give a -2 or a 0 to a student who always scores 98 but then drops to a 96?

Our simple improvement scoring system would have other problems. What of the student who usually scores around 60, but one week scores 90 out of 100? On the next week he scores 80. Would you really want to give him a 0? We need a system which recognizes improvement over <u>usual</u> level of performance, not just this week over last. The 80 should be recognized as improvement; a week-to-week system would fail to recognize it as such.

The ILE Percentile Improvement Scoring System developed by *Robert Slavin* (Johns Hopkins University) compares quiz scores with a running average which is readjusted after every second quiz so it discounts temporary performance swings and gives students points depending on how much they exceed their usual level of performance. In the system zero represents a substantial drop from usual level of performance, not just a failure to beat last week's quiz score.

Improvement Scoring takes a little time and a bit of work to learn. None of the four bite-sized steps in the system are too big; they just take a bit of practice to master. But it is worth it; the system is a very powerful resource -- far more fair and motivating than traditional approaches.

I have trained thousands of teachers in improvement scoring. Those who implement the system consistently report *very* positive results -- especially for the lowest achieving students. What they thought was intellectual deficit in many cases turned out to be only lack of motivation.

On the following pages are the improvement scoring system, an improvement scoring rolebook, and some guidelines for creating multiple choice questions. Following that comes a section on recognition systems -- after all, once you know how to generate and record improvement points, there remains the question: What to do with them?

Spencer Kagan: *Cooperative Learning*©
Publisher: Resources for Teachers , Inc. • 1(800) Wee Co-op

Improvement Scoring Step-By-Step

Step 1: Weekly Quizzes. Students take a weekly quiz of at least ten items. They exchange papers to grade and get immediate feedback. Use quizzes of similar difficulty each week, and quizzes which produce a range of scores -- a good quiz has items which are difficult for the highest achiever, and a few items which even the lowest achiever will answer correctly. The rest of the items are distributed in levels of difficulty. Place easy items at the beginning of the quiz. Any format for the quiz will work, including short answer, performance with manipulatives, matching, and multiple choice. See the guidelines for writing multiple-choice items, following this section.

Step 2: Base Scores. Initial Base Scores are the average percent on past quizzes. If you are beginning, use an initial quiz to determine the initial Base Score. The Base Score is your best guess as to how a student is likely to do.

Step 3: Calculating Improvement Points. Compare Quiz Scores with Base Scores to determine Improvement Points, as follows:

Quiz Score	Improvement Points	Comment
5 or more below base	0	"You can do better!"
4 below to 4 above base	1	"About average for you --but you can do better"
5-9 above base	2	"Better than your average --good work"
10 or more above base or perfect score	3	"Super! Much better than your average!"

95 to 99 points never receive less than 2 Improvement Points
100 always receives 3 Improvement Points

Step 4.
Recomputing Base Scores. After every two weeks recompute the base scores by averaging the old Base Score and the scores on quizzes since assigning the last base. For example, if there had been two Quiz Scores since a student received her old Base Score, recomputing the Base Score would look like this:

(Old Base + Last Quiz + Next-to-last quiz) ÷ 3

Example: Name:	Base	Q1	IP	Q2	IP	Base	Q3	IP	Q4	IP	Base	Q5	IP	Q6	IP
1. Ben	72	70	1	77	2	73	77	1	70	1	73				
2. Tom	62	50	0	58	1	57	90	3	68	3	72				
3. Danny	60	60	1	60	1	60	64	1	56	1	60				
4. Jennifer	95	95	2	100	3	97	94	1	95	1	95				

Improvement Scoring Role Book

!!! The Improvement Role Book above is not correct !!!
How many errors can you find?

Spencer Kagan: *Cooperative Learning*©
Publisher: Resources for Teachers , Inc. • 1(800) Wee Co-op

Improvement Scoring Role Book (page 1)

Name:	Base	Q1	IP	Q2	IP	Base	Q3	IP	Q4	IP	Base	Q5	IP	Q6	IP
1.															
2.															
3.															
4.															
5.															
6.															
7.															
8.															
9.															
10.															
11.															
12.															
13.															
14.															
15.															
16.															
17.															
18.															
19.															
20.															

Improvement Scoring Role Book (page 2)

Name:	Base	Q1	IP	Q2	IP	Base	Q3	IP	Q4	IP	Base	Q5	IP	Q6	IP
21.															
22.															
23.															
24.															
25.															
26.															
27.															
28.															
29.															
30.															
31.															
32.															
33.															
34.															
35.															
36.															
37.															
38.															
39.															
40.															

Spencer Kagan: *Cooperative Learning*©
Publisher: Resources for Teachers , Inc. • 1(800) Wee Co-op

10 Rules For

Writing Multiple Choice Questions

1. Keep the reading level low. Simplify stems and alternatives as much as possible.

2. The item stem should include a single, clear idea. It should stand without the responses which follow.

Good:

Most of South America was settled by colonists from:

A. England   C. Holland
B. France   *D. Spain

Bad:

South America

A. is a flat, arid country
B. imports coffee from the U.S.
C. has a larger population than the United States
*D. was settled mainly by colonists from Spain

3. The item stem should include as much of the item as possible.

Good:

Spanish colonists settled most of South America in search of

A. adventure.   C. lower taxes
*B. wealth.   D. religious freedom

Bad:

Most of South America was settled by Colonists from Spain. How would you account for the large number of Spanish colonists settling there?

A. They were adventurous
*B. They were in search of wealth
C. They wanted lower taxes
D. They wanted religious freedom

4. Avoid negatively stated items.

Good:

Which of the following states is located south of the Mason-Dixon line?

A. Maine   C. Pennsylvania
B. New York   *D. Virginia

Bad:

Which of the following states is not located north of the Mason-Dixon line?

A. Maine   C. Pennsylvania
B. New York   *D. Virginia

5. Make the alternatives similar in form and grammatically consistent with the stem.

Good:

An electric transformer can be used to

A. store up electricity
*B. increase the voltage of alternating current
C. convert electrical energy into mechanical energy
D. change alternating current to direct current

Bad:

An electric transformer can be used

A. for storing up electricity
*B. to increase the voltage of alternating current
C. it converts electrical energy into mechanical energy
D. alternating current is changed to direct current

6. Avoid clues to the correct answer. (verbal association, textbook language, length of alternatives, and grammatical clues)

7. Write distracters (incorrect alternatives) that are plausible to the nonachiever; use common errors and misconceptions.

Good:

Who discovered the North Pole?

A. Ronald Amundsen   *C. Robert Peary
B. Richard Byrd   D. Robert Scott

Bad:

Who discovered the North Pole?

A. Christopher Columbus   *C. Robert Peary
B. Ferdinand Magellan   D. Marco Polo

8. If you use alternatives such as "None of the above," "Both of the above" and "All of the above," include them as the incorrect answer about 3/4 of the time.

9. The correct answer should appear without pattern in each of the alternative positions.

10. The correct answer should appear equally often in each of the alternative positions.

Relation of Improvement Points and Report Cards Grades

Improvement points are part of a classroom recognition system, and should never contribute to the academic side of report cards. The same is true for team grades. Never under any circumstance should a team grade influence an individual's academic report card. There simply is no way to justify that.

For example, if a teacher gives points to teams whose members all get in their homework, those points may be part of a recognition system, but cannot legitimately influence report card grades. Otherwise two students with exactly the same motivation, ability, and performance will receive different grades, depending on the performance of the teammates they happen to have.

Individual report card grades should always be a function of assessing what an individual can do, independent of his/her teammates.

In a moment we will explore a variety of recognition systems which are independent of report cards, but first we will take a detour and examine a recent trend which would have us abandon all use of praise, points, certificates, or rewards in classrooms.

Do rewards really erode intrinsic motivation?

There has been a movement away from rewards, certificates, and even praise in classrooms, based in part on research which has shown that rewards can erode intrinsic motivation. One intelligent man has gone so far as to say, "Verbal reinforcement is worse than nothing, and material reinforcement is worse yet." Before we all play follow the flag waving leader and march right off the end of the pier without life jackets, let's think a bit.

There is a body of research which shows that in certain situations rewards for behavior do erode intrinsic motivation. For example, if children are given rewards for performing some behavior which they would gladly do without rewards, some may change their attributions from internal to external. That is, without the rewards they see themselves as performing the behavior because they enjoy it, but when the behavior is consistently followed by rewards they may see themselves as performing the behavior for the reward. Later, when rewards are taken away, they may conclude, "If I was doing it for a reward, and there is no reward now, then there is no reason to perform the behavior." So rewards in some cases can erode intrinsic motivation.

But it is only a very special kind of situation in which this is true. It is a situation in which students conclude the *only* reason I am doing something is for the reward. If a

"He who praises everybody praises nobody."

-- *Samuel Johnson*

"He who praises nobody has taken the research on rewards and extrinsic motivation too seriously." -- *Spencer Kagan*

student is performing a behavior and enjoys it and happens also to receive praise or recognition, the recognition will not necessarily erode intrinsic motivation. The student knows the reward is not the *only* reason for the behavior. We must be careful not to provide a message to our students that the *only* reason they are studying or cooperating is for external praise or rewards. If a teacher smiles at, praises, or gives a certificate to a student, that recognition can be perceived as a messages from the teacher to the child: "I really appreciate the work you are doing." And the child may conclude "I get to do what I really enjoy doing, and the teacher supports me too."

If I show a child I am pleased he is eating an ice cream, it will not make him less motivated to eat ice cream in the future. The recognition is not perceived as the *only* reason to engage in the behavior. Thus, we should design learning tasks as intrinsically motivating as possible -- tasks the students would love to do with or without rewards. Adding recognition or rewards on top of good learning tasks will not necessarily erode intrinsic motivation. And for some students, the rewards will actually increase intrinsic motivation.

There is a body of research which shows that rewards can actually increase intrinsic motivation. In situations in which the rewards motivate students to engage in behaviors they otherwise would not, when later tested some show *increases* in intrinsic motivation -- they have found rewards in the behavior on their own. In this case the rewards have provided the incentive to get involved in the task, and once involved the students discover rewards intrinsic in the task.

If we ask how rewards actually work in classrooms there is plenty of support for using them. There is not a single study showing that in the context of a real classroom praise for academic accomplishments or prosocial behavior actually decreases those behaviors. In contrast, most of the the research in cooperative learning which has consistently shown academic and prosocial gains has included teacher and/or peer reinforcement in the form of praise, rewards, certificates or grades. If praise and rewards are so bad, why have they been consistently associated with academic and social gains in cooperative learning classrooms?

This is not a plea for massive use of rewards. In fact, I do not use any points or certificates or rewards when I do demonstration lessons. It is a plea only for not abandoning a powerful tool which many teachers find useful.

There has been a pendulum swing both in cooperative learning and in education as a whole. The pendulum has swung away from what is now called "drill and kill" toward constructionist views. Skinner, practice worksheets, high-consensus content, convergent thinking, and rewards, are out; Piaget, non-evaluated experimentation, low-consensus content, divergent thinking, and self-evaluation are in.

If praise and rewards are so bad, why have they been consistently associated with academic and social gains in research investigating cooperative learning classrooms?

I like the movement. I designed Co-op Co-op for use in my own classes at the University of California, in 1972 in part because it allowed students to choose studies in their own zone of proximal development. Instead of completing teacher-directed assignments in order to receive a grade, students began researching in order to acquire personally meaningful knowledge. The motivation was to satisfy one own curiosity and to have something of worth to offer others, not just obtaining a grade.

I believe that we should, to the extent possible, design learning experiences which are intrinsically interesting, and which students would find a joy to do whether or not they received a reward or praise from the teacher. On the other hand, I know that improvement scoring and formal recognition of improvement in the form of points, class thermometers, and recognition ceremonies works very well to motivate some students, and we should explore all tools which enhance learning and development. There are many, many teachers who have reported to me that once they put in place improvement scoring and coupled it with a class thermometer, they have seen very dramatic improvement among certain students -- in many cases improvement beyond what the teacher thought possible!

Recognition Systems -- What to do with the points

Once you have generated improvement points, the question becomes, what to do with them. We move then from scoring systems to recognition systems.

The simplest and perhaps most efficient system is simply to give students two scores on their test each week -- a score in a square, (representing the 0-100 percentile score), and a score in a circle, (representing the 0-3 improvement score). The improvement can be couple with appropriate comments like "You can do better," for a 0 or 1; "Keep up the improvement," for a 2, and "Fantastic improvement, for a 3."

Spencer Kagan: *Cooperative Learning*©
Publisher: Resources for Teachers , Inc. • 1(800) Wee Co-op

Class Thermometer

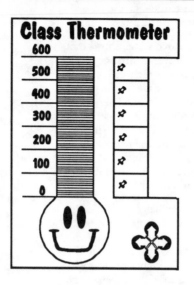

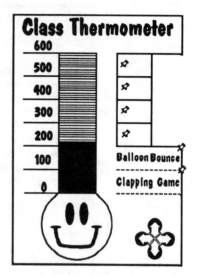

Step 1: Write in
Class Celebrations

Step 2: Cut and fold the
thermometer to hide celebrations

Step 3: Reveal each celebration as
students reach class goals.

If you wish to formalize the recognition, you might have students who have received 1 Improvement Point take a bow for the class, those who have received 2, take two bows, and those who have received 3, take three.

Class Thermometer

Or, in a more formal recognition system, students mark their improvement points on the class thermometer, which records progress toward class goals. See Box. To use the Class Thermometer the teacher first records some class celebrations, such as a co-operative game, a favorite teambuilder, or classbuilder. See Step 1. Next, these celebrations are hidden because the teacher has cut and folded the thermometer (See Step 2). The teacher unfolds the thermometer to reveal each celebration. When the class has accumulated sufficient improvement points to reach a celebration point (See Step 3).

Class Improvement Chart

An alternative recognition system was designed by *Fred Balcom* (Washington Middle School, Vista, California). Fred's Class Improvement Chart, uses a bar graph approach. The improvement points of each

team are plotted on a cumulative bar graph which provides a clear visual display for students. In the box is how the bar graph might look after three weeks.

Fred originally set up his chart in a between-team competition format. That is, the team with the most points received rewards. My suggestion to him was to have both between-team competition and a between-team cooperation. That is, each week the team with the greatest number of total Improvement Points, or the most Improvement Points for the week might receive special recognition.

By drawing goal lines across the graph at 12 point intervals, however, class goals can be set up as well. For example, the teacher could allow a desired class activity to occur each time all teams pass another 12 point interval. The 12 point intervals are suggested as class goals because they represent the maximum number of improvement points a team can receive in a week. The class goals create positive interdependence among teams. Students view themselves as part of a whole class, not just as members of separate teams; they then hope and work for the success of all students because they know the success of others will mean another class celebration.

In the example, in week three the first class goal was reached (all teams passed the 12 point mark), so it would be the occasion for a class celebration.

To calculate team improvement points, just add up individual improvement points. To adjust the points earned for teams of three or five, either add or subtract the team average. For a three person team add their average to their score -- that will tell them what they would have had if they were a team of four. For a team of five, subtract their average from their score, to determine what they would have had if they were a team of four.

Seasonal Charts

Seasonal Charts simply mark points on a path toward class goals. Depending on the season, the seasonal chart takes a different form. For example, during the Halloween season the path has celebration points marked by symbols of the season (black cat, wicked witch, hollow tree, pumpkin patch). The big class celebration would occur when

we work our way all the way to the haunted house.

Content Charts

If we are doing an astronomy unit, the levels of the recognition chart is marked by different planets. A unit on the westward movement will have a recognition chard marked by important landmarks on the trail. The class has a big celebration when it works its way all the way to California.

Additional recognition systems include the Team Standings Chart, The Class Recognition Bulletin, and rewards and certificates, examples of which are on the following pages.

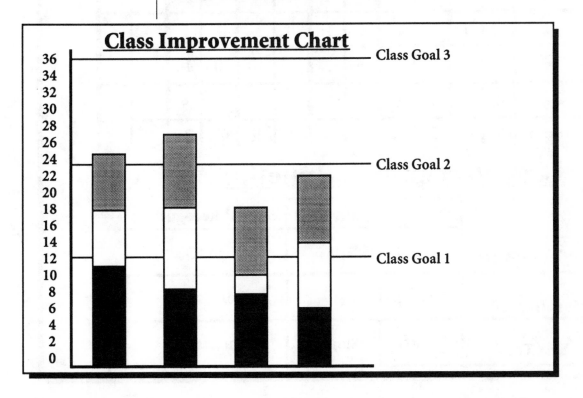

Team Standings Chart & Class Recognition Bulletin

In recording the team scores, you might want to use a Team Standings Chart on which students can record improvement points each week and keep track of cumulative points. The Class Recognition Bulletin displays the names of most improved students and teams each week. See Box.

Note: Each week on the Team Standings Chart the teams post their improvement points. Each individual keeps track of his total points by adding the week's points to the previous total and posting the sum. Special recognition points may be recorded for use of the Skill-Of-The-Week of for any desirable behavior.

The Class Recognition Bulletin displays the weekly best, the most improved this week over last, and the highest total. In the fifth week example, Carlos received the most improvement points, (3), Miguel was most improved (two improvement points this week versus none last week), and Simon has the highest number of improvement points overall (11).

Team Standings Chart

Week:	1		2		3		4		5		6	
Weekly Special Recognition Points:	III		II		NN		NNNN II		NN			
	WK	TOT	WK	TOT	WK	TOT	WK	TOT	WK	TOT	WK	TOT
Total Recognition Pts:	**3**	**3**	**2**	**5**	**5**	**10**	**12**	**22**	**3**	**25**		
Simon	2	2	2	4	2	6	3	9	2	11		
Miguel	1	1	1	2	1	3	0	3	2	5		
Monica	3	3	3	6	1	7	3	10	0	10		
Carlos	0	0	0	0	3	3	3	6	3	9		
Team Improvement Pts:	6	6	6	12	7	19	9	28	7	35		

Class Recognition Bulletin: *Week 5*

	Team	Individual	Special Recognition
Weekly Best:	Box Tops	Carlos	High IQ's
Most Improved:	Box Tops	Miguel	Box Tops
Best Total:	Smurfs	Simon	Smurfs

Possible Rewards

Privileges

Library pass
Free time
Help other students or teachers in building
Help teacher with project
Choose the day's story
Helper for the day
  Pass out papers
  Run errands
  Water plants, etc.

Use playground equipment
Choose class game
Lunch in room with teacher
Choice of music
Play with special game or toy
Use new markers, special paper, easel, etc.
Use clay, paint

Extra Art, PE, Music
AV treat
Choose where to sit
Work in hall
Line up first for:
  Recess, Drinks,
  Go home, Lunch
Cooperative Sports & Game

Recognition

Happy Gram
  to student
  to parent
  to principal
Students of the week
Recognition in daily announcements

Smile
Pat on back
Hug
Standing ovation
Round of applause
Encouraging words

Special Days

Dress up Day   Dress down Day   Hat Day   Joke Day   Stuffed Animal Day

Rewards

Eraser
Pencil
Bookmark
Tokens

Certificates
Willow-in-
  the-Wind
Care Lift

Stars
Stickers
Stamps
Snacks/soft

Drinks in room
Grab bag
Popcorn party
Pencil top

Adapted From: Dee Dishon and Pat Wilson O'Leary's *A Guidebook for Cooperative Learning*, Holmes Beach, Florida: Learning Publications, Inc. 1984.

the Cooperation award

TO

_____

FOR

_____

the Cooperation award

TO

_____

FOR

_____

Spencer Kagan: *Cooperative Learning*©
Publisher: Resources for Teachers , Inc. • 1 (800) Wee Co-op

the c∞peration award

TO

_____

FOR

_____

the 10 x 10 multiplication table, after eliminating 0s, 1s, 2s, 10s and reversals, boils down to only 28 facts. How is it that we have not developed a system in which each of our students learns these simple, necessary facts perfectly by third grade, freeing them to use them without error as they progress to higher level problems? Is it really necessary to take years to learn 28 simple facts -- or are we making some fundamental mistake?

How is memory work presently taught? Basically, teachers assign drill and practice work, such as memorization of the multiplication facts, vocabulary words, states and capitals, as homework. Motivated students learn the facts -- others do not. Those who do not, fall farther and farther behind as they move to more difficult concepts. For example, when students begin long-division, if they are still counting on their fingers for the multiplication, to acquire the concept of division parts of the algorithm, they have little free attention.

The American educational system receives failing marks in the subject of teaching basic skills and facts. Unacceptably large numbers of students cannot locate Spain on a map, tell us the content of our bill of rights, or state how many eggs there are in three half dozen cartons. Why have we failed in the area of acquisition of basic facts? The answer: Basic facts are seldom taught; if taught, they are usually taught very poorly.

Why have teachers relegated such important learning to homework, with predictably poor results? The problem is that "low level" memorization is probably the least favorite type of teaching for most teachers. This is true, in part, because teachers like to see themselves as dealing with higher level concepts, but also in part because teachers generally have not been provided systems for efficiently promoting the acquisition of simple facts.

Color-Coded Co-op Cards

There is a problem in American Education: students are not acquiring basic facts and information. We teach basic information very poorly. The proof of this claim lies in what we do with regard to the multiplication facts. Go to any district and ask when the multiplication facts are taught. Usually work begins by second grade. But then work on the multiplication facts continues in the following grades: third..., fourth..., fifth..., sixth..., and very often remedial work continues on in the seventh..., eighth..., and even beyond.

This unbelievably unsuccessful teaching of a simple set of basic facts, year after year adds up to an incredible waste of time, teacher and pupil self-esteem. Actually

The Color-Coded Co-op Cards are efficient -- they have led to radical improvements in acquisition of basic facts in a variety of subject areas. Almost without exception when the Color-Coded Co-op Cards have been used, students begin to enjoy memory work. Students will ask for the opportunity to work on their cards -- in many classrooms the Color-Coded Co-op Cards have actually become an ongoing reward sponge -- students are allowed to take out their cards and practice, if they complete a team assignment

Spencer Kagan: *Cooperative Learning*©
Publisher: Resources for Teachers , Inc. • 1(800) Wee Co-op

before all the other teams are done. Dull drill becomes a delight; memory work becomes a favorite among students.

At essence the method is simple: for each item missed on a pretest students make up a flash card (using their own colored pen or writing on paper a different color than that of their teammates). Students then drill each other in a systematic way, playing the flash card game. Following this practice, they take a practice test, checking on how much improvement they are making (how many cards they can star), practice again using the flash card game, take a final test, and receive individual, team and class recognition for improvement. The color-coded cards allow students to pool and count their team improvement points. They are a tangible marker of success -- a visible, countable, poolable, yet retrievable reward token. The cards allow even very young students to calculate their team improvement points -- all learned items are placed in the center of the table and counted. The color coding allows easy retrieval by each student of his or her items for future work. At the heart of the method is how students drill each other -- the flash card game. The game is based on well-established principles of learning, including frequent, positive feedback following repeated, distributed trials. The method maximizes the time-on-needed-task for each individual, and includes multi-modal associative links.

THE TEN STEPS OF COLOR-CODED CO-OP CARDS

1. Pretest

Give all students a pretest on this week's memory items, such as vocabulary words, math facts, geography facts, chemistry valences, historical events.

2. Students Create Color Coded Co-op Cards

Have each student on the team make a set of flash cards on the words (or problems) he or she missed on the pretest. Each student on the team has a set of different color cards. Regular bond paper is fine. Note: We are talking about only four of five colors in the classroom; although each student within a team has a different color, across teams the colors can be repeated. (If colored paper is

The 28 Multiplication Facts

X	1	2	3	4	5	6	7	8	9	10
1										
2										
3			9	12	15	18	21	24	27	
4				16	20	24	28	32	36	
5					25	30	35	40	45	
6						36	42	48	54	
7							49	56	63	
8								64	72	
9									81	
10										

3X3=9
3X4=12   4X4=16
3X5=15   4X5=20   5X5=25
3X6=18   4X6=24   5X6=30   6X6=36   7X7=49
3X7=21   4X7=28   5X7=35   6X7=42   7X8=56
3X8=24   4X8=32   5X8=40   6X8=48   7X9=63
3X9=27   4X9=36   5X9=45   6X9=54

                                    8X8=64   9X9=81
                                    8X9=72

too expensive or not available, cut up plain paper and have students mark their cards with a color, or write with different colored marking pens).

3. Students Play The Flash Card Game (3 Rounds)

Round 1: Maximum Cues. Half of the students (called tutees) hand five of their cards to the person across from them (called the tutor). The tutor holds up one card, shows and reads the tutee the front of the card (question or cue) and then shows and reads the back (answer). For young children and kinesthetic learners, the tutee may trace the answer or write the answer. The tutor then turns the card around again, showing the front, and asks for the answer from short term memory. The tutee attempts an answer. If the answer is correct, the tutor gives an exaggerated praise, such as, "You are a fabulous learner," "Super fantastic job," and the card is "won back" (returned to) the tutee. At this point, 90% or more of all answers should be correct, because the student

---

Steps of:

Color-Coded Co-op Cards

1. **Pretest**
2. **Create Cards on Missed Items**
3. **Play Flash Card Game**
   Play rounds 1, 2, and 3
   Switch Roles after Each Round
   Include "Praisers" and "Helpers"
4. **Practice Test**
5. **Initial Improvement Scoring**
6. **Play Flash Card Game On Missed Items**
   Play rounds 1, 2, and 3
   Switch Roles after Each Round
   Include "Praisers" and "Helpers"
7. **Final Test**
8. **Final Improvement Scoring**
9. **Individual, Team, and Class Recognition**
10. **Reflection**
    How Well Did We Work Together?
    How Could We Improve?

---

has been told and shown the answer immediately before being asked for it. If, however, the tutee fails to answer correctly, he or she receives a "helper" rather than a "praiser." Helpers might be hints, showing and telling the card again, an opportunity to trace or write the right answer, reminders, and the joint creation by tutor and tutee of fantastic visual images which are difficult to forget. If a "helper" is given, the card is not won back, but rather placed back in the stack of cards the tutor holds, so that it will be repeated. Note: This method insures time-on-needed-task, as the easy items are quickly returned to the tutee and the more difficult items are repeated as needed. When the tutee wins back all of his or her cards, the tutor and tutee switch roles.

Round 2: Few Cues. After both students have won back all of their cards on round 1, they progress to round 2. In round 2 the same basic procedure is followed, but this time fewer cues are given, and students move from short- to long-term memory. Thus, for example, the tutor shows the tutee the front and asks for the back from memory. Not having just seen the back, the student must produce the information on the back from long-term memory. The same rules prevail, a correct answer produces an exaggerated praise and the card is returned to its maker; a slow or false answer produces a helper, and the card is placed back in the stack of items to master. To keep the game fresh, for both the tutor and tutee, each time a card is won the tutor must make a different, unexpected praise. Students are encouraged to be creative about the praises, so as the teacher circulates, he/she might hear things like, "Ronald Reagan loves you for being so bright." "Our team will always be a winner with you." "You are extraordinarily intelligent."

Round 3: No Cues. Again, after both students win back their set of cards, they move up a round. On the third round, no cues are allowed. So, for example, the tutor might call out the multiplication question or say the vocabulary word without even showing the tutee the card. As in the other rounds, a correct response receives the card as a token of success accompanied by a praiser; a hesitant or false response receives help and repeated work.

4. Practice Test

Following the flash card game, students take a practice test on all of the words (or problems) they have practiced.

5. Initial Color-Coded Improvement Scoring

Each student contributes to the team improvement score by marking with a star and placing in the center of the team table all of the flash cards which he or she has correctly spelled on a practice test. The total represents the improvement score for the team.

6. Repeated Practice on Missed Items

For a few students, following the practice test there will be a need to increase their deck of flash cards -- they will miss a word or two on the practice test which they they did not miss on the pretest. (A right guess on the pretest is sometimes forgotten). These new words are included for the second round of practice, along with flash cards which have not yet earned a star. After a second round of practice and possibly a second practice test, students are ready for the final test.

7 & 8. Final Test & Final Improvement Scoring

Students take the final test and then a simple team improvement score is calculated by having students pool and count their correct cards.

9. Individual, Team, and Class Recognition

Following the final improvement scoring, a full blown recognition ceremony is in order, and recognition is given at three levels:

Individuals. Individuals post their improvement scores on their individual improvement score graphs, and all students who improved more this week than last, as well as very high, stand up and take a bow as they are recognized by the class.

Teams. Teams announce their total improvement scores, post them on their team improvement graph, and on the class improvement chart. The class improvement chart usually takes the form of a thermometer or graph; teams post their contribution toward the class goal, using their team color. During the recognition ceremony, when a team comes up to post its improvement points, members give their "team handshake" and/or "team cheer."

Class. Class progress toward the next class goal is recognized; teams are recognized not for having "beaten" other teams, but rather for having advanced the class toward its next goal. Thus between-team competition is minimized; teams see themselves as all on the same side contributing toward a common goal.

〜 See Chapter 16:
Scoring & Recognition 〜

10. Reflection

Students need time to discuss how they feel using the Color-Coded Co-op Cards. Especially important is an opportunity for students to share what kinds of helpers they find most useful. Some students like fantastic visual images, others prefer mnemonic devices, and so on. If the students are given time to work on their process, they will become more efficient helpers. Also, some students enjoy the game-like format for the Co-op Cards and like to include exaggerated praisers; others are more serious. Processing is the time for students to work out how best to work with each other.

In Sum. Color-Coded Co-op Cards are a useful addition to cooperative learning because it (1) focuses the attention of each student on his or her own most needed learning tasks; (2) provides immediate and frequent tangible and social feedback to each student regarding improvement; (3) provides a simple improvement scoring system which even very young students can manage; and, most importantly, (4) converts dull unsuccessful drill into fun, efficient learning game.

DOMAIN OF USEFULNESS

Although the domain of usefulness of the Color-Coded Co-op Cards is limited to mastery of basic information -- knowledge and comprehension -- the learning and over-learning of basic information stimulates movement to higher level thinking. For some time I had thought the structure was useful only for memorization of simple facts such as the multiplication and addition facts, letter recognition, states and capitals, vocabulary words, spelling words, chemistry valences. Then I got a surprise. The Co-op Cards can support higher level thinking. See box: A Pleasant Surprise.

WHY DO CO-OP CARDS WORK SO WELL?

Many teachers report that use of the co-op card method has made a radical difference in their classroom. Work which was boring is

A Pleasant Surprise

Ken Attebury from the ABC School District has always made the Bill of Rights an important part of his American history course. He is a fine teacher and his students do well. One year he decided to use the Color-Coded Co-op Cards to have students memorize the Bill of Rights. The cards had the number of the ammendment on one side and the principle feature of the ammendment on the other. What followed that semester was quite different from what had happened in the many previous times Ken had taught the course. Always in the past, students had memorized the first ten amendments to the Constitution, taken their test on it, done well, and then moved on to other topics in the course. The Bill of Rights was never again mentioned by the students. After the Co-op Cards were use, students not only did better than any previous class on the quiz, what followed the quiz changed. After the students had memorized the amendments using the co-op cards, as other topics were discussed, they repeatedly referred back to the bill of rights, with comments like, "Wouldn't that violate the first amendment?" By providing a secure information base, the Co-op Cards promote higher level thinking. *Application, Analysis, Synthesis, and Evaluation cannot occur in a vacuum.*

now fun, and students request the opportunity to work on their memory facts. Teachers claim that after the initial extra time taken to have students learn the method, and to insure that all the steps are included, they actually take far less time on memory work than they did previously. For example, a number of teachers report producing almost all perfect papers on spelling lists, vocabulary words, and simple math facts, in as little as two-thirds the time it previously took for them to produce scores averaging around 75-80%.

Why do the Co-op Cards work so well? The method takes advantages of a number of principles of learning, including: repeated trials with frequent, immediate, and varied positive reinforcement; distributed rather than massed practice, time-on-needed task; movement from short to long-term memory; emphasis on improvement; multimodal and affective associative links.

Repeated Trials With Frequent, Immediate Peer Feedback.

In the traditional classroom, students work alone with worksheets or workbooks. The only external reinforcement available for having mastered the work comes in the form of a written grade and possibly teacher and parent praise following the test. In some cases, that grade comes on Monday or Tuesday when the students have forgotten studying for the test. There is little linkage between the study and the reinforcement and reinforcement occurs only once.

In contrast, each bit of progress on the Co-op Cards is rewarded. A student receives three praises for each item learned. And the reinforcement comes from those who mean most for many students -- their peers.

Varied Rewards.

Following each success a students "wins back" a card. The color-coded cards thus serve as a tangible token of success. In addition, students receive praise from two different tutors, individual recognition from the team and the class for improvement, as well as the more traditional, praise and grades from parents and teacher.

Maximum Probability of Success.

On the first round of the flash card game students are told and shown the answer and then immediately asked for the answer back from short-term memory. Only following this initial success do students move toward long-term memory trials. Students move from maximum to minimum cues, or in some formats, students move from recognition to production. In either case, there is an extremely high probability of initial success. For many students, especially those with a history of school failure, a system which creates initial successes and a very high favorable ratio of successes to failures is critical -- it makes them feel their efforts will be rewarded and that it is worth trying.

Distributed Practice.

After both students have won back all of their cards on round 1, they progress to round 2. Further, the co-op cards are practiced on different days. Thus, practice is distributed rather than massed. Research has clearly established that memory work separated over time is far more likely to be retained than is work all massed into one session.

Time-On-Needed-Task; Individualized Pacing.

If a student knows an item it is quickly set aside and attention is focused on items needing work. Thus, the co-op card method individualizes instruction -- each student works on what he or she needs to work on. This is quite in contrast to workbook or worksheet work which provides all students with the same tasks, regardless of need.

Multimodal Input. Students differ in preferred modes of processing information. The color-coded card method provides visual, auditory, and kinesthetic input, maximizing the probability that students will receive input in their preferred mode.

Varied Associative Links. Each time a card is won the tutor must provide a different exaggerated praise. This method produces a game-like, light affective tone. If the praisers are exaggerated enough, they produce affect which in turn is associatively linked to the learning. Further, students are trained in creating fantastic visual images to associate with the learning material. Together students can produce richer associative links better than they can alone. Research shows that materials with a variety of associative links, especially with affective associative links are more likely to be remembered.

Simplified Improvement Scoring. The Co-op cards provide a very simple way of calculating improvement points. Because students count and plot their own improvement points, their points are more likely to be meaningful. Focus on improvement, rather than relative standing in the class, equalizes status: Traditional scoring focuses attention on the question of who will be the "best" students in the class; each student is compared with the best students, insuring a few winners but mostly losers. When improvement scoring is used, all students regardless of ability level have an equal chance to receive recognition. The goal is more likely to be learning, not determining one's relative status.

STAD: Student Teams Achievement Divisions

STAD, Student Teams Achievement Divisions, is an extremely well-researched, effective approach to mastery of basic facts and information. Research of STAD also has revealed very positive effects on ethnic relations and various types of prosocial development. The use of STAD includes enduring teams (usually for about six weeks) and an improvement point scoring system which provides high motivation for students across the range of ability levels. The following is a description of STAD reproduced by permission with only slight modifications from Robert E. Salvin's *Using Student Team Learning, Revised Edition* (Baltimore: The Center for Social Organization of Schools, The Johns Hopkins University, 1980).

OVERVIEW

STAD is made up of five interlocking components: Class presentations, teams, quizzes, individual improvement scores, and team recognition. These components are described below:

1. Class Presentations. Materials in STAD are initially introduced in a class presentation. This is most often a lecture-discussion conducted by the teacher, but could include audio-visual presentations. Class presentations in STAD differ from usual teaching only in that they must be clearly focused on the STAD unit. In this way, students realize that they must pay careful attention during the class presentation, because doing so will help them to do well on the quizzes, and their quiz scores determine their team scores.

2. Teams. Teams are composed of four or five students who represent a cross-section of the class in academic performance, sex, and race or ethnicity. (See Heterogeneous Teamformation, Chapter 6.) The major function of the team is to prepare its members to do well on the quizzes. After the teacher presents the material, the team meets to study worksheets or other material. The worksheets may be materials obtained from the John Hopkins Team Learning Project, or they may be produced by the teacher. Most often, the study takes the form of students quizzing one another back and forth to be sure that they understand the content, or working problems together and correcting any misconceptions if teammates make mistakes.

The team is the most important feature of STAD. At every point, emphasis is placed on team members doing their best for the team, and on the team doing its best to help its members. The team provides the peer sup-

members. The team provides the peer support for academic performance that is important for effects on learning, and the team provides the mutual concern and respect that are important for effect on such outcomes as intergroup relations, self-esteem, and acceptance of mainstreamed students.

3. Quizzes. After approximately one period of teacher presentation and one period of team practice, the students take individual quizzes. The quizzes are composed of course content-relevant questions, that students must answer. They are designed to test the knowledge gained by students from class presentations and during team practice. Students are not permitted to help one another during the quizzes. This makes sure that every student is individually responsible for knowing the material.

4. Individual Improvement Scoring. In addition to the quiz score, students receive an improvement score each week indicating how well they are performing compared to their usual level of performance. Details of how to calculate improvement scores are provided in Chapter 15.

5. Team Recognition. Each week teams receive recognition for the sum of the improvement scores of the teammembers. A newsletter is the primary means of rewarding teams and individual students for their performance. Each week, the teacher prepares a newsletter to announce team scores. The newsletter also recognizes individuals who showed the greatest improvement or got perfect papers, and reports cumulative team standings. In addition to or instead of the newsletter, many teachers use bulletin boards, special privileges, small prizes or other rewards to emphasize the idea that doing well as a team is important.

INTRODUCING STAD TO YOUR CLASS
1. First Lesson

On the day you begin to use STAD, teach the first lesson of the new unit. You may use a lecture, a discussion, demonstrations on the chalkboard, or audio-visual aids to introduce the unit. Make sure that what you teach is closely matched to the objectives

tested by the quiz, and do not spend excessive time on unrelated material. Students must have the sense that they will be held responsible for everything you teach.

The amount of time you spend on introducing the unit is up to you. One full class period should be enough for most units in most classes, but you may take two, three, or even more periods to do the initial teaching if you feel that more time is needed. Remember, though, that students will have opportunities to study the content and practice the skills you introduce, so you need not be exhaustive in your presentation.

1. Introducing Team Assignments and Team Practice

1. Introduce Teams. Explain the concept of teams and teamwork to the students. In your introduction, you might say the following:

"For the next several weeks, we are going to use a new way of learning. It is called Student Teams-Achievement Divisions, or STAD. In STAD you will be working on a team helping each other to learn the material we study in class. You will have worksheets to use in your team practice sessions. To see how well you learn, each of you will take quizzes on the material that I present in class and that you study in your teams. Your quiz score will count toward a team score. The winning teams and the students who contribute the most to the teams' scores will be recognized in a class newsletter."

"Each week you and your teammates will have a chance to work together to practice and help each other get ready to take the quizzes. Today I am going to assign you to teams. Then you will have some time to work together and prepare each other for the quiz that you will take later this week."

2. Inform Students of Their Team Assignments. "Now I will tell you which team you will be on. When I read your name, find your teammates and sit next to them. Then choose a team name. Choose a good one, because you will use it for several weeks."

Read the names of the members of each team and point out a place for the team to assemble. Students should move desks together to face each other or move to common tables. While the teams are deciding on names, pass out two copies of the worksheet and two copies of the worksheet answer sheet for your first lesson to each team. Only two copies are given to each team to emphasize that the worksheets are for team practice, not meant to be filled out and returned. Record the team names chosen by the teams on the Team Summary Sheets.

3. Introduce Team Practice. After the team names have been recorded, continue as follows:

"The purpose of the team you are in now is to prepare its members for the quizzes that we will have each week. The quizzes will give you a chance to earn points for your team. Each team will have time to practice together the day before the quiz. The idea of team practice is to give teammates an opportunity to help each other learn so that the whole team can do well on the quizzes."

Make sure that each team has received its worksheets and answer sheets. Then explain to students how they should work together.

"You may practice in your teams however you wish, but I will show you one way of practicing that may help you."

"You have in front of you a worksheet and an answer sheet for this week's unit. Every team should have two worksheets and two answer sheets for the whole team. Find your worksheets and answer sheets."

Allow time for students to find worksheets and answer sheets. Make sure you have everyone's attention before you continue with the following:

"If you look at the worksheet you will see a set of instructions and a list of items. The quiz will have questions like those on the worksheet. Your job as a team will be to make sure every member of your team can do every item on the worksheet. To do this, you can first work in groups of two or three within your teams. You may study the worksheet together, checking yourselves against the answer sheet. You might want to

quiz each other on the items; or, if the questions require a lot of figuring, you might work the problems one at a time yourself and then check your answers with your team partner or partners. If your partners make any mistakes, try to help them understand why they made the mistake, as well as learn the correct answer. You may look at each other's work and try to figure out where your teammates made their mistakes so that no one will make that mistake again. In other words, you will be each others' teachers."

If the students are doing problems that take time to work out (as in mathematics, for example), have them divide into groups of two or three within their teams and work the problems together one at a time, checking the answer sheet after each problem is completed and correcting any misconceptions if teammates make mistakes. If the content requires short answers, have the students drill each other in pairs, with one student testing his or her partner and then switching roles to be tested, until both students feel confident in their answers. In either case emphasize the following.

1. No one is finished studying until he/she is sure that every one of his/her teammates will make 100% on the quiz.

2. When students have questions, they should try to get answers within their teams before asking the teacher.

3. Teammates should explain answers to each other instead of simply checking each other and then just going on.

If there is still time in the period, continue as follows:

"Now you may divide into groups of two or three within your teams and begin to work with each other on the worksheet items. Use the answer sheets to check your answers. If you don't understand an answer, first discuss it with your teammates, and then you may ask me. The idea is to use the worksheets to learn and to help your teammates learn - you are not finished with your worksheet until you and all your teammates know the material. The quiz on this material will be given tomorrow, so be sure to study well today. Are there any questions?"

"Go ahead and form into groups of two or three in your teams and work on your worksheets." Allow students to work in teams for the remainder of the period. Walk around the room, moving from team to team, to see that students are working well together on the problems, feel free to use or encourage that method. However, try to avoid a situation where students just do their problems independently and do not interact with their teammates. Also, make sure that teammates are explaining missed problems to one another rather than just grinding through the worksheets. Remind students that the worksheets are for studying, and that their goal is to be sure that every student on the team can do the problems on his or her own. At the end of this work period, have the teams collect their worksheets and give them to you to keep for the next practice.

3. Continued Team Practice and Quiz

1. Team Practice. As students come into class, have them move their desks to get into their teams again. You may need to remind students of their team assignments. If you wish, you may take ten or fifteen minutes to review your lesson. Then pass out two copies of the first worksheet and answer sheet to each team. Try to reinforce the idea that the worksheets are study aids, not something that should be filled out and handed in. Let students work in their teams for about half of the period.

One problem that sometimes arises at this point is that some students study or work for five or ten minutes and then say they are finished. If this happens, remind students that they will soon be taking a quiz in which they will need to know the material. If students claim to know the material, remind them to help those on their teams who do not - the whole team has to do well if they are to be successful as a team. If team members try to do the problems independently, remind them that their teammates are there to help them, and encourage them to check each other's work to try to locate and explain errors.

About ten minutes after the team practice begins, have students work with new partners within their teams. This helps reinforce the idea that it is a team effort that is important, rather than just individuals or pairs.

If you have some students who are having substantial difficulty with the subject matter, you may wish to have a resource teacher or aide work with them on the material the class is studying.

2. Quiz. If students appear to have done enough studying and there are at least twenty-five minutes until the end of the class period, have students put away all materials and take the quiz. If there is not enough time left, give the quiz during the next period. Make sure you have enough time for students to complete the quiz. (It should be a "power" test, not a "speed" test.) Have students move their desks apart, if possible, to minimize the possibility of copying.

You may allow students to check each other's papers; or if you wish, you may collect the papers and check them yourself. Either way, it is essential that the papers be corrected in time for the next class period. If you allow students to check each others' papers, have them exchange papers with members of other teams; then, read off the correct answers. Have students mark an "X" through the numeral of each incorrect answer and circle the numeral of each correct answer in pen or colored pencil (so the students cannot change each others' answers). Have the checkers put their names on the papers they check. Then have them return the quizzes to their owners (make sure that the owners do not write on them), and have all students pass their quizzes in. You should recheck the answers after school to be sure they were accurately marked. Again, if you check the papers yourself, be sure to do so in time for the next class period.

Figuring Individual and Team Scores. Individual and Team scores are figured using improvement point scoring; recognition is given through newsletters.

〜 See Chapter 16:
Scoring & Recognition. 〜

TGT: Teams-Games Tournaments

TGT is identical to STAD except quizzes are replaced with academic game tournaments, and individual improvement scores are replaced with a bumping system (details provided by Slavin, 1980). Details of TGT are not included in this book because my own research with the method revealed that cooperative and minority students can suffer negative consequences from the very competitive tournaments. Although students are not told which tournament tables are for the high achievers and which are for the low achievers, many know, and this form of within-class tracking may be responsible for the self-esteem drops we observed for cooperative and minority students. The critical elements which differentiate TGT from STAD are game tournaments and the bumping system.

Game tournaments. Students play games in which they win points by demonstrating knowledge of the academic material which has been practiced in teams. The games are quite competitive. Students can win extra points by correctly challenging their opponents at the weekly tournament table.

Bumping system. The competition is kept among equals via a bumping system. Each week the winner at a tournament table moves to a higher-level table; the loser moves to an easier table. This bumping system insures that all students are winners about equally often.

Warning: Although all students are winners and losers about equally often, and TGT produces academic gains for all students there is a potential problem. The bumping system in TGT can lead to the tracking of students within the class along ability lines and race lines. Having higher achieving and/or white students at the top tournament tables and lower achieving and/or minority students at the lower tournament tables each week may explain why, in my own research, we found that minority students did not like the class climate as well in TGT as in STAD classrooms, and that following TGT they decreased in their feelings of intellectual competence. If teachers wish to have the excitement of an academic tournament, perhaps it should be reserved as a very occasional event so students cannot make a stable internal attribution, such as, "I must be dumb, I always go to the lowest tournament tables."

References:

Slavin, Robert. *Using Student Team Learning.* The John Hopkins Team Learning Project, Baltimore, MD: 1988

Chapter 18

Task Specialization Designs

If each student on a team has a unique contribution to make, several positive outcomes result: Each student in turn occupies a position of high status as he or she shares the unique information, teammates bring forth the best from the student who is presenting because they need what that student can provide, and the team gains the sense of being an integrated working unit.

The task specialization designs occupy a unique place in cooperative learning. They create intense interdependence among teammates because teammates must depend on each others' efforts. The designs vary from simple Pairs, (Within-Team Jigsaw: Each student reads a paragraph, and then teammates do a Roundrobin, reporting to their teammates what they have read) to complex (Double Expert Jigsaw, with heterogeneous teams and heterogeneous expert groups). My suggestion: begin with some simple designs and move up as your needs dictate.

Pairs

Half the students in the class are given material to master (math problem, story, history event) and the other half are given other material to master. Students with the same material sit to-gether, and can help each other. The students then each find a partner who had different material, and teach each other what they have mastered.

Telephone

Barbara Chipps (Orange County Department of Education) called me one day, excited, to tell me about a new structure. Barbara had first trained with me in 1981 and had gone on to train other teachers. One of the teachers she had trained was *Carol Cromwell* (Alhambra High School) who was teaching an ESL classroom and developed a new structure designed to facilitate the development of listening and oral language skills; she called it Telephone.

Telephone is very simple. One student from each team steps out of the room. The teacher reads a very short story to the class. The absent student returns and the teammates teach the student everything they can about the story. Teammates are highly motivated to teach because the student who was absent takes a test on the material, and the score is the team score.

Telephone worked well in Carol's classroom. There was a positive class atmosphere and the students all performed well. Most importantly it promoted listening and expressive oral language as a communicative competence.

Deborah Forster (Culver City Unified School District, Culver City, California) created an important variation of Telephone. Her teams listen to the story on a tape recorder so she could accompany and work with the students who step out of the room.

Partners

As I thought about the original version of Telephone, two things worried me. First, what if the student did not do well -- would not that be too much of a burden on one student: to fail for the whole group? Second, I don't like any structure which involves dead time. To send students out with nothing to do, did not sit well with me, although in Carol's classroom the stories were very brief and it was not a problem. In thinking about these problems, it seemed that they both could be solved at once, if two students were sent out together and were given something to do together while they were outside.

And then it occurred to me that there really was no need to send them out. Why not split a learning unit in half, have two members on each team working on one part, the other two working on the other part, and afterwards have them teach each other. The pairs or partners could sit on opposite sides of the room. As soon as we tried this, an exciting possibility opened up -- the partners, sitting next to partners from other teams working on the same material could consult with each other. Thus, Partners was born.

Steps of:

Partners

1. **Partners are formed within teams.** Often the high and low achiever are partners, as are the two middle achievers.
2. **Class divides: partners sit together.** Topic 1 partners are all on one side of the class; topic 2's on the other.
3. **Materials are distributed.** Materials often consist of some reading and a worksheet. Worksheets are designed to stimulate higher-level thinking.
4. **Students master materials.**
5. **Partners consult with same-topic partners.** Partners consult with other partners sitting next to them; they check for correctness, completeness, and different points of view.
6. **Partners prepare to present & tutor.** Partners analyze critical features and decide on a teaching strategy; students are encouraged to make visuals and other teaching aids; they must evaluate what is important to teach, how to determine if learning has occurred in their teammates.
7. **Teams reunite; partners present & tutor.** Partners work as a team, dividing the labor as they teach the other partner in their team. After presenting material, partners check for understanding and tutor their teammates. Practice is distributed: topic 1 partners share, topic 2 partners share; topic 1 partners tutor, then, finally, topic 2 partners tutor.
8. **Individual assessment.** An individual quiz or essay, or Numbered Heads Together is used to assess individual mastery.
9. **Team processing.** Teammates reflect back over the process: How did we do as teachers? as learners? How could we do better next time? What social skills did we use? Which should we use next time?
10. **Scoring & Recognition.** An optional step, often not included, is to have some form or scoring and/or recognition system. The scoring system can be based on student improvement. The recognition system can recognize individual, team, and class accomplishments.

I especially like the process by which Partners was born: Barbara who had trained with me, trained Carol, who in turn came up with a new structure, which in turn led me to yet another new structure. Partners was the by-product of cooperative learning among teachers and trainers.

STEPS

As we experimented with Partners, it evolved and we found it useful to break it into ten steps, described in the box.

APPLICATIONS:

Partners can be used in almost any subject matter. Some examples:

Literature: Have students each read different short stories by the same author. When they return to their teams, first they teach each other the content, then they can discuss similarities between the two stories. Or, have the partners deal with two authors with different styles, or two poems by the same author, to emphasize contrasts.

Social Studies: One pair might deal with autobiographical information, the other the accomplishments of the person. Following sharing the information they might discuss how historical accomplishments have their roots in personal experience. Or partners might simply work on different parts of a chapter, with the emphasis on sharing information and ideas.

Spencer Kagan: *Cooperative Learning*©
Publisher: Resources for Teachers , Inc. • 1(800) Wee Co-op

Science: Each pair might conduct a different experiment on a related topic; they would then describe their results and discuss what conclusions the results together support.

Math: Each pair learns how to do a certain kind of problem. They then teach the other pair.

Jigsaw

Elliot Aronson first developed a Jigsaw approach to the classroom. Each student on the team specialized in one aspect of the learning unit, met with students from other teams with the corresponding aspect, and after mastering the material returned to the team to teach his/her teammates. The Original Jigsaw was developed to create extreme interdependence among teammates; each expert was the only one to see that part of the learning material. Although this extreme form of interdependence ensured positive relations among students, it was not practical because it involved rewriting the text.

Robert Slavin, gave up some task interdependence in favor of practicality as he created Jigsaw II, which uses existing textbooks. The story goes on: *Billie Telles* developed Partner Expert-Group Jigsaw, in which teammembers work primarily with one other person to master their expert topics and to prepare and practice the presentations which they will make to their teammates.

In order to make Jigsaw more efficient, simpler, and in some cases to adapt Jigsaw to special needs, I developed Within-Team Jigsaw, and Double Expert-Group Jigsaw. Teachers working with me developed Leapfrog Jigsaw and a number of new pieces to Jigsaw such as Team Worksheets, Blooming Worksheet packets, and Experts Share & Tutor.

The list of Jigsaw variations is formidable and still growing. But don't despair. In this chapter the Jigsaw variations are presented in order of complexity, and you can ease into Jigsaw at your own rate, trying some very simple forms first.

Jigsaw Objectives. Jigsaw can be used in a variety of ways for a variety of goals, including mastery, concept development, discussion, and group projects.

For example, in social studies a mastery oriented lesson might divide a textbook chapter into four parts, having each student on a team become an expert in one part, and then having each student teach his or her part to the team. A concept development approach might have the students from the team go to expert groups where they learn the evidence supporting a different potential solution to a problem. When they return to their teams, they interact -- with the aim of producing an animated, informative team discussion which might lead to higher level thinking and possibly a unique solution which respects the values underlying all four points of view. Discussion of a poem within a group will almost certainly be richer if each student first becomes an expert on a different aspect of the poem (rhyme, meter, symbolism, author's life).

Teams

For some Jigsaw variations, illustrations complement the text. Teams will be represented by the second picture.

Team X

Jigsaw Projects

In a Jigsaw on the AIDS issue *Rosemary Zarate-Crevello* and *Teri Marchese* (Pajaro Valley Unified School District, Pajaro California) had students first meet in expert groups to take one point of view regarding the question of what to do regarding a student with the disease. Afterwards, the "school principal," "parent," "doctor," and "parent of a classmate," met within each team to forge a policy statement they could all endorse. The goals of the lesson included knowledge, values clarification, and higher-level analytic and synthetic thinking.

If the aim is a group project which involves a variety of skills, each student may go to an expert group to learn one skill to share with the team. After each student on a team learns a different manual arts skill, they return to their teams to teach the team the skills. The team then uses those skills to design and create the project.

Within-Team Jigsaw

The simplest form of Jigsaw is Within-Team Jigsaw:

Step 1. Independent Work. Each student from a team works independently to master a bit of new material. Students might initially become experts on the new material in a variety of ways -- silent reading, homework, learning centers, computer programs, or performing an independent experiment.

Step 2. Students Share. Students do a Roundrobin within teams to share the new knowledge with their teammates.

Step 3. Individual Assessment. There is assessment of all of the students on all of the material. Improvement scoring as well as individual, team, and class recognition might be included.

This form of Jigsaw is called Within-Team Jigsaw because the teammembers do not work with members of other teams. As with all forms of Jigsaw, students will need help in learning how best to master material, report material to teammates, and to tutor teammates to ensure mastery.

Team Jigsaw

In a second simple form of Jigsaw, Team Jigsaw, each team becomes an expert on one topic and then its teammembers spread out to share share their new knowledge with the rest of the class. For example, in a typical classroom of eight teams, a textbook chapter is divided into four parts and two teams are assigned to each part.

(Teams 1 and 2 have the first quarter of the chapter, Teams 3 and 4 the second quarter....).

After the students have mastered their portion of the material in their teams, they teach the other teams. To teach part one, the high and low achiever from teams one and two each go as a pair to teach teams three and four, and the remaining students from

Team Jigsaw

1. Teams Master Topics. Two teams were assigned per topic.

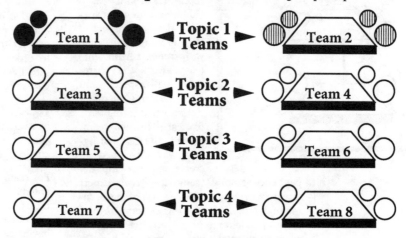

2. Topic 1 Teams Report. All students on a topic spread out to teach -- as pairs or individuals.

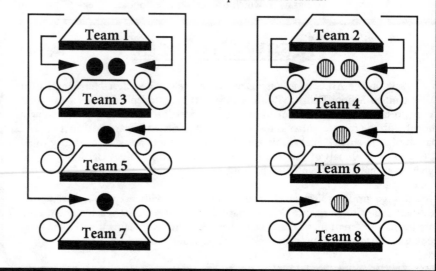

A Jigsaw Teambuilder:

Send-A-Jigsaw Puzzle

1. Teammates each write a fact on one piece of paper.
2. Person 1 rips it in half, turning the paper while tearing to make curved rips.
3. Persons 2 and 3 rip halves in half.
4. Each person rips the quarters in half.
5. The team delivers the jigsaw puzzle to another team to solve.

teams one and two each go individually to teams 5, 6, 7, and 8 (See Box). When it is time to share Topic 2, the members of Teams 3 and 4 spread out in the classroom to teach other teams. Sharing of topics 3 and 4 follow.

If each student in the class is to do a presentation alone, instead of having a pair present to a team, one expert can present to two members of a team while the other expert presents to the other two teammembers.

Workstation Jigsaw

It is so nice when I go into a classroom to consult with a teacher first using a cooperative learning technique and learn a new twist on an old technique -- especially if the new twist is of value to other teachers. When I walked into *Dolores Sasway's* class (Lincoln Middle School, Vista, California), I saw something brand new being done with Jigsaw.

Dolores is an expert in workstations. She has built up a great number of materials which are appropriate for small groups of students to work with on their own. So when she learned about Jigsaw, she modified the approach to include workstations-- *Workstation Jigsaw* was born.

In Workstation Jigsaw, students go to expert groups with a worksheet, but they do not turn to a text for the answers. In Dolores' class one expert team may be viewing a filmstrip, another working with instructional cards, a third with informative articles, and so on. The possibilities are limitless: experts can do experiments, conduct interviews, survey recent magazines.... They then report back to their teams on the information they have learned, as in Original Jigsaw.

Workstation Jigsaw breaks the set of traditional learning for students. Students learn that the sum of knowledge on a topic is not just what they find in a text. At least one workstation would be good as a supplement for any Jigsaw classroom! The teacher could be sure all students get a turn at workstation experiences by rotating groups: a different quarter of the students could have a workstation experience each unit.

For an example of a student-directed cooperative project appropriate for Workstation Jigsaw, see "Surface Tension," Chapter 15.

Leapfrog Jigsaw

We owe this one also to that very resourceful mentor teacher *Doug Wilkinson* (R.H. Dana Elementary School, Dana Point, California). In working with very young children, Doug has one expert from each team come to the back of the room to learn from him an important skill which they bring back to their teammates. The teammates, meanwhile, are working on either the last skill they have learned or an interesting sponge activity Doug has provided. The technique is called Leapfrog Jigsaw because each skill builds on the previous skill. The children make successive leaps toward a learning goal.

For example, in teaching children a lesson about the Mobius strip, the first child learned how to teach his teammates how to use a ruler to create a straight line, the second child learned how to show his teammates how to use the scissors to cut the strip, the third child learned how to show her teammates how to use tape to form the strip, and the fourth member of each group learned how to teach the others how to test the Mobius strip to determine if it really had only one side.

Leapfrog Jigsaw is very attractive for very young children who need a great deal of teacher direction. Even though the children work with the teacher rather than each other to become experts, they experience a great sense of pride as they come back to their teammates to share their new skill. Many primary grade projects involve a sequential set of skills, lending themselves to Leapfrog Jigsaw. Thanks Doug!

Partner Expert Group Jigsaw

Billie Telles (Los Angles County Office of Education) developed Partner Expert Group Jigsaw. The idea is powerful. As in other forms of Jigsaw, curriculum is divided into four parts and each student on a team is assigned one part. Five Steps follow:

Step 1. Partners Formed. The student is assigned a partner from another team.

Step 2. Partners Master Materials. The partners, working as a pair, meet to master the material.

Step 3. Expert Groups Meet. The same-topic pairs meet in expert groups to discuss the material, checking for completeness and agreement.

Step 4. Partners Practice Presentation. The partners meet again to prepare and practice the presentation they will make to their team.

Step 5. Experts Present to Teams. The teams reconvene and the experts make their presentations.

Partner Expert Group Jigsaw has a number of very strong features. Pair work

Partner Expert Group Jigsaw

1. Partners Formed. Each student is assigned a partner from the class.

2. Partners Master Materials. Partners sit together and work as independent pairs to master topics.

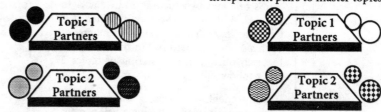

3. Partner Expert Groups Consult. All same-topic partners form expert groups.

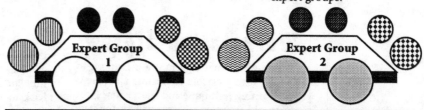

4. Partners Practice Presentation. Partners work as independent pairs to practice presentation

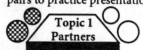

5. Experts Present to Teams. Individuals return to teams to present to teammates.

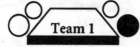
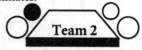

Partner Expert Group Jigsaw

1. Teams
2. Partners
3. Expert Groups
4. Partners
5. Teams

doubles the amount of participation in expert groups; students can be assigned carefully to another student who might be a good partner for academic, linguistic, or social reasons; and the students have support as they practice their presentations.

Besides, never has there been a design with more symmetry, in fact, it is the palindrome of designs.

Double Expert Group Jigsaw

The learning unit is divided into four topics and each student on the team is assigned one topic. For teams of five, the high and low achiever are assigned one topic and are instructed to work together. For three member teams, only three topics are assigned and the members will learn the fourth from another team.

When the students meet in expert groups, it is helpful to have two expert groups per topic, or Double Expert Groups. In the box is a picture of a Jigsaw classroom at two times. Time one pictures students in teams; time two pictures students in their expert groups. Notice, each of the four expert topics has two expert groups. This is the "Double Expert Group" design..

The rationale for Double Expert Groups is that it allows more participation and consulting. Picture for a moment all of the students with Topic 1 in one corner of the room, Topic 2 students in another corner, and so on. In a typical classroom with eight teams, that would mean eight students in each corner of the room, one from each team. We know, though, that a group of eight students is far too large to work well cooperatively. Thus we need to break up the expert groups into two groups, 1A and 1B.

If Jigsaw is to be done only occasionally, it is fine to assign students to topics randomly and to allow the students to break randomly into Expert groups A and B on each topic If, however, the Jigsaw teams are to meet on a regular basis, more care can be taken with assigning students to expert groups. A random assignment or student self - selection could result in the four lowest achievers in

the class working together to master the material. While we could live with this on a one-time basis, if it were to occur on a regular basis both those students and their teammates would not have full access to the curriculum. Thus, there is a need for careful assignment of students to double expert groups. With a little care, the expert groups can be assigned so that a high, two middle, and low achieving student is on each expert group -- maximizing the probability of successful peer tutoring. See Box.

Advantages of Double Expert Group Jigsaw

There are two main advantages to the double expert group structure: First, smaller expert groups mean more participation. Second, the structure allows "Experts Consult." The composition of each expert group is one high, two middle, and one low achiever, just as in the teams. This ensures that each group will get full and correct answers, and lower achievers have high achievers as models and coaches.

Assigning Students to Permanent Double Expert Groups

A method for assigning heterogeneous double expert groups is pictured on page 18:10. In step one, the students from team one are each assigned a different topic, and are assigned to expert groups with the high achiever on topic 1, the middle achievers on topics 2 and 3, and the high achiever on topic 4. In step two, the same procedure is followed, but the low achiever is assigned to topic 2, the middle achievers to topics 1 and 3, and the high achiever to topic 4. It does not matter what topic a student has or if the student is assigned to expert group "A" or "B." All that matters is that all four teams have a different topic, and each expert group has a balance of achievement levels. An assignment sheet with directions is provided. By assigning each student on a team to a different expert topic and also taking care to have each student take the appropriate place of a high, middle, or low achiever on the expert team, each team has every topic covered and each expert group has the full range of ability levels.

Assigning Expert Topics

Double Expert Group Jigsaw

New Piece:

Time 1: Students in Teams.

Time 2: Students in Heterogeneous Expert Groups.

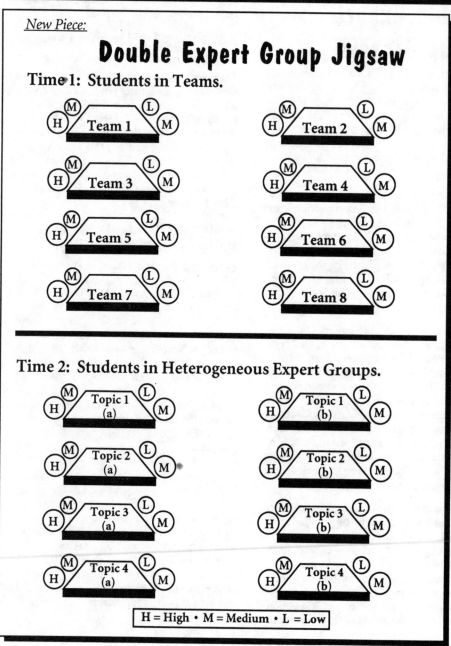

Experts Consult

With students in double expert groups, another New Piece of Jigsaw is possible: Experts Consult. When the students in their expert groups finish their discussion, worksheets or projects, then send a representative to the expert group with their same topic. Expert Groups 1A and 1B exchange consultants as do groups 2A and 2B, 3A and 3B, and 4A and 4B.

Having the expert groups consult via representatives adds several nice features to Jigsaw. Students in an expert group working alone might go wrong, so the teacher must be vigilant or else the experts may take back wrong answers to their group. It is very unlikely, however, that two groups working independently will go wrong in the same way, so they catch each other's errors and take some of the pressure off the teacher. Also, by consulting they come up with more complete answers, and learn some conflict resolution skills. Experts Consult gives students experience in a new role -- the consultant.

Experts Consult also makes class management easier because the consultants check for completeness and accuracy, saving the teacher some work. Only if groups disagree on the answer and exhaust their own resources do they need to call over the teacher.

Experts Create a Teaching Plan

After the students have mastered the material in their expert groups they create and practice a plan for teaching their teammates. The plan may include creation of visuals or manipulatives, working up an outline of the presentation, or simply agreeing on the main points to be presented. They may do some practice teaching to their fellow experts before returning to their teams to teach.

Experts Share & Tutor

Once students return from their expert groups to teams, they have two jobs: 1. To share what they have learned in their expert groups; and 2. To tutor their teammates on their expert topic, making sure every member knows the content. It is important to distinguish "Sharing" and "Tutoring." The temptation for students is to feel the experts have done their job if their teammates write their answers on the worksheet. But their job is only half done; they need to quiz and tutor their teammates to ensure mastery of the material. Each expert is responsible for making sure everyone on the team knows the material he/she has brought to the team. Thus, it is important to divide Jigsaw teamwork into two distinct parts.

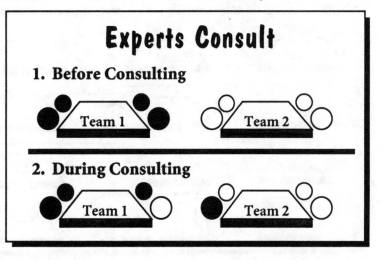

Experts Share. During Experts Share, the experts communicate and explain whatever concepts they have mastered in their expert groups. *Chris Harrison* (Chaparral Middle School, Diamond Bar, California) devised a nice touch to include at this stage. She instructs students to put down their pencils and listen to the expert give a full explanation. Only after they understand the explanation are they allowed to write, and they must write the answer in their own words. Thus, the focus is kept on understanding. Without "Pencils Down," the Experts Share stage can become rote, word-for-word dictation. Some teachers, elaborating on this

Assigning Students to Double Expert Groups

Step 1. Assign each member of Team 1 to a different expert topic.

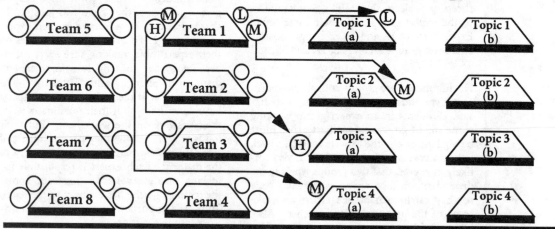

Step 2. Assign each member of Team 2 to a different expert topic.

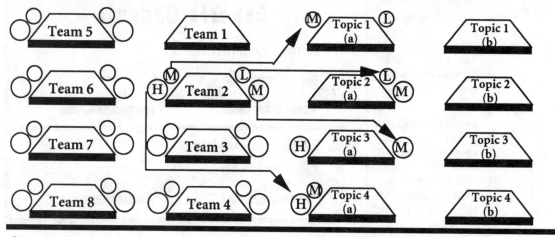

Step 3. Assign each member of Teams 3-8 to a different expert topic.

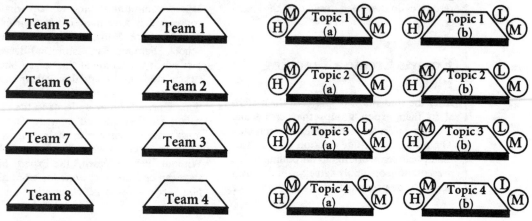

Spencer Kagan: *Cooperative Learning*©
Publisher: Resources for Teachers , Inc. • 1(800) Wee Co-op

Double Expert Group Assignment Sheet

Step 1. Fill in Students Names. Fill in names of students in the provided spaces. Be sure to place the names next to the appropriate achievement level.

Step 2. Assign Students to Expert Groups. First, assign the students in team 1, each to a different topic. Write their names, by their topic below, making sure to place their names on the line according to their achievement level.

Repeat step two for each team to assign all teams to expert groups. Result: each student on a team has a different topic and each expert group has all four levels of achievement.

H = High • M = Medium • L = Low

Teams   **Expert Groups**

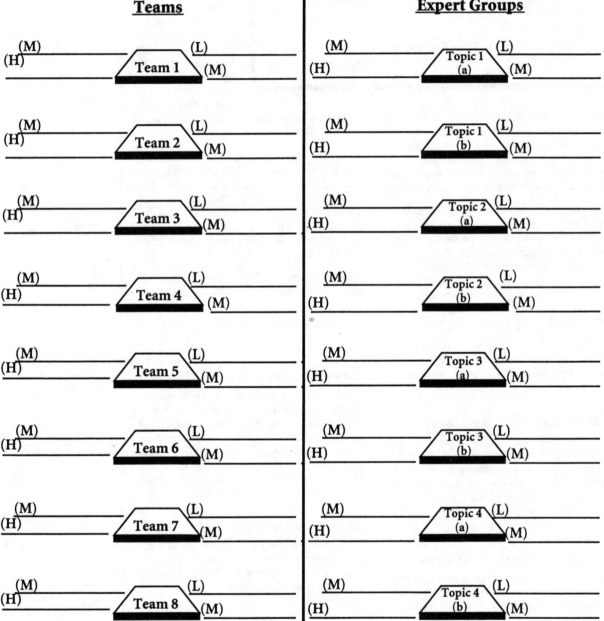

Spencer Kagan: *Cooperative Learning* ©
Publisher: Resources for Teachers, Inc. • 1(800) Wee Co-op

A Suggested Jigsaw Sequence

1. Assign Topics, Using Double Expert Groups
2. Double Expert Groups Meet to Master Material
3. Experts Consult
4. Experts Create & Practice Teaching Plan
5. Experts Return to Teams to Share and Tutor
   (Teams Consult, if necessary)
6. Teammates Work on Team Worksheet
7. Individual Quiz
8. Improvement Scoring
9. Individual, Team, and Class Recognition

technique, use a "Pencil Cup" for each team. The expert instructs teammembers when to place their pencils in the cup, and when to take them out. Students can take their pencils from the cup only after the expert has checked to make sure everyone understands.

Experts Tutor. After an expert has shared and explained his material and each student has written an answer to the worksheet on that topic, the expert has his/her teammates turn over the worksheets. The expert then asks questions and calls on teammates to ensure mastery. One phase follows the other directly; the expert is standing and is in charge of the group during both phases.

The Experts Tutor phase may be formalized to the extent that experts administer and correct a practice quiz to their teammates on their expert topic.

Teams Consult (if necessary)

If there is an absence and the team does not have an expert on a topic, when that topic is presented, the three-member team moves to sit with a team who has the expert present. Usually this is a team with a high ability expert on that topic. Team consultation increases cooperation between teams.

Blooming Worksheet Packets

An easy way to assign expert topics, give students an overall sense of the unit, and to guide work in Jigsaw is to give each student a Blooming Worksheets Packet. The packet contains a blooming worksheet on each of the four Jigsaw topics (see Blooming Worksheets in the Concept Development Chapter). Each student on the team goes to a different expert group to master one of the four different worksheets. Afterwards they come back to help their teammates fill out and master the concepts on their worksheet so that all students mastered the whole unit.

Give students a packet of four Blooming Worksheets, one for their own topic and one for each of the other three topics. The packet lets them see what they need to master and teach, and also provides a place to record answers when students are as experts, and later when they are receiving input from the other experts.

The construction of Blooming Worksheets is described in the Thinking Skills Structures chapter.

 See **Chapter 11: Thinking Skills Structures.**

Teams Contribute

Before students leave for work in expert groups, they may contribute to the worksheet. That is, they may discuss the material as a group and suggest the topic they most want to learn more about. The eight teams may contribute eight questions to the worksheets -- probably the eight questions about which there is the greatest interest.

Experts Construct

In advanced classes, the experts might construct some or even all of the worksheet on a topic. They can take over or help the teacher with the job of deciding what is to be learned.

There is a meta-level learning which takes place when students are given greater responsibility for the learning process: By inclusion of "Team Contribute" and "Experts Construct," students learn how to structure a learning task and they learn that the teacher values their interests.

Manuel Robles (Vista Unified School District, Vista California) routinely has his seventh grade students, while in their expert groups, construct Blooming Worksheets.

Tracking Expert Groups

Jigsaw is built around the concept of getting dissimilar students working productively together. Nevertheless, there are some instances in which tracking the expert groups is desirable. For example, you may have students who cannot speak in English at all and you may not have enough bilingual students to be able to provide a bilingual translator in each team. Or, in some classrooms, students are working on materials which are highly discrepant in ability-level, and it would not be reasonable to have all the students work at one level. In such cases, you can track your expert groups, making sure the high ability students are working with different worksheets and materials than the medium ability students, who in turn are working with different materials than the low ability students. If tracking is done, it should be only a portion of the students' learning experience, otherwise negative stereotypes and negative self-esteem will result.

Team Worksheets

After students have completed the expert worksheets, a team worksheet is given to each team. The team worksheet includes questions which demand that students integrate and synthesize the material in the separate expert worksheets. The idea of a team worksheet was suggested to me by Doug Wilkinson (R.H. Dana Elementary School, Dana Point, California). The idea goes to the essence of Jigsaw -- having students with discrepant information and/or points of view, working together to form an integrated whole. If the team worksheet is constructed well, it draws from the various expert sheets in such a way that integrative and synthetic thought is required of students. For Example, in the Team Worksheet, questions direct students to think about items covered by Expert 1 are related to those covered by Experts 3 and 4.

Two-Week Jigsaw Schedule

Week 1

Monday:	Introduce the learning unit. It may include Roundtable or some other group activity related to the learning unit.
Tuesday:	1) Students sit in teams and skim the whole chapter 2) Students receive expert assignments 3) Teams may contribute questions to expert sheets
Wednesday:	Students meet in expert groups and answer their worksheet questions
Thursday:	Students meet in expert groups and prepare to share and tutor. This includes making visuals.
Friday:	Students return to teams; Experts 1, 2, 3 & 4 share & tutor

Week 2

Monday:	Students work on team worksheet
Tuesday:	Students make up, take, and grade practice quiz
Wednesday:	Teammates tutor and drill (quiz indicates who needs help-- students may go a round of flashcards)
Thursday:	Cooperative Review followed by quiz and scoring of quiz
Friday:	Calculating improvement points; Recognition Ceremony

Jigsaw Twins

Jigsaw Twins is an alternative structure for Double Expert Group Jigsaw which is useful in the following situations:

1. There are a number of very low achieving students in the classroom

2. There are a number of monolingual language minority students in the classroom

3. Students are mainstreamed into an ongoing jigsaw class

In Jigsaw Twins, five members are assigned to each team, and the highest and lowest members are twins. That is, they work as a pair, going to the same expert group, and together presenting the material back to their group.

To assign students to teams of five members, simply take the highest, lowest, and *three* middle achievers to form team one, then cross off their names and repeat to form teams 2 through 6.

The Jigsaw Twins set-up insures that the group will not receive inadequate information from the very lowest achievers. If it is used in the bilingual classroom, the twins are a monolingual and a bilingual student, insuring that the monolingual student will have someone to translate for him or her both in expert group and in the Jigsaw team. The technique can be useful also in dealing with the mainstreamed student, insuring that he/she has a companion to help master the class structure and content.

One Caution: Attention is needed to insure that the low achiever of the twin pair assumes an important role in the team. For example, there can be a rule that each member of the twin pair must present half of the information received in the expert group, even if the higher achiever must translate or help him or her. The higher achiever is a coach or helper, but should not do the work for his/her twin.

5-Member Option

The five-member option differs somewhat from Jigsaw Twins. In Jigsaw Twins each team has five members, but two of the members function as one. They are assigned to the same expert group and they report back to the team as a pair.

In contrast, in the five-member option each of the members is assigned to a different expert group, for example, one to expert group 1A and the other to expert group 1B. When they report back to their teams, the two members with the same topic take turns and share the job of presenting.

DEALING WITH ABSENCES IN JIGSAW

There are two times the Jigsaw classroom can be restructured to deal with absences: absences on expert group day, and absences when experts present their findings to their teams.

Absences on Expert Group Day

When an expert is absent on the day he/she is to present material to the team, rather than trying to have one student fill in on two topics, it is more efficient to simply let the groups function without the missing expert, and then use the Teams Consult option when it is time for reporting back on the topic. If there are two absences from an expert group on expert group day, rather than having a two-person expert group, that group can be collapsed into the other expert group with the same topic. For example, a two-member 2a and a four-member 2b become a six-member 2ab. Alternatively, two three-person expert groups may be formed.

Absences When Experts Present

If an expert is absent on the day he or she is to report to the team, or if the expert is present but was absent on Expert Group day, then use the Teams Consult option. That is, simply have the team with a missing expert sit with another team to get the information. If all four members are present, it may be easiest to send two to one team and the other two to another to learn the topic.

Planning for Frequent Absences

In classrooms in which there is a high absentee rate, some teachers use five member teams, so that on expert group day, all four topics can be covered even if there is an absence. If there is no absence, the highest and lowest achievers are sent to the same topic -- either in the same expert group (as in Jigsaw Twins) or in the "a" and "b" sections of an expert group (as in the five member option). To form heterogeneous five member teams, simply select a high, low, and three middle achievers for each team.

Original Jigsaw

The Original Jigsaw method was developed to place students in situations of extreme interdependence. To do so, each student was provided with only part of the learning materials, but was evaluated on how well he or she could master the whole unit. Each student on a team, therefore, had but one piece of a jigsaw puzzle, but needed to complete the whole picture. Details are provided by Aronson et al. (1978). The elements of original Jigsaw include:

Specially Designed Curriculum Materials. Curriculum materials are designed or rewritten so that each member of a learning team has a unique source which is comprehensible without reference to the other sources. In the original Jigsaw, students read individual sections that are entirely different from those read by their teammates. This has the benefit of making the experts possessors of completely unique information, and thus makes the teams value each team member's contribution that much more. For example, in a unit on Chile one student might have information on Chile's economy, another on its geography, a third on its history, etc. To know all about Chile, a student has to rely on his teammates.

The most difficult part of original Jigsaw, is that each of the individual sections must be written so that they are comprehensible by themselves. Existing materials cannot be used. This makes the Original Jigsaw impractical: books can rarely be divided neatly into sections that make any sense without the other sections. For example, in a biography of Alexander Hamilton, the part that describes his duel with Aaron Burr would assume that the reader knew who both men were (having read the rest of the biography).

Teambuilding and Communication Training. Extensive teambuilding includes roleplaying, brainstorming, and specially designed group activities.

Study Group Leader. The importance of a group leader is stressed. Group leaders are selected by the teacher and receive special training. They organize the group, keep the group on task, serve as group/teacher liaison, model productive social and academic behaviors, and help resolve conflicts.

Teams. Teams range in size from three to seven members; original Jigsaw uses five- or six-member teams and five topics for each unit. Teams are heterogeneous with regard to ability level, racial and sex characteristics, and personality factors such as assertiveness.

Expert Groups. Each teammember is assigned to an expert group composed of members of other teams who have been assigned the same expert topic. Students meet in their expert groups to exchange information and master the material they will present to their teams.

Individual Assessment and Reward. Students take individual tests or quizzes covering all of the material of the learning unit; there is no group score or grade. Original Jigsaw uses very few quizzes (if any), and does not use team scores, improvement scores, or newsletters. Students simply receive individual grades.

Jigsaw II

Most of the material in this section is taken from Robert E. Slavin's *Using Student Team Learning*, Revised Edition, by the permission of the author (Slavin, 1980).

Jigsaw II was adapted from the original Jigsaw to incorporate some features of STAD which were not part of the original Jigsaw and to allow use of existing curriculum materials.

Step 1. Introducing Jigsaw II

1. Introduce the Idea of Jigsaw II. To explain Jigsaw II to the students, you might say the following:

"For the next several weeks we are going to be using a new way of learning. It is called Jigsaw. In Jigsaw, you will be working on a team. Being on a team and helping each other will help you learn better about what you read. Each team member will have a special topic to learn about. After you read the material, you will meet with members of other teams who have the same special topic and discuss your topic, and then you will return to your team as an expert to teach your teammates about your topic. Finally, everyone will be quizzed on all of the topics. The topics are like the pieces of a puzzle - each expert will be working to fit in his/her piece so that the whole team and the students who contribute the most to their teams' scores will be recognized in a class newsletter."

2. Inform Students of their Team Assignments. "Now I will tell you which team you will be on. When I read your name, find your teammates and sit next to them. Then choose a team name. Choose a good one, because you will use it for several weeks."

Read the names of the members of each team and point out a place for the team to assemble. Students should move desks together to face each other or move to common tables. Record the team names chosen by the teams on the Team Summary Sheets.

3. Pass Out Reading Material and Expert Sheets. After the team names have been recorded, pass out the reading material and Expert Sheet to each student. Then continue as follows:

"As I mentioned before, the idea behind Jigsaw is that each student becomes an expert on a particular topic and then teaches it to his or her teammates. The first step in this process is to get a topic and then to read the material, looking in particular for information about that topic. In a moment, I will come around to assign you to topics. When I do, you may begin reading the pages indicated on your Expert Sheets. Be sure to read carefully, so that you may learn about the material in general and your own topic in particular."

4. Assign Topics and Begin Reading. Go from team to team assigning students to topics. Make the assignments randomly; it is not important who gets which topics.

As you assign topics, have the students start reading and let them read until the end of the period. You may assign the rest of the reading for homework or have students complete it at another time such as during reading period, or you may wait until the

next period to have students finish their reading in class. Remind students to be sure to bring their Expert Sheets back for the next class period.

Step 2. Introducing Expert Groups

1. Finish Reading. Let the student finish their reading, if they have not done so for homework or during some other time. Ask those who finish early to go back over the material to be sure they understand it.

2. Introduce Expert Groups. As soon as almost all students have finished reading, introduce expert groups as follows:

"Now you will all have a chance to discuss your topics with others who have the same topic. In a moment, I will ask everyone who has topic 1 to get together, and so on. In these expert groups you will be able to talk about your topic to decide what the most important things are about it. You should share your information so that others will share theirs. I will appoint a leader for each expert group just for today. The leader's job is to get every student in the expert group to help add ideas. Are there any questions?"

Jigsaw II Schedule	
Day 1:	Introduce Jigsaw Lesson Pass Out Reading Materials and Expert Sheets Assign Topics and Begin Reading
Day 2:	Finish Reading Expert Groups Meet
Day 3:	Experts Report To Teams Quiz

Point out a place for each expert group to assemble. If there are more than seven students in one group, divide the group into two groups. Appoint a leader for each group. The leader does not have to be a good student, but should be a student who has the respect of his or her classmates.

When the students are in their expert groups, have them start discussing their topics. Encourage them to try to anticipate what might be on the quiz, and recommend that they make lists of what they feel are important answers to the questions asked in the topics. Work with each expert group, one at a time, to help them structure their task and use the time effectively. You may wish to give the expert groups special hints so that they will have truly unique information to bring back to their teams. Also, you may wish to give the expert groups specific discussion points to help focus them on the main ideas in their readings. Let the students work in their expert groups for the rest of the period.

Step 3. Experts' Reports and Quiz

1. Experts' Reports. Have students return to their teams and report on what they learned in their expert groups. Again, the students should emphasize the main points and anticipate what might be on the quiz in preparing their teammates. If you wish, you may have a class discussion of the material following the experts' reports. If you do, try to draw on the experts in the discussion to emphasize their special skills and knowledge.

2. Quiz. At least fifteen minutes before the end of the period, have students put away their materials and take the quiz.

After Step 3

The procedures for Jigsaw II - figuring individual and team scores, recognizing team accomplishments, returning the first set of quizzes, recomputing base scores after two quizzes, changing teams, and grading - are exactly the same as those for STAD. Because they have already been described in detail for STAD (see Chapter 11), those procedures are not repeated here. The one procedural difference between the two techniques is the weekly schedule after the first week. After you return the first Jigsaw II quizzes and newsletters and discuss the improvement point system, you may begin the next unit.

~

References:

Aronson, Elliot. *The Jigsaw Classroom.* Beverly Hills, CA: Sage Publications, 1978.

Coelho, E., Winer, L. & Winn-Bell Olsen, J. *All Sides of the Issue. Activities for Cooperative Jigsaw Groups.* Hayward, CA: Alemany Press, 1989.

Clarke, J. & Wideman, R. *Cooperative Learning—The Jigsaw Strategy.* Scarborough, Ontario: Scarborough Board of Education, 1985.

Slavin, Robert E. *Using Student Team Learning (Revised Edition).* Baltimore, MA: The Center for Social Organization of Schools, The Johns Hopkins University, 1980.

Co-op Co-op
PHILOSOPHY OF CO-OP CO-OP

Co-op Co-op provides conditions so that the natural curiosity, intelligence, and expressiveness of students will emerge, develop, and guide learning. The emphasis in this philosophy is on bringing out and nourishing the natural intelligent, creative, and expressive tendencies among students. It is an approach quite in contrast to traditional approaches which assume that the student is a void into which educators must pump facts, theories, and methods.

Fortunately, we do not have to choose one or the other. But, if we had to choose, which is better: To have students learn the outcomes of old investigations, or have students acquire the skills to conduct their own? Exclusive study of the products of prior work looks back, disempowering students; conducting creative investigations looks forward, empowering students.

Co-op Co-op is based on the assumption that following one's curiosity, having new experiences that modify one's conception of oneself and the world, and sharing these experiences--especially with one's peers--are inherently satisfying, and that no extrinsic reward is needed to get students to engage in these activities, which are the most important forms of learning.

Through cooperative learning project designs, students can realize their greatest potential as independent learners. They determine the content of study, how it will be studied, and how to formulate and present the results of their investigations. If we are to realize the goal of creating independent learners and thinkers, project designs are indispensable.

There are some project designs beyond the scope of this book. For example, "City Building," is a comprehensive curriculum package which details ways to teach social skills, math, science, social studies and language arts while students cooperate in designing a model city of the future (Nelson, 1984).

The present chapter details lesson designs which are content-free ways of organizing the classroom around cooperative projects

Co-op Co-op, therefore, is structured to maximize the opportunity for small groups of students to work together to further their own understanding and development--usually, but not always, in the form of producing a group product--and then to share this product or experience with the whole class so that the other class members also may profit. Thus, the name Co-op Co-op: Students cooperate within their small teams to produce something of benefit to share with the whole class; they are cooperating in order to cooperate. There is, therefore, a fundamental difference between Co-op Co-op and cooperative learning methods such as STAD or Jigsaw II, in which students cooperate in teams in order to obtain more points as a team than do other teams. In Co-op Co-op, students learn in order to satisfy their own curiosity about themselves and the world and to share with others what they have learned. In STAD and Jigsaw l, learning and cooperating are the means; the goal is winning. In Co-op Co-op, learning and cooperating are the goals.

As the foregoing brief discussion indicates, Co-op Co-op can be viewed as a way to operationalize the ideas of progressive education as described by Dewey. It is experiential. As Dewey (1957, p. 35) noted:

> A primary responsibility of educators is that they not only be aware of the general principles of the shaping of actual experience by environing conditions, but that they also recognize in the concrete what surroundings are conducive to having experiences that lead to growth. Above all, they should know how to utilize the surroundings, physical and social, that exist so as to extract from them all that they have to contribute to building up experiences that are worthwhile.

Co-op Co-op embodies a democratic, cooperative philosophy consistent with Dewey's notion of social intelligence:

> The way is, first, for the teacher to be intelligently aware of the capacities, needs, and past experiences of those under instruction and, secondly, to allow the suggestion made to develop into a plan and project by means of the further suggestions contributed and organized into a whole by the members of the group. The plan, in other words, is a co-operative enterprise, not a dictation. The teacher's suggestion is not a mold for a cast-iron result but is a starting point to be developed into a plan through contributions from the experience of all engaged in the learning process. The de-velopment occurs through reciprocal give-and-take, the teacher taking but not being afraid also to give. The essential point is that the purpose grow and take shape through the process of social intelligence. (Dewey, 1957, p. 85).

Co-op Co-op differs markedly from STAD, Jigsaw II, and Traditional, whole-class structures along a number of dimensions. Those differences are summarized in the table on the next page.

As can be inferred from the table, there is an important metacommunication we make to students via the classroom structure we adopt. How we structure a classroom is an important, perhaps the most important, form of communication we make to students. If we structure the classroom so that the goal of learning is a good team score, we communicate that the most important value is a competitive victory. If we structure so that the teacher is in full control of what and how students study, we communicate that students are empty or that their intelligence and curiosity are not valued. If we choose an autocratic authority structure, we communicate a lack of faith in the potential of students to choose positive directions for development. By taking full responsibility for students' learning, we leave them none. We do not leave students room to come out and become fully engaged in the learning process.

In Co-op Co-op, the structure communicates that we value the interests and abilities of the students. Students become responsible for learning and sharing what they have learned. The structure prepares students for participation in a democratic society.

ELEMENTS OF CO-OP CO-OP

The essence of Co-op Co-op is to allow students to work together in small groups, first to advance their understanding of themselves and the world, and then to provide them with the opportunity to share that new understanding with their peers. the method is designed to be simple and flexible. Once a teacher grasps the philosophy behind Co-op Co-op, he or she may choose any number of ways to apply the approach in a given classroom. Nevertheless, the inclusion of certain elements or steps increases the probability of success of the method. The ten most essential elements or steps of Co-op Co-op follow.

Steps of Co-op Co-op

Step 1. Student-Centered Class Discussion. At the beginning of a class unit in which Co-op Co-op is used, the students are encouraged to discover and express their own interests in the subject to be covered. An initial set of readings, lectures, or experiences prior to the student-centered class discussion is helpful in stimulating and generating curiosity about the topic to be covered. The aim of the discussion is not to lead the students to certain topics for study; rather, it is to increase their involvement in the learning unit by uncovering and stimulating their curiosity. The discussion should lead to an understanding among the teacher and all the students about what the students want to learn and experience in relation to the topic or unit to be covered. In Co-op Co-op, learning is not seen as progress toward a predetermined teacher-defined goal; it is a process that flows out of the interests of the students.

This first step in Co-op Co-op may take more or less time, depending in part on the extent to which the students have differentiated interests related to the topic. The importance of the initial student-centered discussion cannot be underestimated; it is unlikely that Co-op Co-op will be successful for any students who are not actively interested in a topic related to the unit, and who are not motivated to learn more about the topic.

Ideally, if the student-centered initial discussion is successful in uncovering and stimulating the curiosity of the students, the students will see learning as an opportunity to find out more about a topic they wish to explore; the students identify with the learning process. They become more

---

A Comparison:

Co-op Co-op, Traditional, and STAD & Jigsaw II

	Co-op Co-op	**Traditional**	**STAD & Jigsaw II**
Assumptions about Students' Nature:	Intelligent, Curious, Expressive, Probing, Problem Solving	Empty, in need of facts and methods	
Social Structure Modeled:	Democratic: students and teacher together determine what and how to study and evaluate	Autocratic: Teacher alone determines what and how to study and evaluate	
Motivation for Learning:	Curiosity, Interest, Opportunity to share	Individual grades	Outscoring other teams
Motivation for Cooperation:	Opportunity to learn, share	None	Between-Team Competition
Nature of Cooperation:	Planning; group decision making; Sharing, Cooperative analysis & synthesis	None	Dyadic drill; Helping; Sharing
Primary Goal:	Cooperation and Learning	Individual grades	Team Victory

Note: For a more detailed analysis of the dimensions of classroom structures, see Kagan, (1985b).

intrinsically motivated and increase their sense of internal control. A second major reason for the initial discussion is to let students see that their own learning can be of use to their classmates. As they listen to other students express what they would like to know, the students discover that they can be instrumental to the goal attainment of others, that knowledge can lead not only to the satisfaction of their own curiosity but also to helping others.

Step 2. Selection of Student Learning Teams. The students may be assigned to teams or may be allowed to select their teams, depending on the goals of the class. If a teacher has, as a goal, increasing the probability of cross-ability level peer tutoring and improving cross-ethnic relations, it will be useful to assign the students to teams in order to maximize heterogeneity among students. Methods for maximizing heterogeneity are covered in Chapter 6: Teams.

On the other hand, if the greater concern is with the development and differentiation of students in the direction of their own intellectual growth, a teacher may choose to have students select teams on the basis of their interests. There are potential pitfalls, however, in this latter approach. Students may self-segregate along race, achievement, or friendship lines, reinforcing preexisting stereotypes and polarizing the classroom. In general, by maximizing diversity of students within the teams, teachers increase the probability of establishing positive peer tutoring, improving ethnic and social relations, increasing role-taking abilities, and improving self-esteem among students.

Assigning students on the basis of heterogeneity increases the need for teambuilding -- especially at the secondary levels where cross-ethnic and cross-ability-level relations among students may be quite poor.

The Ten Steps of

Co-op Co-op

The essence of Co-op Co-op is structuring the classroom so that students are cooperating within teams in order to cooperate with the whole class in reaching a class learning goal. In order to produce the cooperative within- and between-team structure of Co-op Co-op, ten steps are suggested, as follows:

1. Student-Centered Class Discussion. Initial experiences, including class discussion are designed to uncover and stimulate student curiosity.

2. Selection of Student Teams. As in STAD, this step usually is designed to maximize heterogeneity within teams along the dimensions of ability, sex, and ethnic background.

3. Team-Building and Skill Development. As in original Jigsaw, teambuilding and cooperative skill development is incorporated to increase within-team cooperation and communication skills.

4. Team-Topic Selection. Students divide the learning unit into topics so that each team is responsible for one aspect of the learning unit, and the work of teams will complement each other in moving the whole class toward mastery of the learning unit.

5. Mini-Topic Selection. As in Jigsaw, each student becomes an expert in one aspect of the team learning goal; unlike Jigsaw, students determine how to divide the topic. Mini-topics are se-

lected by students; they are subject to teacher approval, but are not assigned.

6. Mini-Topic Preparation. Students individually gather and organize materials on their mini-topics. There is a bias toward non-text sources such as interviews, surveys, observations, and experiments.

7. Mini-Topic Presentations. As in Jigsaw, students present to the group what they have learned on their topic. There is usually time for feedback from the group and a second round of presentations designed to respond to the needs of the group.

8. Preparation of Team Presentations. Teams synthesize the material of the mini-topics to prepare their team presentation.

9. Team Presentations. Presentations are made to the whole class. Non-lecture formats are preferred, such as demonstrations, learning centers, audio-visual presentations, skits, and debates.

10. Reflection Evaluation. Evaluation is made of (1) individual mini-topic presentations to the team (by teammates); (2) team presentations to the whole class (by classmates); and (3) individual papers or projects on mini-topics (by teacher). Students participate in the construction of evaluation forms; they are evaluating the extent to which individuals and teams helped further the class in reaching its learning goals.

Spencer Kagan: *Cooperative Learning* ©
Publisher: Resources for Teachers , Inc. • 1(800) Wee Co-op

Step 3. Teambuilding and Cooperative Skill Development. Teambuilding and cooperative skill development have been covered in the chapters by that title in this book. The number and type of teambuilding and skill development activities to be used in Co-op Co-op depend on the needs of a particular classroom. Co-op Co-op cannot proceed successfully until the members of each team feel they are a "we." Teambuilding may be needed to build team identity; skill development activities are especially necessary for communication skills, such as active listening, supportive questioning, and helpful criticism, and for conflict resolution skills. Processing should be an ongoing part of Co-op Co-op.

Step 4. Team Topic Selection. After the team members have developed trust and communication skills sufficient for them to work together, they are allowed to select topics for their team. If the team topic selection does not directly follow the student-centered class discussion, students are reminded (via blackboard, overhead, or handout) which topics the class as a whole has indicated are of greatest interest. It is pointed out that the team can cooperate most fully in realizing the class goals if they choose a topic related to the interests of the class. The teammates are encouraged to discuss among themselves the various topics so they can settle on the topic of most interest to themselves as a group.

As the teams discuss their interests and begin to settle on a topic, the teacher circulates among the teams and acts as a facilitator. If two teams begin to settle on the same topic, this can be pointed out, and the teams can be encouraged to reach a compromise, either by dividing that topic or by having one of the teams choose some other topic of interest. If no team settles on a topic which the class deems important, this too can be pointed out and the the students can be encouraged to respond to the need.

When the fourth step of Co-op Co-op is successfully completed, each team has a topic and feels identified with its topic. The teacher may facilitate a spirit of class unity by pointing out how each of the topics makes an important contribution to the class goal of mastering the learning unit.

Step 5. Minitopic Selection. Just as the class as a whole divides up the learning unit into sections to create a division of labor among the teams within the class, so does each team divide its topic to create a division of labor among the students within each team. Individual students select minitopics, each of which covers one aspect of the team topic. Minitopics may have some overlap, and the students within teams are encouraged to share references and resources, but each minitopic must provide a unique contribution to the team effort. As the students settle on minitopics, the teacher may need to be more or less involved, depending on the level of the students. The teacher may require that minitopics meet his or her approval because some topics may not be appropriate to the level of a given student, or because sufficient resources may not be available on a given topic.

It is acceptable and natural for some students to make a larger contribution than others to the total team effort because of differences in abilities and interests, but all members need to make an important contribution. This can be accomplished by various means, including (1) allowing the students to evaluate the contributions of their fellow teammates; (2) assigning an individual paper or project to the students on their minitopics; and (3) having teachers monitor the individual contributions. If the minitopics are selected properly, each student will make a unique contribution to the total group effort, so individuals have peer support for mastering their minitopics.

Step 6. Minitopic Preparation. Once the students have divided the team topic into minitopics, they individually work on their particular minitopics. They each know that they are responsible for their particular minitopics and that the group is depending on them to cover an important aspect of the team effort.

The preparation of minitopics takes different forms, depending on the nature of the class unit being covered by Co-op Co-op. The preparation may involve library research, data gathering via interviews or experimentation, creation of an individual project, introspection, or an expressive activity such as writing or painting. These activities take on a heightened interest because students know they will be sharing their product with their teammates and that their work will contribute to the team presentation.

Step 7. Minitopic Presentations. After the students complete individual work on their minitopic, they present their minitopic to their teammates. This step of Co-op Co-op is similar to the "Experts Share" of Jigsaw. The minitopic presentations within teams should be formal. That is, each teammember has a specific time allotted for minitopic presentation. Each teammember stands while presenting his or her minitopic. Minitopic presentations and discussion within teams are carried out in a way that all teammates are afforded the knowledge or experience acquired by each.

Following minitopic presentations teammates are able to discuss the team topic like a panel of experts. The students know that the minitopics, like the pieces of a jigsaw puzzle, must be put together in a coherent whole for a successful team presentation to the entire class. In the process of interacting with peers over a topic of common concern, some of the most important learning can occur.

During the minitopic presentations, a division of labor within the teams may be encouraged so that one teammate may take notes, another may play critic, another supporter, and another check for points of convergence and divergence in the information presented in the minitopics.

Time may be allotted for a feedback loop: students may report back to the team after they research, redo, or rethink their minitopics in light of the feedback they receive from the team. Teammembers are encouraged to let teammates know what questions remain unanswered regarding the minitopic; teammembers are responsible to their group.

Step 8. Preparation of Team Presentations. The team needs to discuss and integrate all of the material presented in the minitopics presentations in order to pre-

pare their team presentation. Students are encouraged to integrate all minitopic material in the team presentation. For the synergy principle to operate, there must be an active synthesis and integration of the minitopics; in the process of discussion and integration, the team presentation becomes far more than the sum of the minitopic presentations.

Discussion of the form of the team presentation should follow the active synthesis and integration of the minitopic material. Panel presentations in which each teammember reports on his or her minitopic are discouraged; they represent a failure to reach high level cooperative synthesis. The form of the presentation should be determined by the content of the material. For example, if a group cannot come to consensus, the ideal form for their presentation would be to present for the class a debate. Nonlecture formats such as debates, displays, demonstrations, learning centers, skits, and teamled class discussion are encouraged. The use of blackboard, overhead, audiovisual medias, and handouts are also encouraged.

Teams are informed that the classroom is theirs for the time of their presentation; they can rearrange furniture or make use of available resources if that will contribute to making their presentation interesting and informative.Teams may make arrangements with other teams to give them feedback following a formal practice presentation. Teams also may ask for and receive the help of other class members or teams, if that will aid in their presentation.

Step 9. Team Presentations. During their presentation, the team takes control of the classroom. They are responsible for how the time, space, and resources of the class are used during their presentation; they are encouraged to make full use of the classroom facilities.

Spencer Kagan: *Cooperative Learning* ©
Publisher: Resources for Teachers , Inc. • 1(800) Wee Co-op

Because teams have difficulty managing time, there is generally a need to appoint a class timekeeper who is not a member of the presenting team. The timekeeper holds up warning cards when there is just five, one, and no minutes remaining.

The team may wish to include a question-answer period and/or time for comments and feedback as part of its presentation. In addition, the teacher may find it useful, following the presentation, to lead a feedback session and/or to interview the team so that other teams can learn something of what was involved in the process of developing the presentation. Particularly successful teams are held up as models. During post-presentation interviews, the teacher uncovers strategies which might be useful to other teams in future Co-op Co-op units.

Step 10. Reflection and Evaluation. Students are asked to reflect on their use of social skills. Reflection occurs at various times during Co-op Co-op with an aim of improving social relations and skills. Reflection can be facilitated by a simple question from the teacher such as "How well did you stay on task today?" or "Did everyone participate about equally?" Sometimes a reflection form may be used, to be filled out by teammates. See handout "How Productive Were We."

Evaluation in Co-op Co-op takes place on three levels: (1) team presentations are evaluated by the class; (2) individual contributions to the team effort are evaluated by teammates; and (3) an individual write-up or presentation of the minitopic by each student is evaluated by the teacher.

Following each presentation, the teacher may guide a class discussion of the strongest and weakest elements in the content and format of the presentation. Formal evaluation forms are also sometimes used for teammate and team contributions. See the Teammate Evaluation Form, and the Team Presentation Feedback forms for secondary and primary.

Co-op Co-op can run well with anything from great to no emphasis on grades. Some teachers and classes prefer to make learning and sharing its own reward; others prefer formal evaluation. In either case, the class should have considerable say in determining the form of the evaluation to be made.

Scheduling Co-op Co-op

Co-op Co-op units can be scheduled in a variety of ways:

Mini Co-op Co-op projects can be carried out in one day. In this short format teams taking only 10 or 15 minutes to prepare short presentations of 5 minutes or so.

A Co-op Co-op unit may run concurrently with a traditional or Jigsaw class structure, in which case students work one or two days a week on their Co-op Co-op projects which in that format usually take 4 or 5 weeks to prepare.

An intensive two week Co-op Co-op project for the last two weeks of a long unit becomes a welcome addition for the students and teacher. Co-op Co-op projects at the end of the quarter are particularly attractive because they allow students to extend, reinforce, and integrate the knowledge they have acquired over the quarter. Also, the acquisition of knowledge takes on a different tone when students know they will use that information in a presentation to the class.

An excellent format is to have two rounds of presentations. The first round may be relatively highly structured by the teacher, with relatively minimal demands on students; the second round may be less structured as students take more responsibility for their education.

How Productive Were We?

1. Effective Use of Time:

1	2	3	4	5	6	7
Much time spent without purpose		Got off track frequently		Did well, once we got our ideas clear	No wasted effort-
-stayed on target	

2. Development of Ideas:

1	2	3	4	5	6	7
Little done to generate ideas		Ideas were imposed on the group by a few		Friendly session but not creative	Ideas were encouraged and fully explored	

3. Ability to Decide Issues:

1	2	3	4	5	6	7
Poor resolution of difference		Let one person rule		Made compromises to get the job done	Genuine agree-ment and support	

4. Overall Productivity:

1	2	3	4	5	6	7
Did not accom-plish our goal		Barely accom-plished the job		Just did what we had to	Held a highly productive session	

Adapted for : Lee, K., Oakes, J., Cohn,J., Webb, N. & Farivar, S. "Helping behaviors handbook." Los Angeles: Unpublished Manuscript, Graduate School of Education, University of California, Los Angeles, Ca. 1885

Spencer Kagan: *Cooperative Learning*©
Publisher: Resources for Teachers , Inc. • 1(800) Wee Co-op

Team Presentation Feedback - Primary

1. It was loud enough.

2. They looked at me.

3. I could see the project.

4. I liked it.

Spencer Kagan: *Cooperative Learning*©
Publisher: Resources for Teachers , Inc. • 1(800) Wee Co-op

A video, Co-op Co-op, Exploring the Lesson Design in Depth, is available. In the video, a middle school class goes through all the steps of Co-op Co-op.

Group Investigation

Group Investigation is designed to provide students with broad and diverse learning experiences -- quite in contrast to STAD, TGT, and the Jigsaw methods which are oriented toward student acquisition of predetermined facts and skills. Research has revealed that Group Investigation is particularly effective in increasing higher level cognitive abilities among students.

A detailed presentation of the philosophy and technique is presented by Sharan and Hertz-Lazarowitz (1980). Essential to the approach is (1) organization of the classroom into a "group of groups;" (2) use of multifaceted learning tasks; (3) inclusion of multilateral communication among pupils and active learning; and (4) teacher communication and guidance of the groups.

Students in Group-Investigation progress through six consecutive stages:

1. Identifying the Topic and Organizing Pupils into Research Groups. A balance is struck between the need to organize students into heterogeneous groups and the need to allow students choice of inquiry topics.

2. Planning the Learning Task. Group members or pairs of group members determine subtopics for investigation. Groups decided what and how to study. They set the goals of learning.

3. Carrying Out the Investigation. Multilateral communication is stressed as students communicate with collaborators, teacher, other groups, and other resource persons. They gather information, analyze and evaluate the data and reach conclusions.

4. Preparing the Final Report. The investigation culminates in a report, event or summary. Students organize, abstract and synthesize information. Groups decide on content and format of their presentation; a steering committee of representatives of the groups coordinates the work of groups.

5. Presenting the Final Report. Exhibitions, skits, debates, and reports are acceptable formats, as is inclusion of class members not in the group.

6. Evaluation. Assessment of higher level learning is emphasized including applications, synthesis, and inferences. Teachers and students may collaborate on evaluation; the steering committee may work with the teacher in creating the exam.

Co-op Jigsaw

For a number of years I have puzzled over a dilemma. We have watched with dismay the progressive decline of basic skills among our students. Thus, there is justification for the back-to-basics movement. On another hand, many of us remember well that our most important educational experiences occurred when we were given the opportunity to explore in depth an area of interest. I learned reading, writing, and math in the process of following my interests, not in the process of attempting to acquire those skills. Individuals with tremendously large vocabularies have acquired them not by learning lists of words or even by looking up unfamiliar words in the dictionary; words are learned in the context of reading and listening. Limited English Speaking students learn as much or more language in their Jigsaw groups than they do in their language units. Thus, there is justification for the opposition to the narrow back-to-basics approach which has gained the day in some school districts. The basics might well be acquired better in the context of broad educational programs which emphasize the general intellectual development of students.

Nevertheless, if we give students choice over what and how to learn, we cannot be confident they will learn the basic skills and information we deem critical. The dilemma remains: movement toward allowing students to pursue their own interests is almost always movement away from drill and practice. And the press for basic skill

An Example:

Co-op Jigsaw I

In her handout to students Chris indicated the following requirements for the unit on government they were to cover:

Of Each person:

1. A 2-5 page report on their minitopic

Of Each Expert Group:

1. An outline of the major points of the government.
2. A chart showing the organization of the governing body and a list of the strengths and weaknesses.
3. An oral presentation for the class covering the basics of the government.

Of Each Team:

1. A new and unique constitution for a colony on the moon, incorporating the knowledge the group has gained on government.

Each person became an expert on one type of government (Communism, Dictatorship, Democracy, Monarchy, and -- in the case of five member groups -- Socialism). Students were instructed to "be sure to include" the following information about each government they studied:

1. History -- how it began.
2. Basic philosophy.
3. How it is set up, eg., elections, structure.
4. Other countries which have this type.
5. Your opinion of this type of government.

Result: Expert team presentations and posters conveying basic, required information on each type of government and high level discussion of ideas and ideals, including very creative synthesis of elements of various types of governments.

Co-op Jigsaw leads to acquisition of basic information plus high level independent investigation and synthesis -- creative synthesis at its best, for Chris Harrison, and Co-op Jigsaw students.

---

set of educational goals and the other set addresses another.

For some time I had approached this problem by saying that we ought to do Jigsaw and STAD some of the time and Co-op Co-op some of the time, and that no one technique could satisfy all educational goals. In fact my most recent research has been along the lines of looking at the effects of combining techniques. For example, doing Co-op Co-op two days a week and Jigsaw the remaining three, or scheduling a two week Co-op Co-op project following six weeks of Jigsaw and/or STAD. More recently, I have found that mini Co-op Co-op projects can be included quite often within the multi-structural lesson, so that one lesson might include Roundtable, Numbered Heads Together, Group Discussion, and a small Co-op Co-op project.

acquisition has increased in recent years. As greater and greater emphasis has been placed on performance on standardized achievement tests, teachers have narrowed their definition of education. If it does not translate into a higher achievement score, for many it is not education.

The two poles of these apparently conflicting approaches to education are represented within cooperative learning. STAD and Jigsaw usually have narrowly defined goals of increasing achievement as assessed by standardized achievement tests. Co-op Co-op and Group Investigation attempt to develop the student as an independent investigator. Some advocates of the latter methods claim that basic skills and general knowledge will be acquired within the process of pursuing one's interests, but I think that if we are really honest, we must admit that one set of methods addresses one

Co-op Jigsaw I: Experts Report

Chris Harrison broke the set for me of thinking of designs in either/or terms. She developed a Co-op Jigsaw approach which combined the creative and expressive elements of Co-op Co-op with the emphasis on acquisition of information found in Jigsaw. Chris, a teacher at Chaparral Middle School, Diamond Bar, California, developed a combination of the two techniques which has the potential to resolve the basic skills -- independent investigator dilemma. In Co-op Jigsaw, as in Jigsaw, each student first becomes an expert on an assigned topic, meeting with experts on the same topic from other teams. Yet the experts do not stop at gathering basic information. As a group of experts they make a presentation to the whole class. And Co-op Jigsaw does not stop there. When students return to their teams, they put their information together to create a novel group product.

Co-op Jigsaw II: Teams Report

As I began to experiment with Co-op Jigsaw, a second form emerged which for me is even more exciting than the first: In Co-op Jigsaw II, experts do not report to the class, rather teams report to the class, each on a different topic. Students go to expert groups to learn basic principles and information; when they come back to their teams they *apply* those principles and information to a specific problem. Co-op Jigsaw II is very flexible and can be used in almost any subject. It is best understood by examples.

Topic: The Seasons

Let's start with a kindergarten project. The four members of each team are assigned a season, so there is a Fall, Winter, Spring and Summer expert on each team. The students go to expert groups and study their season, using magazines to cut out pictures and discuss topics. In the winter group students are cutting out pictures of snow, fur coats, holiday scenes, and so on.

When students return to their teams, they apply their concept to a topic. Thus, there is a Food Team, Weather Team, Holiday Team, Clothing Team, Plants Team, Sports Team, and a Vacation Team. Within each team students prepare a presentation. So the Clothing Team will tell the class how clothing changes with the seasons, the Weather Team will describe the weather of each season, and so on.

Each student has a unique mini-topic corresponding to his or her expert topic and the report might well be the presentation of four mini-murals. When the class is done with all the reports, the mini-murals are posted to give a complete picture of the seasons along different dimensions.

In Sum:

Co-op Jigsaw can be used at almost any grade-level across the curriculum. It has the advantage of producing comprehensive coverage of a topic while allowing creative expression. The Teams Report version has the particular advantage of allowing application level thinking. Too often we teach principles which are not applied and which, therefore, do not become part of the active repertoire of students. If students learn about geography in general, how high are mountains and how low are deserts, or learn about measurement in general, how to calculate volume and weight, and immediately apply those principles to a new topic, the describing the state of Maryland or describing the difference between a golf ball and a ping pong ball, it is more likely that the new skills will be retained and applied throughout life. Co-op Jigsaw represents a marriage of mastery and concept development; theory and practice.

An Example:
Co-op Jigsaw II

My favorite example is the team newspaper. When the Challenger exploded, *Kathy Reider* had her students do a Co-op Jigsaw newspaper. Each team was to write a newspaper. Because Kathy wanted all of the students to deal with their feelings, they all wrote a letter to the editor about their personal experience. Beyond that, each student became an expert on one aspect of a newspaper. The news experts met together to learn about their topic, as did the human interest columnists, the science editors, and the editorial writers. In their expert groups the editorial writers wrestled with issues like how to weigh the costs against the benefits of undertaking exploration. The news reporters learned the elements of a news story, including how to write a "lead." When the students had mastered their new skills they returned to their teams to make a team newspaper. The newspapers were remarkable products.

Example Topics

Co-op Jigsaw II

Topic: Seasons   **Grade: Primary**

Team Topics	Expert Topics			
	Fall	Winter	Spring	Summer
Weather Foods Holidays Recreation Clothing Vacations				

Topic: Senses   **Grade: Primary**

Team Topics	Expert Topics			
	Sight	Hearing	Taste	Smell
Thanksgiving Dinner Baseball Game School Recess The Beach The Mountains				

Topic: Plants   **Grade: Upper Elementary**

Team Topics	Expert Topics			
	Structure	Needs	Reproduction	Uses
Desert Coastal Forest Plains Mountain Tropical Sea				

For animals: If it is Dinosaurs, the teams might be Brontosaurus, Stegosaurus, Tyrannosaurus Rex, Triceratops, Pterodactyl, and Dimetrodon; the Expert groups might be Food, Size, Special Features, Habitat. For Insects, The Fly Group and the Mosquito Group and the Butterfly Group would each have an expert on Size, Speed, Food, and Reproduction. In the Size expert group, the children learn how to weigh and measure an insect; when they return to their teams they apply those skills to their team insect.

Topic: Western States   **Grade: 5th**

Team Topics	Expert Topics			
	Climate	Resources	History	Geography
California Hawaii New Mexico Utah Nevada				

Much more exciting than the usual state reports -- and more comprehensive.

Spencer Kagan: *Cooperative Learning*©
Publisher: Resources for Teachers , Inc. • 1(800) Wee Co-op

Example Topics

Co-op Jigsaw II

Topic: Careers   Grade: 3rd

Team Topics	Expert Topics			
	Education	Salary	Activities	Conditions
Gardener Doctor Lawyer Accountant Engineer Auto Mechanic				

After learning what to look for in their expert teams, students can describe for the class various career opportunities.

Topic: Nutrition   Grade: 3rd

Team Topics	Expert Topics			
	Milk	Meat	Bread/ Cereal	Fruit/ Vegetable
Breakfast 1 Breakfast 2 Lunch 1 Lunch 2 Home Dinner Italian Dinner Chinese Dinner Dinner in Space				

In their teams, students create a balanced meal; each expert makes sure his/her food group is represented.

Topic: U.S. Government   Grade: Middle School

Team Topics	Expert Topics			
	Powers	Duties	Laws	Qualifications
President Vice President House Senate Supreme Court Federal Courts State Courts				

With this one, the time in expert groups would be brief -- just enough time to discuss the main concepts and agree on some research strategies.

Spencer Kagan: *Cooperative Learning*©
Publisher: Resources for Teachers , Inc. • 1(800) Wee Co-op

Chapter 19. Project Designs

Example Topics

Co-op Jigsaw II

Topic: Measurement   Grade: 3rd

Team Topics	Expert Topics			
	Height	Weight	Volume	Shape
A Baseball A Golfball A Brick A Pen A Wood Block An Eraser				

After students learned their measurement skills in expert groups, they would apply them to specific objects. Each expert would teach teammates a skill. For example, the volume expert would lead the team through a displacement experiment; the weight expert would create a balance scale and use paper clips as the unit of weight...

Topic: Spanish Painting   Grade: High School

Team Topics	Expert Topics			
	Period	Theme	Style	Autobiography
El Greco Goya Dali Ribera Murillo				

Topic: California Missions   Grade: 4th

Team Topics	Expert Topics			
	Founding	Drawing	Life Then	Status Today
Carmel San Juan Capistrano Santa Barbara				

Spencer Kagan: *Cooperative Learning*©
Publisher: Resources for Teachers , Inc. • 1(800) Wee Co-op

19 : 15

Rotation Learning Centers

When I first head a presentation on Descubrimiento, I liked pretty much everything I heard except the heavy price tag, the need for teachers to receive days of training outside their school setting, and that the method was available only for second and third grade. Descubrimiento refers to a lesson design for learning centers and a set of grade-specific, curriculum-specific materials. It seemed to me that many teachers either have or can create their own curriculum materials -- what they would like is a cooperative lesson design which would allow all teams to work each day at learning centers without the need to create a learning center for each team on each topic.

Thus, when Vista Unified School District (Vista, California) asked me to work with some of their teachers in developing a cooperative learning science program, I jumped at the opportunity. Gertrude McClay and Carol Olson, two of Vista's finest teachers agreed to work on the project. Gertrude is a much loved science teacher who at that time was in her first year of retirement from regular teaching; Carol is a creative, energetic science teacher actively searching for better methods for her students.

What resulted from our efforts was what we called Rotation Science Centers. Later I realized that the underlying design had applicability to areas other than science, so I now call the design Rotation Learning Centers.

Science lends itself nicely to teamwork and learning centers because there are so many hands-on instructive projects. In fact, most science teachers group their students some of the time for experiments -- what is lacking often is the formal structure of teamwork. For a typical, student-directed science project appropriate for a learning center, see "Surface Tension" in Chapter 15. Most content areas, though, can be adopted to learning centers. Much of the thrust of our new national math standards is to have students performing hands-on experiments with manipulatives such as Base 10 Kits, Algebra Tiles, and Fraction Bars. In the language arts areas, we can design learning centers which will be the basis for our instructional programs in integrated reading, writing, speaking and listening. The notion of a language arts learning center is in synchrony with the whole language approach.

As we sat down to discuss the possibilities, Gertrude, Carol, and I agreed that a practical design would include the following: (1) The classroom structure would be built around a teacher's existing curriculum materials and text; it would not depend on purchase of special curriculum materials; (2) the structure would convey basic information, but would also maximize the opportunity for students to work in teams to experience, rather than read about the curriculum.

We agreed that the scientific process of observing, formulating hypotheses, testing hypotheses, and rethinking one's view of the world is often not emphasized enough, and that cooperative learning had the potential to have students actively engage in the scientific process. Too often students only read about or experience the outcomes of that process, rather than experience it. This is true even when teachers include "experiments" for students to do because the "experiments" are preplanned by the teacher, with predetermined intended outcomes. Those experiments are really demonstrations which the students perform -- they do not involve students in original hypothesis generation and testing.

The result of our discussion was a plan which was carried out in Carol's classroom, with Gertrude's support in developing materials. In Rotation Learning Centers, students rotate through activity centers. Some time is spent also in direct instruction, Jigsaw, and other cooperative learning structures to master basic concepts and related text material.

Rotation Learning Centers is based on creating content for three different learning centers per curriculum unit. The content is duplicated, so there are nine learning centers in the classroom, three identical centers on each topic. Three teams work at identical centers each day, and then rotate to a new topic the next day.

Typical Weekly Schedule

Rotation Learning Centers

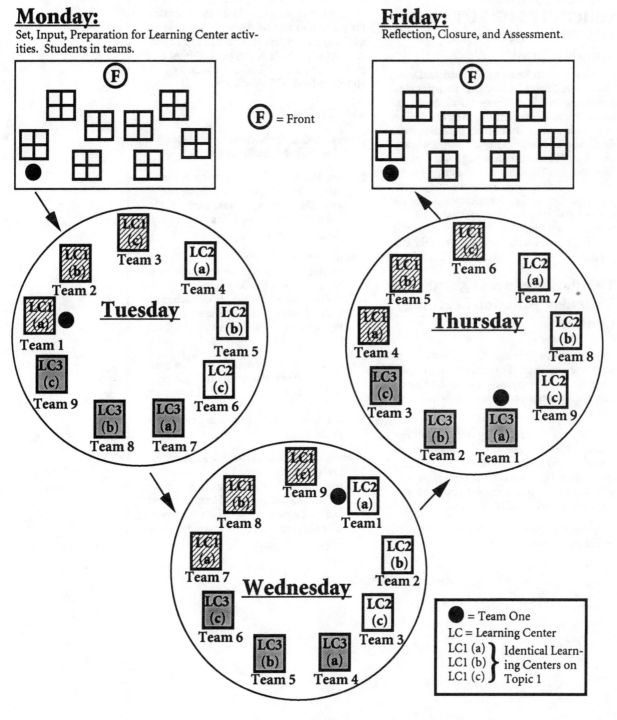

Monday:

Set, Input, Preparation for Learning Center activities. Students in teams.

Friday:

Reflection, Closure, and Assessment.

F = Front

= Team One
LC = Learning Center
LC1 (a)
LC1 (b) } Identical Learning Centers on
LC1 (c) } Topic 1

Spencer Kagan: *Cooperative Learning* ©
Publisher: Resources for Teachers , Inc. • 1(800) Wee Co-op

Also, with only three days a week at activity centers, there is time for teacher demonstrations, and other teamwork.

TYPICAL WEEKLY SCHEDULE FOR ROTATION LEARNING CENTERS:
Monday: Input

Monday consists of an Initial Lecture, Demonstration, Direct Instruction, Partners, Independent Work, or Jigsaw for content. An introduction to the unit may be provided by the teacher who uses lecture, demonstrations, and/or media materials. Students are seated in teams and structures like Think-Pair-Share, Three-Step-Interview, Numbered Heads Together, and Roundtable may be used. The initial demonstration by the teacher and teamwork prepares students so that they can complete the activities of the learning centers with minimum teacher supervision.

Tuesday, Wednesday, and Thursday Rotation Learning Centers

Students rotate through three activity centers, one per day. The activity centers are designed to be independent of each other so that students can participate in them in any order.

On each activity center day one-third of the students are involved in each activity; there is one activity center per team. Those teams working on the same activity centers consult with each other via a representative or as a large group at the end of the day.

Teams rotate through all three activity centers in three days.

Friday: Integration and Assessment

Students work in teams on a team project which integrates the information from the three learning centers. This integrative work may be a blooming worksheet, a report, or an additional project. Some time is taken for evaluation and reflection on learning via a formal quiz or test, or structures like Send-A-Problem, Trade-A-Problem, Numbered Heads Together, Inside-Outside Circle, and/or Individual Projects. ◡

References

Dewey, John. *Experience and education.* New York: Macmillan, 1957.

Nelson, Doreen. *Transformations. Process and Theory. A Curriculum Guide to Creative Development.* Santa Monica, CA: Center for City Building Educational Programs, 1984.

Kagan, Spencer. Co-op Co-op: A flexible cooperative learning technique. In R. Slavin, S. Sharan, S. Kagan, R. Hertz-Lazarowitz, C. Webb & R. Schmuck (Eds.) *Learning to Cooperate, Cooperating to Learn.* New York: Plenum, 1985. (a)

Kagan, Spencer. *The dimensions of cooperative classroom structures.* In R. Slavin, S. Sharan, S. Kagan, R. Hertz-Lazarowitz, C. Webb & R. Schmuck (Eds.) *Learning to Cooperate, Cooperating to Learn.* New York: Plenum, 1985. (b)

Sharan, S., Hertz-Lazarowitz, R. A group-investigation method of cooperative learning in the classroom. In S. Sharan, P. Hare, C. Webb, & R. Hertz-Larowitz, (Eds.), *Cooperation in Education.* Provo, UT: Brigham Young University, Press, 1980.

Chapter 20

Co-op Lesson Planning

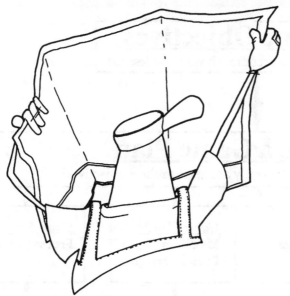

There is a similar developmental process in learning to implement cooperative structures and learning to implement co-op lesson designs. It is natural after using a structure many times to modify it by playing with the elements of the structure. A Think-Pair-Square becomes a Think-Write-Pair-Square. The same process occurs in learning to create original co-op lesson designs. It is natural after using a prefab co-op lesson design many times to modify it by playing with the elements of the design.

Four different approaches to planning cooperative lessons can be adopted, depending on the goals and experience level of the teacher. These different game plans all have validity and may all be used by one teacher with the same class at different times. The four game plans are 1) Insert-A-Structure; 2) Prefab Design; 3) Modified Prefab Design; and 4)Freestyle Design. Co-op lesson planning consists of defining the objectives of a lesson, choosing one of the four game plans, and implementing it. The four game plans for cooperative lesson planning differ in

complexity, and teachers may progress from one plan to another as they gain experience.

Teachers usually begin by taking existing, traditional lessons and simply inserting a cooperative structure. Later they move to choosing and implementing an existing, prefabricated co-op lesson design. After having implemented a prefab lesson design a number of times, teachers begin "tweaking" the design, modifying it, inserting or subtracting design elements. The effectiveness of these innovations is a function of the teacher's understanding of the elements of lesson design. At a later stage of experience teachers move to creating their own freestyle lesson designs—unique sequenced sets of design elements.

There is a strong analogy between structures and lesson designs. A structure consists of a series of structure elements. For example, Think-Pair-Square consists of three elements: Individual Thinks, Pairs Discusses, and Teammates Discuss. Similarly, a lesson design consists of a series of design elements. For example, STAD consists of five design elements: Direct Instruction, Teamwork, Individual Quiz, Improvement Scoring, and Team Recognition.

The difference between an element of a lesson design and an element of a structure, however, is profound. An element of a structure is an action or interaction in a classroom. Several structure elements are combined to form a structure, as in Think-Pair-Share. An element of a lesson design is a sub-objective of the lesson design. Several of these designs are combined to form a lesson design, as in STAD. Each design element of sub-objective can be achieved through many possible means, often including a variety of cooperative learning structures. For example, many different structures could be used to do the teamwork (Guided Practice) called for the second design element of STAD.

Spencer Kagan: *Cooperative Learning*©
Publisher: Resources for Teachers , Inc. • 1(800) Wee Co-op

A Flowchart for
Co-op Lesson Planning

I. Define Objectives
What do I hope to accomplish with this lesson?

II. Choose a Game Plan
Which game plan will most efficiently accomplish these objectives?

Game Plan 1: **Insert-A-Structure**	*Game Plan 2:* **Prefab Design**	*Game Plan 3:* **Modified Prefab Design**	*Game Plan 4:* **Freestyle Design**

III. Implement the Game Plan

1. Examine objectives 2. Examine Chart of Stuctures 3. Choose a structure which matches objectives 4. Insert structure into lesson plan 5. Implement	1. Examine objectives 2. Examine Chart of Lesson Designs 3. Choose a design which matches objectives 4. Structure the design 5. Implement	1. Examine objectives 2. Examine Chart of Lesson Designs 3. Choose Design 4. Examine Chart of Design Elements 5. Insert or subtract design elements 6. Structure the design 7. Implement	1. Examine objectives 2. Examine Chart of Structures 3. Choose series of structures to reach unique curriculum objectives 4. Ask the 'Big 4' questions 5. If necessary, modify the series of structures to meet the 'Big 4' 6. Implement

There is an analogy also between learning to implement cooperative structures and learning to implement co-op lesson designs. It is natural after using a structure many times to modify it by playing with its elements. For example after becoming very familiar with a prefab structure like Think-Pair-Square, a teacher might modify the structure, inserting an element, doing a Think-Write-Pair-Square. Later yet, the teacher may begin to create original, freestyle structures like Think-Write-Roundrobin.

The same process occurs in learning to create original co-op lesson designs. First, a teacher learns well a prefab co-op lesson design, later begins to modify the design, and finally begins to play with design elements to create freestyle co-op lesson designs. For example, after using STAD many times, a teacher may modify it by inserting or subtracting design elements. One teacher may modify the design by inserting an anticipatory set and/or closure, another may take out improvement scoring and insert reflection time on social skills. At the highest stage of co-op lesson planning, teachers create freestyle lesson designs which do not resemble any of the prefab designs. The freestyle designs are unique designs created to meet the requirements of specific curriculum, student needs, and teacher objectives.

To modify structures, it is helpful to have a systematic overview of the various elements which make up structures. The elements of structures are presented briefly in Chapter 5: Three Approaches to Cooperative Learning. It was noted there that a detailed presentation of the Element Matrix and how to work with the matrix to modify and create structures is beyond the scope of this book. It is in preparation by Miguel Kagan and myself as a separate publication: Kagan & Kagan, *The Element Matrix: Creating Cooperative Learning Structures* (In Preparation).

Similarly, to modify co-op lesson designs, it is helpful to have a systematic overview of the various elements of lesson designs. Thus, in this chapter you will find a presentation of the dozen elements of lesson design along with a discussion of how those elements are used to modify prefab co-op lesson designs and create new designs. Knowledge of design elements is the basis for efficiently modifying and creating cooperative lesson designs. The elements of lesson design, however, are not the same as the elements of effective instruction. The elements of effective instruction are general principles which can be used while implementing any lesson design.

No matter which of the four game plans you choose, or which of the various cooperative learning lesson designs you choose, the lesson will be more effective if it it is implemented with respect for the elements of effective instruction. So, before turning to the four game plans, and a presentation of the elements of lesson design, let's briefly review the elements of effective instruction. These principles have been discussed in depth in a variety of sources. For a concise, yet thorough overview, see Gentile, 1988. The elements of effective instruction are summarized only very briefly here.

Elements of Effective Instruction

1. Setting Objectives. The first step to planning a lesson is to decide exactly what you wish to accomplish with the lesson. That is, lesson objectives are established. Ask yourself the question, "What do I hope to accomplish with this lesson?"

There are many possible objectives. You may want students to master basic skills or information, create a project, develop social skills, enhance class or team climate, develop higher-level thinking, or develop communicative skills. In one lesson the objectives may be to stimulate thought at all levels of Bloom's Taxonomy; another lesson may aim only at promoting knowledge and comprehension. Defining the objectives you wish to accomplish gives direction to the lesson.

Objectives are set at the correct level of difficulty. A task analysis is used to assess the essential sub-objectives of the task. Sub-objectives are chosen to begin instruction at a point at which all students can experience success. Attempts are made to match the task to the students, so all children are working at the correct level of difficulty.

2. Teaching to the Objective. The activities in the lesson are sequenced to move toward the objective. Teaching to the objective, though, respects the needs and interests of the students, so time is allowed for student input, teacher response to student needs, and activities which allow student ownership of what is learned.

3. Monitoring and Adjusting. The teacher elicits and checks observable behavior of students to interpret progress toward the objectives. The teacher is responsive to what students have and have not learned, making changes in the input or using different structures, if necessary.

Checking for understanding can occur in many ways including sampling individual responses, choral responses, finger responses, use of slates, and use of a variety of structures such as Numbered Heads Together, and Paris Check.

4. Applying Principles of Learning. Principles of motivation, reinforcement, retention, and transfer are applied. Teachers promote learning by having students ready to learn, and actively involved. The teacher optimizes the level of anxiety, lowering the level of concern if anxiety interferes with learning, raising it if students are not sufficiently motivated. The teacher also integrates cognitive and affective elements of a lesson, alternates periods of input and periods of student output, structures for success, gives immediate feedback, provides time to reflect on how well learning is occurring, and provides closure and transference opportunities. (Whoever said our job was easy?)

Choose a Game Plan

Once we set our objectives, we choose a cooperative learning game plan. We ask, "How can I most efficiently reach the objectives that I have set for this lesson? Will cooperative learning help? What approach to cooperative learning should I take?"

The answer to these questions will depend on the your experience level in cooperative learning, your values, the curriculum to be delivered, and the objectives of the lesson. Once the objectives are defined, there are four different game plans you can adopt. We will take up the four game plans in order, examining the simplest game plan first. Let's look first at lesson planning for a teacher new to cooperative learning.

Game Plan 1:

INSERT-A-STRUCTURE

Teachers just beginning to experiment with cooperative learning in their classrooms, are advised to ease into cooperative learning very slowly. Teachers new to cooperative learning may know only a few cooperative structures. As an example, let's say a teacher knew only one cooperative structure (Think-Pair-Square) and wanted to incorporate some cooperative interaction in a unit on electricity. Co-op lesson planning at this stage begins by asking, "Where in this lesson might a Think-Pair-Square be effective in reaching a lesson objective?"

A Think-Pair-Square is a simple structure: 1) a problem is posed; 2) students think about the question individually; 3) students pair up to discuss the question; and finally, 4) students discuss the question as a team.

At the beginning of the lesson, the teacher wants students to be actively involved, to arouse interest and motivation. To accomplish these sub-objectives, at the beginning of the electricity lesson, the teacher may use a Think-Pair-Square, asking the students questions like: "Where do the lights in your house get power? How do you think electricity works? Where does electricity come from? What are three things in your house that depend on electricity?"

Later in the lesson, students are creating an electromagnet and the teacher is using Think-Pair-Square to have them reflect on questions like: "How can you get this magnet to be more powerful? What would happen if more wire were wrapped around the nail? How many more paper clips would stick to the nail, if the nail was given two more wraps of wire?"

For closure of the lesson, Think-Pair-Square might be used with content like: "What did you learn about electricity? Why is it important to know about electricity? What did you most enjoy about the lesson? What are some questions you still have?"

With just one structure available, a teacher is capable of incorporating cooperative learning in several places in a lesson, and can do so in almost any lesson! Think-Pair-Square

CHART OF STRUCTURES

Resources for Teachers, Inc. • 1(800) Wee Co-op

Spencer Kagan: *Cooperative Learning*©
Publisher: Resources for Teachers , Inc. • 1(800) Wee Co-op

like many simple multi-functional structures can be used to create an anticipatory set, obtain and reflect on a concept, and to provide closure to a lesson.

With time and experience, teachers create a repertoire of structures, knowing which structures are most effective for which objectives. Once more structures are available, a teacher has more options. For example, during closure of the electricity lesson, the teacher could have used a Team Statement or Team Word-Webbing with great effect. As more structures are mastered, teachers have more choices and are more likely to pick the most appropriate structure for the objective at hand.

Having just one structure is somewhat like opening up a toolbox and finding just one tool. If it is a good tool, you can create many things with it. But of course, as more tools are added to the tool box, you become capable of building more things, and building old things in a more sophisticated and refined manner.

Each tool is useful for some things and not for others; that is, each structure has its domain of usefulness. The teacher learns to pull out the right tool for the objective at hand. The Chart of Structures lists the structures by category and is helpful in choosing which structure to insert in a lesson. When deciding which structure to use in a lesson the first question is, "What is my objective?" If the objective is teambuilding, then one of the structures under teambuilding will probably do the job. If the objective is communication building, you may wish to pull out a communication building structure. See Chart of Structures.

As you become fluent in more structures, you begin naturally to insert more structures into your lessons. The movement from inserting just one structure into a lesson to doing multi-structural lessons is a natural movement as more structures are mastered.

Sample multi-structural lessons have been written for math (Andrini, 1991), language arts (Curran, 1991; Stone, 1991) and higher level thinking (Wiederhold, 1991). The Fables lesson (Chapter 15) is an example of a multi-structural lesson in language arts.

Game Plan 2:
PREFAB DESIGNS

A second approach to co-op lesson planning is to select and implement a prefabricated cooperative learning lesson design. Chapters 17, 18, and 19 of this book provide prefab mastery designs, task specialization designs, and projects designs. Those designs and their design elements are summarized in the Chart of Lesson Designs.

Choosing a Lesson Design

Just as with structures, the more lesson designs you are familiar with, the more options you have. Some educators push some designs as *the* way to present a lesson, yet designs, like structures, have their domain of usefulness. Some objectives are best reached by certain designs while other objectives are better reached by other designs. For example, if your objective is to create a project, you might use Coop Co-op or a Co-op Jigsaw. In contrast, if the objective is mastery of facts and information, you might use a design more oriented to practice and mastery, like Color-Coded Co-op Cards or STAD.

Just as with structures, familiarity with lesson designs and the ability to choose the best design for any objective is acquired slowly through experience. A discussion of the domain of usefulness of the various prefab cooperative learning designs is provided in Chapters 17, 18, and 19. But the best teacher is experience. With experience one learns that memory of discrete items is better handled with the Color-Coded Co-op Cards, whereas mastery of broader sets of information and skills might be better accomplished with STAD. Only by working with a design can one learn its domain of usefulness.

IMPLEMENTING THE DESIGN

Having selected the lesson design which best fits your objectives, you plan to implement the design by deciding which structure or structures to use to reach the sub-objective defined by each design element. In preparation for teaching, you choose structures to implement each element of the design. Each

CHART OF LESSON DESIGNS

Chapter 17: **Mastery Designs**

Color-Coded Co-op Cards 17:1

1. Pre-Test
2. Create Cards
3. Flashcard Game
4. Practice Test
5. Count Improvement Points
6. Flashcard Game
7. Final Test
8. Final Improvement Scoring
9. Individual, Team & Class Recognition
10. Reflection

STAD 17:6

1. Direct Instruction
2. Group Work for Practice
3. Individual Quiz
4. Improvement Scoring
5. Team Recognition

TGT 17:10

(Same as STAD except Tournament replaces Quiz, and points are based on out scoring others.)

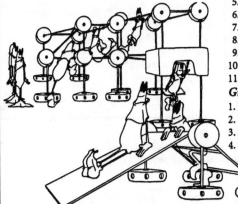

Chapter 18: **Division of Labor Designs**

Telephone 18:1

1. A Student Exits Room
2. Remaining Students Instructed
3. Student Returns
4. Returnee Instructed by Teammates
5. Returnee Tested

Jigsaw II 18:15

1. Direct Instruction
2. Expert Topics Assigned
3. Expert Group Work
4. Experts Teach Teammates
5. Individual Quiz
6. Improvement Scoring
7. Team Recognition

Partners 18:1

1. Form Partners Within Teams
2. Class Division
3. Materials Distributed
4. Partners Work
5. Partners Consult
6. Partners Prepare to Present
7. Teams Reunite
8. Partners Present & Tutor
9. Reflection
10. Individual Assessment

Chapter 19: **Project Designs**

Co-op Co-op 19:1

1. Class Discussion
2. Team Selection
3. Teambuilding/Social Skill
4. Team Topic Selection
5. Mini-Topic Selection
6. Mini-Topic Preparation
7. Mini-Topic Presentation
8. Prepare Team Presentation
9. Team Presentations
10. Evaluation
11. Reflection

Group Investigation 19:10

1. Identify Topic; Team Selection
2. Plan the Learning Task
3. Carry Out Investigation
4. Prepare Final Report

Co-op Jigsaw 19:10

1. Expert Topics Assigned
2. Expert Group Work
3. Experts Return, Share, Tutor
4. Prepare Team Presentation
5. Team Presentations
6. Check for Connections
7. Evaluation
8. Reflection

Rotation Learning Centers 19:16

1. Monday: Input
2. Tuesday: 1st Learning Center
3. Wednesday: 2nd Learning Center
4. Thursday: 3rd Learning Center
5. Friday: Integration & Assessment

Chapter 20: **Multi-Functional Frameworks**

Effective Instruction 20:3

1. Anticipatory Set
2. Instructional Input
3. Check Understanding
4. Guided Practice
5. Closure
6. Independent Practice

Johnson & Johnson 5:9

1. Direct Instruction of Content
2. Teach Social Skills
3. Students Work in Groups
4. Teacher Observes for Social Skills & Content
5. Process Social Skills & Content

Big Four 20:18

1. Class Building
2. Teambuilding
3. Mastery
4. Thinking Skills

Resources for Teachers, Inc. • 1(800) Wee Co-op

Spencer Kagan: *Cooperative Learning*©
Publisher: Resources for Teachers , Inc. • 1(800) Wee Co-op

design element can be implemented with a range of structures. By selecting a structure or structures for each element, you take the barren design and use it as a framework for creating learning experiences. Placing structures into a design is like putting muscles and tissue on a skeleton—the design can take many forms; we make it come alive by structuring it—selecting structures to best reach a set of objectives.

For example, if the design is Co-op Co-op and the design element is student team presentations, I might choose to have each team present to the whole class, one at a time, or I might choose to have each team present to just one partner team, or I might use a Team Inside-Outside Circle. Team Inside-Outside Circle would allow a great deal more learning in the same time, but the learning would be purchased at the expense of not having each team hear every presentation. (For a detailed analysis of this issue, see Chapter 12: Information Sharing Structures). Again, knowing the domain of usefulness of many structures gives me more options, and increases the probability that I will select the best structure at each point in a design to reach my intended objectives efficiently.

Each lesson is a sequence of activities designed to reach the lesson's objectives. This sequence of activities is dictated by the design elements, which are sub-objectives for the lesson. For example, the first sub-objective in a STAD lesson design is direct instruction. This objective could be reached by a teacher standing in front of the class talking; but Teacher Talk is but one of many structures which can be used to provide input. Pair Reading, Videos, Demonstrations, Experiments, and Three-Step Interviews are alternative structures. Again, the more structures a teacher has available, the greater the options, and the more likely it is that the design element will be implemented efficiently, and the sub-objective reached.

A STAD lesson, for example, will take a very different form depending on the structures chosen to implement it. There are a variety of structures possible for each design element of STAD. See Chrt: Structures to Implement STAD. A similar analysis can be done for each lesson design, revealing a wide range of ways to implement each design. Implementation of a lesson design is the

Structures to Implement STAD

Design Element	Possible Structures or Elements
Direct Instruction	• Teacher Talk • Individual Reads • Paired Reading • Roundrobin Reading • Video • Team Presentations
Group Work for Practice	• Numbered Heads　• Send-A-Problem • Pairs Check　• Trade-A-Problem • Flashcard Game　• Fact-or-Fiction • Guess-the-Fib　• Q-Trix • Inside-Outside Circle　• Team Test Taking • Turn-4-Review ～ See Chapter 10: Mastery Structures ～
Individual Quiz	• Individual Test/Quiz　• Individual Essay • Numbered Heads　• Individual Performance 　• Individual Project
Improvement Scoring	• Student Scoring • Computer Lab Scoring • Estimating improvment scores • ILE scoring
Team Recognition	• Certificates • Newsletters • Class Recognition Bulletin • Team Standing Chart • Class Thermometer • Seasonal Charts. ～ See Chapter 15: Scoring & Recognition ～

process of populating it with structures and content, to create a meaningful sequence of activities.

Again, the analogy between lesson designs and structures holds: A structure is content-free and can hold a wide range of content, just as a lesson design is structure-free and can hold a wide range of structures. We place activities (structure plus content) into a lesson design in order to create lessons, just as we place content into a structure to create learning activities. *A lesson is merely a sequence of activities leading toward one or more learning objectives.*

Spencer Kagan: *Cooperative Learning*©
Publisher: Resources for Teachers , Inc. • 1(800) Wee Co-op

LESSON PLANNING FORM

As an aid to lesson planning, Miguel Kagan and I developed a generic lesson planning form. The Co-op Lesson Planning Form can be used with any lesson design or set of design elements. The second page of the form can be duplicated for longer lesson plans which might take several pages.

Using the Co-op Lesson Planning Form

Step 1. Define the Objective. The first step to lesson planning using the Lesson Planning Form is to fill in the box for lesson objectives. This will aid in selecting the appropriate lesson design, and planning the lesson to meet the defined objectives. **Example:** One objective might be for students to review information regarding the American Revolution.

Step 2. Select a Lesson Design. Select the appropriate lesson design to meet the objectives. Each design has a primary function or domain of usefulness. Therefore, the design you choose is dependent upon the objective. Chapters 17-19 describe co-op lesson designs and categorizes them by their primary function. See Chart of Lesson Designs. **Example:** Given a limited objective of reviewing information regarding the American Revolution, I would choose a mastery design.

Step 3. List the Design Elements. In the Chart of Lesson Designs, you will find lesson designs categorized by primary function, and a list of the design elements for each. On the Lesson Planning Form, list the design elements of the design you have chosen on the lines indicated. **Example:** In the case of STAD, the five design elements to be listed at the top of the Lesson Planning Form are 1) Direct Instruction (Input); 2) Teamwork (Guided Practice); 3) Individual Quiz (Assessment); 4) Improvement Scoring (Feedback); and 5) Team Recognition (Feedback).

Step 4. Create Activities. Here's the creative part: You create learning experiences for your students by populating the design with structures and content. List the first design element of the lesson design in the column marked "Design Element." Next, choose a structure to implement that design element. See Box: Structures to Implement Design Element, which lists some of the many possibilities.

Structures to Implement Design Elements

1. Anticipatory Set
- Roundrobin
- Roundtable
- Team Discussion
- Team Interviews

2. Closure
- Individual Share
- Roundrobin
- Think-Write-Share
- Three-Step Interview

3. Reflection
- 4S Brainstorming
- Roundtable
- Team Discussion

4. Input
- Blackboard Share
- Pair Reading
- Partners
- Roam the Room
- Share & Compare
- Teacher Talk

5. Guided Practice
- Flashcard Game
- Inside-Outside Circle
- Match Mine
- Numbered Heads Together
- Pairs Check
- Paraphrase Passport
- Same-Different
- Team Test Taking
- Turn-4-Review

6. Independent Practice
- Blackboard Share
- Individual projects
- Individual Writing
- Numbered Heads Together
- Send-A-Problem
- Stand & Share

7. Assessment
- Blackboard Share
- Choral Response
- Inside-Outside Circle
- Numbered Heads Together
- Slate Responses
- Stand & Share

8. Feedback
- Affirmation Chips
- Certificates
- Class Thermometer
- Improvement Points
- Paraphrase Passport
- Team Handshake

9. Teambuilding
- 4S Brainstorming
- Roundtable
- Team Interview

10. Classbuilding
- Corners
- Formations
- Line Ups
- Mix-Freeze-Group
- Who Am I?

11. Social Skills
- Assignment of Roles
- Gambits Chips
- Match Mine
- Modeling & Reinforcement
- Paraphrase Passport
- Reflection Time
- Same-Different
- Talking Chips

12. Transitions
- Choral Response (Checking)
- Modeling
- Role-Plays
- Roles (Materials Monitor)
- Structuring

Co-op Lesson Planning Form

Lesson Topic:_____ **Date:**_____

Lesson Design: _____

Design Elements: _____ _____

_____ _____

_____ _____

_____ _____

_____

Lesson Objectives:	**Materials:**	**Time:**
		Sponge:

Design Element	Structure or Element	Content	Notes

Spencer Kagan: *Cooperative Learning*©
Publisher: Resources for Teachers , Inc. • 1(800) Wee Co-op

Co-op Lesson Planning Form (continued) Page___

Lesson Topic:_____ **Date:**_____

Lesson Design:_____

Design Element	Structure or Element	Content	Notes

Spencer Kagan: *Cooperative Learning*
Publisher: Resources for Teachers , Inc. • 1(800) Wee Co-op

For example, for Input, you might use Teacher Talk, but there would be a great deal more active participation and learning if, instead, you used a cooperative structure like Pair Reading or Team Interview. Each of the design elements can be implemented with a large number of structures.

Game Plan 3:
MODIFY A PREFAB DESIGN

If a lesson design from the Chart of Co-op Lesson Designs does not quite reach the desired lesson objectives, the question may be asked, "Can I modify one of the prefabricated co-op lesson designs to reach my objectives?" A lesson design may be tailored to fit teacher-defined objectives.

When I was first training teachers in STAD, I did not like the between-team competition and so would say, "Yes, do improvement scoring, but don't set the teams against each other by emphasizing which is best. Rather, take the points the teams earn and sum them -- have them contribute toward reaching a class goal. Use a class thermometer and sum points toward a common goal so you create positive rather than negative interdependence among teams."

In fact, I was not modifying the STAD lesson design by inserting a class thermometer. The design calls for team recognition (Feedback); I was merely substituting one form of team recognition for another. Teams can be recognized for their contribution toward a class goal, rather than for how much better they do than other teams.

Similarly, during the practice time of STAD, following the simultaneity principle, I used to recommend pair work rather than teamwork to double the number of active participants at any one moment. But, again, I was not modifying the STAD design, I was merely recommending another way to implement the design. The design calls for group work (Guided Practice) and I was merely calling for a form of practice which I thought was more efficient.

Design Elements

Co-op lesson designs are merely a sequenced set of design elements. For mastery of a

---

> ## STAD: A Sequenced Set of Design Elements
>
> | Step of Design | Design Element |
> |---|---|
> | 1. Direct instruction | Input |
> | 2. Group Work | Guided Practice |
> | 3. Individual Quiz | Assessment |
> | 4. Improvement Scoring | Assessment & Feedback[1] |
> | 5. Team Recognition. | Feedback |
>
> ---
>
> 1. The scoring of students' performance compared to usual level of performance is valuable *assessment* for the teacher; giving students improvement scores is valuable *feedback* for the student.

---

basic skill or information through STAD there are five steps. The five steps of STAD are merely five of the twelve design elements, sequenced to achieve a type of earning objective. See Box: A Sequenced Set of Design Elements.

To modify a design is not merely to implement it with a different structure, but rather to add or subtract a design element. For example, if I felt the STAD design was too limited for my particular objectives for a class because it did not build social skills, I might add Reflection Time to have students reflect on skills like how well they had been helping and tutoring each other. If at some point I wanted the students to summarize for themselves what they had learned, I might add Closure to the design. Or, if I felt that in my class the students did not need improvement points or team recognition, I might modify the design by discarding those design elements.

Notice, even when you add or subtract design elements, you still can use the Co-op Lesson Planning Form. You simply add more or fewer elements at the outset. It is wise to keep a binder with lesson plans for future use, and when modifying a lesson design, notes can indicate the results, so over time you perfect designs which suit your needs and those of your students.

Successful modification of lesson designs is based on an understanding of the critical attributes of design elements.

Co-op Co-op: A Sequenced Set of Design Elements

Step of Design	Design Element
1. Class discussion	Anticipatory Set, Input
2. Team Selection	Transition
3. Teambuilding	Teambuilding
4. Team Topic Selection	Guided Practice, Transition
5. Mini-Topic Selection	Guided Practice, Transition
6. Mini-Topic Preparation	Independent Practice
7. Mini-Topic Presentation	Input, Independent Practice
8. Prepare Team Presentation	Guided Practice
9. Team Presentation	Input, Independent Practice
10. Evaluation	Assessment, Feedback
11. Reflection	Reflection

It is important to realize that an infinite number of lesson designs can be made from the twelve design elements. STAD, Co-op Co-op, Partners, and the other Co-op lesson designs are merely a sequenced set of design elements.

When we turn to more complex lesson designs, we discover that they too can be conceptualized as merely a sequenced set of the dozen design elements, but certain steps of the design may implement more than one design element. For example, in Co-op Co-op, as students make a team presentation, there is Input (to the class) as well as Independent Practice (Students may be on there own as they do their part of the presentation) and perhaps even Guided Practice (students may provide verbal and non-verbal assistance to their teammates). See Box: Co-op Co-op: A Sequenced Set of Design Elements.

Each of the lesson designs, is composed of a series of design elements. A design element is a sub-objective of the lesson. What distinguishes different designs is which design elements are included, and how they are sequenced.

The twelve most important elements of lesson design are listed in the box: The Dozen Elements of Lesson Design, and are summarized in the section which follows.

By inserting and subtracting design elements, new designs can be created. To do this artfully, familiarity with the dozen elements of lesson design is important.

The Dozen Design Elements
Meta-Cognitive Elements

Meta-cognitive design elements have students think about their learning, providing motivation to learn, summary of learning, and reflection on the skills they are acquiring.

1. Anticipatory Set

Activities which motivate the student to learn the content get them "set" to learn. These include allowing students to link past experience directly to the current learning, stimulation of interest and curiosity about the subject matter, knowledge of how present learning will empower students for future learning and for reaching important life goals.

Students may need little or no set if they are strongly motivated to learn more about the topic; they may need extensive set or repeated sets if they are not interested or if interest wanes. They may need to be set repeatedly for different aspects of the lesson.

Desirable Attributes: Surprise, active participation, experience directly related to the learning objective, and student discovery of the importance of a topic all create a set to learn.

The most important anticipatory set for a lesson is providing some experience which is contrary to expectations. The dissonant experience awakens students' need to make sense of their world -- a natural curiosity and search for an understandable and predictable world which brings forth the scientist within all of us.

The Dozen Elements of Lesson Design

Meta-Cognitive Elements
1. Anticipatory Set
2. Closure
3. Reflection

Content Acquisition Elements
4. Input
5. Guided Practice
6. Independent Practice

Evaluation & Feedback Elements
7. Assessment
8. Feedback

Contextual Elements
9. Teambuilding
10. Classbuilding
11. Social Skill Instruction
12. Transitions

Spencer Kagan: *Cooperative Learning*©
Publisher: Resources for Teachers, Inc. • 1(800) Wee Co-op

Example: At the outset of a lesson on magnetism the teacher holds a magnet behind a piece of paper and a paper clip on the other side. The paper clip "magically" moves through a maze drawn on the paper. Students turn to a partner and discuss how this might be possible.

Later, teams of students try to make strings of paper clips as long as possible connected to the team magnet. They then do a Think-Pair-Share on topics like: How does the magnet pass its power through the paper clips? Have you ever seen a magnet before? What do you guess magnets are used for? What could you do if you had a giant magnet? Why might it be important to learn about magnets and magnetism?

Alternative Structures: Roundtable (What are all the things magnets could pick up?); Team Interviews (What are all the things you would do, if you had a magnet strong enough to pick up a car?); Roundrobin (How do you think the magnet picked up the paper clips?); Team Discussion (If we put two magnets together, would they pick up twice as many paper clips, or more, or less? Why?). Other set providing structures include simulations, role-plays, and guided visualizations.

2. Closure

Activities which allow students to summarize the learning experience, and to relate it to other learnings. Like a set, closure can occur at different points during a lesson. Closure activities help the students "own" the learning -- incorporate it into their own body of knowledge about the topic. Good closure makes it more likely that the learning will be retained.

Desirable Attributes: Active participation, closure congruent to the objective, and a chance to express the personal meaning of the learning or to summarize the learning in one's own words create closure.

Examples: Today we learned what what was meant by a six-inch voice. What did I mean by a six-inch voice? Why was it important that we use it? What part was the hardest for you in using it?

A new student will come into our room tomorrow. Turn to a partner and explain in your own words what we learned in the lesson today.

Alternative Structures: Three-Step Interview, Roundrobin, Think-Write-Share, Individual Write, Inside-Outside Circle.

3. Reflection

Reflection Time is a time to look back over the lesson, assessing how well a skill has been used. The skill could be either social or academic. Reflection time is different from closure. In closure the question is "What have you learned?", and in Reflection Time the questions are "How well have you been using a cognitive or social skill? and How could you use it better?" Reflection comes early in a lesson while a skill is being used; closure may come at different points in a lesson to cement different learnings, but it comes following the learning, not during the learning. Reflection is described in the chapter on Social Skills (Chapter 14).

Desirable Attributes: Students take responsibility for assessing their own progress toward a learning objective and adjust their behavior accordingly, making and following a plan to improve learning.

Example: "We have been working on creating synergy in our groups. Talk over how you have building on each other's efforts to reach beyond what anyone alone could do? Make a plan to increase synergy. Roundrobin specific things you can do to build on each other's ideas."

Alternative Structures: 4S Brainstorming, Roundtable, Team Discussion.

Content Acquisition Elements
The content acquisition design elements are the heart of the lesson, providing information and ideas, and the opportunity to master and apply the ideas first in a supportive context, and later alone.

4. Input

Sometimes called "Direct Instruction" or "Teaching to the Objective." The most important way of providing input to cooperative learning groups is through modeling. Modeling can occur by teacher demonstrating a behavior with other students and having individuals or teams serve as a model to other teams. Other forms of input include films, showing finished products, stimulating questions, answers, student presentations, interviews of teammates and classmates, and teacher focusing the attention of the class on a model student or team.

Desirable Attributes: Input should be congruent to one sub-objective at a time. Input is given in "bite sized pieces," each piece mastered before the next piece is given. Input should be multi-modal, appealing to a variety of senses because some students are visual learnings, while others are auditory, and yet, others are kinesthetic learners.

Example: In your teams, using a Roundrobin, take turns pantomiming one of the ways you found in your home for using electricity. Teammates, it is your job to guess what is being acted out.

Alternative Structures: Paired Reading, Partners, Jigsaw, Co-op Co-op presentations, Teacher talk, Videos, Live Television Programs, Guest Speakers, Presentations by members of an upper grade class.

5. Guided Practice

Teachers or peers monitor while a student or team practices, providing feedback and opportunities to correct or improve responses. The mastery, thinking skills, and communication skills structures are ways of structuring guided practice. See Mastery Structures (Chapter, 10), Thinking Skills Structures (Chapter 11), and Communication Skills Structures (Chapter 13). The methods described in the Social Skills chapter (Chapter 14) provide guided practice for the acquisition of social skills.

The teacher checks for understanding of instructions, as well as the new material, as students begin their guided practice. To check for understanding of directions, the teacher may ask for students to tell a partner what they are to do, or to give a choral response such as when the teacher asks, "Everyone together, tell me the number of the student who will be the team recorder?"

Desirable Attributes: Careful structuring ensures that students experience a high success rate. An attitude is generated in which errors are welcomed and explored as learning opportunities. Students are made to feel that errors are a natural part of the learning process.

Example: During Color-Coded Co-op Cards today, if your partner misses an item, don't give hints. Simply show him the back of the card, and work together to find a way he can remember next time.

Alternative Structures: Pairs Check, Numbered Heads Together, Flashcard Game, Turn-4-Review, Inside-Outside Circle, Same-Different, Match Mind, Paraphrase Passport, Team Test Taking for Practice.

6. Independent Practice

Students work alone on an activity congruent to the objective.

Desirable Attributes: Independent practice should follow guided practice and should not occur until there has been a high degree of mastery during guided practice.

During independent practice students work on one clear objective. There is a high success rate because students are working within their zone of proximal development and there is a clear procedure to follow if there is not immediate success. Students work independently only when they have shown initial mastery of the topic by demonstrating mastery to their teammates, class checkers, or teacher. Resources are available and there is an opportunity to check responses frequently so that incorrect responses are not practiced.

Rather than working on dittos, students make murals, build collages, conduct and analyze surveys, analyze television programs, play with manipulatives, make photo essays, collect samples, construct mobiles, perform experiments, and design mini-learning centers for their teammates.

Example: Find the country at the following longitudes and latitudes, using the method you have practiced in your teams.

Alternative Structures: Send-A-Problem, Independent Writing, Step 4 of Numbered Heads Together, Blackboard Share, Stand and Share, Mini-Topic Presentations, Jigsaw Expert Presentations.

Evaluation/Feedback Elements
The evaluation elements provide a clear message to both students and teacher as to progress toward the learning objectives. The feedback to students provides reward, as well as focuses students on what is yet to master.

7. Assessment

Assessment can be formal or informal and take many forms, including a diagnostic quiz or pretest, tests and quizzes, behavior observations, informal chats and observations of students, collecting portfolios, choral responses, slateboard responses, and improvement scoring. Assessment can be by Teacher, teammates, or classmates.

Checking for understanding in all its forms is evidence that the majority of the class can perform the new skill. Includes improvement scoring in which students' performance is assessed in relation to usual level of performance. Can be informal, "How many of you can tell me..." or formal, Quizzes, Exams, Behavior Observation. See Observation forms (Chapter 14) and Guidelines for tests (Chapter 16)

Desirable Attributes: Occurs several times during input and repeatedly during guided practice. Errors are dignified. Ample correction opportunities.

Example: "Students, at the count of three, everyone show me on the fingers of you left hand, the number   of hydrogen atoms which combine with oxygen atoms to form a single water molecule."

Alternative Structures: Numbered Heads Together, Inside-Outside Circle, Choral Responses, Slate Responses, Blackboard Share, Stand & Share, Teacher Questioning, Behavior Observations, One Minute Time Samples (See Chapter 14: Social Skills) Weekly Quizzes and Improvement Scoring (See Chapter 15: Scoring & Recognition).

8. Feedback

Feedback provides the learner with specific knowledge of results and recognition of accomplishments. Feedback includes appreciations and praise by peers and teacher and celebrations. Feedback can be informal ("Nice job," smile, nod) or formal (Class Thermometer, Certificate, Class Party) See Chapter 16: Recognition Systems.

Desirable Attributes: To be effective feedback must be specific and immediate. Feedback should be followed by correction opportunities. One of the biggest tragedies of traditional approaches is to give feedback at the end of lessons so that it is merely evalua-

tive and does not lead to more or improved learning. Feedback should be frequent during the process of learning. For many students feedback from peers is valued more than marks from a teacher.

Example: "During Pairs Check, if you and your partner both have the same answer as the pair across from you, do a team handshake. If not, figure out where you went wrong, and why."

Alternative Structures: Send-A-Problem, Flashcard Game, Team Discussion.

Contextual Elements

Contextual elements provide a positive context which supports learning, both by motivating it and making it more efficient.

9. Teambuilding

Teambuilding creates the will to work together and creates peer relations which are positive and supportive. See Chapter 8: Teambuilding.

Desirable Attributes: Content related teambuilding is preferable to teambuilding activities which take time from academic tasks.

Examples: Team names are astrological terms for a unit on astrology, Guess-the-Fib is in role as famous historical characters for a history unit, Roundtable on all possible causes for the increased national debt, at the outset of an economics unit.

Alternative Structures: 4S Brainstorming, Content-Related Team Projects.

10. Classbuilding

Classbuilding creates feelings among students of belonging, mutual respect, and security. If students know their ideas will be met with respect, they are freer to express themselves fully and to admit what they do not understand, contributing to learning. See Chapter 9: Classbuilding.

Desirable Attributes: Content related classbuilding is preferable to classbuilding activities which take time from academic tasks.

Example: Students form a line-up based on their estimates of the cost of a war. After talking with the students nearest themselves in the line-up, they fold the estimate line and talk in pairs so that the student with the highest estimate talks with the student in the class with the lowest estimate.

Alternative Structures: Corners, Mix-Freeze-Group, Who Am I?

11. Social Skill Instruction

Social skill instruction makes learning more inclusive, more motivated, and more efficient. For example, by learning the skill of Staying-on-Task, there is a better use of time. By learning the Skill of Giving-A-Good-Helper, guided practice is more efficient. Praising is a skill which provides a motivational context. Gatekeeping ensures that all students participate. See Chapter 14: Social Skills.

Desirable Attributes: Skills should be learned in the context of an academic task rather than as separate units. When learned as separate units, students do not apply them

to team interaction, and there is a great deal of wasted time. Skills are acquired primarily through modeling -- the teacher focuses the attention of the class on good use of a skill.

Example: "Class, I would like you to all look at the Astro-Brilliant Team. They have set their map on the table so everyone can read it easily—no one has to read upside down."

Alternative Methods: Assignment of Roles, Development of Gambits, Modeling, Reinforcement, Reflection Time, Skill related structures such as Paraphrase Passport and Talking Chips.

12. Transitions

Transitions refer to the procedures and directions given during and between the elements of a lesson design. See Chapter 7: Management. One of the most important elements in a cooperative learning lesson is a sponge activity so groups work productively if they finish early. See Box.

Desirable Attributes: Directions are clear and lead students through the procedure step-by-step. Only a few directions are given at a time unless written. The teacher checks for understanding and either models him/herself what needs to be done or has a student or team serve as a model. Directions take a minimal amount of time and are written (blackboard or handout) if more than two steps. The simultaneity principle is applied.

Example: Poor: Teacher hands out papers one at a time. Stronger: Your papers are together with those of your teammates on the materials table, Team Materials Monitors, get the papers for your team.

Alternative Methods: Roles (Quiet Captain, Materials Monitor), Modeling, Structured Role-Plays, Simultaneous Response Modes, including Choral Responses to check for understanding of directions.

Sponges

Purpose: To eliminate dead time with self-directed content related activities when a group or individuals have finished their assigned tasks.

What are they?
- Activities related to structures and/or lesson content
- Used to promote continuous student participation
- Used as a follow-up to a lesson
- Enrichment or reinforcement

Characteristics of Sponges?
- Easy entry, easy exit
- High proportion of success
- Many correct answers
- Congruent to objectives
- Fun
- Short problems
- Easy to monitor

Where can you put them?
- At the bottom of the page
- On transparency/Chalkboard
- In a "Sponge" box
- In a learning center or bookshelf
- Orally from teacher
- On an audio cassette "Mission Impossible"

Sponge Possibilities
- Art activity (illustrate lesson using no words)
- Puzzles and mazes
- Brainstorming (words related to a subject)
- The Kid's Book of Questions (check any bookstore)
- TeamBoggle (letters in a matrix on board)
- How many words can you make from...?
- Task cards
- Game corner (chess, checkers, dominoes, cards)
- Brainstormers
- Extension to curriculum
- Q-Matrix materials
- Log or Journal entries
- List ways to sum three digits to make 11
- List things made with rubber
- How many ways can you make one dollar

Spencer Kagan: *Cooperative Learning*©
Publisher: Resources for Teachers , Inc. • 1(800) Wee Co-op

Game Plan 4:

CREATE A FREESTYLE LESSON

A dozen years ago, when first trying to convince teachers and districts that there was merit in cooperative learning, I did demonstration lessons. For several years, I would not agree to work at a site unless the principal and teachers saw a cooperative learning lesson—I was convinced that the power of seeing students supporting each other and taking joy in learning together was far greater than any words I could provide.

The Big Four Framework

In the process of designing hundreds of demonstration lessons for Kindergarten through twelfth grade, I fell into a formula. Because I wanted to demonstrate the power of structures, I would look at the curriculum and decide which structures would be exciting to use. My criteria for deciding if I had planned a good lesson was to ask myself four questions:

Question 1: Teambuilding. *When I get done with the lesson, will the teammembers feel better about themselves as a team and about working together?*

Question 2: Classbuilding. *When I get done with the lesson, will the students have interacted with classmates other than their teammates in a supportive way, and feel better about being part of this class?*

Question 3: Mastery. *When I get done with the lesson, will the students know something they did not know before, and be able to perform better on an objective test related to the objective?*

Question 4: Thinking Skills. *When I get done with the lessons, will the students have sharpened their thinking skills, be more likely to ask themselves a critical question, more analytic, have a clearer evaluative framework, be more likely to apply information to a new context, or be better able to put discreet bodies of information together in a meaningful category system?*

And that was it. I felt that if during each one hour demonstration lesson, I made progress toward each of the four goals, the lesson was a success. And lesson planning became very easy. All I needed to do was be sure I included in the lesson some teambuilding, some classbuilding, a mastery structure, and a thinking skills structure. Almost always this formula would be very successful. This was true regardless of the grade level or the curriculum area. For efficiency, I almost always made the teambuilding and classbuilding content-related, so all four aspects of the lesson worked together toward the main curriculum objective.

I called my approach 'The Big Four' approach, and began training teachers in the Big Four Formula. Later, when I had the honor of working with Beth Andrini and Jeanne Stone in developing multi-structural lessons for their books in Math and Language Arts, we applied the Big Four Formula, including in each lesson some content-related teambuilding and classbuilding, as well as mastery and thinking skills.

The Big Four Framework allows a great deal of freedom. While planning a lesson, a teacher may include any or all of the dozen lesson design elements in any order, depending on the dictates of the curriculum and the needs of the students. When the lesson is planned, however, there is a final check to see if the Big Four questions have been answered in the affirmative: Does the lesson include Teambuilding, Classbuilding, Mastery, and Thinking Skill Development?

Classbuilding, for example, may come at the end, middle or beginning of the lesson, but I want to be sure that when the lesson is done, the students have made some progress toward one of the aims of classbuilding (getting acquainted, creating mutual trust, creating a positive class identity, valuing individual differences, or developing synergy).

The multi-structural lessons which resulted from working within the Big Four Framework were freestyle lessons. The curriculum and my whims dictated the sequence of structures. I could swim in any direction I wanted and in any style I wanted, as long as by the time I was done, I had made progress toward four goals.

Spencer Kagan: *Cooperative Learning*©
Publisher: Resources for Teachers , Inc. • 1(800) Wee Co-op

Sample Big 4 Lesson

Categorizing

Introduction

What follows is one of my favorite lessons, written using the Big Four Framework. Note, the classbuilding in the lesson occurs in the context of learning from other teams. The teambuilding occurs simply because the activity is fun and the teams get a sense of accomplishment, solving the problem in their own unique way. The mastery occurs as students learn the names and properties of discreet category systems they have discovered. And the thinking skills occur as students classify and reclassify data and discover the properties of alternative ways of classifying data.

As we move increasingly into an information based economy, there will be an increasing demand for individuals to analyze, synthesize, and categorize information.

Notice the design takes an inductive rather than deductive approach. In the process of the lesson, the students discover a Venn Diagram. This inductive approach is quite in contrast to putting a Venn Diagram on the board and telling the students how it works. The traditional, deductive approach starts by telling the students what they are to learn, robbing them of discovery opportunities. The inductive approach provides the students experiences, allowing them to discover what is to be learned. Through structures, we orchestrate learning experiences.

Categorization-- Recategorization

1. Give each team a set of 20 pictures of different animals (or foods, ideas, people --depending on the unit of study). 2. Ask them to categorize the animals any way they wish. 3. Use Teams Tour, Roam the Room, or Carousel so students learn the category systems of other teams. 4. Have them return to their teams and recategorize the animals.

Discover Multiple Category Systems

Have students "discover" the difference among several two dimensional category systems, as follows:

Step 1. Use simple unipolar systems which work.

Have students classify the following eight animals: **Lion, Angora Cat, Butterfly, Alligator, Pit Bull, Irish Setter, Goldfish, Black Widow Spider.** First, have students place the names of the animals on cards or Post-it notes, one animal per slip of paper. Next have students use unipolar Furry–Not Furry lines to place items, as in the figure. Ask them if it was easy. Next, have them reclassify the items in a line marked Dangerous to Humans–Not Dangerous to Humans. In a team of four, have each student place two items. Again, ask them if it was easy. They will say yes.

Step 2. Have students discover a simple bipolar system won't handle the data.

Have them try to place the animals on a third line, a bipolar line marked Furry--Dangerous. When they ask, "Where should we place

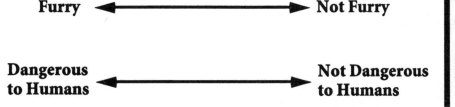

Step 1: Provide unipolar category systems which work.

Furry ⟷ Not Furry

Dangerous to Humans ⟷ Not Dangerous to Humans

Spencer Kagan: *Cooperative Learning*©
Publisher: Resources for Teachers , Inc. • 1(800) Wee Co-op

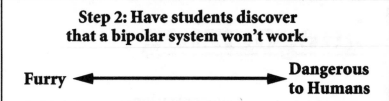

Step 2: Have students discover that a bipolar system won't work.

Furry ⟷ Dangerous to Humans

is different, though, because each of the bits of information were discovered/created by classmates.

Goldfish or Lion?" tell them to do the best they can with the category system. Let their frustration build so they are ready to work to create an alternative system. Ask them if the task way easy. They will say no.

Step 3. Teams Create New, Valid Category Systems.

Provide the students chart paper and markers and challenge them to discover ways to represent both dimensions at once. The instructions are, "You are to design your category system so that anyone viewing your chart paper and seeing where an animal is placed will know how furry and how dangerous it is. Design a system which will work for all animals." Wait until at least four teams have discovered different categorizing systems which work. (Sometimes they need a bit of coaching.)

I circulate among the teams and when I find a team which has discovered a good categorizing system such as A Tree Diagram, Venn, 2x2 Matrix, Graph, Plot, Circle, or some other unique system. See chart on page 20:21. I then give that team a number and name, such as, "You will be Team 1—the Graph Team." or "You will be Team 2 — the Matrix Team."

When four teams have their names and numbers, I ask all teammembers Number 1 to leave their own teams and gather around Team 1; all Number 2's gather by Team 2, 3's around Team 3, and 4's around Team 4. Teammember #1 of Team 1 stays to explain his/her team's categorizing system; Teammember #2 of Team 2 stays, and so on.

Notice, this part of the design is like Jigsaw in that each student is gathering a unique bit of information to share with teammates. It

After the students gather information about the category systems of other teams, they return to their own teams to share. Students then practice in their teams using the new category systems, and later they are each individually accountable for knowing all category systems discovered in the class. For example, using Numbered Heads Together, I probe with questions like, Which systems quantify furryness and dangerousness, and which only classify? Name a time when a graph is better than a Venn, and a time the reverse is true. ◠

References

Andrini, Beth. *Cooperative Learning and Mathematics.* San Juan Capistrano, CA: Resources for Teachers , 1991.

Curran, Lorna. *Cooperative Learning, Lesson for Little Ones.* San Juan Capistrano, CA: Resources for Teachers, 1991.

Gentile, Rondald, J. *Summary and Analysis of Madeline Hunter's Essential Elements of Instruction and Supervision* Oxford, OH:National Staff Development Council, 1988

Kagan, S. & Kagan, M. *The element Matrix: Creating Cooperative Learning Structures.* San Juan Capistrano, CA: Resources for Teachers (In Preparation).

Stone, Jeanne. *Cooperative Learning and Language Arts.* San Juan Capistrano, CA: Resources for Teachers, 1991.

Wiederhold, Chuck. *Cooperative Learning and Critical Thinking: The Q-Matrix.* San Juan Capistrano, CA: Resources for Teachers, 1991.

Step 3: Teams Discover Category Systems.

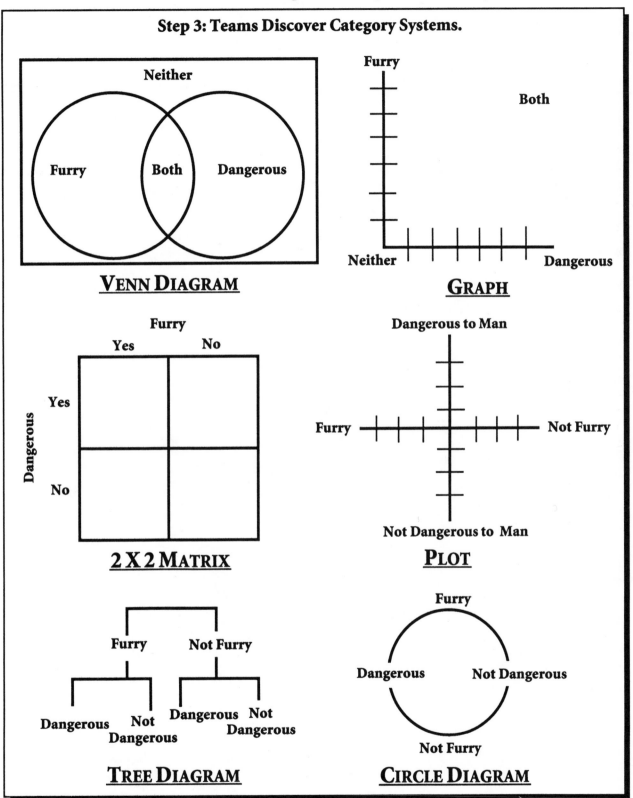

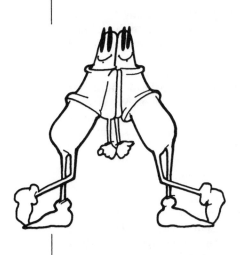

Cooperative learning is for teachers, too.

A variety of school-wide efforts are providing further support. "Cooperative Learning Days" and "Writing Days" focus efforts and allow all members of a staff to communicate and problem solve on a common topic. School staff meetings are being reorganized to make teacher support a primary objective. At staff meetings, just like in class meetings, there is time for mutual sharing, supporting, planning, and problem solving. Teachers, staff, and administrators are dropping their traditional roles and are working together as concerned intelligent educators.

Beyond the school, additional forces are gathering, also with the aim of generating support for teachers. Districts have adopted elaborate Structure-A-Month plans which include demonstration lessons, staff organized training sessions, expert coaching, as well as peer planning, observation and feedback. District-wide efforts are allowing teachers to meet to plan, create, and disseminate curriculum materials and to share tips on teaching.

Just as traditional classroom practices deny students the opportunity to help, support, and care for each other, traditional school practices do not structure for teachers opportunities for mutual mentoring and support.

The traditional social organization of schools was cellular. Each teacher was in charge of his or her cell (classroom). The teachers came to school, entered their cell, worked there, and left. Often they had little knowledge of what was going on in other cells, and had few opportunities to share with, support, and influence other teachers.

Happily the cellular structure of schools is breaking down. The breakdown of the cellular structure is at the core of the reorganization of schools. Teachers are beginning to see themselves as all part of a greater whole, and are feeling the need to coordinate efforts. We are beginning to see teachers supporting teachers.

Teachers are supporting teachers in many ways, including planning lessons together, organizing study groups, sharing successes, problem solving, making videos of their lessons to share with each other, co-teaching, and observing each other with the aim of providing mutual help and support.

Cooperative Staff Meetings

Just as the traditional classroom structure is a model of autocratic and sequential structures, with one person at a time talking, and one person making all the decisions, so too is the traditional structure of staff meetings -- with the same alienating impact.

Traditionally, agendas for staff meetings have been determined by principals, and at the meetings the principals do most of the talking. When others talk, it is one at a time, orientation front, with little interaction among staff. Only a small percent of teachers are actively involved, and the average amount of time for expression per staff member is minimal.

Spencer Kagan: *Cooperative Learning*©
Publisher: Resources for Teachers , Inc. • 1(800) Wee Co-op

By applying the principles of cooperative learning, staff meetings are being transformed radically. The transformations include:

• Using every second staff meeting to plan cooperative lessons, and to reflect on progress toward teacher generated goals such as competency for all teachers in eight new structures each school year.

• Teachers seated in heterogeneous teams during staff meetings with a wide range of structures used to generate the content of the meeting.

• Corners, Folded Value Lines, and Similarity Groups for staffbuilding (getting acquainted, knowing and accepting the range of views represented, providing mutual support).

• 4 S Brainstorming to generate agenda items for the staff meeting.

• Spend-A-Buck to prioritize the agenda items generated.

• Folded, Folded Value Lines to form Heterogeneous teams on the most important issues.

• Three-Step Interview and Paraphrase Passport to make sure all sides of the issues are expressed and heard.

• Teams working on issues and concerns they generate, each team on a different issue.

• Teams reaching consensus on recommendations.

• Team recommendations presented to and affirmed by the whole staff.

• Because everyone knows that the teams represent the range of views on the topics, and that all views have been considered, the staff generally reacts very favorably to the team recommendation, coming to consensus on the issues without a great deal of additional debate and discussion.

Teachers walk away from the staff meeting with a strong feeling of having impacted in a important way on decisions which will directly impact themselves and their students. They feel they have spent their time in a productive way. The principal leaves feeling the support of the staff and knowing that the staff is committed to the decisions made.

Structure-A-Month Clubs

I have encouraged those wishing to implement the structural approach to think long-term. At the heart of the most successful plans is a Structure-A-Month Club. In preparation for the Structure-A-Month Club, two or more teachers make a multi-year commitment to become site-level facilitators. They are given a full year to become fluent in a number of structures, and then facilitate workshops the second year so other teachers at their site have support as they learn the structures, one per month.

Prior to the first year of the plan teachers volunteer to become facilitators of the Structure-A-Month Club. Teachers know that volunteering involves intensive training for a year, following which they will lead others at the site through the Structure-A-Month Club plan. Two or more teachers are selected to become facilitators. In some elementary schools two primary (K-2) and two elementary (3-6) teachers are selected, and there are two parallel sets of workshops which follow. At some secondary sites, the training is conducted within departments, and at least two facilitators are selected per department.

Prior to the first year of the plan, the facilitators receive initial training in the structural approach -- often at a summer training institute. The following school year, the first year of the plan, is the Facilitator Prep Year. The facilitators do not train any other teachers. Rather, they work together to master a range of structures. The criterion for having mastered a structure is if the facilitator feels that with relatively little preparation time he or she can go into a classroom of another teacher and demonstrate the structure, using the curriculum materials of the teacher. In order to reach this level of competence in the structure, during the Facilitator Prep Year, the facilitator is released to "borrow" the classrooms of other teachers. This approach serves to build competence in the facilitator so that the following year he or she can speak with authority when asked how a structure works in different situations. The approach serves also to generate interest among the remaining staff at the site so they are set to get involved when the Structure-A-Month Club begins the following year.

Prior to the second year of the plan, the facilitators receive training at a facilitators' institute. There they develop their Structure-A-Month site-level plan, and learn methods for presenting structures and instituting site-level change.

When the second year begins, the site level facilitators institute the Structure-A-Month Club for volunteers at the site. Volunteers make a year-long commitment to try one new structure many times each month. They know also they will receive support in this learning, from the facilitators.

Each month there is a monthly meeting of the Structure-A-Month Club. At the meeting the following things happen: Teachers role-play being students in a cooperative classroom and experience a new structure with several different curricula contents. Remaining in their teams, the teachers step out of the role of students and talk as teachers about the kinds of learning the structure produced. They plan together in teams how they could use the structure with their own students, and in some cases make the materials necessary. They then practice being a teacher using the structure, role-playing standing before their class and taking their students through the steps of the structure. (For the speed of simultaneity, each teacher teaches only one team, while pretending they were in front of a whole class of teams). Prior successes are shared, and problems are solved.

During the month the facilitators do a number of mini-demonstration lessons in the classrooms of teachers at a range of grade levels and across a range of curriculum materials. These mini-demonstration lessons are limited to a demonstration of only the structure of the month; they may take as little as 15 minutes. Facilitators offer support to teachers using the structures, and set up an information sharing system, such as a bulletin board in the staff room, to share successes and variations developed by members of the Structure-A-Month Club. A great deal of positive energy is released as many teachers focus on learning one structure; the structure becomes a common topic of conversation. Principals use the structure during staff meetings or delegate some time for the facilitators to do so.

By the end of the first year, many teachers are doing multi-structural lessons because they have learned each new structure so well they don't abandon it when they take up the second and then the third structure. Each month they add one new structure to their repertoire. Facilitators and teachers find the Structure-A-Month Club easy because they do not have to give a workshop on, or practice more than one new structure at a time.

About midway in the second year, each facilitator chooses a teacher to become a Facilitator-in-Training so that during the third year the Structure-A-Month Club has twice the leadership, and the new facilitators assume increased leadership. The initial facilitators share the leadership responsibilities. In the third year teachers choose which structure to take up each month, sometimes choosing to revisit structures they had already taken up in the previous year. New teachers wishing to join the club make a year-long commitment. In some cases, there may be a beginning and an advanced Structure-A-Month Club.

Peer Support

When I first started training teachers in cooperative learning, I discovered that there was almost always initial enthusiasm among teachers. When I checked back some months after the training however, in some schools there were more teachers using the techniques than when I had left; experimentation and implementation were flourishing, but in other schools the interest and enthusiasm had waned.

With time it became clear to me the critical difference between schools was the quality of relations among teachers and between teachers and the administrator. If teachers felt free to ask each other for help, observe each other, and if there was a generally supportive attitude among the staff, when new methods were introduced, they spread. The teachers experimented, adapted the methods to their own needs, and built on the methods. They felt free to try, make mistakes, ask for help and try again. If on the other hand, teachers were stuck in the traditional cellular structure, if they were isolated, without others knowing and caring about what they were attempting, if they feared criticism of their administrators and peers, then when they hit a snag with the new methods there was not a built-in support system, no easy way to solve problems. At that point, they were likely to abandon the new methods in favor of the safer traditional methods.

Peer support and mutual mentoring are critical for all teachers. Just as traditional classroom practices deny students the opportunity to help, support, and care for each other, traditional school practices do not provide teachers opportunities for mutual help and support.

Peer support meetings can take many forms, including informal and formal brainstorming, sharing of videos, and support visits designed to help teachers focus on the positive aspects of their teaching.

Support Visits. It is important to distinguish "Support Visits" from "Cooperative Coaching." With Support Visits, there is an agreement to plan lessons together, to observe, and to provide each other support. Support Visits are entirely safe, teachers know that the only input they will receive from the observing teacher is positive, supportive feedback. During a Support Visit meeting, the job of the teacher who has observed a lesson is to get the other teacher to focus on all of the positive aspects of the lesson, and to allow the teacher an opportunity to reflect on the lesson.

Support Visits are a good way to ease into the coaching process, but during Support Visit meetings there is an agreement not to problem solve, give technical feedback, or analyze what could have been done to improve the lesson. Those activities are reserved for the very structured and supportive context provided by Cooperative Coaching.

After a number of Support Visit meetings, teachers may agree to begin Cooperative Coaching which includes problem solving and systematic observations designed to help progress in an area of growth for the teacher. But Cooperative Coaching is structured very carefully to keep it positive and supportive.

Cooperative Coaching

When I realized the importance of peer coaching and support, I began to include Cooperative Coaching as a topic in my cooperative learning training institutes. It has turned out that this work is as important to teachers as cooperative learning is to students.

Some of the best teachers make the worst coaches.   Some fine teachers have gotten where they are because they are self-critical. This self-critical quality has led them to find fault with their own teaching and to seek ways to improve it.   These teachers, when placed in the role of coach, however, bring to others their same critical qualities: The more self-critical a teacher, the more likely it is that he or she will be critical of others. These teachers are likely to focus on the technical aspects of coaching. Although this form of coaching is well-intended, it does not create an atmosphere conducive to experimentation, openness, and discovery. We are all frightened by an observer who has all the answers. Good coaching can occur only after acceptance and support are established. During coaching, both teachers need to feel themselves as part of the same team, working together to solve problems of mutual concern.

THE COACHING CYCLE

There are three phases to the coaching cycle: 1. **Planning**, 2. **Observing**, and 3. **Reflecting.** During Planning Time, a teacher and coach meet to discuss a lesson and to establish a contract for coaching.   During the Observation Time, the coach observes the lesson, recording all the positive aspects of the lesson and making observations on specific behaviors agreed to by the teacher and coach. During the Reflection Time, there is a sharing of the observations and a teacher-centered discussion of the lesson.

1. Planning (Pre-Observation)

The most important aspect of coaching is setting a tone of mutual trust and support.

It is important that the coach know and respect the feelings of the teacher. Teaching is our profession. We are "on the line" each time we are observed. Some anxiety in such a situation is natural, especially the first time a teacher is observed by a coach. Having clear limits and structures helps reduce the risk and anxiety. Therefore, the coach and teacher must have a very clear agreement as to their roles during the observation and afterwards. Some of the most important things to establish are: what the coach will be looking for and doing during the observation session, what he or she will be sharing afterwards, and the fact that there will be complete confidentiality regarding the observation and conferences. See Planning Form, page 21:8.

Planning the Observation. All of cooperative coaching is teacher-centered. That is, the coaching will focus on what the teacher feels he or she would like to work on, not necessarily any concerns of the coach. Therefore, the coaching begins with the coach asking the teacher, how she or he feels about the lesson they are going to work on.

The teacher's response sets the tone for the coaching session. If a teacher is feeling unsure about the lesson and/or the coaching process, then the coach's role should be primarily to provide support. Whatever problem solving is done, should be in a very limited domain, focusing on specific behaviors. See Box, "Good Coaching has a Behavioral Referent."

Problem solving should not occur if it is not requested by the teacher. To begin the coaching process, it is often helpful to take some very limited aspect of a lesson for observation and to make the observation relatively brief. As confidence increases, the range of behaviors observed and the length of the observation time may increase.

Examples of:

Motivational Statements

"Remember how important cooperative learning can be for the low achieving student who rarely or never gets peer support for achievement in the traditional classroom."

"Cooperative learning is a radically different way to teach, so naturally it will be hard at first. With practice, we will both get better."

Support Statements

"You did a great job of using the quiet signal to get full attention before giving directions."

"During your introduction to the lesson, I could see the kids waking up and getting interested in the topic."

Confidentiality. During the Planning Stage, confidentiality between coach and teacher is established. The rule is simple: Nothing observed or discussed at any point in the coaching cycle is to be shared with anyone else. The teacher and coach may decide to wave that rule, but only for special need, and only at the teacher's request.

Time, Place, Roles. Other aspects of the coaching contract which need to be established are exactly when the observation will take place, for how long, the role of the coach during the lesson, and most importantly, what exactly is to be observed and discussed afterwards. At first, it is probably most comfortable for the teacher and coach if it is agreed that only one specific behavior will be observed and discussed. Later, the coaching may open up to extra observations and suggestions, but only by prior agreement.

2. Observing

There are two main jobs of the coach during the observation session: Record all of the positive aspects of the lesson -- the goodies list, and make the specific behavioral observations contracted for during the planning session. See Observation Form, page 21:9.

The list of positive aspects of the lesson, or goodies list, is important for setting the tone during the reflection time. If we focus only on the problems, coaching fails to provide the support we all need; we need a healthy balance between problem solving and support. *"One thing to grow on, ten things to glow on."* Also, as indicated, the observations for problem solving must have a specific behavioral referent. The job of the coach is not to note all the aspects of the lesson which could be improved, but rather to focus on the specific behaviors agreed upon during the planning session.

3. Reflecting

Checking In. It is important to begin the reflection session by checking with the teacher as to his or her feelings. See Reflection Form, page 21:10. Good coaching is teacher-centered; the form it takes depends on the feelings of the teacher. If a teacher is discouraged, little or no technical feedback should occur -- the coaching session should focus on motivation and support statements. See Box. If the teacher is confident, more time might be spent problem solving technical aspects of the lesson, but always there must be a balance between "things to grow on and things to glow on." Checking with feelings early can lead to some important surprises. A defensive teacher may have given what looks like a weak lesson, but want to focus only on the positive aspects of the lesson. It is very important for that teacher to know that the coach has seen and appreciated the positive aspects of the lesson and that the technical feedback be limited to only one or two items in a very supportive context. When technical feedback is given, it is absolutely essential that the feedback have a behavioral referent -- that it be objective rather than evaluative. See Box.

In contrast, a very self-critical teacher may have given what the coach thinks is a great lesson, but in the coaching session that may be inclined to focus only on the problems.

The most helpful thing a coach can do for a self-critical teacher is to have them focus on all the things that went right in the lesson. The highly self-critical teacher will have a hard time hearing or "taking in" his or her accomplishments. For all teachers, an early sharing of the goodies list helps set the positive, supportive context in which to do the limited and focused problem solving.

If a teacher and coach work only on those aspects of the lesson which need improvement, coaching will not provide the positive support we all need. It is very important during the reflection time that the coach has the teacher note and discuss all of the positive aspects of the lesson -- the list of goodies.

Problem Solving. There should never be movement to problem solving until motivation is

strong and an atmosphere of support has been established. The problem solving focuses on what the teacher wants to work on, and it is a mutual discussion and kicking around of ideas -- not a time for an "expert" to tell a novice. Good problem solving is synergistic: A good test of the quality of the problem solving during the reflection time is whether solutions and ideas emerge which neither the coach nor the teacher imagined beforehand.

Good coaching is not just a pat on the back. For some teacher-coach pairs, the temptation is to just focus on what is good. But good coaching doesn't stop at support. Support is necessary to set the context for good coaching, but once there is a "we" feeling and an atmosphere of support, the teacher and coach need to take a good hard look at the

Good Coaching Has a Behavioral Referent

Contrast the following two comments:
1: "Your directions were not clear enough. "
2: "When you gave the directions, I saw some of the groups go to work, but some of the groups were discussing what exactly to do."
The two comments might well be in response to the same observation. But the first comment is evaluative; it focuses on grading the teacher; it invites hurt. The second comment focuses on behaviors of students; it invites problem solving. If teachers know that during the Reflection Session they will receive evaluation, coaching will be a time of anxiety rather than growth. If they know they will receive clear behavioral observations in a predetermined domain of observation, coaching will be an opportunity for problem solving and growth.

Thus, it is quite important in the planning time to establish **behaviors** as the focus of coaching. For example, if a teacher says, "My kids are all always out of control," the statement does not have a clear behavioral referent. If no behavioral referent is established before the observation session, the teacher and coach have set up a situation which invites evaluation -- a focus on the question, is the teacher good at controlling her students? The job of the coach is to move the focus toward behavior -- to ask, "Are they *all* out of control?" After it is established that Johnny, Joe, and Jack are the primary problems, the coach might ask, "Out of control, what do you mean?" It may turn out that out of seat behavior will be the focus of observation, or poking each other, or putting each other down. If clear behavioral referents are established in the Planning Stage, the whole coaching process moves away from evaluation and toward creative problem solving.

Thus there are two reasons that good coaching must have clear behavioral referents. First, they lower anxiety -- I can live comfortably with the idea that someone is going to observe "out of seat behavior" in my classroom; it is much more difficult to live with the idea that I will be evaluated on my management abilities. Second, clear behavioral referents promote positive problem solving -- If we find I have poor management abilities there isn't much we can do, but if we discover certain students are out of their seats too often, it is time for creative problem solving.

lesson, examining all possible ways of improving it. Each point on the coaching form should be taken up with an eye to how the lesson might be improved. A lesson can always be strengthened. If coaching does not increase awareness of alternatives, it is not

Good problem solving is synergistic: A good test of the quality of the problem solving during the reflection time is whether solutions and ideas emerge which neither the coach nor the teacher imagined beforehand.

filling an important function. If the coach and teacher don't end up feeling they took a hard look at all the alternatives for at least one aspect of a lesson, then the coaching may have been all things to glow on with nothing to grow on. The trick, of course is to work on the problem areas only within a context of basic trust and support, and for the teacher, rather than the coach, to define areas of growth and to lead the discussion. Coaching is not a time for the observer to share all that he or she knows; it is a time for the teacher to work with a coach on things of concern to the teacher.

Positive Closure. An important job of the coach is to provide a positive closure to the reflection session. Closure is provided by allowing the teacher time to restate some of the positive outcomes of the lesson and by asking the teacher to formulate some goals for next time (so the coaching cycle turns full circle and sets the stage for the next planning session). The tendency during coaching is to focus too much on the problems, to lose sight of the forest because of the trees. Thus during the "positive closure" time the coach brings attention back to the big picture: The lesson was not technically perfect (the perfect lesson has never been taught) but students were learning and supporting each other.

THE COACHING FORMS

On the following pages are coaching forms which I use in coaching. The planning form is filled out together by the coach and teacher prior to the observation. The Observation Form is used by the coach during the observation. The Reflection Form is a script for the interaction during Reflection Time. The lines are reminders for the Coach as to what information he/she is to illicit from the teacher.

In the context of a supportive atmosphere, the two teachers discuss the various aspects of the observed lesson. They work on the problems the teacher feels are most important. Responsibility for change rests with the teacher, not the coach. The coach is there to support the teacher, to work with the teacher, not to change him or her. Change, paradoxically occurs much more readily when there is no attempt to change, but rather an attempt to understand and accept what has occurred and what options exist.

References:

Wynn, Richard & Guditus, C.W. *Team Management: Leadership by Consensus.* Columbus, Ohio: Charles E. Merrill, 1984.

Johnson, D. & Johnson, R. *Leading the Cooperative School.* Edina, Minnesota, Interaction Book Company 1988.

Goswami, D. & Stillman, P. *Reclaiming the Classroom: Teacher Research as an Agency for Change.* Montclair, New Jersey: Boynton/Cook, 1987.

Joyce, B. & Showers, B. *Student Achievement Through Staff Development.* White Plains, New York: Longman, 1988.

PLANNING FORM

INTRO
How do you feel about the lesson?

_____

What is the object of the lesson?

_____

Describe the lesson -- what will happen first, next,...?

_____

_____

PROBLEM SOLVING
What areas are you working on? _____

_____

_____

THE CONTRACT
1. What would you like me to watch for? What can I watch for or listen for that will give you useful information?

    a._____

    b._____

2. Observation Date & Time

    Date_____Beginning time_____Ending time_____

3. Where would you like me?
☐ Seated or ☐ Circulating   ☐ Next to a group   Which group? _____

4. Role: What would you like me doing?
☐ Observation only   ☐ Talk with group   ☐ Work with group   Which group? _____

5. How do you feel about my taking notes? Would you prefer all notes were left with you? That I don't take notes?

_____

6. Confidentiality: Our agreement is _____

OBSERVATION FORM

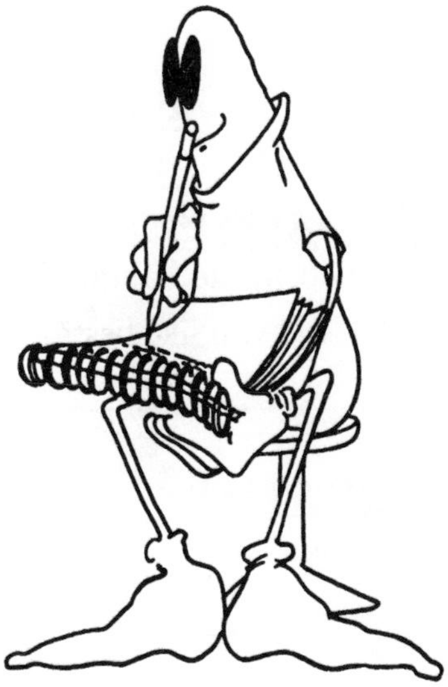

1. OBSERVATIONS FOR CONTRACT

Behavior: _____

Observations: _____

_____

_____

_____

Behavior: _____

Observations: _____

_____

_____

2. GOODIES LIST (EFFECTIVE BEHAVIORS)

(**Think:** Principles, Plan, Progression, Management, Student Behaviors, Structures, Creativity...)

Teacher Behavior	Student Responses
1 _____	_____
2 _____	_____
3 _____	_____
4 _____	_____
5 _____	_____
6 _____	_____

REFLECTION FORM

SELF-ANALYSIS
How do you feel about the lesson? _____

What did you like best? least? _____

_____

GOODIES LIST
Some effective behaviors I observed that you haven't mentioned

were...

Behavior Observed	Student Responses
1._____	_____
2. _____	_____
3._____	_____
4._____	_____
5._____	_____
6._____	_____

OBSERVATIONS FOR CONTRACT
We agreed that I would look for_____. Here is what I saw:

Teacher Behavior	Student Responses
1._____	_____
2. _____	_____
3._____	_____

GOALS FOR NEXT TIME: What goals would you like to set for yourself for next time?
1._____

2. _____

3. _____

POSITIVE CLOSURE:
What did you feel were some of the most positive aspects of the lesson? _____

_____

Chapter 22

Schoolwide Cooperation — and Beyond

If we apply the principles of cooperation to the school as a whole, and beyond, the result is mutual support among students and teachers schoolwide, among schools, and between schools and the broader community.

There are many ways to apply the principles of cooperation to the school as a whole; too often we have turned to competitive models when cooperative modes would produce better results in both the academic and social domains.

SCHOOL IDENTITY BUILDERS

Many of the activities which are presently in the teambuilding and classbuilding chapters are applicable at the school level. Many schools have a school color and a school song. Some have a school charity and community improvement project. Other schoolwide identity builders include school handshakes, mascots, logos, cheers, t-shirts, sweatshirts, jackets, binders, and bookbags. All of those symbols help us see it as "our school."

SCHOOL GOALS

Coordination and cooperation among classes to reach a common goal is a second way to produce the feeling of "our school." The goals might be academic or social. Some possibilities:

Reading Drive. When Diane Wallace became principal of LaBallona Elementary School in Culver City, California, she instituted a school reading drive. Each student who read a book contributed to the school goal. When the goal was met there was a special assembly and "overnight read-in" in the cafeteria

Progress toward schoolwide academic goals can be recorded on a school thermometer. For example, the thermometer can indicate how many new books we (teachers, staff, and students) have read this year. There can be recognition as we reach some minor goals (each 100), but a reward assembly when we reach major goals (each 1000). Reading as well as school spirit would increase. When designing recognition systems, why stop at individual, team, and class recognition? Let's move to the schoolwide level.

Schoolwide Cleanup Drive. Why not have a school-wide clean up drive with recognition at the school level for clean playgrounds and lunch areas? Points on a clean-up thermometer can be recorded for each piece of yard trash deposited in a trash can.

Schoolwide Charity. Students select a recipient (convalescent home; school in a poor neighborhood; poor country), and each grade level choose one way to contribute to the drive. Goals are set and celebrations are held when the goals are reached.

The American Heart Association sponsors "Jump for Heart." School goals can be set, and within classes students can work cooperatively to support the goals. A Roundtable

Spencer Kagan: *Cooperative Learning*©
Publisher: Resources for Teachers , Inc. • 1(800) Wee Co-op

structure can be used while each student on a team jumps for a minute and rests while his/her teammates take their turns.

Fund Drives. Cooperative schoolwide projects can be used to raise money for charities or school improvement projects. Some possibilities: A school pumpkin patch, class and school quilts, crafts bazaar.

Attendance. I was asked to consult with an elementary school which was trying to improve attendance. They had a competitive system going. At each grade level each month there would be a reward for the classroom which had the best attendance. At sixth grade one class had come to hate the members of the other class because they beat them by a few student attendance points each month. The third class which had most frequent absences had given up trying. Attendance was not improving.

I suggested they stick with the one class per month reward system, but that it be rotating, based on if any class beat last month's attendance. That is, everyone knew that if any class beat its own past attendance record, it would earn the reward for the class of the month. Attendance actually improved. More improved was school spirit. Rivalry turned into cooperation; classrooms rooted for the other classes at their grade level to improve in attendance, because they knew if no class did so, it would delay a month their turn for the reward. Why is it that we gravitate to competition when cooperation results in better results and improved social relations?

ACADEMIC FAIRS

Science Fairs. Science fairs are now generally based on a competitive model. They are an opportunity for motivated parents to compete for rewards. The science fair itself is not nearly as instructive as it could be because of the very disparate and unrelated topics covered -- the participants have not coordinated their efforts.

A cooperative science fair has a theme. Let's say it is energy one year, the solar system the next, plants the third, and so on. Further, each grade level has a mini topic. Thus if energy were the topic, the kindergarten stu

dents might be working on magnetism, the sixth grade students working on atomic energy, with the other grade levels working on topics of intermediate complexity such as solar energy, energy in the home; electricity, and so on. Within grades student teams would develop projects. The projects are presented in a coordinated way so that the science fair becomes an instructive experience. If the school has six themes, one a year, students attending the school would have learned a great deal by the time they graduated. Why is the emphasis presently on competition rather than learning?

Reading Week. The whole school reads on a theme. Teachers meet to plan the week. They share their best reading techniques and may do demonstrations in other classes. An assembly features authors, reader's theater, and/or storytelling. A dress-up day allows students, teachers, and staff to come to school as their favorite character. Upper grade students read to lower grade students during reading times. Grandparents come in to school and read to students in the library. Bookmarks, bookcovers, and book illustrations are posted. Students at all grades write and illustrate books to share with other classes. A readathon culminates the event as students bring in their sleeping bags to spend an overnight in the cafeteria.

Cooperative Sports Field Day. The cooperative sports activities become the focus for a fun day for the whole school. If the cooperative sports field day comes early in the school year, it can set positive norms for playground behavior as well as a supportive, non-competitive tone for the whole school.

Career Days. Community members come in to share their jobs with students. Students visit job sites. Students may all dress up in role for their dream career.

Art Week. During art week each student's work is displayed, classes tutor other classes in art techniques. The cafeteria becomes the art gallery and each day it is transformed as different classes take charge. Display tables or easels outside each classroom are used to show the favorite pieces of each child. A wall becomes the home of the school mural to which all students contribute.

Spencer Kagan: *Cooperative Learning*©
Publisher: Resources for Teachers , Inc. • 1(800) Wee Co-op

STUDENT DIRECTED SCHOOLWIDE COOPERATION

The best schoolwide cooperative projects begin with student input. For example, have the students within teams and classrooms brainstorm ideas for school improvement. Let students have input, cooperatively selecting goals, and design their own ways of reaching those goals.

PARENTAL SUPPORT

There are a number of ways parents can support cooperative learning. My favorite is the notion of cooperative homework. Traditionally parent involvement in homework has been parents tutoring, encouraging, or even doing a child's homework. The idea with cooperative homework is to send home a task for parents and child to do together. For example, parent and child together are given a poem to read and then work together to think of extensions such as additional excuses for not taking the garbage out, of additional ways a day could turn out to be a horrid day. (See Holm and associates, 1987 and Stocking and associates, 1979). Co-op play for the home is a refreshing alternative (Crary, 1984).

COOPERATION BETWEEN CLASSES

Luci Bowers (Frank Jewett Elementary School, Bonny Eagle School District, W. Buxton, Maine) met a gentleman from Sweden who was visiting Maine. His child happened to be in the same grade as the elementary school class Luci was teaching that year. So Luci made contact with her counterpart teacher in Sweden and her class began a year long project called the "Swedish Connection." Each student had a pen pal from the other class. The classrooms created and exchanged videos which presented a day in the life of their schools. In the videos, the students also introduced themselves individually, talking directly to their pen pals. Interestingly, over the school year, fewer and fewer students were willing to share correspondence from their pen pals with their class-mates, as the letters became more and more intimate! Many students continued to correspond with their pen pals long after the school year ended.

COOPERATION AMONG SCHOOLS

The California State Department of Education created the Middle School Partnership Network. Ten model middle schools in the state were chosen to disseminate their successful programs to neighboring middle schools. For example, Chaparral Middle School in Diamond Bar California for the last four years has been involved in showing other middle schools how to implement their very successful interdisciplinary team approach (cooperation among teachers) and their cooperative learning approaches. They have give workshops and symposia on cooperative learning, and have served as a visitation center for over 1000 teachers and administrators wishing to see cooperative learning and the interdisciplinary approach in action.

Open-School Days. Several districts working in the Structural Approach have one or more model schools which put on "Open-School Days." Teachers sign up to demonstrate different structures and know that visiting teachers will be coming in to observe at the predetermined times.

Teachers who come to Open-School Days first meet to get a general orientation to cooperative learning, a handout which describes the structures to be demonstrated, and a schedule. They then choose to visit the classes which, to them, are of most interest.

Open-School Days for cooperative learning in the structural approach occur on a regular basis and draw visitors from inside and outside the district at John F. Kennedy Elementary School (Santa Ana Unified School District, Santa Ana, California), Sherwood Park Elementary School (Cumberland County School District, Fayetteville, North Carolina) and Eagle Ridge Elementary School (Douglas County School District, Douglas County, Colorado). ∾

References:

Crary, Elizabeth. *Kids Can Cooperate.* Animal Town Game Co. Healdsburg, CA: 1984.

Faber, A. Mazlish, E. *How to Talk So Kids Will Listen and Listen So Kids Will Talk.* Animal Town Game Co. Healdsburg, CA: 1982

Holm, A., Schultz, D., Winget, P., Wurzbach, L. *Cooperative Activities For the Home: Parents Working with Teachers to support cooperative Learning.* Resources in Special Education. Sacramento, CA: 1987.

Neale, D.C., Bailey, W.J., & Ross, B.E. *Strategies for school improvement: Cooperative planning and organization development.* Boston: Allyn & Bacon, Inc., 1981.

Reid, J., Forrestal, P. & Cook, J. *Small group work in the classroom.* Kewdale, Western Australia, 1982.

Schmuck, R.A., Chesler, M., & Lippit, R. *Problem solving to improve classroom learning.* Chicago: Science Research Associates, 1966.

Schmuck, R.A. *Students as organizational coparticipants.* In S. Sharan, P. Hare, C.D. Webb, & R. Hertz-Lazarowitz (Eds.) *Cooperation in education.* Provo, UT: Brigham Young University Press, 1980.

Schmuck, R.A. & Schmuck, P.A. *A humanistic psychology of education. Making school everybody's house.* Palo Alto, CA: Mayfield Publishing, 1974.

Schwartz, M.N., Steefel, Q., Schmuck, R.A. *The development of educational teams.* Eugene, OR: Center for Educational Policy and Management, 1976.

Stenmark, J., Cossey, R., Thompson, V. *Family Math.* EQUALS. University of California, Berkeley, CA: 1986.

Stocking, H. S., Arezzo, D., Leavitt, S. *Helping Kids Make Friends.* DLM Tabor & Argus Communications. Allen, TX: 1979

Wynn, R. & Guditus, C.W. *Team management: Leadership by consensus.* Columbus, Ohio: Charles E. Merril Publishing, 1984.

Chapter 23

Co-op Play

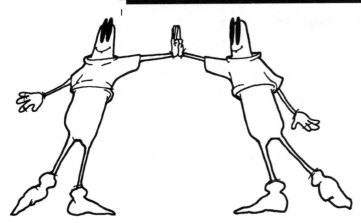

Our students need cooperative sports and games on the playground part of the time. Otherwise they will not experience the full range of positive human interaction -- and they will develop blind to joyful, cooperative possibilities. Play is fundamental to development. Why is there so little play on our playgrounds?

My favorite example of the difference between cooperative games and competitive games is musical chairs. In the traditional version, each time the music stops we create one more loser. The goal of the game: make every player a loser except one, who we call the winner. Like in the traditional version, in the cooperative version each time the music stops a chair is taken away. But, unlike in the traditional version, if you find yourself without a chair, instead of becoming a drop-out, you sit on someone's lap. At the end, everyone feels a sense of unity as everyone is on someone's lap except the person who is on the chair supporting everyone. Cooperative games are a celebration of a basic -- but too often lost -- capacity, the capacity to play.

Kids don't play competitive games; they obey them.

It is sad to note how fully our playgrounds have become void of play. Our playgrounds are battle grounds where students, faces deadly earnest in the struggle, fight to make the other

person or team the loser. We place tetherball poles on our playgrounds and students respond accordingly, individual against individual, they do battle. Not only is there negative interdependence among the students, there is a lack of simultaneity, as only two "play" as the rest watch.

I am not against stiff competition. I set swimming records in college and enjoy a tough racquetball match probably more than most. What I am against on the playground, just as in the classroom, is a lack of balance. Our students need cooperative sports and games on the playground part of the time if they are to experience the full range of possibilities with regard to interaction -- if they are not to develop blind to joyful cooperative possibilities.

There is another problem with adherence to an exclusively competitive play pattern. It robs students of the opportunity to make their own rules, fostering an authoritarian orientation which is contrary to the notion of participatory democracy. The point became clear to me one Thanksgiving day as I observed and participated in a minor power struggle over ping-pong, involving my two youngest children and my grandmother. My grandmother, Mama Clara, a month short of 89 years old at the time (but who would never admit that) was over to the house for the family Thanksgiving celebration. My daughter and son were playing ping-pong. Monica complained that Carlos was hitting the balls too hard, and walked off in a pout. My grandmother defended Carlos, "That is the way you are supposed to play, you are supposed to hit them so the other person can't return them." I said I thought it would be nice if he hit the balls toward her so they could volley. Mama Clara looked at me aghast, "You can't do that; that is not the way you are supposed to play."

Spencer Kagan: *Cooperative Learning*©
Publisher: Resources for Teachers , Inc. • 1(800) Wee Co-op

It occurred to me that there is something very authoritarian about competitive games, or at least the exclusive reliance on competitive ways of structuring games. An almost religious adherence to the rules fosters the notion that there is always just one right way to interact. This is what destroys play. Kids don't play competitive games; they obey them. Reliance on an exclusively competitive format for games can undermine the spirit of participatory democracy and autonomy among children. There is nothing wrong with two people agreeing to hit the ball away from each other, to challenge each other, to make a stiff match. That kind of competition, as *Robert Slavin* has pointed out, may be viewed as a kind of cooperation -- an agreement resulting in pleasure for both individuals. But there is something very wrong if our youth develop with the notion that competition is the *only* way to structure games, then they have been deprived of many joyful alternatives, on the playground and in later life.

Function and Form of Cooperative Sports

With some effort cooperative sports activities all can be classified according to function (getting acquainted, mutual support, synergy), using the same category system I developed to classify teambuilding and classbuilding activities. The process is not very satisfying though, because so many of the activities are multi-functional, and all of them share a basic function -- they are played for fun.

Cooperative sports activities fit more neatly and are better remembered if we classify them not by function, but by form. There are Tag Games, Balance Games, Friendly Fights, and so on. The way I count it there are eight categories of games. In the remainder of this chapter, are some of my favorites in each category, and plenty of references.

1. Tag Games

Freeze Tag

Everyone is IT. Anyone can freeze anyone if they touch them and yell "Freeze." If you get frozen, you must freeze in whatever position you are in. When everyone but one is frozen, that person yells, "Unfreeze," and the game starts again. (Some participants at first need to be reminded about the difference between touching someone and being touched: If you tag someone, they are frozen but you are not.)

Freezer-Unfreezer Tag

Like Freeze Tag, but add a chance to be nice. If you are frozen, you hold your two arms outstretched and yell "Help, Help, Help." Anyone can unfreeze you if they yell "Unfrozen" while ducking under your outstretched arms. Once you are unfrozen you may either freeze anyone who is moving (by tagging them and yelling "Frozen") or you may unfreeze anyone who is frozen (by ducking under their arms and yelling, "Unfrozen").

Variation:

When frozen, place their legs wide apart, and the way to unfreeze them is to crawl through their legs.

Types of
Cooperative Play
1. Tag Games
2. Helping & Support
3. Balance & Coordination
4. Movement
5. Fantasy Play
6. Group Challenges
7. Converted Sports
8. Friendly Fights

"The concept behind cooperative games is simple: People play with one another rather than against one another; they play to overcome challenges, not to overcome other people; and they are freed by the very structure of the games to enjoy the play experience itself. No player need find himself a bench warmer nursing a bruised self-image. Since the games are designed so that cooperation among players is necessary to achieve the objective(s) of the game, children play together for common ends rather than against one another for mutually exclusive ends. In the process, they learn in a fun way how to become more considerate of one another, more aware of how other people are feeling, and more willing to operate in one another's best interests." Terry Orlick (1982, p. 4)

Hug Tag

This one is like common tag: Being IT transfers when you are touched. But Hug Tag has an important twist. You are safe while you hugging someone else. Try this one with several ITs at the same time.

Variations:

If there are too few risk takers (or long hugs), you might add rules: 1) Only three or four pairs can be hugging at any time. 2) You may hug for only 5 seconds.

Humming Tag

Start with about two times as many groups of three as ITs. Groups of three are safe as long as they are holding hands in a circle and humming. When they run out of air, they break up and each one must find two new partners before they get tagged. ITs have their arm up. If anyone is tagged by an IT, the IT holds up their hand and counts to five. They are now an IT and cannot let their hand down until they have tagged someone else. Once they have tagged someone else and passed the ITness to the other person by lifting that persons arm and counting five, they drop their own arm and seek two others who are not ITs. Joining the others they take a deep breath, and begin humming.

Blob Tag

Start with one Baby Blob, (one person), and everyone else free. When Baby Blob tags someone, they stay hooked on in some way, becoming part of the blob. The blob grows up tagging more and more people until only one is left free. At that moment, the one left calls "Baby Blob," becomes the Baby Blob, and everyone else breaks apart, to start the game again.

Variations:

Start with several Baby Blobs and when everyone is tagged, the last person in each blob becomes a Baby Blob and the rest go free to start the game again.

Amoeba Tag

One student is a Baby Amoeba. The game is played in slow motion. The Baby Amoeba begins chanting, "A..Me..BA," with the accent on the last syllable. When he/she tags another student, they link on, becoming a Child Amoeba. The Child Amoeba continues the chant, "A..Me..BA," as it walks in very large, limbering steps, in rhythm to the chant.

When the Child Amoeba catches yet another student, the students links on and the three become an Adolescent Amoeba, continuing the chant. When the Adolescent Amoeba catches the fourth student, it is an Adult Amoeba. Adult Amoebas must split up in a defined way -- The two ends join to become one Child Amoeba, as do the two middles, so that the two new Child Amoebas consist of partners who were not previously together.

Now there are two Child Amoebas walking and chanting, trying to tag others who attempt to escape without breaking the slow motion rule. Children become Adolescents who become Adults who become Children....

Broken Spoke

Students sit in about five lines, with about six students in a line. The lines all extend out from a mid-point, like spokes from the hub of a wheel. IT walks around and then touches the outermost person on one spoke, yelling either "With Me" or "Against Me." All of the students in the spoke get up and race around the outside of the wheel, attempting not to be the last one to sit back down in the spoke. Students race either in the same direction as IT (With Me) or in the opposite direction (Against Me). IT is also in the race, but almost always is the first to be seated. The last one to sit becomes the new IT.

Three Deep

Students form two concentric circles, so each is in a pair and both are facing the center. Two students are on the outside, one is IT and the other hopes not to become IT. IT tries to tag the free student. At any point the free student can join a pair so they are "Three Deep." The person on the inside must run, trying not to be caught by IT. If a Tag is made, IT is free and the free person is IT.

Good Witch, Bad Witch, Sandwich

Participants stand in two parallel lines facing each other, about twenty giant paces apart. The Witch stands in the center. The players chant twice to the Witch, "Good Witch, Bad Witch, Sandwich!"

If the Witch responds with "Good Witch," the players take a giant step forward. If the Witch responds "Sandwich," the players take one step back and must remain backwards until the next command from the witch. If the Witch responds "Bad Witch," the players try to run to the other side without being tagged by the Witch. If they are tagged, they become witches, and on the next round they join the original witch to tag the players who are crossing. After several rounds there are many witches, and quickly everyone is caught. The last to be caught becomes the new witch and the game is played again.

Vampires & Zombies

To simulate night, everyone shuts their eyes and begins to wander about. The Night Watchman keeps people in the designated area. The Night Watchman whispers to someone that they are the Vampire. (Everyone else is a Zombie.) The Vampire keeps her eyes closed and continues to mill about.

If two Zombies bump into each other, nothing happens. But if the Vampire bumps into anyone, she snatches the person and lets out a blood-curdling cry. Now there are two Vampires, and soon there are many, as cries pierce the darkness.

The game does not end quickly, though, because if two Vampires snatch each other, they both become Zombies!

Puri

Everyone wants to become a Puri (PROO-ee). You become a Puri by shaking hands with one. Start with everyone milling around

with eyes closed searching for the Puri. The teacher whispers to one student that he/she is the Puri. The leader then closes his/her eyes and joins the play. The Puri opens his/her eyes and stands in place. If you bump into anyone you shake hands and ask, "Puri?" If they respond by asking "Puri?" you know you have not found the Puri. The Puri is mute.

When you shake hands with someone who does not respond, try a second time to be sure. If you really have found the Puri, you do not let go of the handshake and open your eyes. You are now a Puri standing in place, enjoying watching the remaining students search for the Puri.

If a student tries to shake your hand when you are the Puri, shake hands with your free hand and remain mute. The student has found the Puri, and becomes a Puri. To become a Puri students must find the free hand of the Puri at either end of the growing line. Thus, after a bit there is a line of students watching others groping to find one of the two ends of the line.

Bumper Cars

Students stand in pairs, one behind another. The person in the rear puts his/her hands on the waist of the person in front. Together they are a bumper car. There are about half as many ITs as bumper cars. The ITs are alone and try to tag the person in back of a bumper car. If they do, they latch on and the person in front of the car bumps off, and becomes an IT, trying to latch on to a different bumper car.

Variation:

Elbow Tag

Same game as bumper cars, but it is elbows which connect students. Students link arms, each with his/her hand on hip, elbow bent.

Bumper-Unbumper Cars

Everyone starts as an individual, attempting to tag anyone. If they do, they become a Bumper Car (as in Bumper Cars, above). Bumper Cars attempt to tag other Bumper Cars. If they do, they unbump. That is, they become four individuals who attempt to become Bumper Cars who attempt to become individuals, who attempt to become bumper cars who attempt to ...I can spell banana, but I just don't know when to stop!

Coupled Cars

Students are in pairs, one person with his or her hands on the hips of the other. They are told they are like railroad cards coupled together. When the leader calls go, each pair tries to hook on to pair of cars while avoiding being hooked onto.

The synergistic aspect of this game is the surprise ending: The whole group is running around in a large circle or several small circles. Competition undoes itself, leading to cooperation.

Dragon's Tail

Around a dozen people form the Dragon by standing in a line, hands on the hips of the person in front. A handkerchief (Dragon's Tail) is placed in the back pocket of the person at the end of the line. Now the Dragon lets out a few yells, and at a signal the Dragon tries to catch its own tail. Of course the tail tries to avoid being caught. When caught, the tail becomes the head and the game starts again.

Triangle Tag

Students form groups of four. They choose who is to be the Odd-One-Out, and the other three join hands to form a triangle. One of the three in the triangle is the Target, and the the Odd-One-Out tries to tag the Target. The other two in the triangle protect the Target by keeping him/her away from the Odd-One-Out who tries to go over, under, or around in attempt to make the tag. Once the tag is made, or a time has elapsed, the Odd-One-Out joins the triangle, the Target becomes the Odd-One-Out, and a new Target is chosen.

Smile If You Love Me

Students stand in a circle. IT walks up to one and says, "Smile if you love me," and makes faces, sounds, and motions, attempting to make the other person smile. No touching. If the person smiles, there are two ITS. Soon

there are four, and soon everyone loves everyone.

2. Helping & Support

Willow-in-the-Wind

Around eight students stand in a circle. (I use two teams in the class.) One person stands in the center with eyes closed. They lean back with feet "glued, knees unbent, and arms crossed over the chest. They are gently rolled around the circle. At least two people maintain contact with the center person at all times. The slower the better, as participants are to provide a gentle feeling of support.

Lifeboats

As many students as possible stand on a bench. They are told they are in a lifeboat and there are alligators in the water. If any of them fall in, the alligators will know they are there and they will all die. Their job: line themselves up by height. Or by birthday. Or by the second letter in their first name, or....

Car and Driver

Students work in pairs. One student is the Car, the other is the Driver. The Driver stands behind the Car with her hands on the Car's shoulders. The Car closes her eyes and covers them with both hands. The Driver then directs the Car around the room, using hand signals and whispered instructions. Stress safety and consideration for others in this game. After a few minutes Car and Driver change places. (If children peek to see where they are going, let them. Trust cannot be forced; it must be earned.)

Shoe Scramble

Form a circle. Everyone takes off one shoe and tosses it in the center. All join hands. With hands joined, each person must pick up one shoe, locate the owner of the shoe and return it to them.

Frozen Bean Bag

Give every child a bean bag to place on her head. Ask the children to hop or skip around. If the bean bag drops, the student is "frozen," standing still, calling for help. Another child can crouch down, without dropping his own bag, and replace the bean bag on the frozen child's head. The recipient then says, "Thank you."

Variation:

Row Row Freeze

I like to have participants pretend they are in a row boat and rowing backwards, careful not to drop their captain's hat. Everyone is singing Row, Row, Row Your Boat. If too many are careful I speed up the tempo so they must sing and row faster

Blind Maze

One student from each group of three or four shuts his/her eyes. Beanbags, paper, or other markers are placed about the area, about five large paces apart, in a random arrangement. The Blind student must step on each marker. The rest of the team can call one direction at a time and then must allow the blind student to carry out the whole direction before calling out another direction. This game can be timed and students can try to beat their own record.

Float-A-Friend

Around seven students gather around one, "The Friend," who lays down with his/her arms straight at his/her sides eyes closed. One student uses both hands to support The Friend's Head. The others gather around placing their hands under the legs and back of The Friend. Students are on their knees, and very, very gently float their friend a few inches off the ground, and then begin to gently rock him/her. They are to go so slowly that The Friend never knows when he/she has left earth.

Moonjump

This one is in honor of the decreased gravity on the moon. The Astronaut has hands on hips firmly with elbows bent. The two Assistant Astronauts stand on either side, with one hand holding the wrist of the Astronaut and one hand holding the arm. On the count of three, the Astronaut makes a jump straight up. At the peak of the jump, the Assistants give a slight boost so the Astronaut defies gravity. Assistants need to be warned not to launch the Astronaut.

Moonhop

When Astronauts have become proficient at the moonjump, they advance to the moonhop. The moonhop is like the moonjump except there is forward movement -- the Astronaut takes one hop forward. The Assistants move right along with the Astronaut as he/she hops forward in a hop.

Moonjaunt

When Astronauts have become proficient at the moonhop, they are finally ready to take a moonjaunt. The moonjaunt is like the moonhop except it consists of a continuous series of hops forward. Again the Assistants move right along, giving that added boost at the peak of each hop. Astronauts who have fully mastered the Moonjaunt report they can float across the lunar landscape effortlessly.

3. Balance & Coordination

Pair Balances

One of the simplest and purest forms of positive interdependence are the pair balances. Each person in a pair stands off balance, supporting the other who would fall without the support. Examples:

Palm Lean. Students place palms together and take baby steps back until they are both leaning forward supporting each other. They then let go of first one and then the other hand to the crowd.

Toe Lean. Facing each other with toes together and hands clasped, students lean back until their arms are straight. They then begin to gently rock.

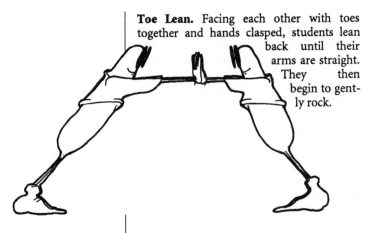

Back-to-Back. Students stand back-to-back and then slowly step forward, keeping their backs together supporting each other.

Shoulder Lean. Students place shoulders together and lean toward each other. They get to a position so they have only one foot on the ground.

Square Balances

Once students master some pair balances, have the pairs pair and create some square balances.

Octi-Balances

Squares square to become groups of eight and do some Octi-Balances.

Yurt Circle

The whole class forms a circle, holding hands. Students number off, 1,2,1,2,1.... All of the number one people at a signal lean slowly in while then number two people lean out to counterbalance them. Lean from the ankles, not the hips so that you would fall if not held. At a signal, the roles shift so the twos lean out and the ones lean in.

The Yurt Circle is named after the tent of the Mongolian nomads. The roof the tent pushes against the walls so that roof holds up the walls while the walls hold up the roof.

Partner Pull-Ups

Partners sit on the ground facing each other, knees bent, toes touching, soles of feet flat on the ground. They reach forward, grasp hands, and pull each other up. They then support each other as they sit down.

Partner Push-Ups

Students stand in pairs facing each other with arms outstretched, palms in contact. They then slowly do push-ups by bending their arms until heads touch.

Catch A Friend

Students are in the same position as in Partner Push-Ups, but this time they fall forward, catching each other by having their palms meet. When they are forward they do a little push away to return to straight up. Each time they catch each other, they move back about three or four inches, to make it a greater challenge.

Balloon Bounce

Groups of four or so hold hands in a circle. They bounce a balloon in the air without letting go of their hands. When they get good, they try to keep two and even three in the air. If the balloon lands on the ground, they must pick it up and get it bouncing again without letting go of their hands.

Ball Balance

Two people carry a ball or balloon between them by using their bodies. They are holding hands and are not allowed to touch the ball with their hands. Once they have made it from one goal to another, they try it with two balls, then three, then....

If a pair drops a balloon, they are frozen and yell for help from another pair who cannot use their hands in assisting them in getting going again.

Touching Toes

Students stand in groups of eight to a dozen, with right foot forward, all toes touching in the center. They attempt to hold each other up so they can get their left feet off the ground. Ask them to count the seconds they are in position and then try to beat the record.

Elephant-Alligator-Monkeys

Students stand in a circle. One student, The Pointer, is in the center. The Pointer points to one student and calls either "Elephant," "Alligator," or "Monkey." The student pointed and the students on either side quickly become the animal called. To be an Elephant, the student in the center uses his/her arms to form the long trunk, while the students on either side use theirs to form the waving ears. Alligators have long mouths in the middle (arms straight ahead opening and closing) and eyes on both sides (fists). Monkeys hold on to a branch with one hand and scratch themselves with the other. The students on both sides of center join hands to form the branch.

The students try to quickly get into position because they know the last one of the three to get in position must go to the center of the circle to become the new pointer.

Twirling Circles

Students hold hands to form circles of about eight. They begin twirling to move forward. This American Indian game can be used for exciting races among groups.

Blanket Ball

Two blankets and at least one ball are the equipment. Students gather around three sides of each blanket. Begin with the fourth edge of each blanket touching. A ball is placed in one blanket. The students around that blanket call "1, 2, Toss" and at the sound of "Toss," they toss the ball to the other blanket. As students become better at blanket toss, they may trade two balls simultaneously, and they may begin longer distance tosses, moving a pace further apart at each catch and a pace chosen together at each miss.

Class Juggling

Students stand in a circle. All students raise one hand. The teacher calls the name of one student and tosses him/her a ball. The student uses the name of another student to get his/her attention and then tosses the ball to that student. The process is continued until everyone has received the ball. The ball is then sent back to the original sender. Students are instructed to remember who they sent the ball to. Next, the class gets as many balls going around the circle as possible, using the same pattern. Students are instructed not to throw a ball unless they are sure the receiver is ready - they can always go slower.

Pencil in Bottle

Students face back-to-back in pairs. A string is tied around their waists so they are separated by about 3 or 4 feet. A pencil on a string is tied to the middle of the first string so it hangs vertically. A soda pop bottle is placed below the pencil. Goal: get the pencil in the bottle. Variation: Use a coffee can, blindfold the pair, and have the teammates provide the cues.

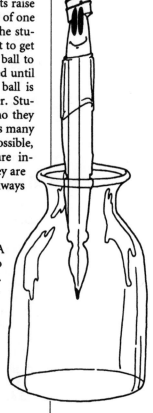

Rhythms

Players sit in a circle. A rhythm is established. All players slap their thighs twice, clap twice, and snap their fingers first on one hand and then the other. Once the rhythm is established, one player begins. This person calls his own first name on the first snap of the fingers, and any other person's name on the second snap. The player called then continues the pattern, stating his/her own name on the first snap and someone else's on the second snap. Try to establish an atmosphere in which it is acceptable to not come in on the very next snap. Let the player who is calling change the pattern if he wishes.

Four Up

All the players need to be able to see one another for this game. Begin the game sitting down. Anyone can stand up whenever she wants to, but cannot remain standing for more than five seconds at a time before she sits down again. Then she can get right up again if she wants to. Your object as a group is to have exactly four people standing at all times.

Pyramids

Students on soft grass or gym mats can build a variety of pyramids. They can start with a three person (2,1) pyramid (two on their hands and knees at the base and one on hands and knees on top), move up to a six person (3,2,1), and graduate with a ten person (4,3,2,1).

4. Movement

Bark-Nose-Hop

Students are in a group of any size. One person calls out a sound, a body part, and a motion, such as "Quack, Knee, Twirl." All students Quack, hold a knee, and twirl around until any student yells "Stop." The student who yells "Stop" then calls out a new set of three, such as "Hum, Eye, Skip."

Follow The Leader

In groups of around four, students follow the leader who may move around skipping, bending, hopping. The leader rotates to the end of the line when he or she wishes, to allow the next person in line to become leader for awhile.

Mirror Mirror

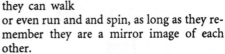

Students begin in pairs facing each other and pretend that the other person is their mirror image. They have their hands up, palms forward so palms almost meet, but the mirror is between. Then they begin moving. After a time they can walk or even run and and spin, as long as they remember they are a mirror image of each other.

Shadow Shadow

Like Mirror Mirror, except one student is behind the other.

Mirror Mirror Shadow Shadow.

Start as in Mirror Mirror but then add a shadow to each side.

Jelly Roll

Students stand in a circle, holding hands. The leader drops the hand of the person on the left and begins a clockwise spiral around the inside of the circle. At each revolution, the spiral gets smaller until the whole group is a tightly wound Jelly Roll.

Split Jelly Roll

Students hold hands and stretch out as far as they can in a line. Both ends begin to roll in, without letting go. The middle of the line splits. Two Jelly Rolls are formed.

Jelly Role Races

Two human jelly roles race to pick up a ball placed in the center between the two. The ball can be picked up only by the person in the center. When one team picks up the ball the two jelly roles play catch without letting go of their hands and without unwrapping.

Jelly Role Nibble

Students are reminded not to let go, centers of the Jelly Role duck under all hands and lead everyone out.

Spiral Unspiral

The leader begins as if a jelly role is to be formed but when the center gets tight he/she reverses directions and leads the group out, with the outward spiraling people walking between the inward spiraling people. This is a nice way to lead a class in from play.

5. Fantasy Play

Imaginary Toss

Students are in a circle. I usually begin this one by holding my hand up cradling an imaginary egg, saying "I have an egg in my hand. It isn't cooked, so when I toss it to you, please be very careful. Don't drop it or you will make a mess. Susan, are you ready to catch the egg? Are you sure? You know that if you miss we are looking a big mess. And raw egg mess is hard to clean up. Are you sure you are ready?" Each time the egg is tossed, a member of the circle is to be sure the receiver is ready, by doing a similar speech. While the egg is doing its rounds, I introduce a second object, such as a paper airplane which will do loops before being caught. Pretty soon the calm circle is chaos because I have introduced more and more objects, such as bubbles which are blow and caught with imaginary bubble wands, hot potatoes which can burn the hands, live chickens, gentle butterflies which flutter, bowling balls, snow balls which freeze the hands.

Rope Tricks

Pairs or small groups are given an imaginary rope. They are first to jump rope, then to create a variety of activities with their rope. They spin each other like tops; they walk the tight rope, and hang and break pinatas. After awhile I get the small groups to tie their ropes into one long strong rope and we do a tug of war. Participants have to be reminded that the rope cannot stretch so both sides must observe the other carefully so there is a realistic give and take.

Jazz Band

Students each choose an imaginary instrument from the jazz band to practice. When they have practiced enough, they get together to do a pantomime jazz concert.

6. Group Challenges

All-On-The-Ball

A small ball or soda can is produced and the class is challenged to have everyone "on the ball." That is, they all must be touching the ball at once. When they have succeeded, intensify the challenge, asking them to be All-On-The-Ball with none touching each other. Similar challenges include, how many people inside a hula hoop, and how many people can get the toes of their right foot touching at once.

Crunch

Students stand in a circle. They are challenged to take three giant steps forward together and remain standing.

Circle Run

Student stand in a circle holding hands, with the leader in the center. The leader faces one person and indicates that person is The Marker. The group is challenged to make a complete revolution so The Marker is again facing the leader. Time is kept, and after the first trial the group is challenged to beat its record. The group is challenged repeatedly until it discovers that the task can be accomplished in just two or three seconds if The Marker races forward toward the leader and then darts around, rather than traveling the long distance around the outer circumference of the circle.

Pretzel

A pair of students, The Unpretzelers, turn their backs on a group of five or more, the Pretzel Makers. The Pretzel Makers hold hands in a circle. Without letting go they twist about and step over and under arms to form a human pretzel. When they are well pretzeled, they call over the Unpretzelers to do their work. The Unpretzelers have not seen how the Pretzel Makers got pretzeled, and they must direct them out of the pretzel without having anyone let go of the their hands.

Knots

Team members stand in a circle shoulder to shoulder. They reach out and grasp hands, each one holding the hands of two others, each of whom is not on either side of the themselves. They then must untangle the knot. At first it may seem impossible. I think sometimes it is. The first time the team may have one member who serves as a director. When the team gets good, they can do it with their eyes shut.

Formations

Ask students to become a clock showing 2:00, by holding hands. Now ask them to time it perfectly as they move from 2:00 to 3:30. Or ask them to become a fish, moving through the water, or....

Body English

Students use their bodies to spell out a word, and then the unused letters try as a group to guess what was spelt. There are two ways words can be spelt: 1) Overhead Spelling: Students stand in position so that someone above could read their word or phrase. The whole class can be part of words spelt overhead. 2) Vertical Spelling: Students stand so that each person is a part of a letter. For ex-

ample, the letter "A" is formed by three students. Two are facing each other with their arms straight above their heads, leaning forward, arms touching, to form the frame of the "A." A third student is behind one of the other students, hiding, showing own his/her arms to form the crossbar of the "A."

Roundup

The fence is down and the cows and ducks have escaped the barnyard. They mill and mingle until the leader says "Stop, it has become night, so you all must close your eyes. Now, you need to group for protection. You cannot open your eyes, but you can find your group if you make a 'Moo' or a 'Quack' I will be timing you, let's see how long it takes until all the cows are holding hands in a group while all the ducks are holding hands in another group. Remember, you cannot open your eyes."

When the groups have formed, the elapsed time is announced, and the teacher challenges the class to beat its record as it plays Roundup again.

7. Converted Sports & Games

Pin-the-Tail

A simple way to convert this traditional game into a co-operative activity is to have the group call out directions to the blindfolded person. You do not need to use a picture of a donkey. Try seasonal motifs: Pin the lid on the jack-o-lantern, pin the hat on the snowperson, or pin the flower on the stem. Keep the group small. This is an effective way for children to learn their directions - higher, lower, right, left, and so on. It may be used as activity center.

Paired Balloon Baseball

Introduction of sports is made easier for the little ones with balloons rather than hard balls. But for big ones too, the variety is fun. Your fist is your bat, and the balloon is the ball.

For Paired Balloon Baseball the rules are the same as regular baseball, except at all times you hold hands with a partner.

Balloon Volleyball

Yarn becomes the net, two players become the net posts, and a balloon is the volleyball. When players get good, introduce a second balloon, then a third, and then more and more until chaos breaks out.

Touch Baseball

This one is played with balloons also. There are only about four people on a side. Once the ball is hit, all players in the outfield must touch the balloon and then yell "Stop." The runner stops wherever he/she is, even if that is between the bases. Once all four players have been up, the outfield comes to bat for the second half of the inning.

Rotation Baseball

There are only four people in line to bat and everyone else is in the outfield. This can be played with balloons or real baseball equipment. There is a rotation order among those in the field. As soon as you score, you go to the outfield, and the pitcher joins the line of four to bat. If you are out, you go immediately to the outfield, and everyone rotates.

Rotation Volleyball

Each time a point is made, the players rotate, but they rotate as an entire group, so two players change sides.

Variation:

Quick Rotation (also called Chaos): Every time you hit the ball you must quickly change sides while the play continues.

Bump & Scoot

This one is like the Quick Rotation Volleyball, but the object is not to make the other team miss. Rather, the object is to achieve a complete rotation of sides before the ball touches the ground.

Variation:

Team Bump & Scoot. There are several minor teams of three or four players are on each side of the net. Each mini-team has its name. When anyone on a mini-team hits the ball, he/she yells the team name, and the whole mini-team must scoot to the other side.

Infinity Volleyball

Players count as they hit the ball and try to set ever higher records for the number of times they hit the ball before it touches the ground.

8. Friendly Fights

Snowball

Half the class writes their name on a piece of red paper, and half on blue paper. They then make snowballs by crumpling the paper. Those with red stand on one side of an imaginary line, and those with blue stand on the other side. At the signal they have a snowball fight, attempting to make sure that more snowballs end up on the other side of the line. When the fight is over, each person gets one snowball of the color opposite that which they started with. Those who now have a red snowball are to find and interview the person whose snowball they have. Afterwards, at a signal, those with blue snowballs are to find and interview their new friend.

Variation:

Have students play a matching game as in states and capitals, inventors and inventions, dates and events, words and definitions. In this case students work in pairs to begin with, and create two snowballs, the red one with something that matches the blue one. After the snowball fight, they are each to find their new partner - the person who has the matching bit of information.

Hagoo

This one is my favorite, given to us by the Tlingit Indians of Alaska. "Hagoo" means "Come here."

Two teams of about a dozen members each stand facing each other a very giant step apart. A member from one team steps to one end of the gauntlet, and a member of the other team steps to the other end. They stare at each other until one issues the challenge, "Hagoo." They are both to walk the entire gauntle with a stern very frown. If they smile, they are won over by the other team. The object of the game is to win over all the other teammembers. Players cannot touch each other, but they make faces and say whatever might get the frowning serious person to crack a smile. ～

References

Animal Town Game Company. *The Animal Town Game Company catalog of board games.* Santa Barbara, CA: Animal Town Game Company, 1984.

Deacove, J. *Cooperative Games Manual.* Perth, Ontario, Canada: Family Pastimes, 1974.

Deacove, J. *Sports Manual Of Co-operative Recreation.* Perth, Ontario, Canada: Family Pastimes, 1974.

Family Pastimes. *Family Pastimes Catalog of Cooperative Games.* Perth, Ontario, Canada: Family Pastimes, 1985.

Fluegelman, A. (Ed.) *The New Games Book.* New York: Dolphin/Doubleday, 1976.

Fuegelman, Andres (Ed.) *More New Games.* Garden City, NY: Doubleday, 1981.

Gwilliam, J. Hughes, G. Jenkins, D. Koczka, W. & Nicholls, L. *"Working Together, Learning Together: The Cooperatively Structured Classroom."* Regina: Department of Cooperation and Cooperative Development -- Education Unit, Saskatchewan Co-operation and Co-operative Development, 1983.

Harrision, M. *For the Fun of It! Selected Cooperative Games for Children and Adults.* Philadelphia, PA: Philadelphia Yearly Meeting of the Religious Society of Friends, 1975.

LeFevre, Dale N. *Playing for the Fun of It.* Marvin LeFevre, 505 Orchard Court, Des Plaines, Ill., 1983.

Lentz, T.F. & Cornelius, R. *All Together. A Manual of Cooperative Games.* St. Louis, MO: Character Research Association/Peace Research Laboratory, 1950.

Michaelis, B. & Michaelis, D. *Learning Through Noncompetitive Activities and Play.* Palo Alto, CA: Learning Handbooks, Pitman Learning, 1977.

Orlick, Terry. *Every Kid Can Win.* Chicago: Nelson Hall Publishers, 1975.

Orlick, Terry. *The Cooperative Sports & Games Book: Challenge without competition.* New York: Pantheon, 1978.

Orlick, Terry. *The Second Cooperative Sports and Games Book.* New York: Pantheon, 1982.

Orlick, Terry. *Winning Through Cooperation: Competitive Insanity; Cooperative Alternatives.* Washington, DC: Hawkins & Associates Publishers, 1977.

Sobel, J. *Everybody Wins: 393 Non-Competitive Games for Young Children.* New York: Walker, 1983.

Torbert, Marianne. *Follow Me: A Handbook of Movement Activities for Children.* Englewood Cliffs, N.J.: Prentice Hall, Inc. 1980.

Weinstein, M. & Goodman, J. *Playfair: Everybody's Guide to Noncompetitive Play.* San Luis Obispo, CA: Impact, 1980.

Where a person has distinguished him/herself as willing to provide additional references in the area, they have been indicated as the "Networking Specialist."

I. Theory

R. Brandt. (Ed.). *Cooperative learning. (Educational Leadership*, 1989-90, *47, special issue)* Alexandria, VA: Association for Supervision and Curriculum Development, 1989.

Brubacher, M., Payne, R. & Rickett, K. (Eds.) *Perspectives on small group learning. Theory and practice.* San Diego, CA: Dominic Press, 1990.

Dewey, John. *Experience and education.* New York: Macmillian, 1957.

Glasser, William. *Control theory in the classroom.* New York: Harper and Row, 1986.

Graves, N.B. & Graves, T.D. *The cultural context of prosocial development: an ecological model.* **In D. Bridgeman.** (Ed.) *The nature of prosocial development: Interdisciplinary theories and strategies.* New York: Academic Press, 1983.

Graves, N.B. & Graves, T.D. *Creating a cooperative learning environment: An ecology approach.* **In R. Slavin, S. Sharan, S. Kagan, R. Hertz-Lazarowitz, C. Webb, & R. Schmuck.** (Eds.) *Learning to cooperate, cooperating to learn.* New York: Plenum, 1985.

Johnson, D. & Johnson, R. *Learning together and alone: Cooperation, competition, and individualization.* Englewood Cliffs: Prentice Hall, 1975.

Kagan, Spencer. *The dimensions of cooperative classroom structures.* **In R. Slavin, S. Sharan, S. Kagan, R. Hertz-Lazarowitz, C. Webb, & R. Schmuck** (Eds.) *Learning to cooperate, cooperating to learn.* New York: Plenum, 1985.

Kagan, Spencer. *Cooperative learning and sociocultural factors in schooling.* In *Beyond language: Social and cultural factors in schooling language minority students.* Los Angeles, CA: Evaluation, Dissemination, and Assessment Center, California State University, 1986.

Cooperative learning resources which have not been included in the prior chapters, are provided here, presented in nine sections.

This chapter is based heavily on the work of Nan and Ted Graves. The Graves for years have distinguished themselves, creating from their peaceful home in Santa Cruz, California, the world's center for networking in Cooperative Learning. Their publication *Cooperative Learning: A Resource Guide* (Graves, 1990) contains over 200 annotated resources of work central to cooperative learning. The guide itself is but one issue of their excellent magazine, *Cooperative Learning*, which is an ongoing treasure chest of articles, reviews, new releases, networking and workshop opportunities.

For the resource guide and a subscription to *Cooperative Learning*, call or write Nan and Ted, the executive editors. They may be reached at Cooperative Learning, 136 Liberty St., Santa Cruz, CA 95060. (408) 429-6550. Additional Co-op newsletters are listed in Section VIII of this chapter.

Kohn, Alfie. *No contest: The case against competition.* Boston: Houghton Mifflin, 1986.

Mead, Margaret. *Cooperation and competition among primitive peoples.* New York: McGraw-Hill, 1936.

Nelson, L. & Kagan, S. *Competition: The star spangled scramble.* **Psychology Today,** 1972, *90(1),* 53-6.

Schmuck, R.A. & Schmuck, P.A. *Group processes in the classroom.* Dubuque, IA: William C. Brown, 1983.

Sharan, S., Hare, P., Webb, C.D., & Hertz-Lazarowitz, R. (Eds.), *Cooperation in education.* Provo, UT: Brigham Young University Press, 1980.

Sharan, S. & Sharan, Y. *Small-group teaching.* Englewood Cliffs: Educational Technology Publications, 1976.

Sherif, Muzafer. *Superordinate goals in the reduction of intergroup conflict.* *American Journal of Sociology,* 1956, *63,* 349-356.

Slater, Philip. *The pursuit of loneliness.* Boston MA: Beacon, 1976.

Slavin, Robert. *Cooperative learning. Theory, research, and practice.* Englewood Cliffs, NJ: Prentice-Hall, 1970.

Slavin, Robert E. *"Small group instruction."* In *The international encyclopedia of education, research and studies; Vol.8.* New York: Pergamon Press, 1985.

Sloan, Douglass (Ed.) *Educating for peace and disarmament: Toward a living world.* New York: Teachers College Press, 1983.

Torbe, M. & Medway, P. *The Climate For Learning.* London: Ward Lock, 1981.

Tutko, T. & Burns, W. *Winning is everything and other American myths.* New York: Macmillian, 1976.

Theory Videos

An Interview with Dr. Robert Slavin. Team Learning Project. The Johns Hopkins University, 3505 N. Charles St. Baltimore, MD 21218.

ASCD Cooperative learning series. ASCD, 1250 N. Pitt Street, Alexandria, VA 22314.

Circles of learning. Cooperative Learning Center, University of Minnesota, 202 Pattee Hall, 150 Pillsbury Drive SE, Minneapolis, MN 55455.

Cooperative learning: An overview. Interactive Concepts, 2114 Sunridge Circle, Riverside, CA 92503.

Together we learn. Curriculum Resources, Metropolitan Toronto School Board, 45 York Mills Rd, Ontario, Canada.

II. Research

Johnson, D.W., Johnson, R. & Maruyama, G. *Interdependence and interpersonal attraction among heterogeneous and homogeneous individuals: a theoretical formulation and a meta-analysis of the research.* **Review of Educational Research,** 1983, *53,* 5-54.

Johnson, D.W., Maruyama, G., Johnson, R., Nelson, D. & Skon, L. *Effects of cooperative, competitive and individualistic goal structures on achievement: a meta-analysis.* **Psychological Bulletin,** 1981, *89,* 47-62.

Kagan, S., Zahn, G.L., Widaman, K.F., Schwarzwald, J. & Tyrrell, G. *Classroom structural bias: Impact of cooperative and competitive classroom structures on cooperative and competitive individuals and groups.* In **R. E. Slavin, S. Sharan, S. Kagan, R. Hertz-Lazarowitz, C. Webb & R. Schmuck** (Eds.) *Learning to cooperate, cooperating to learn.* New York: Plenum, 1985.

Madden, N. & Slavin, R. *"Effects of cooperative learning on the social acceptance of mainstreamed academically handicapped students."* **The Journal of Special Education** *17* (1983): 171-182.

Pepitone, Emmy. *Children in cooperation and competition.* Indianapolis, IN: Lexington Books, 1980.

> *If ever I am a teacher, it will be to learn more than to teach.*
> *--Dorothee De Luzy (1747-1830)*

Salmon, P. & Claire, H. *Classroom collaboration.* London: Routlege and Kegan Paul, 1984.

Sharan, Shlomo. *Cooperative learning in small groups: recent methods and effects on achievement, attitudes, and ethnic relations.* **Review of Educational Research,** 1980, *50,* 241-271.

S. Sharan., P. Hare, C. Webb, D. Clark & R. Hertz-Lazarowitz. (Eds.). *Cooperation in Education.* Provo, UT: Brigham Young University Press, 1980.

Sharan, S., Kussell, P., Hertz-Lazarowitz, R., Bejarano, Y., Raviv, S. & Sharan, Y. *Cooperative learning in the classroom: research in desegregated schools.* New York: Erlbaum, 1984.

> *If you have knowledge let others light their candles at it.*
> *--Thomas Fuller (1608-1661)*

Slavin, R. E. *Cooperative learning.* New York: Longman, 1983.

Slavin, R. E. *When does cooperative learning increase student achievement? Psychological Bulletin*, 1983, *94*, 429-445.

R. Slavin S. Sharan, S. Kagan, R. Hertz-Lazarowitz, C. Webb, & R. Schmuck. (Eds.) *Learning to cooperate, cooperating to learn.* New York: Plenum, 1985.

Research Networking Specialist:

Karl Smith heads an AERA Special Interest Group on Cooperative Learning Theory and Resources. Cooperative Learning Center, 202 Pattee Hall, 150 Pillsbury Drive SE, Minneapolis, MN 55455.

Research Video

Foundations of cooperative learning: An Interview with Spencer Kagan. Resources for Teachers, Inc., 27128 Paseo Espada Suite 602, San Juan Capistrano, CA 92675.

III. Methods

Aronson, E., Blaney, N., Stephan, C., Sikes, J. & Snapp, M. *The Jigsaw classroom.* Beverly Hills, CA: Sage, 1978.

Aronson, E. & Goode, E. *Training teachers to implement jigsaw learning: A manual for teachers.* In R. Slavin, S. Sharan, S. Kagan, R. Hertz-Lazarowitz, C. Webb, & R. Schmuck (Eds.) *Learning to cooperate, cooperating to learn.* New York: Plenum, 1985.

Burns, Marilyn. *Groups of four: Solving the management problem.* **Learning Magazine.** 1981, 10(2), 46-51.

Cantlon, Teresa. *Structuring the classroom successfully for cooperative team learning.* Portland, OR: Prestige Publishers/C&M Education Consultants, 1989.

Caplan, R & Keech, C. *Showing writing: A training program to help students to be specific.* Berkeley, CA: Bay Area Writing Project, U.C. Berkeley, 1980.

Clarke, J., Wideman, R., & Eadie, S. *Together we Learn.* Ontario, Canada: Prentice-Hall Canada , 1990

Cohen, Elizabeth. *Designing groupwork. strategies for the heterogeneous classroom.* New York: Teachers College Press, 1986.

Dishon, D., & O'Leary, P.W. *A guidebook for cooperative learning: A technique for creating more effective schools.* Holmes Beach, FL: Learning Publications, Inc., 1985.

Gartner, A., Kohnler, M.C. & Riessman, F. *Children teach children: Learning by teaching.* New York: Harper & Row, 1971.

Graves, N. B. & Graves, T. D. *"Creating a cooperative learning environment. An ecological approach."* **In R. Slavin, S. Saran, S. Kagan, R. Hertz-Lazarowitz C. Webb, & R. Schmuck,** (Eds.) *Learning to cooperate, cooperating to learn.* New York: Plenum, 1985.

Graves, N. & Graves, T. *What is cooperative learning? Tips for teachers and trainers.* Santa Cruz, CA: Cooperative College of California, 1990.

Graves, N. & Graves, T. *A part to play. Tips, techniques and tools for learning Co-Operatively.* Victoria Glen Waverley Australia: Latitude Media & Marketing Pty Ltd., 1990.

Healey, M.K. *Using student response groups in the classroom.* Berkeley, CA: Bay Area Writing Project, U.C. Berkeley, 1980.

Hertz-Lazarowitz R. & Davidson, J. *Six mirrors of the classroom. A pathway to Cooperative learning.* Westlake Village, California: Joan B. Davidson, 1990.

R.T. Johnson & D.W. Johnson. (Eds.) *Structuring cooperative learning: Lesson plans for teachers.* Minneapolis, MI: Interaction Book Company, 1984.

Johnson, D.W., Johnson, R. T., Holubec, E. J. & Roy, P. *Circles of learning.* Alexandria, VA: Association for Supervision and Curriculum Development, 1984.

Johnson, D. W. & Johnson, R. T. *Learning together and alone: Cooperation, competition, and individualization.* New Brighton, MN: Interaction Book Company, 1975.

Johnson, D. W. & Johnson, F. P. *Joining together, group theory and group skills.* New Brighton, MN: Interaction Book Company, 1982.

Johnson, R. T. & Johnson, D. W. (Eds.) *Structuring cooperative learning: Lesson plan for teachers.* New Brighton, MN: Interaction Book Company, 1982.

Kagan, Spencer. *Co-op Co-op: A flexible cooperative learning technique.* **In R. Slavin, S. Sharan, S. Kagan, R. Hertz-Lazarowitz, C. Webb, & R. Schmuck** (Eds.) *Learning to cooperate, cooperating to learn.* New York: Plenum, 1985.

Poirier, G. A. *Students as partners in team learning.* Berkeley, CA: Center of Team Learning, 1970.

Rodes, J. & McCabe, M. *Simple co-operation in the classroom: Beginner's guide to establishing co-operative groups.* Willitis, California: ITA Publications, 1985.

Reid, J., Forrestal, P. & Cook, J. *Small group work in the classroom.* Kewdale, Western Australia: The Manager, 1982.

Saskatchewan Department of **Co-operation and Co-operative Development.** *Working together, learning together.* Saskatoon, Saskatchewan, Canada: The Stewart Resources Centre, 1983.

Schniedewind, N. & Davidson, E. *Open minds to equity: A source books of learning activities to promote race, sex, class and age equity.* Old Tappan, NJ: Prentice Hall, 1983.

Sharan, S. & Hertz-Lazarowitz, R. *A group-investigation method of cooperative learning in the classroom.* **In S. Sharan, P. Hare, C.D. Webb, & R. Hertz-Lazarowitz** (Eds.) *Cooperation in education.* Provo, Utah: Brigham Young University Press, 1980.

Slavin, R.E. *Student team learning: A manual for teachers.* **In S. Sharan, P. Hare, C.D. Webb, & R. Hertz-Lazarowitz** (Eds.) *Cooperation in education.* Provo: Brigham Young University Press, 1980.

Slavin, R. E. *Team-assisted individualization: combining cooperative learning and individualized instruction in mathematics.* **In R. Slavin, S. Sharan, S. Kagan, R. Hertz-Lazarowitz, C. Webb, & R. Schmuck** (Eds.) *Learning to cooperate, cooperating to learn.* New York: Plenum, 1985.

Stein, S. K. & Crabill, C.D. *Elementary algebra. A guided inquiry.* Boston, MA: Houghton Mifflin, 1972.

Weissglass, J. *Exploring elementary mathematics. A small-group approach for teaching.* San Francisco CA: W.H. Freeman, 1979.

Methods Videos

Co-op Co-op: Exploring the lesson design in depth. Resources for Teachers, Inc. 27128 Paseo Espada Suite 602, San Juan Capistrano, CA 92675.

> *The method of teaching which approaches most nearly to the method of investigation, is incomparably the best; since, not content with serving up a few barren and lifeless truths, it leads to the stock on which they grew.*
> --Edmund Burke (1729-1797)

Cooperative learning: From a student's point of view. Educational Activities, Inc. Box 392, Department EL, Freeport, NY 11520.

Cooperative learning: Strategies for instructional excellence. Personal Learning Institute, Box 3905, Englewood, CO 80155.

Managing instruction for equity and excellence. PBS- Educat. Services Dept., Francis Thompson, 1320 Braddock Place, Alexandria, VA 22314.

Numbered heads together: Exploring the structure in depth. Resources for Teachers, Inc. 27128 Paseo Espada Suite 602, San Juan Capistrano, CA 92675.

> *If you would thoroughly know anything, teach it to others.*
> *--Tryon Edwards (1809-1894)*

Pairs check: Exploring the structure in depth. Resources for Teachers, Inc. 27128 Paseo Espada Suite 602, San Juan Capistrano, CA 92675.

Student team learning. Team Learning Project. The Johns Hopkins University, 3505 N. Charles St. Baltimore, MD 21218.

Video Networking Specialist:

Jeanne Bauwens, Professor, Department of Teacher Education, Boise State University, 1910 University Dr., Boise, ID 83725. (208) 345-8654.

IV. Curriculum

Computers

Anderson, Mary. *Partnerships: Developing teamwork at the computer.* Santa Cruz, CA: Educational Apple-cations, 1988.

Male. M., Johnson, D., Johnson, R. & Anderson, M. *Cooperative learning & computers. An activity guide for teachers.* Santa Cruz, CA: Educational Apple-cations, 1986.

Male, Mary. *Special magic: Computers, classroom strategies, and exceptional students.* Santa Cruz, CA: Educational Apple-cations, 1990.

Environmental Education

Cohen, Michael. *Connecting with nature.* Eugene, OR: The World Peace University, 1989.

Cornel, Joseph. *Sharing children with nature.* Healdsburg, California: Animal Town Game Co, 1979.

Johns, F., Liske, K. & Evans, A. *Education goes outdoors.* Reading, MA: Addison-Wesley Publishing Company, 1986.

Jorgenson, E., Black, T. & Hallesy, M. *Manure, meadows and milkshakes.* Los Altos Hills, CA: Hidden Villa Environmental Program, 1986.

Knapp, Clifford. *Creating humane climates outdoors.* Charleston, WV: ERIC- CRESS, 1988.

Matre, Steve Van. *Acclimatization: A sensory and conceptual approach to ecological involvement.* Warrenville, IL: The Institute for Earth Education, 1972.

Matre, Steve Van. *Sunship Earth: An acclimatization program for outdoor learning.* Warrenville, IL: The Institute for Earth Education, 1979.

Matre, Steve Van. *Earth education: A new beginning.* Warrenville, IL: The Institute for Earth Education, 1990.

Project Adventure Staff. *Teaching through adventure.* Hamilton, MA: Project Adventure, Inc., 1976.

Language Acquisition

Christison, M. & Bassano, S. *Look who's talking.* Hayward, CA: Alemany Press, 1987.

Christison, M. & Bassano, S. *Purple Cows & Potato Chips: A multi-sensory language acquisition.* Hayward, CA: Alemany Press, 1987.

Coelho, E., Winer, L. & Olsen, J. *All side of the issue: Activities for cooperative jigsaw groups.* Hayward, CA: Alemany Press, 1989.

Kagan, Spencer. *Cooperative learning for students limited in language proficiency.* **In M. Brubacher, R. Payne, & K. Rickett** (Eds.) *Perspectives on small group learning. Theory and practice.* San Diego, CA: Dominic Press, 1990.

Language Acquisition Video

We can talk: Cooperative learning for LEP classrooms. Resources for Teachers, Inc. 27128 Paseo Espada Suite 602, San Juan Capistrano, CA 92675.

Language Arts

Barnes, Douglas. *From communication to curriculum* Monclair, NJ: Boynton/Cook, 1976.

Britton, James. *Prospect and retrospect.* London: Heinemann, 1982.

Brod, S. & Tuck, P. *Story strategies. Adventures in critical thinking and cooperative learning.* Topeka, KS: Econo-Clad Books, 1990.

Dias, Patrick X. *Making sense of poetry: Patterns in the process.* CCTE Monographs and Special Publications, 1987.

Healy, Mark. *Using student response groups in the classroom.* Berkeley, CA: Bay Area Writing Project, 1986.

Hill, William. *Learning thru discussion: Guide for leaders and members of discussion groups.* Newbury Park, CA: SAGE Publications, 1977.

Johnstone, Keith. *IMPRO. Improvisation and the theatre.* New York: Theater Arts Books, 1979.

Landor, Lynn. *Children's own stories: A Literature-based language arts program.* San Francisco, CA: San Francisco Study Center, 1990.

Moffet, J. & Wagner, B. *Student-centred Language Arts and Reading, K-13: A handbook for teachers.* Burlington, MA: Houghton Mifflin, 1976.

Norton, Michael. *Take 5 for thinking time.* Rolling Meadows, IL: Blue Ribbon Press, 1990.

Reid, Ian. *The making of Literature.* Australian Association for the Teaching of Literature, 1984.

Norwood, M. & Abromitis, B. *Our favorite things series: Notions & News (1988); Cereal box capers (1989); Ribbons & Rainbows (1989); Slippers & Shoes (1989).*Rolling Meadows, IL: Blue Ribbon Press

Stone, Jeanne. *Cooperative learning & language arts: A multi-structural approach.* San Juan Capistrano, CA: Resources for Teachers, Inc., 1989.

Watson, M., Tuck, P. & Morris, E. *Good books for good kids.* San Ramon, CA: Developmental Studies Center, 1986.

Wells, Gordon. *Learning through interaction.* Cambridge University Press, 1981.

Whisler, N. & Williams, J. *Literature and Cooperative learning: Pathways to literacy.* Sacramento, CA: Literature Co-op, 1990.

Language Arts Videos

Cooperative integrated reading and composition. Team Learning Project. The Johns Hopkins University, 3505 N. Charles St. Baltimore, MD 21218.

Fairy tale express: A multi-structural language arts lesson. Resources for Teachers, Inc. 27128 Paseo Espada Suite 602, San Juan Capistrano, CA 92675.

Math

Andrini, Beth. *Cooperative learning and mathematics.* San Juan Capistrano, CA: Resources for Teachers, Inc., 1991

Burns, Marilyn. *The I hate mathematics book.* New Rochelle, NY: Cuisenaire Co. of America, 1975.

Burns, Marilyn. *The book of think.* New Rochelle, NY: Cuisenaire Co. of America, 1976.

Burns, Marilyn. *The good times math event book.* Oak Lawn, IL: Creative Publications, 1977.

Burns, Marilyn. *Math of smarty pants.* New Rochelle, NY: Cuisenaire Co. of America, 1982.

Burns, Marilyn. *A collection of math lessons from grades 3-6.* New Rochelle, NY: Cuisenaire Co. of America, 1987.

Burns, M., Tank, B. *A collection of math lessons from grade 1-3.* New Rochelle, NY: Cuisenaire Co. of America, 1988.

Burns, M., Mclaughlin, C. *A collection of math lessons from from grades 6-8.* New Rochelle, NY: Cuisenaire Co. of America, 1990.

Burns, Marilyn. *The math solution: Using groups of four.* **In N. Davidson.** *Cooperative learning in mathematics.* Reading, MA: Addison-Wesley Publications, 1990.

Chakerian, G.D., Crabill, C. & Stein, S. *Geometry. A guided inquiry.* Pleasantville, NY: Sunburst Communications, 1989.

Clark, C., Betsy C. & Sternberg B. *Math in stride.* Grades 1-6. Menlo Park: Addison-Wesley, 1988.

Cook, Marcy. *Talk it over.* Balboa, CA: Marcy Cook Math, 1987.

Cook, Marcy. *Do talk it over.* Balboa, CA: Marcy Cook Math, 1988.

Cook, Marcy. *Cooperative 100-chart explorations.* Balboa, CA: Marcy Cook Math, 1988.

Cook, Marcy. *Clues & Cues.* Balboa, CA: Marcy Cook Math, 1988.

Cook, Marcy. *Follow the clues with tiles.* Balboa, CA: Marcy Cook Math, 1989.

Cook, Marcy. *Linking logic & geometry.* Balboa, CA: Marcy Cook Math, 1989.

Cook, Marcy. *Team estimation & analysis.* Balboa, CA: Marcy Cook Math, 1989.

Cook, Marcy. *Detective/Problem solver.* Balboa, CA: Marcy Cook Math, 1990.

Cook, Marcy. *Communicating with tiles.* Balboa, CA: Marcy Cook Math, 1990.

Cook, Marcy. *If, then, think and think again.* Balboa, CA: Marcy Cook Math, 1990

Davidson, Neil. *Cooperative learning in mathematics.* Reading MA: Addison-Wesley Publishing Co., 1990.

> *Let our teaching be full of ideas. Hitherto it has been stuffed only with facts.* --Anatole France (1844-1924)

Downie, D., Slesnick, T. & Stenmark, K. *Math for girls and other problem solvers.* Berkeley, CA: EQUALS, 1981.

Erickson, Tom. *Get it together, math problems for groups grades 4-12.* Berkeley, CA: EQUALS, 1989.

Kaseberg, A., Kreinberg, N. & Downie, D. *Use EQUALS to promote the participation of women in mathematics.* Berkeley, CA: EQUALS, 1981.

Meyer, C. & Salee, T. *Make it simpler. A practical guide to problem solving mathematics.* Oak Lawn, PA: Creative Publications, 1983.

Serra, Michael. *Discovering geometry.* Berkeley, CA: Key Curriculum Press, 1989.

Slavin, Robert. *Student team learning in mathematics.* The Johns Hopkins Baltimore, MD: Team Learning Project.

Weissglass, Julian. *Exploring elementary mathematics. A small-group approach for teaching.* Dubuque, IA: Kendall/Hunt Publishing Company, 1990.

Math Videos

Just a sample: A multi-structural mathematics lesson. Resources for Teachers, Inc., 27128 Paseo Espada Suite 602, San Juan Capistrano, CA 92675.

Mathematics: With manipulatives. Cuisenaire Co. of America, 12 Church St - Box D, New Rochelle, NY 10802.

Mathematics: for middle school. Cuisenaire Co. of America, 12 Church St - Box D, New Rochelle, NY 10802.

Team accelerated instruction (TAI). Team Learning Project. The Johns Hopkins University, 3505 N. Charles St. Baltimore, MD 21218.

Math Manipulatives

Kagan, S. & Robertson, L. *Fraction bar kit.* San Juan Capistrano, CA: Resources for Teachers, Inc., 1991.

Kagan, S. & Robertson, L. *Base 10 kit.* San Juan Capistrano, CA: Resources for Teachers, Inc., 1991.

Robertson, L. & Rodriguez, C. *Match mind.* San Juan Capistrano, CA: Resources for Teachers, Inc., 1991.

Science

AIMS Education Foundation. Currently publishes 24 books for K-9 grade (each book is about 70 pages long; each contains lessons, teacher's manual, and student work sheets for duplication. Write for a full catalogue. AIMS Education Foundation, PO Box 7766, Fresno, CA 93747.

The American Forest Council. *Project learning tree.* Washington, D.C.: American Forest Council, 1989.

DeAvila, Edward. *Finding Out Descubrimiento.* Compton, CA: Santillana Publishing, Co.

Hassard, Jack. *Science experiences.* Reading MA: Addison,Wesley Publishing Co., 1990.

Jaffe, R. & Appel, G. *The growing classroom.* Reading MA: Addison-Wesley Publishing Co., 1990.

National Center for Health Education. *Growing Healthy.* New York, NY 10016.

Project WILD. *Elementary and secondary activity guides.* Boulder, CO: Project WILD,1986.

Social Studies

Cooperative College of Canada. *Cooperation and community life.* Toronto, Ontario, Canada: The Ontario Institute for Studies in Education,1980.

Cooperative College of Canada. *Cooperative outlooks.* Toronto, Ontario, Canada: The Ontario Institute for Studies in Education, 1983.

Interact. *Learning through involvement.* P.O. Box 997F, Lakeside, CA 92042.

McLeroy, Jerry. *Project ES-TEAM. Eliminating stereotyping through educational activity management.* Central Education Support Center. Encino, CA 91436.

Miller, Rick. *Educating for citizenship K-4; A series of graded curriculum guides.* Law-Related Education Program. Baltimore, MD 21228.

Nelson, Doreen. *City building education.* Santa Monica, CA: Center for City Building Education Programs, 1982.

Nelson, Doreen. *Transformations. Process and theory.* Santa Monica, CA: Center for City Building Education Program, 1984.

OLoughlin, C. & Oslakovic, C. *A stately adventure.* Rolling Meadows, IL: Blue Ribbon Press, 1989.

Schniedewind, N. & Davidson, E. *Open minds to equality.* Englewood Cliffs, NJ: Prentice Hall, Inc., 1983.

Schniedewind, N. & Davidson, E. *Cooperative learning-cooperative lives.* Somerville, MA: Circle Books, 1987.

Thinking Skills

N. Davidson & T. Worsham. (Eds.) *Enhancing thinking skills through cooperative learning.* New York: Teachers College Press, 1992.

Wiederhold, Chuck. *Cooperative learning and higher level thinking: The Q-Matrix.* San Juan Capistrano, CA: Resources for Teachers, Inc., 1991

> *The true aim of every one who aspires to be a teacher should be, not to impart his own opinions but to kindle minds.*
> *--Frederick William Robertson (1816-1853)*

Thinking Skills Manipulatives

Robertson, L., & Rodriguez, C. *Match mind.* San Juan Capistrano, CA: Resources for Teachers, Inc., 1991.

Wiederhold, Chuck. *Q-Materials packet.* San Juan Capistrano, CA: Resources for Teachers, Inc., 1991.

Wiederhold, Chuck. *Q-Spinners.* San Juan Capistrano, CA: Resources for Teachers, Inc., 1991.

V. Grade Levels

Preschool - Kindergarten

Adcock, D. & Segal, M. *Play together, grow together.* Rainer, MD: Gryphon House, Inc., 1983

> *Scratch the green rind of a sapling, or wantonly twist it in the soil, and a scarred or crooked oak will tell of the act for centuries to come. So it is with the teachings of youth, which make impressions on the mind and heart that are to last forever.*
> *--Henri Frederic Amiel (1821-1881)*

Kindergarten - Second

Curran, Lorna. *Cooperative learning lessons for little ones: Literature-based language arts and social skills.* San Juan Capistrano, CA: Resources for Teachers, Inc., 1990.

Primary Education Networking Specialist: Chambers, Bette Associate Director, Center for the Study of Classroom Processes, Concordia University, 1455 de Maisonneuve Blvd. W, Montreal, Quebec, Canada J7V 5E8.

Middle School

Falsetto, N., Montalban, C. & Tyler, P. *Interactive concepts.* Riverside, CA: 1989.

Kerewsky, William J. *T.E.A.M.* ***The Early Adolescent Magazine.*** Clarksville, MD 21029.

High School

Cooperative College of Canada. *Cooperation and community life.* Toronto, Ontario, Canada: The Ontario Institute for Studies in Education, 1980.

Crabill, Calvin D. *Small-group learning in the secondary mathematics classroom.* Menlo Park, CA: Addison-Wesley Publishing Company, 1990.

Hill, William F. *Learning thru discussion: guide for leaders and members of discussion groups.* Beverly Hills, CA: Sage Publications, Inc., 1977.

Stanford, Gene. *Developing effective classroom groups: A practical guide for teachers.* New York: Hart Publishing Co., 1977.

Stanford, G & Stanford, B. *Learning discussion skills through games.* (out of print.) New York: Citation Press.

Stein, S., Crabill, C. *Elementary Algebra, A guided inquiry.* Boston, MA: Houghton Mifflin Co., 1972.

College/University

Bouton, C., Garth, R. *Learning in groups.* San Francisco, CA: Jossey-Bass, Publisher, 1983.

Cooper, J., Prescott, S., Cook, L. & Cuseo, J. *Cooperative learning and college instruction.* Long Beach, CA: Institute for Teaching and Learning, 1990.

Cooper, J. & Mueck, R. *Annotated bibliography of cooperative/collaborative learning, research and practice (Primarily) at the collegiate level.* Carson, CA: School of Education California State University Dominguez Hills, 1989.

Jacques, David. *Learning in groups.* Kent, England BR3 1AT: Croom Helm Ltd. Beckenham, 1984.

Johnson, R.T., Johnson, D.W. & Smith, K.A. *Cooperative learning: An active learning strategy for the college classroom.* Minneapolis MN: Cooperative Learning Center, 1988.

Johnson, D., Johnson, R. & Smith, K. *Cooperative learning in college: The state of the Art.* ASHE-ERIC Higher Education Report, 1990.

Higher Education Networking Specialist: Copper, James. School of Education SCUDH, 1000 E. Victoria Street, Carson, California 90747.

Adult

Freire, Paulo. *Education for critical consciousness.* New York: Seabury, 1973.

Freire, Paulo. *Pedagogy of the oppressed.* New York: Herder & Herder, 1968.

VI. Special Populations

Dalton, John. *Adventures in thinking: Creative thinking and cooperative groups.* Australia. Melbourne 3000: Thomas Nelson, 1985.

Dalton, J. & Smith, D. *Extending children's special abilities: Strategies for primary classrooms.* North Melbourne 3051: The Victorian Government Bookshop, 1986.

Male, M. & Anderson, M. *Fitting in.* Santa Cruz, CA: Educational Apple-cations, 1990.

Putnam, J.W. & Farnsworth-Lunt, J. *Co-operative learning and the integration of students with disabilities.* Missoula, MT: 1989.

Special Population Networking Specialist: **Sapon-Shevin, Mara.** Inclusive Elementary and Special Education Teacher Preparation Program, Syracuse University, 50 Huntington Hall, Syracuse, NY, 13244-2340.

Mainstreaming Video

Belonging. Cooperative Learning Center, University of Minnesota, 202 Pattee Hall, 150 Pillsbury Drive SE, Minneapolis, MN 55455.

VII. Co-op Books

This section lists children's books which have as their theme cooperation or other prosocial behavior. The list is based heavily on the work of **Susan and Tim Hill**, *The Collaborative Classroom, A guide to cooperative learning,* Portsmouth, NH: Heinemann, 1990. Many entries were provided by Laurie Robertson and Sally Scott.

Albert, Burton. *Mine, yours, ours.* Chicago, IL: A. Whitman, 1977.

Alexandra, Lloyd. *The Prydain Chronicles.* London: Heinemann, 1966-1979.

Alexandra, Martha, G. *I'll be the horse If you'll play with me.* New York: Dial Press, 1975.

Aliki. *We are best friends.* London: Piccolo, 1984

Barkin, C. & James, E. *Sometimes I hate school.* Milwaukee: Raintree Pubs. Ltd., 1975.

Barkin, C. & James, E. *Doing things together.* Milwaukee: Raintree Pubs Ltd, 1975.

Barrett, Judi. *Benjamin's 365 birthdays.* NY: Atheneum, 1974.

Base, Graeme. *The eleventh Hour.* New York: Abram's, Inc, publishers, 1989

Bawden, Nina. *A handful of thieves.* London: Gollancz, 1967.

Beim, L. & Beim, J. *Two is a team.* New York: Harcourt Brace Jovanovich, 1974.

Berry, Joy Wilt. *Fighting.* Danbury, CT: Grolier, 1982.

Blaine, Marge. *The Terrible thing that happened at our house.* New York: Scholastic, 1975.

Bonsall, Crosby Newell. *Who's a pest?* World's Work, 1978.

Boston, Lucy. *A stranger at Greene Knowe.* London: Faber & Faber, 1961

Brandenberg, Franz & Aliki. *The hit of the party.* London: Piccolo, 1985.

Brandenberg, Franz & Aliki. *Nice new neighbors.* London: Hamish Hamilton, 1979.

Brown, Fern. *You're somebody special on a horse.* Chicago: A. Whitman, 1977.

Browne, Anthony. *Piggybook.* London: Julia MacRae, 1986.

Bunting, Eve. *The Wednesday surprise.* NY: Ticknor & Fields, 1989.

Burningham, John. *Mr. Gumpy's outing.* London: Cape, 1970.

Byars, Betsy. *The eighteenth emergency.* London: Bodley Head, 1974

Byars, Betsy. *The pinballs.* London: Bodley Head, 1977

Carle, Eric. *Rooster's off to see the world,* Saxonville MA: Picture Book Studio, 1972

Carlson, Nancy. *Harriets halloween candy,* New York: 1982.

Chambers, Aidan. *The present takers.* London: Bodley Head, 1983.

Cleaver, V. & Cleaver, B. *Dust of the Earth.* New York: Lippincott Junior Books, 1975.

Clifford, Ethel. *The rocking chair rebellion.* Boston: Houghton Mifflin, 1978.

Coleridge, A. & Harvey, R. *The friends of Emily Culpepper.* Melbourne: Five Mile Press, 1983.

Corbett, Pie. *The playtime Treasury. (A collection of playground rhymes, games, and action songs.)* New York: Doubleday, 1989

Corey, Dorothy. *Everybody takes turns, We all share.* Chicago: A. Whitman, 1980.

Godden, Rumer. *Mr. McFadden's Halloween.* New York: Viking, 1975.

Croll, Carolyn. *Too many babas.* New York: Harper & Row, 1979.

Croser, J. & McLean-Carr, C. *Crunch the crocodile.* Gosford: Ashton, 1986.

DeTrevino, E. I, Juan de Pareja. *Farrar.* New York: Straus & Giroux, 1965.

Drett, Jan. *The wild Christmas reindeer.* NY: Putnam, 1990.

Emberley, B. & Emberley, E. *Drummer Hoff.* London: Bodley Head, 1970.

Fleischman, Paul. *Joyful Noise. (Poems for two voices)* New York: Harper & Row, 1988.

Fleischman, Paul. *I am Phoenix (Poems for two voices).* New York: Harper & Row, 1989.

Fleischman, Cid. *The scarebird.* NY: Greenwillow Press, 1988.

Geraghty, Paul. *Look out Patrick.* NY: MacMillan, 1990.

Fox, M. & Ellis, L. *Feathers & Fools.* Melbourne: Ashwood House, 1989.

French, Simon, Cannily, Cannily. *Angus & Robertson,* Sydney: 1981.

Hawkesworth, Jenny. *The lonely skyscraper.* NY: Doubleday, 1980.

Heine, Helme. *Friends.* London: Collins Picture Lions, 1984.

Heine, Helme. *The most wonderful egg in the world.* London: Collins Picture Lions, 1985.

Hoban, Russell. *Harvey's hideout.* Harmondsworth: Puffin, 1976.

Hughes, Shirley. *Alfie gets in first.* Collins London: Picture Lions, 1982.

Hughes, Shirley. *Alfie gives a hand.* London: Collins Picture Lions, 1985.

Hughes, Shirley. *Dogger.* London: Bodley Head, 1977.

Hughes, Shirley. *Helpers.* London: Collins Picture Lions, 1978.

Hutchins, Pat. *The best train set ever.* London: Bodley Head, 1979.

Hutchins, Pat. *The doorbell Rang.* New York: William Morrow & Co. Inc., 1986.

Kastner, Erich. *Emil and the detectives.* London: Cape, 1959.

Keats, Ezra Jack. *Peter's chair.* London: Bodley Head, 1986.

Kelleher, Victor. *Taronga.* Melbourne: Penguin, 1986.

Kerr, Judith. *Mog, the forgetful cat.* Collins, 1986.

Klein, Norma. *Visiting Pamela.* New York: Dial, 1979.

Klein, Robin. *Boss of the pool.* Adelaide: Omnibus, 1986.

Lawrence, Louise. *Children of the dust.* New York: Harper & Row, 1985.

Lewis, C. S. *The Narnia Chronicles.* London: Collins, various dates. Long, Judy. Volunteer Spring. Archway, 1977.

Lionni, Leo. *Swimmy.* Westminster, MD: Pantheon, 1963.

Lobel, Arnold. *Frog and toad are friends.* New York: Harper & Row, 1979

Lobel, Arnold. *Frog and toad Together.* New York: Harper & Row, 1979

Lobel, Arnold. *Frog and toad all Year.* New York: Harper & Row, 1984.

Mattingley, Christobel. *The angel with a mouth organ.* Sydney: Hodder & Stoughton, 1984.

Mazer, Harry. *The war on Villa Street.* New York: Dell.

McKee, David. *Tusk, Tusk.* London: Collins, 1978.

Melton, David. *A Boy Called Hopeless.* Independence, MO: Independence Press, 1976.

The seeds of knowledge may be planted in solitude, but must be cultivated in public. --Samuel Johnson (1709-1784)

Hoban, Russell. *The sorely trying day.* New York: Harper & Row, 1964.

Hoban, Russell. *Tom and the two handles.* World's Work, 1977.

Hoban, Russell. *A mouse and his child.* New York: Harper & Row, 1967.

Minarik, Else Holmelund. *No fighting, No biting!* World's Work, 1969.

Needle, Jan. *My mate Shofiq.* London: Collins, 1978.

Needle, Jan. *My mate Shofiq.* London: Collins, 1978.

Nixon, Joan Lowery. *If you were a writer.* NY: MacMillan, 1988.

Oppenheim, Joanne. *"Not Now!" Said the Cow.* New York: Byron Preis"s Book, 1989

Ormerod, Jan. *101 Things to do with a baby.* Harmondsworth: Kestrel, 1984.

Park, Ruth. *Callie's Castle.* Sydney: Angus & Robertson, 1985.

Park, Ruth. *Callie's family.* Sydney: Angus & Robertson, 1988.

Polacco, Patricia. *Babushka's doll.* NY: Simon Schuster, 1990.

Polacco, Patricia. *Just plain fancy.* NY: Bantam Books, 1990.

Renner, Beverly Hollett. *The hideaway summer.* New York: Harper & Row, 1978.

Rylant, Cynthia. *The relatives came.* NY: Bradbury Press, 1985.

Rubinstein, Gillian. *Space demons.* Adelaide: Omnibus, 1986.

Rubinstein, Gillian. *Answers to Brut.* Omnibus, 1988.

Rubinstein, Gillian. *Skymaze.* Melbourne: Penguin, 1989.

Sharmat, Marjorie. *I'm not Oscar's friend anymore.* New York: Dutton, 1975.

Sharmat, Marjorie. *Sometimes Mama and Papa fight!* New York: Harper & Row, 1980.

Sharmat, Marjorie. *The trip.* New York: Macmillan, 1976.

Sharmat, Marjorie Weinman. *The 329th Friend.* NY: Four Winds Press, 1979.

Sherman, Ivan. *I do not like it when my friend comes to visit.* New York: Harcourt, Brace, Jovanovich, 1973.

Silverstein, Shel. *Where the sidewalk ends.* Harper & Row, 1974.

Silverstein, Shel. *A light in the attic.* Harper & Row , 1974.

Steadman, Ralph. *The bridge.* Collins, 1975.

Steig, William. *Amos and Boris.* Farrar, New York: Straus & Giroux, 1971.

Tobias, Tobi. *The quitting deal.* Harmondsworth: Puffin, 1979.

Udry, Janice May. *Let's be enemies.* New York: Harper & Row, 1961.

Vigna, Judith. *The hiding house.* Chicago: A. Whitman, 1979.

> *The highest function of the teacher consists not so much in imparting knowledge as in stimulating the pupil in its love and pursuit.* --*Henri Frederic Amiel (1821-1881)*

Vincent, Gabrielle. *Bravo, Ernest and Celestine.* London: Collins Picture Lions, 1983.

Vincent, Gabrielle. *Ernest and Celestine.* London: Collins Picture Lions, 1983.

Waber, Bernard. *Ira sleeps over..* Boston: Houghton Mifflin, 1972..

Waber, Bernard. *Bernard.* Boston: Houghton Mifflin, 1982.

Wagner, J. & Brooks, R. *John Brown, Rose and the midnight cat.* Melbourne: Penguin, 1986.

Wells, Rosemary. *Shy Charles.* NY: Dial Books for Young Readers, 1988.

Wildsmith, Brian. *The hunter and his dog.* Oxford University Press, 1984.

Wildsmith, Brian. *The Lion and the Rat.* Oxford University Press, 1986.

Zolotow, Charlotte. *The new friend.* New York: Abelard, 1968.

Zolotow, Charlotte. *The quarreling book.* New York: Harper & Row, 1963.

Zolotow, Charlotte. *The unfriendly book.* New York: Harper & Row, 1975.

VIII. Newsletters

Classroom Connections: The Co-operative Learning Resource Bulletin. Editors, David Bell, John Maschak, Tom Morton, Harry Seddon. John Maschak, Burns View Jr. Secondary, 7658 - 112th St., Delta, BC, Canada V4C 4V8.

Co-operative Classroom The Great Lakes Association for the Study for Co-operation in Education, Sue Ferguson, Area East Office, Toronto Board of Education, 885 Dundas St. East, Toronto, Ontario MSM 1R4

The Co-op Forum Newsletter of the Co-operative Resources Centre at The Ontario Institute for Studies in Education, 252 Bloor St. West, Room 12-110, Toronto, Ont. M5S 1V6

Our Link. Co-operative Learning Network, Pat Roy, Co-operative Learning Centre, Minnesota, 55455

The Linking Clue. Department of Elementary Education, Utah State University, Logan, Utah 84321.

The NNENFCL Cooperative Learning Newsletter. Harrison, ME: Northern New England Network For Cooperative Learning. PO Box 243, Harrison, ME 04040.

Northwest Cooperative Learner. Cooperative Learning Institute, Office of Continuing Education, P.O. Box 751, Portland State University, Portland, Oregon 97207-0751.

Student Team Learing Newsletter. Johns Hopkins Team Learning Project, from the Centre for Social Organization of Schools, 3505 N. Charles Street, Baltimore, Maryland, 21218

IX. Co-op Learning Organizations

Australasian Association for Cooperative Education, Private Bah 12, Hawthorn, Victoria, 3122.

British Columbia Cooperative Learning Association. 4019 Dunbar, Vancouver, BC V6S 2E5.

California Association for Cooperation in Education, Box 1582t, Santa Cruz, California 95061-1582.

Cooperative Learning in Utah Education. Dept. of Elementary Education, Utah State University, Logan, Utah 84322-2805.

Cooperation Throughout Nevada. 230 Drum Lane, Fullon, Nevada 89406.

Great Lakes Association for Cooperation in Education. 885 Dundas St. East, Toronto, Ontario M4M 1R4.

International Association for the Study of Cooperation in Education. 136 Liberty Street, Santa Cruz, California 95060.

Mid-Atlantic Association for Cooperation in Education. 2644 Riva Road, Annapolis Maryland 21401.

New York Association for Cooperation in Education. 10 Cimonelli Drive, New Windsor, New York, 12553.

Northern New England Network for Cooperative Learning. P.O. Box 243, Harrison, ME 04040.

Teacher's Learning Center. 3095 SW Underwood Dr., Portland, Oregon 97225.

Texas Association for Cooperation in Education. 122707 Carvel Lane, Houston, Texas 77072-4515.

> *Many earnest persons, who have found direct education for themselves fruitless and unprofitable, declare that they first began to learn when they began to teach, and that in the education of others they discovered the secret of their own.*
> *--Gamaliel Bradford (1863-1932)*

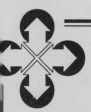

⇨ More Cooperative Learning Books

Cooperative Learning & Literature
(Lessons for Little Ones)
Lorna Curran

◆ *Language Arts*

◆ *K-2*

A special book of cooperative learning activities and lessons for primary children. This is the only comprehensive book on cooperative learning for primary grades. The teacher's manual has 36 lessons which focus on language development and social skills. Adaptions of structures for young children make cooperative learning possible for primary students who have not yet mastered the reading and writing skills. The lessons are based on childrens' literature. Blackline masters are included. $15.00

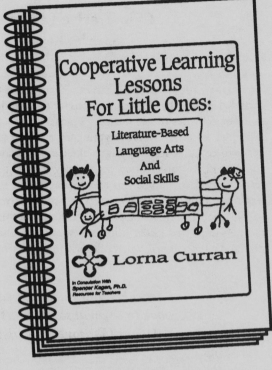

Cooperative Learning & Language Arts:
A Multi-Structural Approach
Jeanne Stone

◆ *Language Arts*

◆ *K-8*

An integrated Language Arts Teacher's Manual which includes 185 activities with 18 cooperative learning structures plus 23 Multi-structural lessons integrating listening, speaking, reading and writing. This book covers a variety of genre: fairy tales, fables, poetry, nonfiction, and auto-biography along with four domains of writing: sensory/descriptive, imaginative/narrative, practical/informative, and analytical/expository. Black line masters are included. $15.00

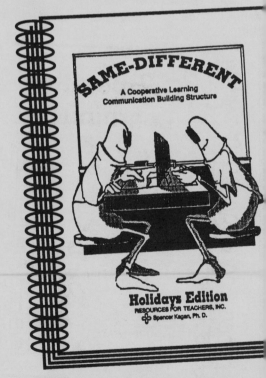

Same-Different, Holidays Edition
Spencer Kagan

◆ *Second Language Acquisition, Analytic Thinking, Fun*

◆ *K-12*

A book of blackline masters with a pair of pictures for each school holiday. Students work in pairs to discover what's the same and what's different in each pair of pictures. A variety of Same-Different methods are described. Includes instructions for making hundreds of same-different activities. Great for English as a Second Language students. Develops analytic skills, vocabulary, and the ability to take the role of another. $10.00

Resources for Teachers, Inc. • 27128 Paseo Espada, Suite 622, San Juan Capistrano, CA 92675 • 1(800) Wee Co-op

⇨ Cooperative Learning & Critical Thinking

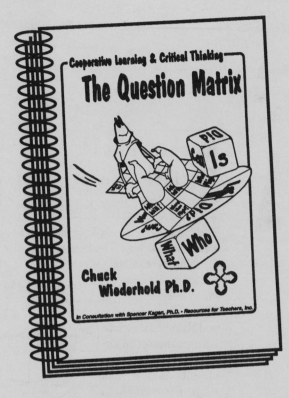

Cooperative Learning & Critical Thinking
Chuck Wiederhold

◆ *Higher Level Thinking*
◆ *2-University*

A revolutionary combination of cooperative learning and critical thinking. This book includes the theory and rationale behind the Question Matrix and explanations of how the Q-Materials are used within cooperative learning structures. Also included are ten lesson plans for the implementation of the Q-Materials into the classroom and numerous activities to generate higher level thinking **$15.00**

Combo Discount: Order Q-Matrix book (Regular $15) and Q-Matrix Packet (Regular $15) and receive both for $25.00!

Q-Matrix Packet

◆ *Question Prompt Manipulatives; Higher Level Thinking*
◆ *2-University*

Includes materials for 9 teams of 4 to produce higher level thinking through student generated questioning. Each team receives its own color-coded heavy card stock set including The Q-Matrix, Quadrant Cards, Q-Chips, Horizontal and Vertical Q-Strips, Q-Dice, and Q-Spinners. The question prompts are the most direct road to higher level thinking. **$15.00**

Quality Q-Dials

◆ *Question Prompt Manipulatives; Higher Level Thinking*
◆ *2-Univeristy*

The set of two Quality Q-Dials allows students to form a different set of questions with each spin such as How Will? How Might? Who Will? Who Might? The two dials produce 36 different questions to stimulate higher level thinking. The dials may be used on an overhead by the teacher or by student teams. The Quality Q-Dials come as a set of two dials. **$6.00**

Recorder

Front view

Recorder	**Role:** Record team decisions and answers.
Gambits:	
1. "Say that again so I can write it down."	4.
2. "Let me record that."	5.
3.	6.

Back view

Role-Cards Packet

◆ *Social Skills Manipulatives*

◆ *K-12*

Role-Cards Packet includes twelve color-coded social role cards for each of nine teams. For each role card, the role and picture of the role are printed on one side and gambits printed appear on the other side. The 108 role cards include Encourager, Praiser, Cheerleader, Gatekeeper, Coach, Question Commander, Checker, Taskmaster, Recorder, Reflector, Quiet Captain and Materials Monitor. The cards stack for easy storage and are reversible too, so each team may create an additional 12 unique roles with gambits. Instructions are included for rotating roles, setting up a social skills center, and how to develop social skills. **$10.00**

Turn-4-Learning Kit

◆ *Two Games for Mastery, Thinking Skills, and Discussion Skills*

◆ *2-12*

Includes two games which provide a fun, easy way to ensure mastery of information and promote high level thinking. The kit includes 18 Gameboards and 864 colorful Gamepieces, enough for 9 teams of 4. Instructions for the two games are included:

Game 1: Turn-4-Review. Used for high consensus questions. Good for review of factual information.

Game 2: Turn-4-Thought. Used for low consensus, creative thinking questions.

Games foster Thinking, Listening, Speaking, Questioning, Augmenting, Praising, Taking Turns and Discussion Skills. **$15.00**

Numbered Heads Together Spinner

◆ *Teacher Tool*

◆ *All Grades*

The Numbered Heads Together Spinner is a welcome addition for teachers who regularly use Numbered Heads Together in the classroom. Place the spinner on the overhead, give it a spin, and Numbered Heads becomes more fun for everyone. An added benefit -- the teacher no longer needs to keep track of which numbers have been called. The spinner selects the number, giving an exciting equal chance for all numbers to be chosen. **$3.00**

Turn-4-Learning Kit©

By: **Spencer Kagan, Ph.D.**

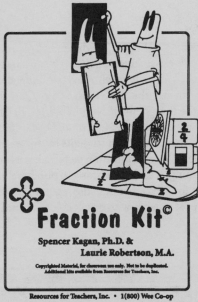

Fraction Kit©
Spencer Kagan, Ph.D. &
Laurie Robertson, M.A.
Copyrighted Material, for classroom use only. Not to be duplicated.
Additional kits available from Resources for Teachers, Inc.

Resources for Teachers, Inc. • 1(800) Wee Co-op

Fraction Kit

◆ *Math Manipulatives to Realize NCTM Standards*
◆ *K-8*

A complete fraction kit for every student in a classroom of 36. Each student receives their color-differentiated, heavy card stock set of ten fractions (1, 1/2, 1/3, 1/4, 1/5, 1/6, 1/8, 1/10, 1/12, 1/16) The fractions are set up for groups of four so distribution is easy. In addition, each kit contains a fraction dice and spinners at both the concrete and symbolic level — 2,448 pieces for just $15 may be the second biggest bargain in all of education.   **$15.00**

Match Mind

◆ *Games for Concept Development and Language Acquisition*
◆ *K-4*

Concept Development and Language Development through play. Especially for primary students and those acquiring a second language. This simple game of Match Mind will increase vocabulary, verbal communication skills, spacial relations, math skills, direction giving, active listening, cooperation, and the ability to take the perspective of another. Includes 64 Gameboards and 1,632 colorful Gamepieces.   **$15.00**

Match Mind©
by
Laurie Robertson, M.A.
Illustrated by
Celso Rodriguez

Kit Includes:	64 Match Mind© Gameboards
	1632 Match Mind© Game Pieces
Designed to Foster	Concept Development Through Play
Copyrighted Material	For classroom use only. Not to be Duplicated.
	Additional Kits Available from Resources for Teachers, Inc.

Match Mind Kit © • Resources For Teachers, Inc. • 1(800) Wee Co-op

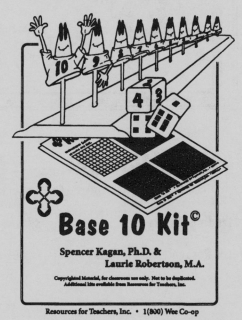

Base 10 Kit©
Spencer Kagan, Ph.D. &
Laurie Robertson, M.A.
Copyrighted Material, for classroom use only. Not to be duplicated.
Additional kits available from Resources for Teachers, Inc.

Resources for Teachers, Inc. • 1(800) Wee Co-op

Base 10 Kit

◆ *Math Manipulatives to Realize NCTM Standards*
◆ *K-8*

Resources for Teachers has broken the price barrier on Base 10 manipulatives! They are now within reach of every teacher. A complete set of Base 10 manipulatives for a whole classroom of 36 students. Each student in the class receives 5 Flats, 20 Rods, and 100 Units. Flats, Rods and Units are made of heavy, color-coded card stock. In addition, there are Base 10 Spinners to make a range of addition, subtraction, multiplication, and division games. 4,518 pieces for $15 may be the greatest bargain in all of education.   **$15.00**

⇨ Videos (Format: VHS)

◆ *Structure Videos:*

Numbered Heads Together

An in-depth look at the rationale and practice of the structure -- How to use it at all grade levels and subject areas. Many variations. **$69.00**

Pairs Check

An in-depth look at the rationale and practice of the structure. How to use it at all grade levels and in content areas ranging from math manipulatives and language arts to physical education. Video includes a wide range of classroom settings, and models step-by-step how to introduce Pairs Check to your classroom. **$69.00**

◆ *Multi-Structural Lessons:*

Co-op Co-op

We follow an eighth grade social studies class for several weeks as they carry out all of the ten steps of this Complex Lesson Design. **$45.00**

Just A Sample

Author Beth Andrini demonstrates a multi-structural Mathematics lesson from her book *Cooperative Learning & Mathematics.* Teams are involved in six structures as they work on a statistics project in which they collect data, construct graphs, and analyze the results of a survey. **$69.00**

Fairy Tale Express

Author Jeanne Stone demonstrates a multi-structural Language Arts lesson from her book *Cooperative Learning and Language Arts.* We view a classroom as it moves through structure after structure of the multi-structural lesson **$69.00**

◆ *Theory & Practice:*

Foundations of Cooperative Learning

Spencer Kagan surveys the research and theoretical underpinnings of cooperative learning. He describes his own research and that of others in the areas of academic achievement, ethnic relations, and prosocial development. **$45.00**

We Can Talk

Cooperative Learning for language and academic gains for students limited in English proficiency. Many classroom variations across grades and subject areas. **$45.00**

⇨ Posters

Resources for teachers offers dozens of colorful classroom posters at a very reasonable price. The posters represent the steps of many structures with easy-to-understand graphics. Students can use the posters to keep on track as they go through the four steps of Numbered Heads and the Eight Steps of Pairs Check. The eight modes of Conflict Resolution are a great reminder when students hit snags. Reducing the times table to 28 multiplication facts makes it fun rather than overwhelming. Teachers wishing to purchase 10 posters can have them for $15 rather than the regular $20 price. They are on white poster paper with bright colored printing. 17 x 22."

**$2.00 each or
10 for $15.00**

⇨ Poster Packages

Sets of 6 posters, 17" x 22", Black Ink on Colored Poster Paper.

Team Standing Charts $5.00 per set of 6

Classroom Recognition Bulletins $5.00 per set of 6

⇨ Binders & Stuff

⇨ Transparency Binder

◆ *Teacher Tool - Blacklines for Handouts, Transparencies*
◆ *K-12*

For teachers who wish to create handouts or overhead transparencies of the structures or posters, there is *Transparencies for Teachers*. The indexed loose leaf binder makes it easy to take out a page to Xerox for handouts or transparencies. Among the many pages are modes of conflict resolutions, dozens of structures, the quiet signal, the 28 multiplication facts, and class rules.

⇨ Workshop Binders

◆ *Teacher Tools: Workshop Organizers*
◆ *All Grades*

Each of these three binders are used in Dr. Kagan's workshops on the structural approach. The indexed, tabbed binders contain materials for beginning, intermediate, and advanced workshops in the structural approach. Contain blacklines.

Transparencies for Teachers
Blackline Masters $15.00

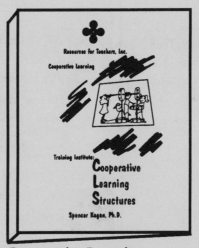

Cooperative Learning Structures
Beginning Workshop Binder $15.00

Cooperative Lesson Designs & Lesson Planning
Intermediate Workshop Binder $15.00

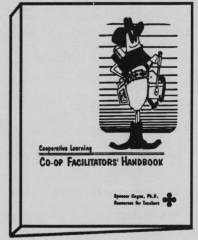

Co-op Facilitators' Handbook
Advanced Workshop Binder $15.00

⇨ T-Shirts

With **Cooperative Learning Logo**, 100% Cotton   ___L ___XL
                                        $15.00 each

⇨ Certificates

Kiddie Recognition (K-2)	(5 x 8" light bond, 4 types, 10 each)	**40 for $2.50**
Elementary Recognition (2-6)	(5 x 8" light bond, 5 types, 6 each)	**30 for $2.00**
Special Recognition (K-12)	(5 x 8" light bond, 3 types, 10 each)	**30 for $2.00**

Resources for Teachers, Inc. • 27128 Paseo Espada, Suite 622, San Juan Capistrano, CA 92675 • 1(800) Wee Co-op

Dr. Kagan is the author of Cooperative Learning and numerous books, book chapters, and scientific journal articles on cooperative learning. He has been featured in *Educational Leadership*. A former Professor of Psychology and Education, University of California, Dr. Kagan is internationally acclaimed as a researcher and presenter. He developed the structural approach to cooperative learning and many cooperative learning structures including: Pairs Check, Color-Coded Co-op Cards, Numbered Heads Together, Team Inside-Outside Circle, Partners, Three-Step Interview, Send-A-Problem, Roundtable, Turn-4-Learning, and Co-op Co-op.

Who Should Attend

All K-12 Classroom Teachers, Chapter 1 Teachers, Curriculum Coordinators, and Administrators. **Adaptations for Special Populations:** Low Achieving, Mainstreamed, Behavior Problems and Limited English Proficient Students.

Training Includes

For All Participants—

- **Book:** *Cooperative Learning*, 1992 Edition
- **Binder:** Unique specialized tabbed binder for each training institute
- **Training materials:** Handouts, wall charts
- **Reception:** Monday evening hospitality cocktail party
- **Refreshments:** Morning rolls and coffee and afternoon lemonade

Weekly Schedule

Monday, 5pm-8:30pm: Reception & Registration, Teambuilding, Classbuilding, Orientation.

Tuesday - Thursday, 8:30am-3:30pm: Full Day Workshops. Experience Cooperative Learning.

Friday, 8:30am-Noon: Workshop and Closing.

Some afternoon sessions will be led by Resources for Teachers author/presenters

6th Annual Summer Institutes

LEVEL 1

The Structural Approach Institute
Grades/Dates: Secondary/July 6-10; Elementary/July 13-17
Prerequisite: None

For teachers beginning the structural approach — Learn Teamformation, Teambuilding, Classbuilding, Classroom Management, Social Skill Development, Improvement Scoring, Recognition Systems, Co-op Sports, and dozens of Cooperative Learning Structures. The next step after an initial one day training.

LEVEL 2

Advanced Structures Institute
Grades: K-12   *Date:* July 20-24
Prerequisite: Level I

For teachers who have completed Level I who are currently using a number of structures regularly with success. Learn to modify and create original structures with the powerful Element Matrix. Also: Advanced Structures and Q-Trix for higher level thinking.

LEVEL 3

Co-op Curriculum Institute
Grades: K-12   *Date:* July 27-31
Prerequisite: Level I

For teachers who have completed Level I who are currently using structures regularly with success. Learn specialized structures for NCTM Standards, Math with Manipulatives, Whole Language, Writing Process, Co-op Reading, Social Studies, Hands-On Science — The Curriculum Through Structures.

LEVEL 4

Co-op Lesson Designs Institute
Grades: K-12   *Date:* August 3-7
Prerequisites: Level I & either Level II or III

For teachers using simple and advanced structures regularly with success. Learn Co-op Lesson Designs, including: STAD, Pairs, Partners, Jigsaw, Co-op Jigsaw I & II, Rotation Learning Centers, and Co-op Co-op. Learn to play with the Dozen Design Elements to modify and create Co-op Lesson designs and create original lesson plans.

LEVEL 5

Co-op Facilitators' Institute
Grades: K-12   *Date:* August 10-14
Prerequisites: Levels I and II

For facilitators wishing to give workshops in the structural approach. Create district and site level training plans, generate administrative and parental support, set up Structure-A-Month Clubs, hone presentation skills, and practice coaching.

Register Now!!!

Dates: July - August, 1992
Location: The Hyatt Newporter
1107 Jamboree Road
Newport Beach, CA 92660

Hotel Rates: $105 Single Occupancy;
$115 Double, per night.

Participants must make reservations directly
with the Hyatt Newporter (714) 644-1700.

University Credit: Offered by the
University of California Extension, Riverside.

Discounts for Early Registration
By 1-31-91   Fee: $350.00
By 4-15-92   Fee: $400.00
After 4-15-92 Fee: $450.00

Setting: The Hyatt Newporter Resort is a world-class resort and has been highly celebrated by trainees each summer. We have our own garden patio and access to spacious grounds and recreation. We are walking distance from sailing, windsurfing, paddle boats and beach recreation. We are near the finest in dining, shopping and recreation. Children under 16 stay free; child care is available all hours. The Newporter provides a free shuttle to and from John Wayne Airport and to shopping and restaurants.

How To Register

Send the information below to Resources for Teachers, Inc. Include either a $100 deposit or your registration fee. Send a check or Purchase Order marked "Non-refundable after June 18, 1992." Purchase Orders may be faxed. For institutes beyond Level I, you will receive an application form; registration is not confirmed until your application has been accepted.

Send Registration to:

Resources for Teachers, Inc.
27128 Paseo Espada, Suite 622
San Juan Capistrano, CA 92675
Fax Number: (714) 248-9662
1(800) Wee Co-op

Name_____ Phone No._____

Address_____

City_____ State_____ Zip_____

School_____ Phone No._____

School Address_____ Grade_____ Subject_____

City_____ State_____ Zip_____

I am registering for: ☐ Wk 1 (July 6-10) ☐ Wk 3 (July 20-24) ☐ Wk 5 (Aug 3-7)
☐ Wk 2 (July 13-17) ☐ Wk 4 (July 27-31) ☐ Wk 6 (Aug 10-12)

☐ Yes, I would like Resources For Teachers to help me arrange for a roommate.

Please send confirmation to ☐ Home ☐ School ☐ District

Resources for Teachers Sends ...

Great Workshops

... To Your School or District

Workshops: Co-op Learning and...

- Computers • Community Building
- Critical Thinking • Hands on Science
- History/Social Sciences • The Year 2000
- Language Arts • Math with Manipulatives
- National Mathematic Standards
- Peer Coaching • Restructuring Schools
- Self Esteem • Social Skills
- Staff Relations • Whole Language • Writing Process

Co-op Learning for Special Populations

- At Risk • Behavior Problems
- Chapter I • ESL
- LEP • Low Achievers
- Mainstreaming • Primary (K-2)

Special Institutes

- **Level I:** The Structural Approach Institute (secondary)
- **Level I:** The Structural Approach Institute (elementary)
- **Level II:** Advanced Structures Institute
- **Level III:** Co-op Curriculum Institute
- **Level IV:** Co-op Lesson Designs Institute
- **Level V:** Co-op Facilitators' Institute

Call **Resources for Teachers,**
or mail or fax us the request below.

Resources for Teachers, Inc.
27128 Paseo Espada, Suite 602
San Juan Capistrano, CA. 92675

Toll Free: 1(800) Wee Co-op
Fax: 1 (714) 248-9662

✂ (cut along dotted line)

Contact Person _____

School Phone _____ Home Phone _____

2nd Contact Person _____

School Phone _____ Home Phone _____

District/School _____

Address _____

City _____ State _____ Zip _____

Type of Presenation:

Key Note ☐ 1/2 Day ☐ Full Day ☐ Follow Up ☐ Series ☐

Location of Workshop: _____

Dates of Workshop: _____

_____ Times of Workshops _____

Description of Topics to be covered: _____

Number of Participants: _____

Prior Experience in the Structural Approach:

Novice ☐ Simple Structures ☐ Complex Structures ☐ Trainers ☐ Other ☐

RESOURCES FOR TEACHERS

27128 Paseo Espada, Suite 622 Fax: (714) 248-9662
San Juan Capistrano, CA 92675 (714) 248-7757

Order Form

11-13-91

Toll Free: 1(800) Wee Co-op

⇨ Cooperative Learning Books

Andrini:	**Cooperative Learning & Mathematics: A Multi-Structural Approach** (K-8)	_____ x $15. _____
Curran:	**Cooperative Learning Lessons for Little Ones: Literature Based Lessons** (K-2)	_____ x $15. _____
Kagan:	**Cooperative Learning** (The Basic Book. K-Universtiy)	_____ x $25. _____
Kagan:	**Same-Different, Holidays Edition: A Communication Building Structure**	_____ x $10. _____
Stone:	**Cooperative Learning & Language Arts: A Multi-Structural Approach** (K-8)	_____ x $15. _____

⇨ Cooperative Learning & Critical Thinking (Book & Materials)

Book: Wiederhold: Cooperative Learning & Critical Thinking: The Question Matrix	_____ x $15. _____
Packet: Q-Materials Packet Manipulatives for 8 teams: Q-Matrix, -Dice, -Spinners, -Strips...	_____ x $15. _____
Combo Discount (Book + Packet above, only $25. Regularly $30 if bought separately.)	_____ x $25. _____
Quality Q-Dials 2 plastic overhead projector spinners and overhead for Q-Matrix questions	_____ x $6. _____

⇨ Binders [Workshop Binders and Blacklines; $15 each]

____**Kagan: Transparencies for Teachers** [Blacklines] ____**Kagan: Co-op Lesson Designs** (Tabbed)

____**Kagan: Cooperative Learning Structures** (Tabbed) ____**Kagan: Co-op Facilitators' Handbook** (Tabbed)

⇨ Videos [Format: VHS]

Total number of Binders _____ x $15. _____

Co-op Co-op	(30 min.)	_____ x $45. _____	**Just A Sample** (33 min.)	_____ x $69. _____	
Fairy Tale Express	(19 min.)	_____ x $69. _____	**We Can Talk** (45 min.)	_____ x $45. _____	
Numbered Heads Together	(30 min.)	_____ x $69. _____	**Foundations of Co-op Learning**		
Pairs Check	(30 min.)	_____ x $69. _____	(58 min.)	_____ x $45. _____	

⇨ Posters [17x22" Colored Ink on White Poster Paper; $2.00 each]

__ Numbered Heads	__ Classbuilding	__ Roundtable	__ 8 Modes of Conflict Resolution
__ Pairs Check	__ Line-Ups	__ Roundrobin	__ Class Thermometer (Cut & Hide)
__ Think, Pair, Share	__ Corners	__ Three-Step Interview	__ The 28 Multiplication Facts
__ Think, Pair, Square	__ Formations	__ Inside-Outside Circle	__ Class Rules
__ 4 S's Brainstorming	__ Social Roles	__ Q-Matrix	__ Quiet Signal

Discount 10 Posters for $15. _____ Total number of $2 Posters _____ x $2. _____

Team Standing Charts (Set of 6; 17x22" ; Black Ink Colored Paper; $5 a set) _____ Sets x $5. _____

Classroom Recognition Bulletins (Set of 6; 17x22" ; Black Ink Colored Paper; $5 a set) _____ Sets x $5. _____

⇨ Kits, Packets, Manipulatives, Games

Numbered Heads Together Spinners (1 plastic Numbered Heads overhead spinner)	____ x $3. ____
Role-Cards Packet (108 Role-Cards, color-coded for nine teams - 12 Role-Cards per team)	____ x $10. ____
Turn-4-Learning Kit (18 Gameboards & 864 Cards to play Turn-4-Review & Turn-4-Thought)	____ x $15. ____
Fraction Kit (36 Sets of 10 Fraction bars;1000's of pieces + Fraction Dice & Spinners)	____ x $15. ____
Base 10 Kit (5 Flats, 20 Rods, 100 Units for each of 36 Students + Concrete & Symbolic Dice)	____ x $15. ____
Match Mind (Concept Development Game; 64 Gameboards; Hundreds of Gamepieces)	____ x $15. ____

Cost of Materials (Minimum Order $10) _____

State Sales Tax (California Residents Only, .0775 x Cost of Materials) _____

Handling (10% x Cost of Materials. Orders over $200 pay 5%. All orders outside Continental U.S. Pay 15%) _____

Total (Cost of Materials + State Sales Tax + Handling) **U.S. Funds Only, please.** _____

⇨ Resources ships latest editions of books and materials. Also, Resources is producing new books, videos, and materials. Please call for new releases. Prices and materials are subject to change without notice. Faxed purchase orders are welcome. Send your check or purchase order to Resources for Teachers. Phone orders by Visa and Mastercard will be accepted beginning January 1992.

YOUR ORDER WILL BE SHIPPED TO THE ADDRESS BELOW:

Phone Number (optional) ( ) _____-_____

NAME: _____

STREET: _____

CITY, STATE, ZIP _____

✤ RESOURCES FOR TEACHERS

27128 Paseo Espada, Suite 622   Fax: (714) 248-9662
San Juan Capistrano, CA 92675   (714) 248-7757

Order Form

11-13-91

Toll Free: **1(800) Wee Co-op**

➡ Cooperative Learning Books

Andrini:	Cooperative Learning & Mathematics: A Multi-Structural Approach (K-8)	____ x $15.____
Curran:	Cooperative Learning Lessons for Little Ones: Literature Based Lessons (K-2)	____ x $15.____
Kagan:	Cooperative Learning (The Basic Book. K-Universtiy)	____ x $25.____
Kagan:	Same-Different, Holidays Edition: A Communication Building Structure	____ x $10.____
Stone:	Cooperative Learning & Language Arts: A Multi-Structural Approach (K-8)	____ x $15.____

➡ Cooperative Learning & Critical Thinking (Book & Materials)

Book: Wiederhold: Cooperative Learning & Critical Thinking: The Question Matrix ____ x $15. ____

Packet: Q-Materials Packet Manipulatives for 8 teams: Q-Matrix, -Dice, -Spinners, -Strips... ____ x $15. ____

Combo Discount (Book + Packet above, only $25. Regularly $30 if bought separately.) ____ x $25. ____

Quality Q-Dials 2 plastic overhead projector spinners and overhead for Q-Matrix questions ____ x $5. ____

➡ Binders [Workshop Binders and Blacklines; $15 each]

____**Kagan:** Transparencies for Teachers [Blacklines]   ____**Kagan:** Co-op Lesson Designs (Tabbed)

____**Kagan:** Cooperative Learning Structures (Tabbed)   ____**Kagan:** Co-op Facilitators' Handbook (Tabbed)

➡ Videos [Format: VHS]

Total number of Binders ____ x $15. ____

Co-op Co-op	(30 min.) ____ x $45. ____	**Just A Sample**	(33 min.)	____ x $69. ____
Fairy Tale Express	(19 min.) ____ x $69. ____	**We Can Talk**	(45 min.)	____ x $45. ____
Numbered Heads Together	(30 min.) ____ x $69. ____	**Foundations of Co-op Learning**		
Pairs Check	(30 min.) ____ x $69. ____		(58 min.)	____ x $45. ____

➡ Posters [17x22" Colored Ink on White Poster Paper; $2.00 each]

__ Numbered Heads	__Classbuilding	__ Roundtable	__ 8 Modes of Conflict Resolution
__ Pairs Check	__Line-Ups	__ Roundrobin	__ Class Thermometer (Cut & Hide)
__ Think, Pair, Share	__Corners	__ Three-Step Interview	__ The 28 Multiplication Facts
__ Think, Pair, Square	__Formations	__ Inside-Outside Circle	__ Class Rules
__ 4 S's Brainstorming	__Social Roles	__ Q-Matrix	__ Quiet Signal

Discount 10 Posters for $15.____   Total number of $2 Posters ____ x $2. ____

Team Standing Charts   (Set of 6; 17x22"; Black Ink Colored Paper; $5 a set) ____ Sets x $5. ____

Classroom Recognition Bulletins (Set of 6; 17x22"; Black Ink Colored Paper; $5 a set) ____ Sets x $5. ____

➡ Kits, Packets, Manipulatives, Games

Numbered Heads Together Spinners (1 plastic Numbered Heads overhead spinner) ____ x $3. ____

Role-Cards Packet (108 Role-Cards, color-coded for nine teams - 12 Role-Cards per team) ____ x $10. ____

Turn-4-Learning Kit (18 Gameboards & 864 Cards to play Turn-4-Review & Turn-4-Thought) ____ x $15. ____

Fraction Kit (36 Sets of 10 Fraction bars;1000's of pieces + Fraction Dice & Spinners) ____ x $15. ____

Base 10 Kit (5 Flats, 20 Rods, 100 Units for each of 36 Students + Concrete & Symbolic Dice) ____ x $15. ____

Match Mind (Concept Development Game; 64 Gameboards; Hundreds of Gamepieces) ____ x $15. ____

Cost of Materials (Minimum Order $10) _____

State Sales Tax (California Residents Only, .0775 x Cost of Materials) _____

Handling (10% x Cost of Materials. Orders over $200 pay 5%. All orders outside Continental U.S. Pay 15%) _____

Total (Cost of Materials + State Sales Tax + Handling) **U.S. Funds Only, please.** _____

➡ Resources ships latest editions of books and materials. Also, Resources is producing new books, videos, and materials. Please call for new releases. Prices and materials are subject to change without notice. Faxed purchase orders are welcome. Send your check or purchase order to Resources for Teachers. Phone orders by Visa and Mastercard will be accepted beginning January 1992.

YOUR ORDER WILL BE SHIPPED TO THE ADDRESS BELOW:

Phone Number (optional)   ( ) ____-_____

NAME:_____

STREET: _____

CITY, STATE, ZIP _____